WEBSTER'S NEW WORLD™
AMERICAN IDIOMS HANDBOOK

WEBSTER'S NEW WORLD™
AMERICAN IDIOMS HANDBOOK

by Gail Brenner

WILEY

Wiley Publishing, Inc.

Webster's New World™ American Idioms Handbook

Copyright © 2003 by Wiley Publishing, Inc., Indianapolis, Indiana

Published by Wiley Publishing, Inc., Indianapolis, Indiana
Published simultaneously in Canada

For general information on our other products and services or to obtain technical support please contact our Customer Care Department within the U.S. at 800-762-2974, outside the U.S. at 317-572-3993 or fax 317-572-4002.

Wiley also publishes its books in a variety of electronic formats. Some content that appears in print may not be available in electronic books.

ISBN: 0-7645-2477-1

Library of Congress Cataloging-in-Publication Data is available from the publisher.

Manufactured in the United States

10 9 8 7 6 5 4 3 2 1

ACKNOWLEDGMENTS

"No man [or woman] is an island. . . ." And this was well proven during the monumental adventure of writing *Webster's New World American Idioms Handbook*. The support, encouragement, and exceeding competence of family, friends, colleagues, and editors gave me the impetus and much-needed assistance to write this book.

First, I must thank Acquisitions Editor Roxane Cerda for inviting me to the task, and for her mastery in getting the project rolling. She handled all of the initial details and follow-up with her usual skill, ease, and aplomb. It was a great pleasure working with you again, Roxane. (And thanks for that terrific list of idioms!)

Secondly, I thank the heavens for sending Project Editor Ben Nussbaum. His expertise and cool-headed management of this project made all the difference. I'm very grateful for his commonsense advice and keen take on what makes for clear reading. His skill, dedication, and easy-going manner greatly contributed to the successful and timely completion of this book. Ben, as editors go, "you rock!"

Copy Editor Mark Enochs did an expert job, along with Ben, editing this formidable manuscript, and clarifying many a vague and awkward line. Thanks, Mark. And thanks also to Jan Zunkel, Bethany André, and Blair Pottenger, who participated in editing portions of the manuscript. Also thanks to the entire production crew who put it all together.

Warm thanks to my colleagues who assisted me in so many ways. First and foremost, I'm very grateful to Lori Colman for her invaluable commitment of time and energy researching idioms, writing innumerable definitions and sample sentences, and offering suggestions. I couldn't have done it without you . . . and that's a fact! To Patricia Sullivan, Lynn Clausen, and Joyce Flager, who reviewed portions of the manuscript, I greatly appreciated your expert feedback and your help clarifying technical points and locating errors. Many thanks to Peggy Miles, "grammarian extraordinaire," to editor Wallace Baine for movie slang, and to Sarah Phelan, my "British idioms consultant," who helped set me straight on a host of Britishisms.

I gratefully thank my Generation X "language consultants" Forrest, Josh, Sid, Skye, Larson, and Betsy. And I'm equally grateful to Dottie Yingling, the coolest 90 year old around, for enlightening me on slang from The Greatest Generation. My fabulous friends gave their unflagging support, inspiration, and encouragement, as well as idiom book loans, slang suggestions, "The Story of English," and late-night chats. Much gratitude and thanks to Deborah Abbott and Rebecca Tavish, to Chuck Ernst (my computer hero) and Joanne Tanner, to Sharon Webber, Adrienne Zihlman, and finally to Joyce Flager and Jan Fitzgerald for putting their foot down on Christmas Day and making me turn off the computer.

And lastly, on the home front, I'm very thankful for the enduring support and encouragement of my son Joshua Harris, who helped sustain my spirit, made me laugh, and saw that I took a break now and again. And who, along with pal Sid, brought me lively idioms "from the street," and from the kitchen, innumerable steaming cups of tea. Awesome, you guys. Thanks!

DEDICATION

For Laurann and Saundri, Jess, and Bret

TABLE OF CONTENTS

PART I

INTRODUCTION

*I*n this part, you learn the basics about idioms: what they are, what they're not, and why they exist. This part also gives you a guide for the rest of the book.

CHAPTER 1

AN INTRODUCTION TO IDIOMS

American English is a rich and ever-changing tapestry. And like most languages, much of its vivid color, texture, and flexibility comes from the rich storehouse of idioms.

American English, like most languages, is filled with idioms and idiomatic expressions. There are over 10,000 idioms in American English, and some of them have been in use for more than 2,000 years, while others are brand new. Idioms are what give language much of its fluid nature: New expressions appear and go out of fashion, street slang becomes popularized by music or film and gains more formal status, new technology brings a wave of fresh jargon, older expressions evolve to new meaning or usage.

Idioms are a major component of American speech patterns and are abundant in everyday chat as well as formal conversation and all forms of writing. There are idioms for nearly every occasion, life situation, and human activity and emotion — birth, death, work, play, success, failure, love, time, money, and so on. In fact, some conversations consist entirely of idioms!

How has American English become such an idiom-rich language? Idioms and expressive language thrive in part because American society is a mobile society. Wherever people move, they bring along their regional and colloquial expressions. Widespread access to mass media, television, radio, film, and more recently the Internet all provide a swift avenue for new jargon and slang that's on the street one day and on everyone's lips the next. America's relatively open society and lax social controls on language help keep idiomatic speech alive and open to experimentation, while America's admiration for individuality and industriousness provides the perfect environment for new and creative language to flourish.

The survival of ancient idioms in today's speech and the enormous scope and variety of idioms in American English suggest that idiomatic language may serve some important function in society. At the very least, people use idioms and expressive language simply to find fresh, vivid, humorous, or cutting ways to say what they want to say. Certain jargon and specialized ways of speaking may be a way of preserving one's identity, or providing a sense of belonging and familiarity among the speakers. Also, casual or familiar speech can reduce tension in a difficult situation. And perhaps it's simply human nature to play with language, shape it to one's use, and take advantage of the full range of expression that a language allows.

People use idioms to make their language richer and more colorful and to convey subtle shades of meaning or intention. Idioms are used often to replace a literal word or expression, and many times the idiom better describes the full nuance of meaning. Idioms and idiomatic expressions can be more precise than the literal words, often using fewer words but saying more. For example, the expression *it runs in the family* is shorter and more succinct than saying that a physical or personality trait "is fairly common throughout one's extended family and over a number of generations." The expression *a nine-to-five job* communicates much more than simply the hours one works. It says that the job is ordinary, unchanging, and perhaps boring or humdrum (the same every day).

Having a solid working knowledge of idiomatic language is essential to understanding and interacting in American English. But learning idioms and using them correctly is often the most formidable and daunting task for language learners. Equally, language instructors preparing to teach idioms often wonder where and how to begin. *Webster's New World American Idioms Handbook* is designed to give language learners, instructors, and others interested in language study a framework and organizational tool (and enjoyable guidebook) for studying and teaching the vast and varied lexicon of American idioms.

Each of the four main parts of this book presents idioms in a slightly different format to accommodate differences in learning, teaching, and language acquisition styles — and to offer a variety of choices for studying idioms. Idioms are arranged into categories by theme, key word, or concept. The chapters and the segments within chapters are arranged in logical "bite-sized" portions, so that any one segment can be read and understood as an independent unit. One goal of this design is to help reduce the sense of intimidation that people often have about learning idioms. It also provides a coherent layout that allows the reader to locate idioms easily, compare related idioms, and to use the book as a reference, a text, or a handbook for studying idioms and English or to just read for enjoyment and interest.

What Is an Idiom?

What is an idiom? Even many native English speakers aren't clear what constitutes an idiom — they simply use them. Some people are more familiar with the meaning of *idiom* as a style or genre of thought and artistic expression. Among various dictionary sources, there is some disagreement and confusion about how to define an idiom. That's understandable, considering the fluid nature of so many words and phrases in American English.

One common, basic definition for an idiom is: *two or more words together that, as a unit, have a special meaning that is different from the literal meaning of the words separately.*

For example, the idiom *stand out* does not mean to stand or to be outside; it means to be prominent, obvious; to be easily noticed because of a unique or different feature.

> **idiom:** His bright red hair really *stands out* in a crowd (is easy to notice, prominent).
> **literal meaning:** He is *standing out* in the yard (standing outside).

This definition of an idiom is a good starting point, but it's not enough to include all of the words that American English speakers use idiomatically. For example, not all idioms consist of two words; some are only one word, like *scratch* meaning money. Other idioms, like *close down,* are almost literal but they stretch or extend the literal meaning. *Close down* does, in fact, mean to close something, but it generally implies to close or quit a business permanently.

Considering all of the words, constructions, and expressions that are used idiomatically in American English, idioms might best be defined as having one or more of the following characteristics:

- Idioms have a meaning that is different from or extends the literal meaning of the individual word or words.
- Idioms break or stretch the rules of grammar, word order (syntax), and semantics to a certain degree.
- Idioms change meaning when translated word for word into another language.

Other terms that are often used interchangeably with *idiom* are *slang, jargon, colloquialism, expression,* and *saying,* to name some. Going back to the *Webster's New World Dictionary,* many of these terms have similar or overlapping definitions, but following are the definitions that most distinguish one term from the other:

- **slang:** highly informal speech that is outside standard or conventional usage
- **jargon:** specialized vocabulary and idioms used in the same profession, work, or group
- **colloquialism:** casual local or regional expressions
- **expression:** a particular word, phrase, or sentence that is idiomatic
- **saying:** an expression of wisdom and truth

In this handbook, the term *idiom* is used throughout, the term *slang* is used occasionally to refer to very informal words and phrases, and *expression* is used for longer idiomatic phrases, except for those that offer words of truth or wisdom, which are referred to as *sayings.*

The Idioms in This Book

The idioms included in this book represent a range of language that is used idiomatically, from long-established expressions to some fresh new slang; from pure idiomatic phrases to ones that just slightly stretch the literal meaning; and from common verbs to colorful greetings, warnings, curses, and praises.

Some idioms included in this book, like *in-law* (the blood relatives of one's spouse) and *clean off* (remove everything from or clean the top surface of something) may not appear to be true idioms, but they are unconventional in a way that is unfamiliar or confusing to language learners.

For example, the expression *in-law* doesn't follow a normal grammatical pattern. *In-law* looks similar to the expressions *in business* and *in medicine*, both of which refer to a person's occupation, but *in-law* doesn't refer to practicing law or being a lawyer. Neither *in-law* nor *clean off* have an exact literal translation.

The idiom *clean off* certainly means to clean, but specifically to clean and clear the surface of something. The preposition, *off*, adds a new dimension to the very common word *clean*. It can become mind-boggling for a language learner to sort out the subtle difference in meaning between expressions like *clean off, clean up, clean out*, and simply *clean*. So this book includes idioms of this type.

USING THIS HANDBOOK

You may begin wherever you like. It is not necessary to read the chapters in order. You can turn to any page randomly and read about idioms.

Here are some terms and conventions used in this book:

♦	marks sentences and dialogues that show examples of the idioms in context
[ ]	used for all cross-references that tell where in the book to find related idioms and information
Grammar Note:	gives essential information on the grammatically correct way to use an idiom, and on variations in word order and tense that can be used with the idiom
Note:	offers additional information on an idiom and the appropriate context in which to use it; also, Notes include warnings to help one avoid common, and sometimes embarrassing, mistakes

The glossary of grammatical terms in the back of the book gives a clear and concise explanation of terms used in this book. An extensive index provides quick access to individual idioms so that you can find them easily. You can use this index to look for a specific idiom that you've heard; you can check out groupings of idioms that begin with the same word; or simply browse this index for fun and interest.

Idioms take time, patience, and practice to master, but you can speed your mastery in a number of ways. You will acquire idioms much faster if you are using them in your conversations and writing. Decide to learn and use one idiom (or more) every day. Join, or create, a study group that meets regularly to speak English and study idioms. You can use this book to help you choose study topics or specific idioms to discuss.

Film and videos are filled with idioms. Choose a film with one of the themes featured in this book (money, romance, family, education) and listen for idioms that you've read about in the corresponding chapter. Invite a co-worker to lunch. Attend lectures, poetry readings, museum tours, anything that will allow you to hear normal speech and conversation. You can improve your skills and learn lots of idioms by volunteering at a non-profit agency or school. If you have time, it's a great way to hear casual conversation, practice English, and help out, too. And following are a few other suggestions — some fun and useful ways that you can use this handbook:

- Choose a theme or chapter that interests you, and then select a small group of idioms under one of the subheadings in the chapter. After you've studied about them, teach them to someone else.
- Use a newspaper to locate idioms (the comics page can be a good source, as can a movie review).
- Check cereal boxes, or other product containers and any kinds of ads. Advertisements are full of idioms. Then find the idiom in this book.
- Write love letters (or talk to someone you love) using idioms from Chapter 8. Plan a date with idioms from Chapter 7.
- Discuss your future with idioms from Chapter 12.
- Keep a list of the idioms that you encounter, and then find them in this book, using the index. Study them and check them. In time you will see how your list of learned and checked idioms begins to grow.
- Choose one or two idioms or phrasal verbs per day that you will practice in conversation. If an opportunity to use your idioms doesn't occur naturally, ask someone to listen to and correct your use of the idioms. That will probably get you talking more about idioms.
- Open this book to the index and check off idioms that your hear while watching TV or a video. Then study the idioms that you heard.
- Open the book randomly to any page, close your eyes, and point to an idiom. Then learn it.

This handbook is bursting with idioms of every type, and includes as many of the most commonly used idioms as could be packed between the pages. Still, this represents just one small portion of the huge lexicon of American idioms, idiomatic expressions, and slang. So feel free to add more whenever you discover a new one that isn't featured here. Jot them in the margins, the blank pages, in a related chapter, wherever you like. There are plenty to add.

Finally, and most importantly, use *Webster's New World American Idioms Handbook* in any way that suits your purpose and interest. And enjoy the lively, colorful, adventure of communicating with idioms!

IDIOMS FOR EVERYDAY ACTIVITIES AND OCCASIONS

*I*n American English, there is an idiom for nearly every occasion, life situation, and human activity — for life and death, work and play, love and marriage, and so on.

Part II contains eight separate chapters, each devoted to an aspect of everyday life. Within these chapters you'll find close to a thousand idioms and idiomatic expressions that Americans use to talk about the people and things that are a part of their daily lives. Idioms are organized around topics such as family and friends, food and dining, home and housekeeping, sleep, hygiene, health and illness, love and marriage, school, work, money, travel, and others. Chapter 9 offers a collection of common phrases and slang expressions that are used extensively in casual conversation.

CHAPTER 2

FAMILY MATTERS: FAMILY, HOME, AND LIFE STAGES

Starting *closest to home* (closest to that which affects us most personally and intimately), there are plenty of idioms and expressions that refer to family and family life, to one's house and home, and to the life stages that one experiences while growing up and growing old. This chapter presents more than 100 common expressions that are used to talk about these important aspects of everyday life.

Family and Friends

In this section, you'll find idioms, expressions, and some colloquial terms to refer to oneself, one's family members, family structure and family types, and one's role in the family. There are also idioms used to refer to friends and to oneself.

FAMILY

People sometimes refer to their family or relatives as *the relies* or *the clan*. People also refer to the *mother's side* or the *father's side,* meaning the relatives or ancestors of the mother or of the father. Following are a few other expressions that refer to family and family types.

blood

> **(n)** family, people who are related by blood; generally used to suggest strong family loyalty or responsibility ♦ *Of course I'll help him; he's* blood. ♦ *We're* blood, *so we have a responsibility to each other.*

flesh and blood

> **(n)** one's children, also sometimes used for one's parents, brothers, and sisters. Often said as one's *own flesh and blood.* Sometimes used jokingly to remind people of their family obligations, as in the second example that follows. ♦ *You can't cut her out of your life. She's your* flesh and blood. ♦ *Come on, Dad, let me borrow the car. You can't refuse your own* flesh and blood.

Types of Families

As family structure has changed over time, so have expressions that are used to talk about families. Terms for traditional American family structures include *nuclear family,* meaning parents and their related or adopted children, and *extended family,* meaning parents, their children, other relatives, and sometimes very close friends that are like family.

A few terms for non-traditional family structures are *single-parent family*, where, as the term implies, there is only one parent and his or her children, and *blended family,* meaning the combined unrelated children (from previous relationships or marriages) of two people. When a person who has no children marries someone with children, it's sometimes said that the childless person has a *ready-made family.*

Note: These expressions, and some of the ones that follow, are not purely idiomatic, but include an adjective that gives special meaning to the word *family,* as in, *immediate family* (one's parents, brothers and sisters, and closest relatives): "Only my *immediate family* was invited to the wedding."

A family in which the members are very close and are involved in each other's lives is often called a *close-knit family.* On the other hand, a family with problems that prevent the family from functioning normally or harmoniously might be called a *dysfunctional family* (this term comes from the field of psychology, but is now in common usage).

Family Members

People don't always use the literal terms *mother, father,* and so on when talking about family members. They sometimes use colloquial terms such as *the folks,* referring to parents, or *my brood,* referring to all one's children collectively. American English does not have special words or required forms of address to show the status or role of family members, as many languages have. Following are a few more common terms used to refer to family members. Some of these terms, like *baby of the family,* are not purely idiomatic, but they are used in an informal or colloquial way, generally in conversation. ***Grammar Note:*** Most of the following idioms require the article *the,* or a possessive pronoun like *my* or *her.*

> **the baby (of the family):** the youngest child in the family
> **in-laws:** the parents of your spouse
> **my better half:** one's spouse
> **my old man:** (slang) one's father; one's husband or male partner
> **my old lady:** (slang) one's wife or female partner
> **the old folks:** grandparents

Types of Dads and Moms

Some expressions have developed to describe different types of parental status. People use the terms *biological parent* or *natural parent* to mean the genetically related parent of a child. The term *non-biological parent* refers to a parent not genetically related. More specifically, the terms *stepmother* and *stepfather* refer to a person whose spouse has children from a previous marriage or relationship (also said as *stepmom* and *stepdad*).

A term that applies to fathers is *family man*. The term usually refers to married men with children, and is used to emphasize that the man has family responsibilities, is devoted to his family, and involved in family activities.

Other terms typically apply only to mothers. It is the mother's role in society that has changed most drastically in recent decades (and therefore has inspired new idioms):

stay-at-home mom: a mother who doesn't work outside the home
working mom: a mother who has a job outside the home
soccer mom: a mother who spends a lot of time taking her children to after-school activities such as soccer, baseball, swimming, or dance
supermom: a mother who seems to tirelessly manage her home and family, her outside job, and her many other responsibilities

Family Likeness

The following common expressions and sayings describe the similarity in appearance, personality, or behavior of related family members.

run in the family

to be genetic, inherited; said of a physical characteristic, personality trait, or talent that is common among related family members and passed from one generation to the next. Sometimes said as ridicule or light teasing. ♦ *Rebecca's mom plays the flute, and Rebecca plays the guitar. Musical talent seems to* run in her family. ♦ *Diabetes* runs in his family, *so he's careful of his diet.*

have someone's eyes (or any other trait)

to have an inherited characteristic or trait that closely resembles that of a parent, grandparent, or other family member of an earlier generation ♦ *Simon wrote a novel when he was 12. He* has his grandfather's creative mind. ♦ *Hopefully the baby will* have its mother's good looks — *not my ugly face!* **Note:** If there is no resemblance to either side of the family, people sometimes say something like **"I don't know whose eyes she has!"**

Daddy's Girls and *Mama's Boys*

The expressions *daddy's girl* and *mama's boy* look similar, but they have very different connotations. A *daddy's girl* is often indulged by her father or has a very close relationship with him. She may be a little spoiled, but the term *daddy's girl* is basically positive.

Mama's boy, however, is not viewed with the same fondness or tolerance. A *mama's boy,* traditionally, was thought to be too close to or needy of his mother, too sensitive — not manly enough. Today, many people oppose criticizing a boy for these characteristics, and reject the negative connotation of *mama's boy*. But the very different meanings and implications of the two terms reveal something about traditional American attitudes toward girls and boys.

be the spitting image of someone

to look exactly like someone, to be a perfect likeness of another person. Also said as *be the spit and image of someone*. ♦ *She's* the spitting image of *her grandmother. They look exactly alike!* ♦ *It's amazing. He's* the spitting image of *his uncle.*

like father, like son *or* **like mother, like daughter**

A proverb referring to a son who resembles his father in intelligence, emotion, behaviors, or interests (now also applied to a daughter who resembles her mother in these areas). Also, this saying can refer to a son or daughter who follows the same career as the father or mother. Sometimes the saying is changed to fit the situation, as in "like father, like daughter" or "like mother, like son." ♦ *Josh is running for public office* — like father, like son. ♦ *Well,* like mother, like daughter. *Liz wants to be a veterinarian, too.* **Grammar Note:** This saying generally comes before or after a complete sentence. **Note:** A similar expression is *a chip off the old block.* For example: "You're really *a chip off the old block.* You think just like your father."

FRIENDS

Very close and trusted friends may say to each other, "We're *family.*" The meaning is clear — we are as close as family members (maybe even closer, for some people); we think of each other as family. One's closest or most important friend is often called one's *best friend*. Here are a few more idioms to describe good friends:

bosom buddy

(n) a very close friend whom one can confide in and depend on. The term can refer to either gender. ♦ *She's my* bosom buddy. *I tell her everything.* ♦ *We're* bosom buddies, *so we're always there to help each other out.*

blood brother

> **(n)** a person who has vowed to be like a brother (or sister) to another and has promised loyalty. *Blood brothers* can apply to either gender. There is no idiom *blood sisters,* though someone might say it. ♦ *As* blood brothers, *they vowed to stand by each other.* ♦ *The three kids became secret* blood brothers, *using red ink for blood.* **Note:** This term alludes to a pact in which a person is bonded to another in a ceremony that typically includes the mingling of one person's blood with the other.

fair-weather friend

> **(n)** a person who is a reliable friend only when times are good, but not when there are troubles or when times are hard. ♦ *Russ won't help you; he's only a* fair-weather friend. ♦ *Sharon will stick by you no matter what happens; she's not just a* fair-weather friend.

THE SELF

Surprisingly, not many idioms refer to the self, even though most people regard themselves as central, or at least the reference point from which they see and experience the world. There are many more idioms to describe money, for example. The following are a few idioms that people use to refer, generally playfully, to themselves.

number one (*or* **#1**)

> **(n)** oneself. Generally used in the expressions *looking out for number one* or *taking care of number one*. This idiom can imply putting one's own interests first, before others' interests, or taking care of oneself primarily. It can be said egotistically, jokingly, or to imply responsibility to oneself. ♦ *Sorry, I can't loan you any money right now. I'm just trying to take care of* number one. ♦ *Ian is such a pain to work with. He's always looking out for* number one. **Grammar Note:** *Number one* is generally used as an object rather than the subject of a sentence.

yours truly

> **(n)** me; used informally and often playfully to refer to one's self ♦ *Guess who won first prize?* Yours truly! ♦ *Hi. It's* yours truly *calling.* **Grammar Note:** *Yours truly* is generally used as an object, rather than as the subject of a sentence. **Note:** The phrase *yours truly* is a common closing to an informal business letter. It was originally meant to imply the sincerity, trustworthiness, or goodwill of the person writing the letter.

me, myself, and I

myself alone, without the help or companionship of others. Generally said as an answer to a question like, "Who did this great (something)?" or "Who helped you?" It's meant to highlight that one did something without assistance or the companionship of others. ♦ *Who paid for my education?* Me, myself, and I! ♦ *I traveled through China alone, just* me, myself, and I.

Home Sweet Home

Home Sweet Home is a saying that brings to mind the comfort and security of having a home and being in one's own home. People occasionally say it when they return home after a trip or a busy day away from home. Sometimes people refer to a home or living place as *a roof over one's head* or *a place to lay one's head.* These expressions refer to having the basic shelter of a place to live (as opposed to being homeless). A person might say, "I'm glad to have *a roof over my head*" or "He doesn't have *a place to lay his head.*"

This section includes common idioms and expressions that people use to talk about the concept of home and having and maintaining a house.

HOME

The following expressions refer to the concept of home. In some expressions, the word *home* describes more than simply a place to live; it's also a concept that includes a sense of security, familiarity, sanctuary, and comfort.

(at) home

to be in one's own house or residence, neighborhood, city, town, state, or country. Also to have returned from being away, as in the announcement "I'm home," said by someone who has just stepped through the door of their home after being gone. ♦ *She had a great vacation overseas, but she's glad to* be home. ♦ *I wasn't* at home *when you called.* ♦ *My kids* are home *doing their chores.*

Grammar Note: The expression to be *home* is an exception to standard grammar rules that require a preposition, such as *at* or *in* before certain nouns (like "at school," "at work," or "in the house"). Depending on how this idiom is used, the preposition *at* is understood. Also common are the expressions *come home, go home, get home,* and *stay home.*

Make Yourself at Home

Make yourself at home is commonly said to a guest who comes to visit someone's home. It's a polite invitation to sit down, relax, and be informal. For an extended visit, it can also be an invitation to freely use the house as if it's the guest's own home. In other words, get something to eat, use the bathroom, use the phone, and so on, without asking or waiting for the host to offer. A host might say "Help yourself" (serve yourself or take whatever you need), as in "*Help yourself to* anything you want in the kitchen."

The expressions *make yourself at home* and *help yourself* highlight an American concept that guests should be made to feel like part of the family, as if they are at home. Treating a guest like family is a way of honoring the person. But in some cultures, where a guest is treated more formally and is served and waited on, this casual attitude may seem like an insult. Generally, a guest in an American home *does* get served and attended to while also being invited to make oneself at home.

feel at home

to feel relaxed and comfortable in a place (as if one is in one's own home); to feel welcome ♦ *Thanks for visiting. I hope we made you* feel at home. ♦ *She's traveled so much that she now* feels at home *anywhere she happens to be in the world.* ♦ *Although I lived overseas for 10 years, I never* felt at home *there.*

home away from home

(n) another house, city, town, state, or country where one visits so often that it's almost like a second home; a place where one feels very comfortable ♦ *Forrest visits us so often that we've become his* home away from home. ♦ *Sue has made Mexico her* home away from home. *She stays there every winter.*

homesick

(adj) to be desperately missing and longing for one's home and family when one is far from home. Often said as to *feel homesick.* ♦ *Were you* homesick *when you were studying overseas last year?* ♦ *Whenever I feel* homesick, *I write a letter to my family.*

THE CONDITION OF A HOUSE

A few idioms describe a house when it's in good condition, clean, and well cared for. But many more idioms describe a house in poor condition, one that is dirty or needs repair. When such a house is for sale (or *on the market*), it's often described to possible buyers as *a fixer-upper* (a house that needs fixing up or repair). A less "friendly" way to describe a house that needs repair is to say that it's *run down*. And if it's especially bad, it might be called *a dump* (alluding to a garbage dump).

A house or anything else that's broken, *run down*, or needs repair could be described in one of the following ways:

in bad shape ♦ *This roof is* in bad shape. *We need to fix it before it rains.*
needs work ♦ *They bought the house, although it* needs work.
falling apart ♦ *Our house is* falling apart! *Something always needs repair.*

Note: The idiom *falling apart* actually means disintegrating, with pieces or parts becoming disconnected and falling off. So, people often use *falling apart* as an exaggeration.

Grammar Note: In the expression *in bad shape*, the adjective *bad* could be replaced by a number of other adjectives: *worse, terrible, better, good, great,* and so on.

A house or anything else that's in good condition might be described with one of the following expressions:

in good shape ♦ *The foundation is* in good shape.
well kept up ♦ *Our house was always* well kept up.

Grammar Note: In this context, the idiom *to keep up* and its adjective form, *kept up*, mean to maintain a house in good condition; to keep it orderly and clean. In its verb form, *keep up* is used as in this example: "We try to *keep up* the house."

KEEPING HOUSE

Keeping house or *housekeeping* isn't about "keeping" (not selling) a house. Instead, *keeping house* means to maintain a clean and orderly house. A house that's very clean and tidy may be called *spotless*: "Her house is always *spotless!*"

On the other hand, a very dirty house may be called a *pig sty* (like a place where pigs live) or *disaster zone*, a term applied to a place that has experienced a natural disaster, like an earthquake or tornado. If the house or other space is this dirty, then it needs to be *cleaned from top to bottom* (cleaned thoroughly, completely, in every part).

If a house is just *messy* (disorderly, untidy), then one of the following phrasal verbs with the preposition *up* might best describe what to do:

straighten up: to make more orderly, neater ♦ *I want to* straighten up *the living room before our guests arrive.*

tidy up: to make more tidy, more orderly, cleaner ♦ *Let's* tidy up *and go home for the day.*

clean up: to clean and tidy ♦ *Saturday morning, everyone helps* clean up *the house.* ♦ *Please* clean *your room* up *before you go out to play.*

To talk about specific cleaning jobs in the house, people often use the verb *to do,* as in *do housework* or *do the dishes.*

[See Appendix I for more on *do*.]

The following expressions are often used to describe varying degrees of housecleaning:

a (quick) once over

> **(n)** a light and often quick cleaning of the whole house or a specific area within the house. Often used with the verb *give,* as in *give a quick once over.* ♦ *He gave the house a quick once over before his guests arrived.*

a going over

> **(n)** a light or a thorough cleaning of the whole house or any part of the house. Often said as *a good going over* to mean a thorough cleaning. Often used with the verb *give.* ♦ *We'll give the carpets a good going over after the party.*

spring cleaning

> **(n)** a very thorough cleaning, often (but not necessarily) done in the spring, and including big jobs such as clearing out closets, washing windows, and so on. Spring cleaning can often take many days. This idiom is often used with the verb *to do.* ♦ *I'm exhausted from all the spring cleaning that we've been doing lately.* ♦ *After keeping the house closed up all winter, it's time for some spring cleaning.*

WHO DOES THE WORK

Some people hire a *housekeeper* (a person who does professional housework) to keep their house clean. *Cleaning lady* is an outdated term for *housekeeper,* but it's still used. It includes the word *lady* because professional housekeepers traditionally were women. In the past, a *housewife* (a married woman at home taking care of the house) generally did all of the housework, but today the housework is usually shared by both husband and wife. And because some husbands and wives have switched roles, now there are *househusbands,* too.

Housework and *Homework*

Two words that are commonly confused by people learning English are *housework* and *homework.* They both refer to work done at home, but refer to completely different types of work. If you're doing *housework*, then you're making your house clean: sweeping, vacuuming, dusting, and so on. If you're doing *homework*, then you're a student, and you're studying, doing schoolwork that's meant to be done after class (or at home). A student with a family does both housework and homework!

LOOKING FOR A PLACE TO LIVE

When people are looking for a new place to live, they might say "We're *house-hunting*" (looking for a house to buy or rent) or "We're *apartment-hunting*" (looking for an apartment to rent). After moving to a new residence, people sometimes have a *housewarming party* (a party to celebrate buying a new home or moving into a new residence). The simple verb *move* is used, as in the following examples, to talk about relocating to a new residence:

move

> (v) to relocate to a new residence or community ♦ *We need some packing boxes because we're* moving *next month.* ♦ *Ben helped his mother* move *to a new house.*

move out

> (v) to leave a current place of residence; to stop living with one's parents ♦ *Sid used to live in this house, but he* moved out *months ago.* ♦ *She asked her renters to* move out *because they were too noisy.* ♦ *I* moved out *at the age of 18.*

move in

> (v) to start living in a new residence or community; often put *moved into* ♦ *The house was empty for a long time, but someone finally* moved in. ♦ *Our son* moved *back* in *after living on his own for a year.*

Ages and Life Stages

From infancy to old age, the various stages of life are often expressed in idioms. Old age is the time of life that people often discuss indirectly, so there tend to be many more idioms and expressions for old age than for youth.

To express one's age, use the verb *to be:*

> ♦ *I* am *25 years old.*
> ♦ *My grandmother* is *70.*

Caution: Don't say "I *have* 25 years" to mean that you are 25 years old. That can imply that you have 25 more years to serve in prison!

When someone has a birthday, he or she might say "I just *turned* 25." In this context, the verb *to turn* means *to become.* Children like to feel that they are *grown up* (mature, adult). So, if you ask their age, they often say something like "I'm five *going on* six," meaning "Although I'm five years old, I'll soon be six!"

To ask someone's age, ask *"How old are you?"* or *"What's your age?"* It's often impolite to ask the age of a woman or of someone who appears much older than you are. However, in very familiar situations you can ask *"Do you mind if I ask your age?"*

BABIES AND TODDLERS

Newborn babies are sometimes called *a bundle of joy,* for example, "Congratulations on your little *bundle of joy.*" Here are a few other idioms for infants and babies:

> **new little one** ♦ *They have a* new little one *in their house.*
> **babe in arms** ♦ *I was just a* babe in arms *when we moved to the United States.*
> **bambino** ♦ *What a beautiful little* bambino.
> **bouncing baby boy/girl** ♦ *How is your* bouncing baby boy?

Toddlers are babies who are able to walk and are often called *tots* (short for toddlers). A funny, slightly derogatory slang term for a toddler is *rug-rat.* This refers to the fact that little children often play on the floor, crawling and scampering on the carpet or rug. An American TV cartoon program called *Rugrats* features a group of energetic toddlers and their wild misadventures.

ADULTS

Adults are often categorized as *young adults* (people in their 20s and 30s), *middle aged* (people in their 40s and 50s), and *seniors* (people in their 60s and beyond). The following are some idioms that refer to these stages.

Young Adults

20-something

> somewhere between the ages of 20 and 29 ♦ *This music appeals to the* 20-something *crowd.*

30-something

somewhere between the ages of 30 and 39 ♦ *Many of my* 30-something *friends are settling down to have families.*

Note: The expressions *20-something* and *30-something* are used as adjectives, as in the examples above. They can also be used as nouns, as in this example: *A lot of* 20-somethings *work at this company.*

in one's 20s

aged 20 to 29 ♦ *She was* in her 20s *when she started her own business.*

in one's 30s

aged 30 to 39 ♦ *Most people* in their 30s *have already started their careers.*

in the prime of life

in the best years of one's life, at the peak of one's success or power ♦ *I have everything I've always wanted, and I'm still* in the prime of my life. ♦ *That boy had so much to look forward to, but he was killed* in the prime of his life. *Note:* Today this idiom is sometimes applied to people who are middle aged, too.

Middle-Aged Adults

People who are middle aged are sometimes said to experience a *midlife crisis;* a sense of anxiety and uncertainty about one's identity, values, and relationships. A midlife crisis is generally characterized by inappropriate or irresponsible behavior, oftentimes acting younger than one's age. For example, "He seemed to be having a *midlife crisis* when he left his family and hitchhiked around the country."

Midlife crisis is often used jokingly, such as "I wanted the red convertible, but then I thought, 'Uh oh, *midlife crisis!'* So, I bought the sensible sedan."

Another term that's often used humorously is *over the hill*. It alludes to the top of the hill as age 40 or midlife, and implies that from there life goes downhill or deteriorates. Here are two examples:

♦ *Of course I can play volleyball with you. I'm not* over the hill *yet!*
♦ *Now that he's turned 40, his kids say he's* over the hill.

Two more terms that may be used when referring to people who are middle aged are *the big four-oh* and *the big five-oh*, referring to the fortieth and fiftieth birthdays as major milestones in life. For example, "Lynn just celebrated *the big four-oh,* but she still looks great!"

SENIORS

Age 62 marks the official *senior citizen* age — the legal age at which one can retire or collect Social Security benefits. *Senior*, the most common term for an older adult, is short for *senior citizen*. *Mature adult* is another term used to refer to an older adult. People tend to talk about old age with idioms and expressions, and they generally prefer not to use the word *old*. But here are some common idioms that do include the word *old*. **Grammar Note:** In these examples all of the following idioms are used as nouns, except *as old as the hills*, which is a simile and an adjective. The expressions *old age* and *old folks* can also be used as adjectives.

> **old timer** ♦ *I like to talk with the other* old timers *down at the Veterans Hall.*
> **oldster** ♦ *This movie is for youngsters and* oldsters *alike.*
> **old age** ♦ *We want to be healthy when we reach* old age.
> **old folks** (always plural) ♦ *There were lots of* old folks *at the memorial picnic.*
> **as old as the hills (adj)** ♦ *He's* old as the hills, *but you should see him play the fiddle!*

Similar, but more negative, terms are *old geezer* and *old codger,* sometimes just said as *geezer* or *codger.* These are slang expressions for a grouchy, tough, or eccentric old man: "Grandpa is an *old geezer,* but we love him."

Today, many adults in their 60s and 70s (or older) are very active, health conscious, and financially secure. So, some derogatory expressions used to describe people in this age group don't always apply. One such expression is *past one's prime,* meaning no longer in the prime of life, no longer active or a fully productive member of society. Here are some examples:

> ♦ *These old board members are* past their prime. *They should resign and let some younger ones take over.*
> ♦ *I may be* past my prime, *but I can still beat you at tennis!*

Sometimes this term is applied to a younger person who can no longer perform a physical skill as well as before, for example:

> ♦ *Professional athletes are often* past their prime *by age 30.*

The following expressions all refer metaphorically to the final stage of one's life, but they have different connotations:

declining years

> a period of declining health ♦ *He enjoyed writing his memoirs in his* declining years. ♦ *Her* declining years *were happy, though she was not very well.*

Little Old Ladies

While old men might be called *old timer* and *old geezer,* old women are often called *little old ladies.* This expression implies a small, fragile old woman who may be meek, but also possibly outspoken. The word *little* alludes to the fact that many older women (and men) shrink and lose weight as they age, so they literally become shorter and smaller. *Note:* Some people consider this expression demeaning, though it is often used endearingly.

 ♦ *People sometimes wonder how a* little old lady *like Mother Teresa could have so much impact on the world.*

 ♦ *Don't treat me like a* little old lady. *I'm quite capable of caring for myself!*

golden years

 used to imply richness, happiness, and security in the later years of life ♦ *They spent their* golden years *traveling to many parts of the world.* ♦ *We look forward to the contentment and security of our* golden years.

twilight years

 the very last years of one's life. Alludes to the time of late evening just before night; implies a period of less activity and worsening health. ♦ *In her* twilight years *she made many friends at the retirement home.* ♦ *I want my parents to be comfortable in their* twilight years.

autumn of one's life

 a period of maturity and gradual decline, but a happy and active period ♦ *No one wants to have financial troubles in the* autumn of his or her life. ♦ *He said, "I hope to spend the* autumn of my life *with children and grandchildren nearby."*

AGES AND AGES

Certain life stages are sometimes expressed as *an age.* The following are some common idioms that use the word *age* to mean a period or stage of life:

awkward age

 (n) adolescence, puberty; refers to the awkward and often difficult transition from childhood to teen years; often phrased *that awkward age* ♦ *He's at* that awkward age, *and afraid to talk to girls.* ♦ *We all went through* that awkward age.

in-between age

> (**n**) any transition age from one life stage to the next for young people; adolescence; the period between adolescence and older teen, or teen and young adult ♦ *He's at that* in-between age — *not a child, but not yet an adult.* ♦ *Three is really an* in-between age *from babyhood to childhood.*

underage

> (**adj**) not old enough to legally do activities such as driving, voting, and drinking ♦ *There's not much for* underage *kids to do at night for entertainment.* ♦ *The restaurant can lose its liquor license if it serves alcohol to anyone who's* underage.

voting age

> (**adj**) old enough to vote, 18 years old; often phrased *of voting age* ♦ *If you're of* voting age, *then remember to register to vote.* ♦ *I'll be* voting age *next year, and I intend to vote.*

college age

> (**adj**) approximately 18 to 22 years old, the age of traditional students attending college ♦ *Cancun is filled with* college-age *kids during spring break.* ♦ *Most of the people living in these apartments are* college age.

ripe old age

> (**n**) quite old; implies relative good health in old age ♦ *My aunt lived to the* ripe old age *of 103.* ♦ *I hope I live to a* ripe old age.

Blue Hairs

The older set are sometimes referred to by their hair color, as in "The auditorium was filled with *gray hairs* for the senior talent show." Older ladies who use white or gray dye on their hair often end up with hair that is slightly blue or purple. This common phenomenon inspired the idiom "blue hairs" for old ladies.

> ♦ *All the little* blue hairs *were there at the senior center luncheon.*

Note: Depending on the tone of voice or context, these names could be considered disrespectful, though seniors sometimes use them to describe themselves.

In the following examples, the word *age* does not refer to a stage of life, as in the preceding section. Here, age simply refers to the process of aging or to a chronological age:

age gracefully

> **(v)** to age with dignity; to look good or youthful even while one is aging ♦ *Many movie stars* age gracefully. ♦ *My grandmother has* aged *very* gracefully; *she is one cute lady!*

act one's age

> **(v)** to behave appropriately to one's age; usually said to children in an effort to improve their behavior, but can also be said of adults ♦ *Stop whining, Tommy, and* act your age! ♦ *He's trying to dress like the college kids. He should* act his age.

look one's age

> **(v)** to appear no older or younger than one actually is; generally used in the negative to say that one doesn't look as old as one is. This expression can be said as a compliment to an older person or simply as a statement of fact. ♦ *You don't* look your age. *That's why they always ask you to show your ID in clubs.* ♦ *I thought she was much younger than she is. She sure doesn't* look her age.

show one's age

> **(v)** to appear to be aging or to look old; implies that one actually looks older than his or her age. This idiom is said of people middle aged or older. ♦ *He looked youthful into his 70s. He certainly didn't* show his age. ♦ *Boy, look at these wrinkles! I'm really beginning to* show my age.

be ageless

> **(adj)** to seem not to grow old or look one's age, to seem not to be associated with any particular age; implies that one doesn't act like an old person ♦ *No one can figure out how old he really is. He's* ageless. ♦ *She seems* ageless, *and has friends of all ages.*

TALKING ABOUT MY GENERATION

People born during a specific time period belong to the generation connected to that era. Generations are commonly referred to by nicknames that say something about the era in which those people were born. Here is a list of generation names:

the Greatest Generation: people born in the '20s and '30s who experienced the Great Depression and World War II.

the Post-War Generation: people born after World War II. Also called *Baby Boomers*.

Baby Boomers: people born after World War II during a great increase (or "boom") in the birth rate. The years from 1945 to the late '50s are sometimes referred to as the *Baby Boom*.

the Me Generation: may include people born in the '50s, '60s, and '70s. This group of people and the era is sometimes characterized as being materialistic and self-serving (only concerned about "me" — oneself).

Generation X: people born in the '60s and '70s; the children of Baby Boomers. Also referred to as *Gen Xers*. Some Xers say that *X* refers to having nothing big with which to identify — no war or other significant historical event.

Generation Y: a somewhat unofficial name for people born in the '80s. Some people of this generation say that *Y* is a sarcastic follow up to *X* of Generation X. *Y* can also stand for the question *why?*

Generation Gap

Each generation has its own unique set of ideals, attitudes, and experiences. So, communication and understanding between generations is sometimes lacking. The *generation gap* is the difference (or gap) in understanding between older and younger generations. When parents and their children disagree, they sometimes blame the *generation gap.* Or, parents might say "I don't understand my kids," or "What's the matter with kids today?" demonstrating that the *generation gap* is widening.

Some expressions that are often said in reference to the *generation gap* are *child of the '60s* (or *'70s* or *'80s*, and so on) and *child of the twenty-first century.* Just about any decade or period of time can follow the words *child of,* for example, *child of the Depression.* This idiom is used to convey that a person's values were shaped by a particular period in American history. For example, "She's truly a *child of the '60s* with a strong belief in equal rights and world peace." You can see how a *generation gap* could exist between a *child of the Depression* and a *child of the '60s,* for example!

CHAPTER 3

CARING FOR THE BODY: EATING, SLEEPING, AND GROOMING

What more basic needs exist than to eat and sleep? There are plenty of idioms to talk about these necessities of life, as well as idioms to discuss bathing, dressing, and personal hygiene. This chapter includes approximately 150 different expressions that can be used to talk about taking care of basic needs and personal grooming.

Eating and Enjoying Food

Eating, drinking, and sharing a meal are so much a part of everyday activity that many idioms and idiomatic expressions exist to talk about them. There are expressions for hunger, thirst, food and food preparation, eating, and dining at home or at a restaurant. This section includes the most common of these idioms.

EATING

Speakers of American English often use the French expression *"Bon Appetit!"* or maybe the Italian *"Mange!"* to invite diners to enjoy the food. Or they may simply say *"Let's eat!"* Here are a few other informal expressions that mean "You are invited to start eating, and enjoy the food."

> **dig in** ♦ *Okay, everyone! Let's* dig in! ♦ *We had just started* digging in *to our food when the phone rang.*
> **chow down** ♦ *The food at the party was great. We really* chowed down.
> **eat up** ♦ Eat up! *There's plenty more.* ♦ *Kids, stop talking now and* eat up.

Eating Like a Bird, a Horse, or *a Pig!*

Some idiomatic expressions describe the manner in which people eat. For example, some people are said to:

eat like a bird: to eat very small portions, only big enough for a bird

eat like a horse: to eat large quantities, enough to fill a horse

eat like a pig: to eat huge portions, with poor table manners; to be a sloppy and noisy eater

be a light eater: to eat small portions and often light food

be a big eater: to need to eat a lot of food; the opposite of a light eater

be a picky eater: to like only a few specific foods, and not eat anything else

It's acceptable to be a *big eater* or to *eat like a horse*, but it's rude and unacceptable to *eat like a pig*. To describe how quickly or slowly someone finishes his or her meal, a person might say, "I'm a *fast eater*" or "I'm a *slow eater.*"

The act of eating is sometimes expressed as one of the following:

feed one's face

(n) to eat; implies to satisfy hunger rather than eat to enjoy a meal; also said as *stuff one's face* ♦ *Eric can't come to the phone right now. He's* feeding his face! ♦ *When we finish* feeding our faces, *let's go downtown.* **Grammar Note:** This idiom is most often used in a progressive (verb + *-ing*) tense. **Note:** This expression is often used as an answer to a question like "What are you doing?" or "Where were you?"

break bread

(n) to enjoy a meal together, especially with friends or family or at a holiday meal ♦ *Thanks for inviting me to* break bread *with you and your family.* ♦ *Let's plan to* break bread *together during the holidays.*

eat someone out of house and home

to eat up someone else's (or the family's) food supply very quickly; to eat so much as to deplete the host's financial resources (usually said as a light scolding or complaint) ♦ *Our teenagers are* eating us out of house and home! ♦ *They nearly* ate us out of house and home *when they came for the weekend.* **Note:** This idiom generally refers to another person, not to oneself.

HUNGER

Idioms that express hunger range from the mild statement *I could eat* to the dramatic *I'm starving,* or even *I'm starving to death!,* even though only people who have never known starvation would use it so lightly. A very hungry person might also say *I'm so hungry I could eat a horse.*

When people are no longer hungry (when their hunger is satisfied), they might use one of the following expressions:

> **I'm full** (informal) ♦ *I only had a small salad, but* I'm *already* full.
> **I'm stuffed** (slang) ♦ *After Thanksgiving dinner, we all were stuffed.*
> **I can't eat another bite** (said when there is still more food to eat; also put more politely as *I couldn't eat another bite.*) ♦ *Everyone ate until they couldn't eat another bite.* **Note:** This expression is never said in the affirmative as "I could eat another bite!"

A few expressions that use the word *fill* refer to satisfying hunger in a specific way:

fill up on

(v) to become full, generally by eating one specific food or snack ♦ *Don't* fill up on *candy before dinner.* ♦ *There was no food at the party, so we* filled up on *chips.*

to eat one's fill

(v) to eat until one is full; to be able to eat as much as one wants of a particular, possibly scarce or expensive, food. Also put as *to have one's fill.* ♦ *After we'd eaten our fill, we sat around the table and talked.* ♦ *There were so many blackberries on the vine that we ate our fill.*

Being Full and *Filling Up*

Language learners often have trouble knowing whether to use *full* or *fill.* The two words sound similar, and both mean the opposite of *empty,* but here's the difference: *Full,* as in the expression "I'm *full*" (no longer hungry) is an adjective: It describes a state of being. *Fill,* as in the expression "We *filled up* on snacks" (satisfied hunger), is a verb: It describes an action.

EXPRESSING THIRST

Saying "I need a drink" implies that a person wants a strong alcoholic drink to steady his or her nerves. So, for general thirst, people usually say "I need (*or* want) something to drink." Intense thirst can be expressed with one of these idioms:

dry as a bone ♦ *After the hike, we were all* dry as a bone.
dying of thirst ♦ *I'm* dying of thirst! *Where can I get some water?*

[For idioms on alcoholic drinks and drinking, see Chapter 4.]

EATING AT A RESTAURANT

Eating at a restaurant, particularly for dinner, is often expressed with the general idioms to *eat out* and to *go out to eat*. *Dine out* is similar to these idioms, but it implies dinner at a nicer restaurant. Here are examples in sentences:

♦ *Let's* eat out *tonight.*
♦ *We* go out to eat *every Friday night.*
♦ *We don't* dine out *very often. It's too expensive.*

A variation of *go out to eat* is *go out for* something, such as dinner, breakfast, a pizza, coffee. This expression can mean to go to a restaurant or bar, or to go and buy take-out food. Here are some examples:

♦ *We* go out *for breakfast every Sunday.*
♦ *Would you like to* go out *for a drink?*
♦ *Brian* went out *for pizza, but he'll be back soon.*

Following are a few other restaurant and fast-food related idioms:

take an order

(v) for a waiter or waitress to write down or hear what a patron wants to eat and drink ♦ *May I* take your order? ♦ *Your waiter will be here soon to* take your order.

place an order *or* **give an order**

(v) to tell a waiter or waitress what one wants to eat or drink ♦ *Are you ready to* place your order? ♦ *May we* give you our order?

doggie bag

(n) a container in which to carry home food from one's restaurant meal ♦ *Waiter, may I have a* doggie bag? ♦ *Shall I bring you a* doggie bag *for that chicken?* **Note:** This idiom refers to a custom of taking leftover meat home to give to one's dog. Today, people usually take the food home for themselves, not their dog.

for here or to go?

> the typical question asked to all patrons at a fast-food or take-out restaurant. It means, "Do you plan to eat the food here, or eat it away from the restaurant?" The patron's answer tells the server whether to put the food on a plate or in a bag; also (in some states) it determines whether to charge tax (for food eaten in a restaurant) or no tax (for food taken out). Also said by the patron as *make that to go* or simply *to go*, as shown in the second example that follows. ♦ *Do you want that* for here or to go? ♦ *I'd like a cheese sandwich* to go, *please.*

Food and Food Preparation

In this section, you'll find idioms for describing certain types of food, preparing and serving a meal, setting the table, and sitting down to eat. Also included are expressions to use at the table to ask for more and ask that an item be passed your way.

FOOD

Considering the importance of food in daily life, one would expect to find many idioms for the word *food*, but there are only a few common ones. Here are two slang expressions for food:

> **grub** ♦ *I'm hungry. I'm going to make some* grub.
> **chow** ♦ *The* chow *is ready. Let's eat.*

These are old expressions, but they're still used sometimes. And people sometimes say *"Chow time!"* instead of "Time to eat." A common expression that refers to a small meal or snack is *a bite to eat,* as in, "Would you like *a bite to eat?*" or "I'm hungry; I think I'll have *a bite to eat.*"

A large, delicious meal might be called a *feast* or a *banquet,* as in "What a great meal. It was a *banquet!*" (Literally, feasts and banquets are large dinners or celebrations involving lots of people and food.)

PREPARING FOOD

Typically, the verbs *make* and *fix* are used to talk about food preparation, as in these examples:

> ♦ *It's time to* make *dinner.*
> ♦ *He* fixed *a great meal.*

Here are a few other idioms that refer to preparing food:

put in (*or* on)

> **(v)** to place food in the oven to cook, or to place a pot or kettle on the stove to heat ◆ *I* put *the casserole* in *at 5:00, so it's almost ready.* ◆ *She* put *the kettle* on. ***Grammar Note:*** *Put on* and *put in* are separable phrasal verbs; they can be separated by a direct object.

nuke

> **(v)** to cook something in a microwave. Alludes to the term "nuclear," jokingly, as a source of fast heat. ◆ *For how long should I* nuke *this potato?* ◆ *If I want to cook something fast, I just* nuke *it.*

throw together

> **(v)** to quickly prepare a meal or dish; to compose a meal with little planning or few ingredients ◆ *We'll just heat up some soup and* throw together *a salad for dinner.* ◆ *She can* throw *the best meal* together *in less than an hour.* ◆ *There's not much food in the house, but let's see what we can* throw together. ***Grammar Note:*** *Throw together* is a separable phrasal verb; it can be separated by a direct object.

whip up

> **(v)** to prepare a meal or dish very quickly and easily ◆ *My grandmother often* whipped up *some cookies before we came to visit.* ◆ *I need at least an hour to make dinner. I can't just* whip *something* up. ***Grammar Note:*** *Whip up* is a separable phrasal verb; it can be separated by a direct object.

slave over a hot stove (all day)

> **(v)** to work very hard, long, and diligently (like a slave) to complete a task; to spend a lot of time and effort preparing a big meal. Often used jokingly when someone has actually spent little time preparing a meal, as in the second example that follows. ◆ *I don't enjoy* slaving over a hot stove all day. *I'd rather go to a restaurant.* ◆ *I'm glad you like the sandwiches.* I slaved over a hot stove all day *making them!*

[For information on separable and non-separable phrasal verbs, see Part V.]

THE TABLE

Following are common expressions for preparing the table for a meal and cleaning up the table afterward:

Let's Sit Down

When a meal is ready and it's time to invite everyone to sit at the table, people commonly use expressions like *time to sit down, let's sit down, come eat,* and *time for dinner (breakfast, lunch, etc)*. In the context of dining, the idiom *sit down* means to come to the table and start eating. For example, if you're invited to a dinner, the host might say, "Come anytime before 7:00. We'll *sit down* around 7:30." Or at home, someone might say, "Okay, everyone, wash your hands. We're going to *sit down* in a minute."

set the table

(v) to put the plates, glasses, silverware, and other items on the table in preparation for a meal. Also said as *the table is set.* ♦ *Josh, would you please* set the table? ♦ The table is *all* set, *so let's eat!*

put out *or* **put on**

(v) to put specific items on the table in preparation for eating ♦ *We still need to* put out *the glasses.* ♦ *Don't* put out *any plates, just bowls for soup.* ♦ *He forgot to* put on *some napkins.* **Grammar Note:** *Put out* and *put on* are separable phrasal verbs; they can be separated by a direct object.

clear (off) the table

(v) to take everything off the table after a meal. Often put in the passive form, *the table is cleared.* ♦ *Did you* clear *everything* off the table? ♦ *When* the table is cleared, *we'll get out a board game to play.* **Grammar Note:** *Clear off* is a separable phrasal verb; it can be separated by a direct object.

clear (off *or* **away)**

(v) to take specific table items or foods off the table after a meal. Often put in the passive form, as in "The dishes *were cleared away.*" ♦ *The waiter* cleared away *the plates and brought some coffee.* ♦ *Let's* clear off *these dishes before we have our dessert.* ♦ *After the dessert* was cleared away, *they left the table.* **Grammar Note:** *Clear off* and *clear away* are separable phrasal verbs; they can be separated by a direct object.

[For information on separable and non-separable phrasal verbs, see Part V.]

SERVING FOOD

Serving food, especially from the kitchen area, is often said as *bringing out* the food. For example: "You sit down; I'll *bring out* the food." When all the food is served, then it's *on the table*. This is not meant to describe the location of the food, but to say that the food has been served and is ready to eat. A person might say, "Okay, come eat! The food is *on the table*."

A typical American style of dining is to *pass* or *pass around* the food (the serving dishes) from one person to the next, as each puts some on his or her own plate. To ask for something that is on the table, but not close by, one can say, for example, "Please *pass* the salt."

A serving or portion of food is also called *a helping*, as in, "Just give me a small *helping*." People often refer to the first plate of food as the *first helping*. When it's finished, if they have more food, that's the *second helping*, and so on. The expression *a second helping* is often shortened to *seconds; a third helping* is shortened to *thirds*, and so on. Here are some examples showing how to use these expressions:

- ♦ *I'd like a* second helping *of lasagna.*
- ♦ *Who wants* seconds?
- ♦ *The pie is so delicious. May I have* thirds?

Sleeping and Waking

Because sleep consumes one-third of a person's life, it makes sense that there are so many idioms and expressions that refer to sleeping, waking, and the need for sleep.

The state of being asleep is sometimes described as *being in dreamland*. Someone who is sleeping well is *sleeping soundly* or *sleeping like a baby*. For example, "I didn't hear the phone last night. I was *in dreamland, sleeping like a baby*."

Another expression for sleeping well is *dead to the world*, meaning to be completely unaware of the world around you, as in "I was so tired that by 9 p.m. I *was dead to the world*."

Someone who is sleeping soundly and, particularly, snoring, is *sawing logs*. "John was in bed *sawing logs* when I got home." *Sawing logs* alludes to the sound made by cutting logs.

An older expression for sleep is *shut-eye* (suggesting shutting one's eyes). This idiom is usually expressed as *getting some shut-eye*, as in "I need to *get some shut-eye*."

FEELING TIRED

There are plenty of idioms to describe feeling tired or sleepy. If you are tired from work or a long day, you might say that you are *bushed, zonked,* or *all in.* Or you might use one of these expressions with the word *out:*

I'm pooped (out).
I'm tuckered out.
I'm tired out.
I'm wiped out.
I'm worn out.

For example:

♦ *After working all day,* I'm pooped.

Grammar Note: The idioms meaning to be tired are generally used in the adjective form. *Pooped out, wiped out,* and *tuckered out* can also be used as passive verbs, as in "That work really *tuckered* me *out.*"

Here are a few other expressions to describe being sleepy:

half awake ♦ *You look* half awake. *Did you get enough sleep last night?*
eyes are at half mast (alludes to a ship's sail, or a flag, being halfway down the mast or pole) ♦ *You should go to bed; your* eyes are at half mast.
ready for bed ♦ *Gee, I'm* ready for bed, *but it's only 7 p.m.* **Note:** Literally, *ready for bed* means prepared for sleep (in night clothes, teeth brushed, and so on), but people often use it to mean *sleepy* and may say it anytime before they're truly *ready* to get into bed.

GOING TO BED

When it's time for bed, people *turn down the sheets* (open the bedding) and *crawl* (or *climb*) *into bed* (get into bed). If you want to say that you're going to the bedroom to go to sleep, you might use one of these idioms:

go (off) to bed ♦ *It's late. I'm* going to bed. *Grammar Note:* Don't say "go to *the* bed."
hit the sack (*or* hay) ♦ *I* hit the sack *early last night.*
call it a night ♦ *When the guests left, we were glad to* call it a night.
turn in ♦ *I'm not ready to* turn in *yet, but you go ahead.*
go beddy-bye *or* **go nighty-night** (generally said to children) ♦ *It's time for you to* go beddy-bye.

FALLING ASLEEP

The most commonly used idioms that mean to start sleeping are to *fall asleep* and to *go to sleep*. The following examples show how to use them:

- *She* fell asleep *while doing her homework.*
- *The baby finally* went to sleep *after crying for 10 minutes.*

Other idioms that mean to *fall asleep* are two-word verbs that use the preposition *off*. People often use the following idioms to refer to unintentionally falling asleep, or to having a light sleep or short nap:

drop off ♦ *Just as I started to* drop off, *the phone rang and woke me up.*
nod off ♦ *I want to watch this program, but I'm* nodding off.
doze off ♦ *He was* dozing off *during his class.*
drift off (to ease into sleep) ♦ *Shhh. The baby is finally starting to* drift off.

Note: These idioms are often used with the verb *to start* as *starting to drop off, nod off,* and so on.

Falling asleep easily or quickly is often expressed with one of the following idioms:

be out like a light ♦ *I was so tired, I was* out like a light.
be out in a second ♦ *As soon as she got into bed, she was* out in a second.
be out (*or* **asleep**) **the minute one's head hits the pillow** ♦ *I'm generally* asleep the minute my head hits the pillow.
crash *or* **crash out** (slang) ♦ *The girls* crashed out *after the soccer game*

BEING UNABLE TO SLEEP

If you lie awake unable to sleep, you can say that you:

toss and turn (all night) ♦ *She* tossed and turned *all night worrying.*
count sheep ♦ *I was up* counting sheep *half the night.* **Note:** Alludes to trying to fall asleep by counting something repetitious, like sheep jumping over a fence.
couldn't sleep a wink ♦ *Our neighbor's party was so loud we* couldn't sleep a wink *all night.* **Note:** Always put in the negative and almost always in the past tense.

STAYING UP

The opposite of *going to bed* is *staying up* (staying awake late or later than others). Also, one can *stay awake* or *sit up (late)*. A person who likes to stay up late is often called a *night owl* (like an owl, which is nocturnal, meaning active at night). There's no similar idiom for someone who likes to go to bed early.

Grammar Note: Don't say "I *slept late* last night." This doesn't make sense, because the idiom *sleep late* means to sleep later than usual in the morning! Instead you can say "I *stayed up* late," "I *went to sleep* late," or "I *went to bed* late."

Staying up late to work on a project is described as *burning the midnight oil* (alluding to an oil lamp that is still burning at midnight because someone is awake).

WAKING UP

There are fewer idioms to describe *waking up* than there are for *going to bed*. Here are the most common ones:

wake up

> to awaken, though not necessarily getting out of bed ♦ *I usually* wake up *around 7 a.m.* ♦ *What time do you want me to* wake *you* up? ♦ *He was snoring so loudly that he* woke *himself* up. **Grammar Note:** *Wake up* is a separable phrasal verb that can be separated by a direct object: *wake* someone *up.*

come to

> to awaken; to stop sleeping ♦ *I generally* come to *before my alarm goes off.* ♦ *It was already noon by the time he* came to. ♦ *Don't wake her up, but if she* comes to *in the next hour, please ask her to call me.*

get up

> to wake up and get out of bed ♦ *She likes to* get up *early, even on the weekend.* ♦ *If I don't wake up when my alarm goes off, would you come in and* get *me* up? **Grammar Note:** *Get up* is a separable phrasal verb that can be separated by a direct object: *get* someone *up.*

[For more information on separable phrasal verbs, see Part V.]

get out of bed

> to wake up and get up; to start one's day, by literally getting out of bed; also put *crawl* (or *climb*) *out of bed* ♦ *He usually makes a cup of coffee as soon as he* gets out of bed. ♦ *Sometimes you just don't want to* get out of bed *in the morning.*

When someone tries to wake another person up, he or she might say *"Rise and shine!"* This means "come on, get up and be bright, active, and productive."

Some people wake up early, as the sun is coming up. A few colorful expressions describe getting up very early. You can place the verbs *wake, get,* or *be* in front of either of these expressions:

up at the crack of dawn ♦ *We have to* get up at the crack of dawn *to catch our flight.*

up with the chickens ♦ *She* wakes with the chickens *every morning.*

Personal Hygiene and Grooming

Everyday activities like bathing, grooming, and, in particular, using the toilet are usually expressed with idioms. The more private an activity, the more likely people are to use idioms to talk about it, rather than literal terms.

IN THE BATHROOM

The most basic of basic needs, *using the bathroom,* or going to the toilet, is generally expressed in indirect ways in American English. For example, native speakers of American English prefer not to use the specific word "toilet." So, rather than say "Where is the toilet," which sounds a little crude, it's much more common and polite to say:

♦ *Where's the* men's room (*or* ladies' room)? (said in public places)
♦ *I need to find a* restroom. (said in public places)
♦ *May I use your* bathroom? (said in a private home)

Some slang expressions for toilet or bathroom that can be used among friends are:

the head
the can
the john

Note: American English does not use the term *loo* for toilet.

Going to the Bathroom

In the sentence "I have to *go to the bathroom,*" the words *go to the bathroom* can mean find a bathroom, but *go to the bathroom* has also become synonymous with urinate and defecate. So you might hear a seemingly impossible sentence like "The little boy couldn't wait and accidentally *went to the bathroom* in his pants."

People often shorten "I have to *go to the bathroom"* and simply say "I have to go" or "I gotta go."

SOAP AND WATER

Using good old-fashioned soap and water or keeping oneself clean can be expressed with the following idioms that mean to wash oneself:

take a shower (*or* bath)

> to wash in the shower or bathtub; sometimes said as *take one's bath* ♦ *Some people* take a shower *in the morning, but I prefer to* take mine *in the evening.* ♦ *You can* take your bath *first, I'll go after you.* **Note:** In American English, people generally don't say *have a bath*.

give someone a bath

> to bathe someone, usually a child, a person who is incapable of bathing him- or herself, or a pet ♦ *After she* gave the baby a bath, *she put her to bed.* ♦ *I tried to* give my cat a bath, *but it was a bad idea.* **Note:** One cannot easily give someone a shower, so there is no such expression.

get under (*or* in) the shower

> to take a shower ♦ *After working on the construction site, I can't wait to* get in the shower. ♦ *He said, "I'll be ready soon; I just need to* get under the shower *for a few minutes."*

Using the preposition *up* with some verbs helps give the verb its precise special meaning, as in the following idioms:

wash up *or* clean up

> to quickly wash one's hands and face, usually before a meal or after getting one's hands and/or face dirty. Sometimes used for a quick shower, but most often used to mean washing oneself at the sink. ♦ *She said, "You kids go* wash up *for dinner."* ♦ *I'd like to* clean up *a little before we go to the store.* **Note:** In American English, *wash up* does not mean to wash dishes.

soap up

> to use soap and create plenty of lather, washing well ♦ *I had just* soaped up *when the water shut off unexpectedly.* ♦ *He gave his son the soap and said, "Soap up *your hands well, and I'll help you rinse them."*

freshen up

> to do a light washing, perhaps in the sink and maybe reapply make-up ♦ *I need to* freshen up *a little bit before going out again.* ♦ *Her schedule was so busy, she didn't even have time to* freshen up *going to the concert.*

GROOMING

A number of grooming idioms use the verb *do*, as in *do one's hair*, meaning to brush, comb, or arrange one's hair. In such expressions, the word *do* means to maintain in a specific way. Here are some grooming idioms that use *do*:

do one's hair

> to arrange one's hair by brushing, combing, styling, and so on; to dye one's hair ♦ *She often* does her hair *into a bun.* ♦ *I'll be ready as soon as I* do my hair. ♦ *Last week he had green hair, and this week he* did his hair *blue.* **Note:** This term is generally used for female hair styling, but it can be used for men too.

do one's nails

> to manicure and, generally, to polish one's nails ♦ *I can't touch anything; I just* did my nails. ♦ *She often* does her nails *in rainbow colors.*

do one's teeth

> to brush one's teeth, and possibly floss ♦ *Her mother said, "Go* do your teeth. *Then I'll read you a bedtime story."* ♦ *The dentist suggested that he use mouthwash after* doing his teeth.

do one's make-up

> put on one's make-up ♦ *She usually drinks a cup of coffee while she's* doing her make-up. ♦ *It takes her only about five minutes to* do her make-up.

More on Hair and Make-Up

"I'm having *a bad hair day!*" That's what people (mostly women) say when they are unhappy with the way their hair looks. When one's hair is stuck into an odd shape after sleeping, it's sometimes called *bed head* or *mattress hair*.

The common expression *put on make-up* means to apply cosmetics or make-up. Occasionally people use the funny expression "I have to *put on my face*." Be careful not to say *put on a face* or **make a face**. Those expressions mean to make a facial gesture that shows displeasure or disgust.

[See *put on* and *take off* in Part V.]

Shaving

A person with a *heavy beard* (dark, thick, and/or fast-growing facial hair) may need to shave more than once a day to look clean-shaven. If his beard is already starting to show again in the afternoon, he has a *five-o'clock shadow* (alluding to the dark shadowy look of unshaven facial hair).

GETTING DRESSED

Although you *put on* clothes or *put* clothes *on,* you don't put clothes off. This is incorrect. Instead, you *take off* clothes or *take* clothes *off.* For example, "In the morning, I *took off* my pajamas and *put on* my work clothes." Some other items that can be *put on* or *taken off* are glasses, contact lenses, jewelry, body products, perfume or cologne, topical medications, and bandages:

- *Let me* put *my glasses* on *so I can read that report.*
- *She* took off *the ruby earrings that belonged to her grandmother.*
- *After her shower she* put on *some deodorant and lotion.*
- *Some people* put *too much perfume* on.
- *You can* take *that bandage* off *now. The cut is healed.*

DRESSING UP OR DOWN

Dressing casually and informally is sometimes called *dressing down,* as in "It's just a casual party, so you can *dress down.*" "Friday is casual day in the office and we *dress down.*" The opposite of *dressing down* is *dressing up* (wearing formal or fancy clothes). For example, "Everyone *dressed up* for the graduation." To *dress up* is sometimes said as *get dressed up:* "We enjoy *getting dressed up* to go out."

Some other expressions that mean to be dressed up or to look great in very nice clothes are the following (usually put in the adjective form):

(all) decked out ♦ *They were* decked out *for the family photo.*
dressed to kill ♦ *She was* dressed to kill *and caught everyone's attention.*
dressed to the nines ♦ *Everyone was* dressed to the nines *at the opera.*
look sharp (or smart) ♦ *He wanted to* look *especially* sharp *his first day on the job.* **Note:** In American English, people say "You *look* very smart," not "You *are* very smart" (which means "You are intelligent").
look like a million dollars (or bucks) ♦ *Wow! You* look like a million bucks *in that outfit.*

The expressions *dress up* or *be dressed up* also mean to put on a costume or disguise. Children like to *play dress up* (put on adult clothes and costumes).

- *Everyone* dressed up *in costumes for the parade.*
- *The kids were* dressed up *in their Halloween costumes.*
- *The children loved the old hats and ties for* playing dress up.

Someone who loves clothes and has a lot of them might be called a *clotheshorse* or a *clothes hound.*

Hand-Me-Downs

If you grew up in a family with older brothers, sisters, or cousins, you may be very familiar with *hand-me-downs* (clothes given to you, usually because an older family member or friend has outgrown them). *Hand-me-downs* are *handed down* (or passed) from one person to, usually, a younger or smaller person. Any clothes that once belonged to someone else and were given away can be called *secondhand clothes.*

♦ *Kristy got all of her older sister's* hand-me-downs.

♦ *Some people enjoy finding quality* secondhand clothes *in thrift shops.*

[See *secondhand* in Chapter 13.]

CHAPTER 4

HEALTH MATTERS: GOOD HEALTH, ILLNESS, AND ADDICTION

Today people are *health conscious,* concerned about staying healthy and active into old age. Everyone knows (but does not always follow) the basic recipe for good health: *eat right* (eat healthy, wholesome foods), *maintain your weight* (don't gain or lose an unhealthy amount of weight), *stay active* (exercise), and *reduce stress* (try to avoid stressful situations).

Physical Health and Well-Being

Maintaining good health is often referred to with the terms *fit* or *in shape,* which mean to be in good physical health, generally as a result of exercise and a healthy diet. These adjectives are generally used with the verbs *to get, to be, to keep,* and *to stay,* and they have slightly different meanings depending on the verb that is used to create the idiom. The following examples show how to use these idioms:

get in shape

> to make an effort to become physically healthier or stronger, often by losing weight; to train or prepare for a physical challenge ♦ *After years of being sedentary, my parents are trying to* get *back* in shape. ♦ *I've been running every day to* get in shape *for the 10K race.*

be in shape *or* **be fit**

> to be physically healthy and strong, generally as a result of physical activity ♦ *I'm exercising now so I'll* be in *better* shape *for the holiday parties.* ♦ *You can't* be fit *if you sit in front of the TV all day.* **Grammar Note:** In this context, an adjective, such as *good, better,* or *great,* often separates the idiom *in shape,* as in "He's *in* great *shape* for a man 78 years old!"

keep in shape *or* **keep fit**

> to maintain good health and a strong, healthy body, generally as a result of physical activity and proper eating habits ♦ *We love to walk. That's how we* keep in shape. ♦ *Dancing* keeps *me* fit.

stay in shape *or* **stay fit**

> to maintain good health and a strong, healthy body ♦ *Playing tennis three times a week helps me* stay in shape. ♦ *It's hard to* stay fit *if you never exercise.*

The opposite of being *in shape* is being *out of shape,* which might include being too heavy or not having enough strength, energy, or stamina. People *get out of shape* when they don't exercise or don't eat wholesome foods, and when they have unhealthy habits like smoking and drinking. The following examples show how to use the expression *out of shape*:

> ♦ *If you don't exercise, you're going to get* out of shape *fast.*
> ♦ *I let myself get* out of shape *when I was working at a desk job.*
> ♦ *He's was too* out of shape *to go on the hike.*

EATING HABITS

Eating habits (what and how much one regularly eats) are important for good health. When people say they are *watching what they eat,* they don't mean that they are looking at their food; they mean that they are paying close attention to the amount, type, and quality of food they eat. Good eating habits are often advised with expressions like the following:

> ♦ *Eat a* **balanced meal!** (a meal with a balance of nutrients needed for good health)
> ♦ *Don't* **overeat!** (eat too much food)
> ♦ *Avoid* **junk food!** (packaged and processed food with no nutritional value, such as chips, soda, candy, pastries, greasy and fried foods, and fast food)

LOSING WEIGHT

Maintaining one's weight means trying to stay at a comfortable and healthy weight for one's own body type and genetic make-up. In other words, a person should try to avoid being *overweight* (having too much weight for one's body type) or *underweight* (having too little weight for one's body type).

But when people say "I'm *watching my weight,*" they generally mean they are trying not to gain weight. For example, "No dessert for me, thank you. I'm trying to *watch my weight.*"

The following idioms mean to lower or reduce body weight:

lose weight ♦ *I* lost *ten* pounds *on our month-long hiking trip.*
shed pounds ♦ *I either have to* shed some pounds *or buy some larger clothes!*
take off pounds ♦ *His doctor advised him to* take off a few pounds.
trim down ♦ *Actors often have to* trim down *or gain weight for a movie role.*
keep one's weight down ♦ *She was dieting most of her life trying to* keep her weight down.

A common way that people try to lose weight is by *dieting* or *going on a diet,* which means reducing the amount of food one eats, or eating only specific or specially designed foods that one believes will reduce weight. A person who is dieting is said to *be on a diet.*

Here are a few examples showing these terms:

♦ *I've* been on this diet *for a month, and I've lost a little weight.*
♦ *She was tired of always* being on a diet, *so she decided to quit dieting and enjoy her larger figure.*

Note: Dieting or being on a special diet is not always done for the purpose of losing weight. Sometimes people eat special diets to gain weight, to put on muscle, or to help control a health problem such as diabetes.

GAINING WEIGHT

These expressions mean to increase body weight:

gain weight

to add body weight ♦ *I* gained 10 pounds *on my vacation.* ♦ *Her doctor told her that she has to* gain some weight *before he can do the operation.*

put on pounds

to add body weight ♦ *She has* put on a few pounds *since I saw her last.* ♦ *Many young women are so worried about* putting on a few pounds *that they become ill from not eating.*

fatten up

to gain a little weight, often deliberately ♦ *He's so thin, perhaps he should* fatten up *a little.* ♦ *Actor John Travolta had to* fatten up *for his role in the movie* Pulp Fiction.

BABY FAT, BEAN POLE, AND RELATED IDIOMS

These slang expressions describe some different body conditions. It's generally impolite to use these expressions to a person directly. However, people often say them about themselves.

These expressions have to do with being heavy or having extra fat. All of them are used as compound nouns:

baby fat: the natural plumpness that babies and many children have
spare tire: extra roll of fat around the middle, alluding to a car tire
love handles: extra fat on either side of the body
pot belly: a stomach that protrudes or sticks out, also called a *paunch*
beer belly: same as a pot belly, but bigger; may be the result of drinking too much beer

These expressions are somewhat derogatory terms for being thin. All of them are used as adjectives, and generally said with the verb *to be:*

skin and bones
a bean pole
stick-thin

Note: It's impolite to comment on a person's size or weight. Words like *fat* for a very large person or *skinny* for a very thin person are considered insulting and rude. If you must refer to a person's size, use *large* or *big* and *thin* or *slender.*

IN GREAT HEALTH

When you feel good, healthy, and vibrant, you might say:

♦ *I* feel like a million bucks.
♦ *I'm* in perfect health.

Or you might use one of these comparisons, which are called *similes:*

♦ *I'm* healthy as an ox.
♦ *I'm* fit as a fiddle.

These four expressions can all be used to talk about oneself or other people. An idiom with similar meaning is *the picture of health.* This idiom is typically only used when talking about other people. For example: "Since she stopped smoking, Nancy has been *the picture of health.*"

Illness and Poor Health

If a person says "I have *health issues*," that means he or she has health problems. The health problem could be a brief illness, a *chronic illness* or *chronic condition* (a continuing health problem), or a *life-threatening* disease (a disease that can be fatal or cause death). If one's health is not good for any reason, one might be described as being *in poor health*. A similar expression, *in bad shape*, can refer to poor health or injury. Here are a few examples of these expressions to show how they're used:

- *We are worried about my uncle, who is in* very poor health.
- *The car accident left him* in pretty bad shape.

Feeling Poorly and Related Idioms

When people are *feeling poorly*, they are not feeling well; they feel a bit sick.

run down (adj) physically exhausted and tired; often used with the verb *to feel* ♦ *I've been feeling* run down *for days. Maybe I'm getting sick?*
come down with (v) become sick with a specific illness ♦ *I came down with a cold last night.*
fight off (v) for the body's immune system to combat an illness like a cold or flu ♦ *Vitamin C seems to help me* fight off *colds.*

[See more about colds and flu later in this chapter.]

Under the Weather and Related Idioms

These expressions mean that one is feeling a little sick, but not terribly ill. All of these expressions are adjectives that are generally used with the verb *to be* or *to feel*:

under the weather ♦ *When you're feeling* under the weather, *it's best to stay home and rest.*
out of sorts ♦ *I don't know what's wrong; I've felt* out of sorts *all day.* **Note:** The expression *out of sorts* (without the word *feeling*) often means to feel grumpy, irritable, or in a bad mood.
not 100% ♦ *This cold has lasted so long, I don't think I'll ever feel* 100% *again.*

Out of It and Related Idioms

These expressions mean feeling very sick, often with a cold, flu, or other common ailment:

out of it

> (adj) not coherent, stable, or present; also used to mean very tired or mentally exhausted ♦ *No, he can't come to the phone. He's too* out of it. ♦ *I felt so* out of it *yesterday that I went to bed at 6 p.m.*

feel rotten *or* **feel miserable**

> (v) to feel very bad physically; to feel very sick ♦ *Poor Baby, she just* feels miserable *with that cold.* ♦ *Man, I* feel rotten! *I'm going to call the doctor.*

sick as a dog

> (adj) very sick, nauseated, or vomiting ♦ *He was* sick as a dog *with that pneumonia.* ♦ *Something I ate in that restaurant made me* sick as a dog.

IDIOMS FOR COLDS AND FLU

Colds are so common that there is even an expression, *the common cold*, meaning the typical cold, the type of cold that most people get when they have a cold. This expression is generally used in medical and news reporting, for example, "Medical science has not yet discovered a cure for *the common cold*." The *flu* is also quite common; *flu* is short for influenza, which is caused by a virus. ***Grammar Note:*** People generally say *a cold* and *the flu*, as in "I have *a cold*" and "I have *the flu*." One exception is the expression *the common cold*, as used in the example sentence above.

Winter is called *cold and flu season*, but you can have *a winter cold* or *a summer cold* depending on the season in which you get sick.

Here are some other idioms related to colds and the flu:

catch a cold

> (v) to get a cold virus and become sick ♦ *If you're sick, stay home. We don't want to* catch your cold. ♦ *I* caught a cold *from my friend.* ***Grammar Note:*** After catching a cold, a person has a cold.

going around

> (v) circulating, as a virus, among a community, school, or workplace, causing a number of people to become sick; generally spoken in the continuous tense ♦ *Something has been* going around, *but I haven't caught it yet.* ♦ *There's a virus* going around. *A lot of people from the office are sick at home.*

[See also *come around* later in this chapter.]

Bedridden

Someone who must stay in bed is *bedridden*, or *sick in bed*. You could say "She's been *sick in bed* all week. Poor thing; no one likes to be *bedridden*." Occasionally people say that a sick person *took to his bed*, but a tired person simply *goes to bed*. Someone who's home sick but not necessarily in bed might say "I've been *house-bound* all week with this cold!" (forced to remain inside the house)

runny nose

(n) excessive mucus in the nasal passages, often a symptom of a cold; also phrased one's *nose is running*. ♦ *You've been sniffling. Do you have a* runny nose? ♦ *I told my doctor that my body aches, my* nose is running, *and I'm coughing.*

take one's temperature

(v) to use a thermometer to check one's body temperature for fever ♦ *Let's* take your temperature *to see if you have a fever.* ♦ *Your head feels hot. Have you taken your temperature?*

burning up

(v) to be very hot from a high fever; to have a high fever; almost always said in the continuous tense ♦ *Gee, you're* burning up! *Let's try to cool you down with some damp cloths.* ♦ *He was* burning up *with fever.*

COME AROUND AND RELATED IDIOMS

When a sick or injured person begins to *get better* or improve, one of the following expressions is often used to describe the person or his or her condition. ***Grammar Note:*** These idioms are often in the continuous tense (verb + *-ing*) or are preceded by *starting to*, as in "He was very sick, but now he's *starting to get better.*"

come around

(v) to improve, regain consciousness; generally used to describe a person ♦ *After her long illness, she's beginning to* come around. ♦ *We prayed that he'd* come around, *but he never woke from his coma.*

turn around

(v) to show a positive change or reversing of one's medical condition; to get better rather than worse. This idiom is used to describe a situation or condition; often phrased *turn things around.* ♦ *After his heart surgery, his critical situation began to* turn around. ♦ *His doctors think that the new medication will* turn things around.

look up

(v) to look hopeful, positive or better. This idiom is used to describe a situation or condition; almost always used in the continuous tense (verb + -ing). ♦ *The situation is* looking up. *His condition is not as bad as we thought.* ♦ *At first her doctor's prognosis was not good, but now it's beginning* to look up.

out of trouble (*or* danger)

no longer in a critical or life-threatening condition, not going to die; generally said of a person ♦ *As soon as we know she's* out of trouble, *we'll move her to a regular hospital room.* ♦ *He's* out of danger *now, but he'll have a long recovery from the accident.*

The following expressions mean specifically that the person is going to recover and probably have a *full recovery* (complete recovery and return to normal health).

on the mend

healing, mending, going to recover ♦ *The accident left him with some cuts and bruises but he's* on the mend.

on the road to recovery

recovering, going to survive or recover ♦ *I heard that you were sick. I'm glad to see you are* on the road to recovery.

GOOD AS NEW AND RELATED IDIOMS

When people are completely well or mended, they can use one of these expressions suggesting they are restored to their original health.

I'm as good as new.
I'm better than ever.
I'm back in business.
I'm back to my old self again.
I'm back to the land of the living.

Here's an example of how these idioms might be used:

♦ *I broke my leg while I was skiing, but now* I'm back to my old self again.

GOING DOWNHILL AND RELATED IDIOMS

If a person doesn't improve or begins to *get worse* (become more seriously ill or have other physical complications), one of following expressions can describe his or her situation:

go downhill

> **(v)** to get worse, to become serious; usually said of the person or the condition ♦ *Her condition is* going downhill. *Now she can barely walk.* ♦ *If he begins to* go downhill, *we'll call the specialists.*

take a turn for the worse

> **(v)** to start to get worse, usually suddenly; said of the person or the condition. This idiom is often phrased in the continuous tense (verb + -*ing*). ♦ *After the operation, he* took a turn for the worse. ♦ *She had been improving well when suddenly she* took a turn for the worse.

at death's door

> close to death, likely will die; sometimes said as exaggeration; generally said of a person ♦ *He was* at death's door, *but then he began to recover.* ♦ *He wanted me to come in to work when I was* at death's door *with the flu!*

MEETING ONE'S MAKER AND RELATED IDIOMS

People often prefer to speak indirectly and metaphorically about death, especially the death of someone they know or love. Rather than saying that someone has died, people might say that someone *has departed, has left us,* or *is gone.* They might also use one of the expressions (presented in past tense form) in the following list:

Note: Although the following idioms are all used to talk about death, you should be very careful when using them. The most acceptable and polite way to say that people have died is to say that they've *passed away.* The other idioms listed here can be very offensive if used inappropriately.

passed away

> **(v)** died; a general term that can be used in almost any situation; sometimes phrased *passed on, passed over,* or simply *passed.* The use of *passed,* rather than *passed away* and so on, is somewhat regional. ♦ *She is going home to see her grandfather before he* passes away. ♦ *I'm so sorry to hear that your mother has* passed on.

didn't make it

(v) didn't survive, recover; often used to mean that a person died suddenly or traumatically. In this context, the affirmative form, to *make it,* means to survive. ♦ *He's very ill, and he probably* won't make it. ♦ *I may be sick, but I'm* going to make it. *I'm not ready to die yet!*

met one's Maker

(v) died; a reference to meeting God after death to be judged ♦ *The old guy finally* met his Maker *at the age of 103.* ♦ *Tell that surgeon to do his best. I'm not ready* to meet my Maker!

breathed one's last

(v) died; literally, to take one's last breath ♦ *Her family was with her when she* breathed her last. ♦ *I'm not giving up until I* breathe my last.

gave up the ghost

(v) died; a reference to one's spirit or ghost leaving the body at death. This term is often used in a way that implies the person may hold on to life, choosing when and where to die. ♦ *He was such a good old dog, but eventually he had to* give up the ghost. ♦ *The old man was sick, but he was tough and didn't plan to* give up the ghost.

These slang expressions meaning to die can be said casually in an impersonal way, but it would be extremely rude and insensitive to say any one of them to a dying person or his or her loved ones.

kicked the bucket ♦ *In the final scene of the movie, the hero* kicked the bucket.
bought the farm ♦ *He lost control of his car during the race. It hit the wall, and he* bought the farm.
punched out ♦ *That wonderful old blues musician finally* punched out, *and we're going to miss him.*

Safety

Better safe than sorry is a common and handy expression meaning that one should anticipate possible dangers or hazards and act safely rather than ignore them and regret it later. The following idiomatic expressions are often used to express this safety warning:

take precautions

> **(v)** to be careful, anticipate hazards, and try to prevent them; often phrased *take precautions against* ♦ *Reduce the possibility of a burglary by* taking *the simple* precaution *of locking your doors.* ♦ *We* take precautions against *sunburn by using sunscreen.*

play it safe

> **(v)** to act safely to help prevent accidents, injury, or death ♦ Play it safe, *and wear your seatbelt.* ♦ *Most skateboarders don't want to wear a helmet, but their parents make them* play it safe.

for safety's sake

> for the purpose of being safe and trying to prevent accidents ♦ For safety's sake *we frequently check the smoke alarms in our house.* ♦ *Everyone must wear a life jacket in the boat* for safety's sake.

be on the safe side

> when faced with two options, to choose the safest, most cautious one; to act safely to avoid accidents ♦ *This food still smells fresh, but let's* be on the safe side *and toss it out.* ♦ *Our house has never been flooded, but to* be on the safe side, *we have flood insurance.*

Note: Expressions like *play it safe* and *be on the safe side* are also used in more general contexts where planning and forethought help to avoid troubles or inconvenience. For example:

> ♦ *I* play it safe *and have backup disks for everything on my computer.*
> ♦ *Just to be* on the safe side, *always pack some toilet paper when you travel.*

WORDS OF WARNING

The following terms are often said when there is immediate and possibly serious danger:

> **watch out!** ♦ Watch out! *There's a lot of broken glass here.*
> **look out!** ♦ Look out! *A snake!*
> **watch it!** ♦ Watch it *with that golf club. You almost hit me!*
> **hold it!** ♦ Hold it! *There's a car coming.*

Heads up! has a similar meaning but can imply that the danger is from above: "*Heads up!* Watch out for the baseball."

These expressions are used as a general warning or for less-serious hazards:

take care

> **(v)** to be careful, to take care of oneself; often phrased *take care not to* or *take care with* ♦ *Any time you work with power tools, you have to* take care. ♦ Take care not to *burn your mouth on that hot soup.* ♦ Take care with *that knife; it's really sharp.* **Note:** Said by itself, *take care* usually means goodbye.

watch your step

> **(v)** to pay attention to where you are walking because of a hazard; to be careful or wary, in general ♦ Watch your step. *There's some water spilled on the floor here.* ♦ *The new supervisor wants to replace you, so* watch your step.

watch your head

> **(v)** to lower your head to avoid bumping it; to pay attention to a hazard above ♦ Watch your head. *This doorway is low.* ♦ *You have to* watch your head *on this sailboat so that you don't get hit by the boom.*

Bad Habits and Addictions

Most people have a bad habit or two, like biting their nails or not hanging up their clothes. They may even have a mild addiction, like watching too much TV or drinking too much coffee. Some bad habits, like smoking, are addictive and damaging to one's health. Smoking, drinking, and drug use have inspired a host of slang terms and idiomatic expressions. This section includes some of the most common ones.

SMOKING

Smoking any kind of tobacco has been proven to cause cancer. That's why cigarettes are called *cancer sticks* (a "stick" that causes cancer) and also *coffin nails* (alluding to the long slender shape of cigarettes, and the fact that smoking can be deadly). Here are a few slang names for cigarettes:

> **smoke** ♦ *Do you have any* smokes? ♦ *Man, I need a* smoke.
> **squares** ♦ *Can I have one of your* squares? *I just smoked my last one.* ♦ *How much for a pack of* squares?

Cigarettes come in three types, which are often referred to colloquially as *lights* (with lower amounts of chemical additives), *filters* (with a filter on the end), and *straights* (no filter, just tobacco).

The following expressions describe types of *smokers* (people who smoke):

light smoker: a person who smokes some but not a lot of cigarettes per day
social smoker: a person who only smokes socially, like at a party or bar
heavy smoker: a person who smokes a lot of cigarettes per day
chain smoker: a person who smokes one cigarette after the next, continuously

You might hear the expression *pack a day,* which means that the person literally smokes a pack of cigarettes a day. A heavy smoker might smoke *two packs a day.* People who smoke this amount of cigarettes *smoke like a chimney.*

Idioms for the Act of Smoking

Most people buy cigarettes in packs or cartons, but some people *roll their own* (make their own cigarettes with cigarette papers and loose tobacco). To smoke a cigarette, one has to *light* it first. The following are three smoking-related idioms using the word *light:*

light up

(**v**) to light a cigarette; to smoke; to begin smoking for the first time ♦ *Sorry, you're not allowed to* light up *in here. This is a no smoking area.* ♦ *Studies show that fewer teenagers are* lighting up *today than a decade ago.*

give someone a light

(**v**) to light someone else's cigarette for him or her, or to give someone a lighter or matches ♦ *Do you mind* giving me a light? ♦ *Here. Let me* give you a light.

a light

(**n**) matches or a lighter to light a cigarette; generally used with the verbs *to have* or *to need.* This idiom is often phrased *"Have you got a light?"* or simply *"Got a light?"* ♦ *If you need* a light, *I have one.* ♦ *Hey, does anyone have* a light?

The act of smoking a cigarette, pipe, or cigar can be described with one of these idioms:

drag on

(**v**) to smoke with a long, slow, deep inhale. The noun form is *a drag.* ♦ *He stood there* dragging on *a cigarette.* ♦ *Advertisers appeal to young smokers with images of a rugged man* dragging on *a cigarette.*

take a drag

> **(v)** to inhale the smoke deeply; generally followed with the preposition *off* or *of* ♦ *Hey, let me* take a drag off *your cigarette.* ♦ *He* took *one last* drag of *his pipe and gave up smoking for good.*

puff

> **(v)** to smoke with short shallow breaths, without many pauses between inhales; to smoke a pipe; often followed by the preposition *on* or *with* ♦ *He* puffed on *his pipe in front of the fire.* ♦ *In the past college students used to* puff away *during the class.*

take a puff

> **(v)** to inhale or draw in smoke from a cigarette, cigar, or pipe ♦ *The first time I* took a puff *on a cigarette, I coughed for five minutes.* ♦ *Mind if I* take a puff?

Other Smoking-Related Idioms

The following are other idioms and expressions that refer to smoking and smokers:

bum a cigarette

> **(v)** to ask someone to give you a cigarette; also phrased to *bum a cigarette off* someone ♦ *Hey, can I* bum a cigarette? ♦ *Why are you always* bumming cigarettes off *me? Go buy your own!*

put out a cigarette

> **(v)** to extinguish a cigarette, to stop it from burning ♦ *He* put out his cigarette *and went back to work.* ♦ *Would you please* put your cigarette out? *The smoke is bothering me.* **Grammar Note:** *Put out* is a separable phrasal verb. It can be separated by a direct object, as in the last example above.

butt

> **(n)** the end that is left after the cigarette has been smoked ♦ *The fire started from a smoldering cigarette* butt. ♦ *Hey, don't throw your* butts *on the grass; put them in the ashtray.*

nicotine fit

> **(n)** symptoms related to a craving or intense physical need for nicotine; an addictive need for a cigarette; also said in the shortened form, a *nic fit* ♦ *He was having a* nicotine fit *after four hours in the plane.* ♦ *Give me a cigarette please! I'm having a* nic fit.

smoker's breath

> **(n)** bad-smelling breath related to smoking ♦ *I've tried chewing mints, but they don't get rid of my* smoker's breath. ♦ *I like him, but I'll never kiss him because he has* smoker's breath.

smoker's cough

> **(n)** a persistent cough related to smoking ♦ *When mom's* smoker's cough *got worse, her doctor told her to quit smoking.* ♦ *His constant* smoker's cough *was annoying everyone in the office.*

secondhand smoke

> **(n)** smoke from cigarettes that is released into the air for others to breathe ♦ *Recent studies show that* secondhand smoke *is as dangerous to a person's health as smoking.* ♦ *Most restaurants, airports, and public buildings don't allow smoking because of the dangers of* secondhand smoke.

DRINKING

When the verb *to drink* is used without naming the type of drink, it generally means to drink alcoholic beverages, as in the examples that follow.

> ♦ *Do you* drink?
> ♦ *I'm not old enough* to drink.
> ♦ *I don't* drink.
> ♦ *She quit* drinking.
> ♦ *He shouldn't* drink.
> ♦ *Have you been* drinking?

Types of Alcoholic Drinks

There are plenty of informal terms and slang for alcoholic drinks. Here are some of the most common:

> **(the) drink:** alcohol, in general; any alcoholic drink
> **booze:** any alcoholic drink
> **hooch:** usually low-quality or homemade liquor
> **vino:** wine, from the Italian for "wine"
> **brew** (also *brewski*)**:** beer
> **hard liquor:** strong liquor with high alcohol content, not beer or wine
> **cocktail:** mixed drink that contains hard liquor and possibly wine, juice, or soda

Types of Drinkers

People who drink alcohol are generally described as one of the following:

social drinker: a person who drinks alcohol only at social occasions like a party, date, or dinner

heavy drinker: a person who drinks frequently and drinks a lot at one time

People who never drink alcoholic beverages might use one of these sentences to describe themselves:

- *I'm a* teetotaler.
- *I* don't drink.
- *I* never touch the stuff.

Social Drinking

Going out for a drink and *having a few with friends* are two ways to talk about social drinking. A *cocktail party* (where cocktails are served) is another occasion for social drinking. An event or reception with a *no-host bar* means guests pay for their own bar drinks, and usually soda, coffee, and other beverages. Drinks are free for everyone at an event with an *open bar.*

Heavy Drinking

A *heavy drinker* might be considered an alcoholic depending on how much or how often alcohol is consumed and how dependent the person is on drinking. The following are some common slang terms for a person who regularly drinks too much or is an alcoholic:

boozer ♦ *She was a real* boozer, *and booze finally killed her.*
drinker ♦ *There are a lot of big* drinkers *in that family.*
lush ♦ *He was a* lush *for years until he got help and quit drinking.*
drunk (also *drunkard*) ♦ *A* drunk *was sleeping in the park.*
souse ♦ *Poor old* souse. *She just can't stop drinking.*
alky (short for *alcoholic*) ♦ *No wonder his marriage split up; the guy's an* alky.

In describing a heavy drinker, someone might say:

- *She* likes to tip the bottle.
- *He* likes his drink.

People who drink an excessive amount at one time without appearing to be drunk or without passing out (being unconscious) are often described with one of these idioms:

- *She can* hold her liquor.
- *He'll* drink you under the table.

Want a Drink?

If you or your friends are thirsty and you want to suggest getting some water, a cool soda, or ice tea, avoid saying "I'd like a drink" or "Do you want a drink?" Unless you are standing at a drinking fountain or soda machine when you say this, they may give you a strange look. Why? Because *a drink* often implies *an alcoholic beverage.* Instead say, "Would you like (to get) something to drink?" or "Are you thirsty?" so that there is less chance of being misinterpreted.

Getting Drunk

After a few alcoholic beverages, one might begin to feel *tipsy* (somewhat unsteady and mentally foggy). People may say "I'm *feeling it,*" "I'm *getting a buzz,*" or "It's *going to my head,*" meaning they are feeling the effects of the alcohol and are a little *light-headed* (dizzy). With more drinking, the person will get *drunk* (overcome by the alcohol; no longer in control of his or her faculties).

Here are some common expressions that mean a person has had too much to drink and is drunk. The form of the idiom shown is the common form in which it's generally used:

had too many (v) ♦ *I'm going to drive Jack home. He's* had too many.
feeling no pain (v) ♦ *I was* feeling no pain *after a few strong drinks.*
soused (adj) ♦ *I think some of the guests are getting* soused.
wasted (adj) ♦ *It's stupid to get* wasted *and make a fool of yourself.*
smashed (adj) ♦ *He was in big trouble with his parents when he came home* smashed.

Three sheets to the wind is one colorful expression to describe people who are intoxicated — so drunk they have lost control of their faculties. It alludes to sheets on a clothesline flapping in the wind like a drunk might stumble and weave around, unable to walk straight. The following expressions also describe someone in this drunken state:

drunk as a skunk
roaring drunk: noisy and intoxicated
dead drunk: so intoxicated that one is unconscious

Getting Help

AA is how most people refer to Alcoholics Anonymous, one of the more prominent organizations that helps alcoholics stop drinking. Its program has 12 specific steps or stages, so it's often called simply *12-step*, as in "My brother was in *12-step*." A person in such a program is said to be *in recovery,* or be *a recovering alcoholic.* A similar program for drug users is NA, or Narcotics Anonymous. Recovered drug users and alcoholics often say that they're *clean and sober* to describe their addiction-free status.

CHAPTER 5

NOSE TO THE GRINDSTONE: SCHOOL AND WORK

Keeping one's *nose to the grindstone* means working hard and diligently until a task is done, whether that be a school- or a work-related task. Education and occupation are two major endeavors in everyone's life, and they have inspired plenty of idioms, expressions, and special terms. In fact, entire texts have been written on business-related idioms alone. In this chapter, you'll find some of the most common idioms and expressions that people use to talk about their schooling, their work, and their experiences in these two environments.

School-Related Idioms

School is a huge part of American life. From learning *the three R's* (the basics of reading, writing, and arithmetic) to *living in the ivory tower* (spending so much time in an academic setting that one loses touch with the rest of the world), this section shows you the most common idioms that are related to schools and learning.

LEARNING YOUR ABCS AND RELATED IDIOMS

Learning your ABCs — a reference to learning the alphabet — is a light expression that refers to attending school and getting an education. This expression generally refers to elementary- and secondary-level education.

- ♦ *She said to her kids, "Time to get up and go* learn your ABCs.*"*
- ♦ *Some children are* learning their ABCs *at home in homeschooling programs.*

Another expression is *the three R's*, meaning reading, 'riting (writing), and 'rithmetic (arithmetic), but referring more generally to basic academic subjects. Someone might say, "Students need to spend more time on *the three R's.*" Another person might say, "Children need to study languages, music, and art, not just *the three R's.*"

Studying and doing schoolwork in general is often expressed with one of these idioms:

hit the books

> **(v)** to study, do schoolwork, often with special concentration ♦ *I have to* hit the books — *I've got a big test on Friday.* ♦ *Johnny, it's time to turn off the video games and* hit the books.

crack the books

> **(v)** to study or start studying ♦ *You haven't* cracked the books *all weekend. Don't you have homework?* ♦ *I rarely* cracked the books *in high school, but somehow I graduated.*

put (*or* have *or* keep) one's nose to the grindstone

> to work especially hard and long on something, often applied to academic study ♦ *In this program, they really* keep your nose to the grindstone. ♦ *I've had* my nose to the grindstone *for a week doing this report.*

have one's nose in the books

> to study with great concentration ♦ *She's* had her nose in the books *all day studying for exams.* ♦ *I'll play some soccer this afternoon, but I'll* have my nose in the books *tonight.* **Note:** This expression is also said in the singular as *have one's nose in **a book**.* The singular version can also mean to study a particular book for school, but typically it's used to talk about being absorbed in an interesting book that one may be reading for pleasure.

PULLING AN ALL-NIGHTER AND RELATED IDIOMS

Staying up all night (or *pulling an all-nighter*) to study for exams or complete a project is a common practice for university students in the United States. Another expression is *burning the midnight oil* (alluding to an oil lamp burning after midnight while one works). A *cram session* usually doesn't last all night — it's intense study before an exam, and it sometimes involves a number of people studying together.

The following examples show how these expressions are used in context:

> ♦ *I'm exhausted! I just* pulled an all-nighter *studying for the test.*
> ♦ *I'll have to* burn the midnight oil *to get this paper finished.*
> ♦ *There's a* cram session *for the final at Natalie's house tonight. Want to go?*

SUBMITTING WORK

At every level of education (elementary, secondary, and higher education) students are required to do homework or projects and submit them to the instructor. The work is corrected, graded (usually), and then given back to the student. The word *submit* is rarely used. Instead, the following expressions are used:

turn in *or* **hand in**

> **(v)** to submit completed work ♦ *Please* turn in *your research papers before Friday.* ♦ *Has everyone* handed in *their essay?*

pass in

> **(v)** to submit while in the class; to pass to the front of the class ♦ *Should we* pass in *our homework now?* ♦ *Time is up. Please* pass in *your exam.*

Grammar Note: Turn in, hand in, and *pass in* are separable phrasal verbs.

After reviewing and grading students' work, the instructor will *hand* or *pass* it *back:*

> ♦ *After class, I'll* hand *your essays* back.
> ♦ *First, I have some homework to* pass back *to you.*

[For more information on separable phrasal verbs see Part V.]

QUIZZES, TESTS, EXAMS

Quizzes, tests, and exams are all designed to test what the student knows. Short quizzes might happen any time, while tests and exams generally occur at the end of a unit of study or in the middle or end of the school term.

Although people use the words *test* and *exam* interchangeably, *exam* usually refers to tests that come at the end of the term, often called *final exams* or *finals*. Tests that come in the middle of the term are called *midterm exams* or *midterms*.

Here are a few ways to talk about tests: An instructor *gives a test* while students *take a test*. After a test is corrected, graded, and *handed back*, the instructor might *go over* the test (review the questions and answers).

Test questions may be one (or a combination) of the following types: *True/false questions* require marking a statement as true or false. *Multiple choice questions* require choosing the right answer out of three or four choices. *Fill-in-the-blank* questions require supplying information to complete a statement or to answer a question. An *essay test* requires writing short essays to discuss an issue or answer a question. At the university level, many tests are of this type, and may be written in a blue booklet called a *blue book*. Finally, *oral exams* or *orals* are spoken tests that are often required by some programs for graduation.

Here are some idiomatic terms for other types of tests:

pop quiz *or* **test:** a surprise test that students aren't expecting
make-up test *or* **exam:** a special test given for students who missed a previous test
open-book test: a test where students can use books and notes to help find answers to the test questions. The opposite is a *closed-book test,* but tests are usually closed book so this term isn't often used.

"How'd you do on the exam?" is a question often heard after a test. One might have done well, poorly, or just okay. But, if the results are great, or terrible, one of the following slang expressions (all verbs) might be heard:

ace the test: to do very well, get a high grade, pass the test easily ♦ *I think I aced the final; it seemed easy to me.*
bomb the test: to do very poorly, get a low grade, fail the test ♦ *I didn't study enough, so I probably* bombed the test.
flunk (the test): to fail, not pass the test; also to give someone a failing grade ♦ *He* flunked *the exam, so he'll need to do extra work to pass the class.* ♦ *Professor Jones* flunked *the three students who cheated on the test.*

DOING WELL IN SCHOOL . . . OR NOT

A student who *gets good grades* (usually As and Bs) is *doing well in school.* One who gets excellent grades or gets *all As* might be called by one of these names:

a straight-A student ♦ *For my sister, it was easy to be* a straight-A student.
a brain ♦ *He's no* brain, *but he tries very hard.*
brainy ♦ *The* brainy *kids always eat lunch and talk together.* **Note:** This adjective is most often used in front of *kid,* as in the example.
an Einstein ♦ *She brags that her granddaughter is a little* Einstein. **Note:** *Little* is often placed in front of *Einstein* when the person being described is a child.
in the 90th percentile (in the top 10 percent of the class) ♦ *She tested* in the 90th percentile, *so she'll go to a top university.*
a walking encyclopedia ♦ *Ask Jen if you don't know the answer. She's* a walking encyclopedia!

TEACHER'S PET AND RELATED IDIOMS

A student who seems to be the teacher's favorite might be called the *teacher's pet.*

On the other hand, a student who *gets bad* or *poor grades* (usually Ds and Fs) is *doing poorly in school.* Today, this student might be called *a low achiever* rather than a more demeaning term like those that follow. People sometimes use these names to criticize themselves or to tease or humiliate another.

bonehead ♦ *I was a real* bonehead *on that last test. I couldn't remember the material.*

dunce ♦ *The poster said, "Don't be a* dunce. *Study hard and stay in school!"*

numbskull ♦ *What a* numbskull! *How could you miss those easy questions?!*

"Be cool. Stay in school" is a saying to encourage students to finish high school or college. A young person who doesn't complete his or her education and graduate is called a *high school dropout* or a *college dropout.* The verb *to drop out* means to quit school before graduation. A person who fails a number of classes and is dismissed from school *flunks out.* (This expression has no noun form. There is no such thing as a flunkout). Failing an exam or class is *to flunk.*

♦ *Today high school* dropouts *can get their diplomas through continuation programs.*

♦ *She* dropped out *of college to join a dance company.*

♦ *If you* drop out *after the deadline, you'll lose your tuition.*

♦ *He failed most of his classes and* flunked out.

In School or *at School?*

Being *in school* generally doesn't mean that one is on the campus or sitting in the classroom at that moment. "I'm *in school*" is another way of saying "I'm a student" (usually a college student). If you're talking to someone on the street and you say "I'm *at school*," he'll probably say something to the effect of "What? No you aren't. You're right here!" Being *in school* can also mean attending school in general.

♦ *Are you* in school *or working?*

♦ *My daughter is* in school *in New York.*

♦ *I'm not* in school *this semester.*

♦ *I was* in school *in the early '90s.*

Being *at school* means being physically on the campus or in the classroom — just as being *at work* or *at the store* mean being physically in those places.

♦ *He's* at school *right now. He'll be back later.*

♦ *I was* at school *when you called.*

Note: People sometimes do use these expressions interchangeably, and one common exception is the use of *in school* with the following:

♦ *What did you do* in school *today?*

Most students stay in school and complete their education, but they don't always attend all their classes. In many schools and even some college classes, attendance is mandatory, so *missing class* (not going to class) can get one into trouble. And missing a lot of classes can lower one's overall grade. Still, it's common, and there are a number of common idioms for it too. ***Note:*** The expressions *ditch* and *play hooky* are usually used when attendance is mandatory. *Play hooky* is also playful slang that can simply mean to take a day off from school or work.

> **cut class** *or* **cut school (v)** ♦ *We sometimes* cut class *on Friday and go to the beach.* ♦ *Just before high school graduation, most of us* cut school *and called it Senior Cut Day.*
>
> **ditch class** *or* **ditch school (v)** ♦ *The kids who* ditched school *were sent to talk to the principal.*
>
> **skip class (v)** ♦ *I'll probably* skip class *today so I'll have time to finish my research paper.*
>
> **play hooky (v)** ♦ *Everyone, we'll have a little quiz tomorrow, so don't* play hooky!

Work-Related Idioms

Work-related expressions and business idioms are so numerous that entire books have been devoted to them. This section introduces common idioms for describing work, having and not having a job, established working hours, types of work and workers, and for being hired, fired, and paid.

"What do you do?" (What is your occupation?) is the most common way to ask people about their work or occupation. It's perhaps a short form of "What kind of work do you do?" In response, people typically don't say "I *do* (something)." They say "I *am* (something)," as in "I'm a teacher." They also might describe their occupation, like "I teach English." Another way people describe their general *line of work* (type of work) is to say *"I'm in . . ."* as in "I'm in construction."

Work, or how one earns money to live, is often referred to as *a living, earning a living,* or *making a living.* Here are some examples that show how these terms are used:

> ♦ *What do you do* for a living?
> ♦ *My work is kind of boring, but* it's a living.
> ♦ *She* makes *her* living *painting houses.*
> ♦ *He's been* earning a living *as a writer.*

Work is sometimes called *the daily grind,* or just *the grind,* as in "Well, our break is over; let's get back to *the grind.*" These expressions emphasize the tiring quality of daily work.

Here are some common ways to say that someone is employed or has a job:

> **have work (v)** ♦ *After looking for two months, I finally* have work.
> **be working (v)** ♦ *In today's economy, I'm thankful* to be working.

Here are some common ways to say that someone is unemployed, or does not have a job:

> **be out of work (adj)** ♦ *So many people are* out of work *right now.*
> **not have work (v)** ♦ *He* hasn't had work *for six months.*
> **not be working (v)** ♦ *Our daughter* isn't working; *she's going to school.*

Grammar Note: Be careful. The expressions *out of work* and *out of a job* have different meanings. *To be out of a job* generally means to be fired or laid off from a job.

WORKING HOURS

A regular day job is often called *a nine-to-five job,* referring to the common working hours of 9 a.m. to 5 p.m. (though the actual work times could vary). Saying "I have a *nine-to-five job*" indicates that one works regular working hours and *full time* (eight hours per day, five days per week). Saying "I work a *40-hour week*" or "I have a *full-time job*" expresses the same thing as a *nine-to-five job.*

Some people who are employed but who don't work *full time* (a *40-hour week*) work *part time* or have a *part-time job.* Even if they work from 9 a.m. to 5 p.m. a few days per week, they usually don't say "I have a *nine-to-five job*" because that implies full-time work.

People use the general, literal terms *day job* and *night job* to describe when they work. Some businesses operate 24 hours a day and have three or four work *shifts* (work periods). Employees use the term *day shift* for any shift that begins in the morning and ends in the afternoon or evening. The following terms are used to describe the types of *night shifts:*

> **swing shift: (n)** from about 4 p.m. to 12 a.m. (midnight)
> **graveyard shift: (n)** from about midnight to 8 a.m.
> **split shift: (n)** two shorter shifts during a 24-hour period, with a break of three or four hours in between shifts

JOB IDIOMS

Following are some job-related idioms:

> **work-a-day job:** a daily, routine, humdrum, boring job ♦ *His work isn't very exciting. It's just a* work-a-day job.

desk job *or* **office job:** a job done at a desk in an office; clerical work ♦ *I enjoy working outside. I wouldn't want a* desk job.

dead-end job: a job with no possibility of advancement or with very limited advancement. Also referred to as a job that *is going nowhere.* ♦ *He's in a* dead-end job; *he'll never be able to advance.* ♦ *I'm looking for a job with plenty of room for advancement; no* dead-end job *for me.* **Note:** *Dead-end* refers to a street or passage that has no exit or way out (called a *dead-end street*).

grunt work: (n) hard physical labor; routine, low-prestige work ♦ *He's the newest employee, so he does most of the* grunt work. ♦ *His dad said, "If you don't want to do* grunt work *all your life, get an education."* **Note:** This term originally referred to low-ranking U.S. soldiers, often called *grunts.*

slave labor: (n) hard physical labor with long hours, poor working conditions, and very low pay, as a slave might have worked; working without pay. This idiom is sometimes used sarcastically to refer to household chores. ♦ *Working in that factory was like* slave labor. ♦ *When we were kids, we had to do* slave labor *every weekend by helping to clean the house.*

THE WORKPLACE

People who work in an office might logically say, as they go to work, "I'm off to the office." But people whose jobs aren't in an office (like teachers, firefighters, construction workers, and so on) may also say this as a lighthearted and idiomatic reference to their work environment. *I'm off to the office* has come to mean more than simply "I'm going to my office." A related idiom is *life at the office,* as in "How's *life at the office?*" or "It's Monday. Back to *life at the office.*" In both examples, *life at the office* means work or workplace.

Following are a few other expressions that describe the workplace:

salt mines

(n) any workplace, but in particular, any place where one works hard; also one's work in general. Usually used in the expressions "I'm off to the *salt mines*" or "I'm home from *the salt mines.*" This expression is generally used in the first or second person (I or you). ♦ *Ah, here you are . . . home from the* salt mines. *Sit down and relax.* ♦ *It's great to have a vacation and take a break from the* salt mines. **Note:** *Salt mines* refers to a place where salt is mined or harvested and the expression alludes to hard, physical labor.

sweat shop

(n, adj) a workplace where one works long hours for low pay and in very poor working conditions; any workplace where one works hard for low pay ♦ *I'm glad I quit that factory job. It was a* sweat shop! ♦ *Police arrested two men who were running a* sweat shop *in the basement of their store.*

Note: *Sweat shop* alludes to a place where workers sweat or perspire a lot because of hard work and poor air circulation. In reality, a sweat shop is illegal, though they do exist. Workers in such situations are frequently undocumented immigrants who might be afraid or unable to demand better pay and work conditions.

THE WORKFORCE

The workforce, or the population of working people in a company, community, or the nation, is sometimes separated into categories of professional and non-professional. A few idiomatic expressions are used to describe working people.

(the) working class

(n) (adj) a category of workers that includes manual laborers and trades people; non-professionals ♦ *For her research on work-related injuries, she surveyed members of* the working class. ♦ *I grew up in a* working-class *neighborhood.* ***Grammar Note:*** Use the article *the* before *working class* when *working class* is a noun. Hyphenate *working class* when it is used as an adjective and comes before the noun it modifies.

Jack of all trades

(n) a person who is skilled at many things, who can do many different types of jobs; a person who knows a little about many jobs but isn't well skilled at any one job. Generally refers to manual labor, crafts, and trades. ♦ *I'll have my son fix that plumbing problem for you. He's really a* Jack of all trades. ♦ *She has her own repair and maintenance business, so you could say she's a* Jill of all trades. ***Note:*** *Jack of all trades* is derived from the saying "He's a jack of all trades, master of none." Today, with more women in the trades and doing jobs that were once considered men's jobs, a woman may playfully adopt the term and say that she is a *Jill of all trades*.

a grunt

(n) a person who does *grunt work* (hard physical labor, routine, low prestige work); a somewhat uncomplimentary term. ♦ *I was just a* grunt *starting out, but I eventually worked up to a better position.* ♦ *They assign all of the dirty, strenuous work to the* grunts.

GETTING HIRED

When a person is actively looking for a job (sending out résumés and going to job interviews), the effort is sometimes described as *pounding the pavement* (alluding to

Blue-Collar and White-Collar Workers

The tradition of laborers wearing a blue work shirt (with a blue-collar) and professionals wearing a white dress shirt (with a white-collar) inspired the terms *blue-collar worker* and *white-collar worker*. *Blue-collar workers* are people who do manual labor or are in a trade. *White-collar workers* are people who work in business offices or are in a profession. These terms are often used to talk about segments of society, for example: "The candidate for governor is hoping to win the vote of *blue-collar workers*."

excessive walking on the sidewalk or pavement, going from business to business looking for work). For example: "I've been *pounding the pavement* for three weeks now, and I haven't found a job yet." Finding a job, receiving a job offer, or being hired is typically described with one of the following expressions:

be in

(**adj**) be hired; to become an employee ♦ *Great news! The firm I applied to just called me to say that* I'm in! ♦ *They were very impressed with her experience, so hopefully* she's in. ***Grammar Note:*** Generally used in the affirmative rather than the negative. Almost always said with a contraction: *I'm, you're, she's,* and so on.

get the job

to be hired for a job for which one has applied ♦ *I like the company, so I hope that I get the job.* ♦ *Out of 200 applicants, she* got the job!

get an offer

to be offered a job, often with a specific salary and benefit plan ♦ *She* got offers *from three different companies.*

give an offer

to offer to hire someone at a specific salary and often specific benefits plan ♦ *They* gave *me a* good *offer. I think I'll take the job.* ***Grammar Note:*** This idiom is also said in the passive form, *be given an offer,* meaning to be offered a job, often with a salary and benefit plan: "They seemed very interested in hiring me, but I haven't *been given an offer* yet."

Make an offer is similar to *give an offer,* but is rarely put in the passive voice. Also, it can be said as *make* their *offer, make* our *offer,* and so on: "After they *make* their *offer* I'll decide whether or not to work for the company."

Grammar Note: An indirect object is often placed after the verb in the idioms *give an offer* and *make an offer,* for example:

> give **Adam** an offer
> make **me** an offer

Also, an adjective such as *good, acceptable,* or *unacceptable* may be placed before the word *offer:* "We *made him an* **acceptable** *offer,* but he refused it."

Two more idioms that mean to hire someone are to *sign on* and *bring on.* These idioms are typically used to refer to hiring someone by a signed contract, often temporarily for a specific or specialized task. *Grammar Note: Sign on* and *bring on* are separable phrasal verbs that can be separated by a direct object. These idioms are often used in the passive voice, *be signed on* and *be brought on.* Here are a few examples:

- ♦ *We recently* brought on *two specialists to analyze marketing strategies.*
- ♦ *We need help with this project, but our budget won't allow us* to bring anyone else on.
- ♦ *I was* signed on *to the job last week.*

[For more information on separable phrasal verbs, see Part V.]

A new employee might logically be called *a new hire* or, more symbolically, *the new kid on the block.* For example: "You're still *the new kid on the block* so don't be afraid to ask questions." *New kid on the block* alludes to a child who has just moved into a neighborhood and is unfamiliar with relationships and the dynamics of the children who play together there. It also implies that *the new kid* still has to prove him or herself before being fully accepted.

WORKING HARD

To be *on the job* can mean simply to be at work or at the workplace. But *on the job* also means to be busy and concentrating on a specific job or task, as in "Take a break; you've been *on the job* all morning." Someone who's always working extra hard might be called *a workhorse,* as in "Jean is a real *workhorse.* She gets a lot accomplished."

Working especially hard and energetically to complete a task is often described with the following colorful expressions:

work one's tail off (also the less polite *work one's butt off*) ♦ *We* worked our tails off *to get this project done.*
work like crazy ♦ *I've been* working like crazy *preparing for the conference.*
work like gangbusters ♦ *Everyone is* working like gangbusters *to have the play ready for opening night.*
work day and night ♦ *She* worked day and night *to finish her master's thesis.*

The Pecking Order

A few common expressions describe the person with the least seniority (years working with a company; level of authority) or the person who has the lowest position. In such a case, one is said to be *the low man on the totem pole* (alluding to the bottom-most, or lowest, figure carved on a totem pole). Other similar expressions are *the low rung on the ladder* (alluding to the bottom-most, or lowest, step on a ladder) and *at the bottom of the pecking order* (alluding to the hierarchy of domestic poultry where a bird of higher status pecks birds of lower status). ***Note:*** The expressions *the totem pole, the rungs of the ladder,* and *the pecking order* all refer to the hierarchy of authority. Here are a few examples:

♦ *When you're the low man* on the totem pole, *you get the jobs no one else wants.*

♦ *These training courses will help you move up the* rungs of the ladder.

♦ *During the economic crisis, everyone near* the bottom of the pecking order *was laid off.*

work around the clock (refers to the numbers on a clock face, but means working 24 hours a day, both day and night) ♦ *The road crew has been* working around the clock.

Grammar Note: In all of the preceding expressions (except to *work one's tail off*) the verb "go" is often used instead of the verb "work," as in *going like crazy, going day and night,* and so on.

When the work is physically very hard, people might use one of these expressions:

work like a dog ♦ *I* worked like a dog *all weekend cleaning out the garage.*
work one's finger to the bone ♦ *She* works her fingers to the bone *cleaning other people's houses.*

A GOOD-PAYING JOB

If you have a *good-paying job* (earn a good salary) you might say "*I make good money.*" Even better, earning a high salary or making a high profit might be expressed as

make bank (v) ♦ *The location of their property is so desirable that they really* made bank *on the sale of their house.*
make big bucks (v) ♦ *His business is* making big bucks *after only one year!*
rake it in (v) ♦ *She's* raking it in *on that new line of products.* ***Note:*** Sometimes put as *raking in the money* (or *dough* or *bucks*).
make money hand over fist ♦ *His computer company was so successful, it was* making money hand over fist.

A similar expression is *make* (or *pull in*) *six figures,* meaning to make a yearly salary that contains six digits ($100,000 or more). For example: "In her new job, she'll be *pulling in six figures!*" This idiom is usually put in gerund form, *making six figures* or *pulling in six figures.*

A LOW-PAYING JOB

If you have a low-paying job, you might be making minimum wage (the minimum wage per hour that an employer can legally pay in the U.S.). A person earning a very low wage might say "I'm *working for peanuts,*" implying that his or her pay has the same value as peanuts.

The following expressions imply that one's salary or hourly wage is enough to pay for basic needs:

make a living wage

> **(v)** to earn enough to pay for basic living expenses ♦ *He wasn't* making a living wage *at his first job, but now he's doing much better.* ♦ *I don't need to make a lot of money, but I do need to* make a living wage.

make ends meet

> **(v)** to be able to take care of financial needs with the money one makes ♦ *With both Matt and Lisa working, they're able to* make ends meet. ♦ *Many people can't* make ends meet *even though they work full time.*

LOSING ONE'S JOB

Plenty of idioms exist to express the unfortunate event of *losing one's job* or *being out of a job* (being fired or dismissed from a job).

The following idioms mean that someone has lost a job due to a company-based reduction in the number of employees (often to reduce expenses), and sometimes referred to, generally, as *job reduction:*

laid off

> **(v)** to be asked to leave one's job temporarily or indefinitely because the company is reducing its number of employees ♦ *She was one of the last employees to* be laid off. ♦ *The factory just* laid off *2,000 more workers.* **Grammar Note:** *To be laid off* is the passive form of the expression *to lay off,* which is what the employer does. *A layoff* is the noun form.

cut

> **(v)** to have one's position reduced in pay or scope, or eliminated altogether. Often put as *one's job* or *position was cut from the payroll.* ♦ *To avoid bankruptcy, the company* cut *one third of its workforce.* ♦ *My position* was cut *to half time, so now I need a second job.*

downsized

> **(v)** have the workforce reduced or decreased in size ♦ *He didn't want to tell us that we were fired, so instead he said, "You've been* downsized." ♦ *I haven't been* downsized *yet, but just in case I'm going to start looking for another job.* **Note:** This modern idiom is meant to sound more friendly than *fired* or *laid off,* but means the same and is often used cryptically.

The following idioms mean to *lose one's job,* to *be fired* or *laid off* from a job for any reason:

> **be let go** ♦ *He was* let go *along with the two other newest employees.* ♦ *Your company will be sorry that they* let *you* go. *You were one of their best.*
> **be (***or* **get) canned** ♦ *Ann* got canned *for continuing to smoke on the job after she was asked to stop.*
> **be (***or* **get) sacked** ♦ *He was given two warnings about his behavior, then he* got sacked. **Note:** This idiom may allude to being given one's sack or box of tools and being told to leave.
> **get the ax** ♦ *Everyone with less than 10 years in the company* got the ax *today.*
> **get the boot** ♦ *The company is downsizing, and we're just waiting to see who will* get the boot.
> **get the heave-ho** ♦ *Dan finally* got the heave-ho *after years of minimum productivity.* **Note:** Alludes to an expression used when heaving and tossing out something.
> **get one's walking papers** ♦ *The company is having trouble, but no one has* gotten their walking papers *yet.* **Note:** Refers to written notice of dismissal.

Grammar Note: The last four idioms above are also commonly used in their passive form: *be given the ax, be given the boot,* and so on. Here are two examples:

> ♦ *Tom was a troublemaker, and was finally* given the ax.
> ♦ *Once the project is finished some of the team will be* given *their* walking papers.

Grammar Note: All of the idioms in this section can be put in an active form, or used with a different verb, to mean to fire someone. In this alternative form, they would be *to lay off, to cut, to downsize, to let someone go, to can* (or *sack*) *someone, to give someone the ax* (or *the boot,* and so on.)

[See other work-related idioms in Chapter 5.]

CHAPTER 6

PEANUTS AND DOUGH: MONEY

A common saying, "money isn't everything," suggests that there are more important things in life than money or monetary gain. By contrast, the saying "money makes the world go 'round" implies that money is essential to the function of the world and everyday life. No matter what one's philosophy, money — getting it, using it, and losing it — has inspired *a wealth* (a rich supply) of idioms, slang, and sayings.

In American English, money is often called one of these slang words:

bread
dough
moola
greenback
that green stuff
scratch
loot

In addition:

A dollar bill is often called *a buck,* as in "The concert tickets cost 25 *bucks* each."
A credit card is often called *plastic,* as in "I don't have much cash with me. I'll use *plastic.*"

Making Money

Making money is the common expression for earning money or making a profit from a business venture. A quantitative adjective (showing an amount) can come before the word "money," as seen in bold in the following sentences:

♦ *I need to* make ***some*** *money while I'm going to school.*
♦ *I didn't* make ***much*** *money as a lifeguard, but it was a great summer job.*

The *breadwinner* is the person or persons in a family whose paycheck supports the family. For example:

♦ *Today, it often takes more than one* breadwinner *to support a family.*
♦ *My father was the* breadwinner *while my mother managed the house.*

Here are a few other expressions meaning to support oneself or one's family:

bring home the bacon

to be a breadwinner. Alludes to an old custom of winning a pig or pork as a prize. ♦ *Who* brings home the bacon *in your family?* ♦ *I don't always enjoy my work, but one has to* bring home the bacon.

earn one's bread and butter

to earn a living; support oneself. Alludes to bread and butter as a staple or necessity of life. ♦ *He asked his son, "How do you plan to* earn your bread and butter?" ♦ *I've sold some of my artwork, but it's not how I* earn my bread and butter.

earn one's keep

to earn enough to pay one's share of expenses or to work in exchange for one's living expenses. Often used lightly to mean doing chores for someone. ♦ *When I was a student, I* earned my keep *by working at night.* ♦ *Her husband said jokingly, "I have to do the dishes to* earn my keep."

MAKING MONEY DECEPTIVELY

Money that's made dishonestly or by deceiving others is sometimes called *dirty money*. Here are a few other expressions that refer to making money deceptively:

make a fast buck

make a quick profit illegally or by cheating others ♦ *He was always trying to* make a fast buck *with some deceptive scheme.* ♦ *They thought they could* make a fast buck *smuggling drugs, but they were caught and sent to prison.*

feather one's nest

to make a profit only for oneself, especially by taking advantage of others or one's position ♦ *Many elderly people lost their money in bad investments, while CEOs* feathered their nests. ♦ *It should be illegal for lawmakers to* feather their own nests *with pay raises while cutting money for education and social services.*

[See more idioms for making money in Chapter 5.]

Having Money

Having money, either a little or a lot, is almost always talked about with idioms. Money is a personal matter. It's impolite to ask people how much (or how little) they have. It's also considered poor manners to discuss one's own financial situation, except with close friends or family. So, idioms allow people to discuss almost any money situation indirectly.

MAKING ENDS MEET

The following idioms mean to have barely enough money to pay for basic living expenses, with little or no money left over for other expenses. This financial situation is often described as *low-income* (an income level that barely meets one's financial needs).

Grammar Note: All of these idioms are verbs, and they're often put in the continuous tense, as in *to be getting by, to be making ends meet,* and so on.

get by ♦ *My family was poor, but we* got by. ♦ *We tried to* get by *on one income, but we couldn't.*
scrape by ♦ *They've just been* scraping by *since he lost his job.* ♦ *We* scraped by *during hard times, but we survived.*
make ends meet ♦ *If I keep expenses down, I can* make ends meet *working part time.* ♦ *With hospital expenses, they weren't able to* make ends meet.
manage ♦ *They're* managing *on her salary while he finishes school.* ♦ *Somehow they* managed *every month on their low pay.*
live from hand to mouth ♦ *They were* living from hand to mouth *until they discovered oil on their property.*

[See idioms that mean "having no money," later in this chapter.]

LIVING COMFORTABLY

To live comfortably, to do okay, and *to do well* mean to have enough money to pay for basic expenses, enjoy some luxuries, and probably save some money too. This financial situation is often described as *middle-income* (a midrange income level that adequately meets one's financial needs).

live comfortably (also put as *be comfortable*) ♦ *Our family wasn't rich, but we* lived comfortably. ♦ *I don't care about being rich; I just want to* be comfortable.
do okay ♦ *Luckily we're still* doing okay, *even in this stressed economy.*
do well ♦ *They both have good jobs, so they're* doing *quite* well.

Note: Do okay and do well can have approximately the same meaning, but *doing well* often implies that a person has more money than *doing okay*.

LIVING IN THE LAP OF LUXURY

People who make plenty of money might describe their financial situation as *high-income* or *upper-income* (a top income level that more than meets basic needs and provides for many expensive extras). The following idioms mean to have a lot of money, to be wealthy or rich:

well off (adj) ♦ *They're not* well off, *but they do okay.*

well to do (adj) ♦ *Being* well to do, *she made a huge donation to the children's fund.*

loaded (adj) ♦ *He started with nothing, but his business grew, and now he's* loaded.

made of money (v) (this idiom is always expressed in the passive form) ♦ *The guy is* made of money; *he has millions!*

have money (v) ♦ *They must* have money; *have you seen their fantastic house?!*
Grammar Note: The verb *got* is often added to this idiom, as in "My aunt is CEO of a company, so she has definitely *got money*."

have money to burn (v) ♦ *If your new CD is a success, you'll* have money to burn!

rolling in money *or* **rolling in dough (v)** (this idiom is always expressed in the continuous tense; it implies having so much money that one can play in it or roll in it) ♦ *Some of these professional athletes are* rolling in money.

Living Large

Some people with a lot of money (even temporarily) like to show off their wealth, spending it lavishly and excessively. You can say they're *living large, living high off the hog* (sometimes said *living high on the hog*), or *living a life of luxury*. If they're living pampered lives with many luxuries and no financial worries, you can say that they're *living in the lap of luxury* or *living like a king* (or a *queen*). Here are a few of these expressions in context.

♦ *They've been* living high off the hog *since they won the lottery.*

♦ *He was* living large *on his inheritance, until he spent it all.*

♦ *She's always* lived the life of luxury, *so she's used to having expensive things.*

People with a lot of money are sometimes referred to with one of these idioms:

a person of means (n) ♦ *Lucy is* a woman of means *and lives elegantly.*
money bags (n) (often used in the place of the person's name) ♦ *If you need a loan, you should ask Uncle Jack,* Mr. Money Bags. ***Note:*** Not polite to say directly to someone, except as light teasing.

[See also "Big Spenders," later in this chapter.]

Saving Money

Putting away money is another way to say *saving money*; you're putting it in a safe place for the future. For example "She's trying to *put away* $100 each month." Here are a few other expressions that refer to saving money.

The verbs below are all separable, meaning that the two words of the idiom can be separated by a direct object:

lay away ♦ *We're* laying away *money for our kid's education.*
sock away ♦ *I try to* sock *money* away *in my IRA account every chance I get.*
squirrel away ♦ *My grandmother used to* squirrel *money* away *in an old coffee tin.*
stash away ♦ *He's going to use the money he* stashed away *to buy a car.*

 A similar verb is *save for a rainy day*, which means to save in case of future hardship: "Don't spend all your money. You should *save* some *for a rainy day.*"

A noun that is related to saving money is *nest egg,* which generally refers to money saved for retirement or old age: "They hope that their *nest egg* will support them after they retire."

Spending Money

Everyone has to spend money, but some *spend foolishly* or *waste money,* while some *spend wisely* or *watch their money.*

In General . . .

Following are some general expressions for spending money — wisely, foolishly, willingly, or reluctantly. These are all verbs:

drop

usually, to spend a large amount at one time, often unplanned ♦ *Wow. We* dropped *a lot of money on that little weekend trip.* ♦ *I just* dropped *$500 on a new stereo system!*

fork over *or* **fork out**

to have to pay or give money, usually unwillingly ♦ *Our taxes are already high, and this candidate wants us to* fork over *more money to the government.*

lay out

usually, to pay a lot of money for a necessary expense ♦ *We* laid out *thousands of dollars for our daughter's education.*

run up the bills (*or* the credit cards)

to have large expenses or to buy a lot of things on credit until the balance due is very high ♦ *Using the heater really* runs up the electric bills *in the winter.* ♦ *We* ran up all of our credit cards *when we were on vacation.*

shell out

to pay someone, often unwillingly, or to pay a relatively large amount of money ♦ *I had to* shell out *$100 for that traffic ticket!* ♦ *I can't believe my friend* shelled out *$800 for a comic book!*

SPENDING MONEY LIKE THERE'S NO TOMORROW

If you're spending money extravagantly or foolishly, it could be said that you're acting *like there's no tomorrow.* Another way to put this is to say that money is *burning a hole in your pocket* — you want to spend it as soon as possible.

The following verbs are also used when one is wasting money or spending it too quickly:

blow money

to waste money or to spend it on something worthless or unnecessary ♦ *You can* blow *a lot of* money *gambling at Reno.* ♦ *I just* blew *$25 on a used TV that doesn't work.*

throw money away

to waste money or to spend it on something worthless; typically, a possessive pronoun separates *throw* and *money* ♦ *That car is a piece of junk. Don't* throw your money away *on it.* ♦ *I don't mind investing in a small risk, but I don't want to* throw my money away.

throw money down the drain

> to spend money and get nothing in return ♦ *If you don't pass your college classes, we're just* throwing money down the drain. ♦ *You're just* throwing money down the drain *on that car. It constantly breaks down.*

spend it as fast as one can make it

> spend money as fast as one can make it; spend money very quickly ♦ *We have so many bills, we're* spending it as fast as we can make it. ♦ *He* spends it as fast as he can make it *on CDs and other things.*

spend like there is (*or* was) no tomorrow

> spending a lot without thinking about the future ♦ *On our vacation, we* spent like there was no tomorrow. *Now we have to pay for it!* ♦ *They were* spending like there was no tomorrow *until his company failed.*

PENNY PINCHERS

People who have money but are *tight with their money* or are *cheap* (rarely spend or share their money) might be called one of these uncomplimentary names:

> **Scrooge** ♦ *Mom, you're a* Scrooge! *You never let us buy candy.*
> **tightwad** ♦ *What a* tightwad. *He only left a dollar tip for the meal!*
> **penny pincher** ♦ *Dad was a* penny pincher, *but he saved a lot.* **Note:** This expression is not always uncomplimentary; it can simply mean someone who is careful with money.
> **skinflint** (implies someone who might be dishonest in money dealings) ♦ *We don't do business with him anymore. He's a* skinflint.

Making Every Penny Count

Are you *watching your money?* If so, you're spending carefully, wisely; you're not buying unnecessary extras. People *watch their money* when their income is low, when they have big bills or unexpected expenses, or when they're saving for something. One way to *watch one's money* is to *make every penny count,* in other words, to never pay the highest price for something, to look for bargains and sales, and to not waste money. *Pinching pennies* is another idiom that describes this cautious spending. *Pinching pennies* can be smart and necessary.

BIG SPENDERS

People who spend their money freely, sometimes to show off their wealth, might be called one of these names:

big spender

> a person who spends a lot, typically on luxury goods or to impress other people ♦ *He's a* big spender; *he's always throwing lavish parties.* ♦ *I know you like to treat your friends, but you don't need to be a* big spender.

sugar daddy *or* **big daddy**

> one who spends a lot of money supporting and buying gifts for someone, often a love interest ♦ *He was a big* sugar daddy *and bought her anything she wanted.* ♦ *When we are tired from working all day, we start joking about finding a* big daddy.

Losing Money and Going Broke

There are plenty of ways to *lose money* (or see one's savings or investments disappear). One can make bad investments or bad financial decisions, experience loss during a weak economy, and so on. Here are a couple idioms for losing money:

> **eat it (v)** ♦ *He really* ate it *on that bad business deal.*
> **lose one's shirt (v)** ♦ *We* lost our shirts *in the stock market.*

BEING CAUGHT SHORT

When people don't have enough money to pay their expenses, or have very little money left, one of the following idioms can describe the situation:

> **strapped** ♦ *With six kids to support they always feel* strapped *for money.*
> **caught short** ♦ *If you spend all your money before payday, you'll be* caught short.
> **short on money** ♦ *He was careless with his money, so when it was time to pay his bills he was often* short on money.
> **down to one's last cent** ♦ *They were* down to their last cent *when he finally found a job.*

GOING BROKE

When someone's money is gone, one of the following idioms can describe the situation:

go broke: to lose or spend all one's money ♦ *They were careless with their money and they eventually* went broke.

broke: to have no money ♦ *He's always* broke. *Where does all his money go?*

tapped: to have no available cash, may be a temporary situation ♦ *I'm* tapped. *Could I borrow a few bucks until next week?*

run out of money: to use up or spend all available money ♦ *When she* ran out of money, *she called her parents for help.*

out of money: to have no available money, may be temporary ♦ *Well, no more shopping for me today; I'm* out of money.

have a cash-flow problem: to have no available cash even though one has assets or money invested. This can be a polite way to refer to financial problems. ♦ *I'm* having a *little* cash-flow problem. *So, could I get an extension on this bill?*

Grammar Note: When *go broke* and *run out of money* are used in the present continuous form (*going broke, running out of money*) it means that one's money is almost gone; that it's going fast.

FALLING ON HARD TIMES

The following idioms imply that one is experiencing financial hardship because of bad luck or other misfortune.

down and out

to be destitute and have no money ♦ *Last time I saw him, he was really* down and out. ♦ *The homeless shelter tries to help people who are* down and out.

down on one's luck

to be experiencing bad luck that causes financial hardship or destitution; may be temporary ♦ *You helped me when I was* down on my luck, *and now I want to help you.* ♦ *Be kind to people who are* down on their luck. *Someday, it could be you.*

fall on hard times

to be experiencing difficult times financially and, usually, in other areas of life as well ♦ *The bad economy has caused many people to* fall on hard times. ♦ *When we* fell on hard times, *some family members helped us out.*

be hard up

to have financial hardship; to be poor ♦ *If you have a marketable skill, you'll never* be hard up. ♦ *During the Depression, almost everyone was* hard up.

Owing Money and Paying Debts

No one (whether an individual or a business) wants to be *in the red*. That means owing more money than one has. *In the red* refers to the red ink used for showing a negative balance — not enough money — in account books. By contrast, having more money than one owes is called being *in the black*, which refers to the black ink used for showing a positive balance.

The following idioms are commonly used when talking about owing money, or being *in the red*:

in debt

> to owe money; to have unpaid debts; also put as *deep in debt* if a lot of money is owed. Often expressed as *get into debt* or *stay in debt*. ♦ *Studies show that over 50 percent of the American population is* in debt. ♦ *After completing graduate school, many people are* deep in debt.

in the hole

> to owe money or have unpaid bills; to have a financial loss of a specific amount ♦ *He's so far* in the hole *right now that he hasn't paid his rent for a few months.* ♦ *I paid your share of the utilities, so you're* in the hole *to me for $30.*

ASKING FOR A LOAN

If you are *a little short of cash* (need some money), you might do what one clever four-year-old suggested, "Go to the bank and get some more!" But when that's not possible, you may need to *take out a loan* (borrow money). At a bank, you can ask to *take out a loan, secure a loan,* or simply to *borrow money*.

For a short-term loan from friends or family, the following expressions are commonly used:

foot someone a loan

> to loan someone money ♦ *Could you* foot me a loan *until next week?*

cover someone

> pay for someone else, sometimes without expecting to be paid back ♦ *I've just spent my last dollar. Would you* cover me? *I'll pay you back tomorrow.* ♦ *He often wants me to* cover him, *but he rarely pays me back.*

tide one over

> to get a loan or monies to help pay expenses until one has more money; also put as *carry one over* ♦ *She needs something to* tide her over *until next month, so I loaned her a little money.* ♦ *Thanks for the loan. That will* carry me over *for awhile.*

[See *mooch off* and *sponge off* in Chapter 11.]

The High Cost of Living

The cost of living — the total expense of maintaining everyday life — is almost never referred to as the low cost of living; people usually talk about the *high* cost of living. Individual costs for housing, food, utilities, insurance, medical care, transportation, and so on are one's *living expenses.* Though the cost of things seems always *on the rise* (increasing), sometimes you can still *get a deal* (find a bargain or good price).

COSTING A FORTUNE

The following expressions are often used to describe something that is very expensive or high priced:

cost a fortune

> sometimes used when one can't afford the expense ♦ *He wanted to go to private school, but it* costs a fortune.

cost a pretty penny

> sometimes this idiom refers to money you did not intend to spend, such as on a home repair or traffic citation; also, you might use this idiom when trying to persuade someone not to spend money ♦ *That speeding ticket is going to* cost *him* a pretty penny. ♦ *Buying that new car will* cost *you* a pretty penny. *If I were you, I'd keep the car you have.*

cost an arm and a leg

> implies that one might have to sacrifice something else to pay the expense ♦ It costs an arm and a leg *to maintain a sailboat.*

pay through the nose

> often refers to the expense of a necessity or financial obligation ♦ *We had to* pay through the nose *for this insurance policy.*

GETTING A RAW DEAL

When people feel that they have been cheated by having to pay too high a price or by paying too much for poor quality, they might say *I got a raw deal!* The following expressions are also often used to describe this situation:

> **It's highway robbery!** ♦ *You paid $2 for that head of lettuce?!* That's highway robbery!
>
> **It's a rip off!** ♦ *That movie was* a rip off; *it was so boring.* **Note:** The verb form, *to rip someone off,* means to steal from or cheat someone.

GETTING A REAL DEAL

When people buy something at a tremendous saving, they might say *I got a real deal.* The following expressions are also often used to describe something that is surprisingly inexpensive or on sale at a huge discount:

> **It's a steal** ♦ *Look at the sale price on this bike.* It's a steal.
>
> **I got it for a song** ♦ *At the thrift shop you can get things* for a song.
>
> **I got it for peanuts** ♦ *You can get books and CDs* for peanuts *over the Internet*
>
> **I paid next to nothing** (also put as *it costs next to nothing*) ♦ *We paid* next to nothing *to stay in the youth hostel.* ♦ *This table that I got at a garage sale* costs next to nothing. **Note:** The word *practically* can be used instead of *next to,* as in: "You should join the union. *It costs practically nothing* for a lot of benefits."
>
> **They're practically giving it away** ♦ *The camera shop is going out of business, and* they're practically giving stuff away. **Grammar Note:** *Practically* is unnecessary, but is typically part of this idiom.

CHAPTER 7

TAKING IT EASY: ENTERTAINMENT, LEISURE, AND TRAVEL

Taking it easy, or relaxing with no stress or worries, is something everyone likes to do. In fact, people often say *take it easy* to each other when they part. From *taking a nap* (a little sleep during the day) or *taking in* a show (attending a show) to *taking off* (leaving on a vacation or short trip), idioms about leisure, entertainment, and travel are abundant. This chapter is full of such idioms, which people use to talk about the many ways to relax and *take it easy.* You'll also find idioms related to transportation.

Out on the Town

People often enjoy living in big cities because of the *nightlife* — the nighttime activity and entertainment, including great restaurants, bars, clubs, theaters, concerts, and other *nightspots* (places to go at night). *Going out on the town* means going out at night to enjoy the nightlife.

go out

> **1. (v)** to enjoy nightlife and other activities outside the home ♦ *We generally* go out *on Saturday night.* ♦ *My parents rarely* go out. *They like to stay at home and go to bed early.*
> **2. (v)** to date ♦ *Laura and I have been* going out *for about a year.* ♦ *I* went out *with her a few times, but we didn't continue dating.*

take in

> **(v)** to attend a movie, play, concert, or other similar event. Often used when the decision to go to the event is spontaneous. *Take in* is generally used when the activity is passive, not active. ♦ *After dinner, we could* take in *a movie if you like.* ♦ *Whenever I go to New York, I* take in *a Broadway play.* **Note:** Do not use this phrase with the words *bar, club,* and *dance.*

see

> (v) to view, to watch an event or performance. Often said as *go to see*. ♦ *We went to* see *a great play last night*. ♦ *Have you ever* seen *Bonnie Raitt in concert?* ♦ *Hey,* seen *any good movies lately?* **Note:** Although the word *watch* clearly describes the act of concentrated looking, the idiom *to see an event* (to experience or attend) is most commonly used. *Watch* is often used when talking about viewing TV and videos. Don't use *look at* to describe viewing movies, plays, concerts, and other events.

hit the bars (*or* clubs *or* parties)

> (v) to visit, often briefly, various places of night activity; to check various places or go from place to place to find the best social scene. This idiom typically implies the consumption of alcohol. ♦ *When my buddies come to town we always* hit all the clubs. ♦ *Let's* hit a few nightspots *and then have a late dinner.* ♦ *When the movies let out, people often* hit the bars and restaurants.

[See also *bar hopping* and *club crawling*, later in this chapter.]

go dancing

> (v) to go to a nightclub, bar, or restaurant where one can dance ♦ *There's a fantastic dance band playing at the Night Vault. Do you want to* go dancing? ♦ *We love to* go dancing. *We do it almost every weekend.*

eat out

> (v) to eat at a restaurant ♦ *The restaurants are packed on Saturday night with lots of people* eating out. ♦ *We* ate out *every night on vacation.*

dine out

> (v) to eat dinner at a restaurant, generally a quality or high-priced restaurant ♦ *If you like* dining out, *there are plenty of elegant restaurants in the city.* ♦ *We should* dine out *more often.*

At the Movies

When people say that they're going to the theater, they mean, *live theater* (a play or musical), though occasionally they may mean *movie theater* (cinema). When people want to see a movie they usually say "We're going to *the movies*."

Following are some general terms related to the movies:

flick

(n) (slang) a movie ♦ *We saw a great* flick *last night.* ♦ *I haven't seen a* flick *for a long time. Let's go see one.*

showing

(n) a presentation of a movie. A theater usually has several showings of the same movie in one day. ♦ *There are five* showings *of this movie on Saturday.* ♦ *Let's get tickets for the 7:30* showing.

showtime

(n) the time when a movie (or concert, play, or musical) begins ♦ *Let's hurry, or we'll miss* showtime. ♦ Showtime *was delayed for the animation festival because of a problem with the projector.*

box office

(n, adj) the place where one buys tickets for a movie, concert, play, and so on; generally used to refer to the power of a show to attract a paying audience or the economic success of a movie ♦ *I like to work in the* box office *selling tickets, when the customers are nice.* ♦ *This movie has been a* box-office *success.* ♦ *They didn't expect this movie to do well at the* box office, *but it did.*

soundtrack

(n) the sound portion of a film, specifically, the music or songs in a movie ♦ *The movie wasn't that great, but the* soundtrack *was wonderful.* ♦ *I bought the* soundtrack *for the movie* The Red Violin. *Do you want to hear it?*

special effects

(n) the artificial visual effects of a movie. Typically said in the plural. ♦ *Some movies have great* special effects, *but not much else.* ♦ *The* special effects *in that movie weren't done very well.*

trailer

(n) a preview of an upcoming movie ♦ *I saw the* trailer *for that movie; it looks like it's going to be good.* ♦ *We're a little late, but we probably won't miss any of the movie because they'll show* trailers *for the first 10 minutes.*

moviegoer

(n) a person who goes to movies often or regularly. Often used in the plural. ♦ *I'm not much of a* moviegoer, *but I see a movie occasionally.* ♦ Moviegoers *have flocked to see this new movie.*

The Movies

Do you wonder why Americans say "I'm going to the *movies*" (plural) when they are only going to see one movie? Well, some people think it's because most movie theaters today have a number of movie screens and several movies show at one time. But, in fact, the word *movies* existed long before multiscreen movie theaters. Early films were called *moving pictures* so *movies* became a kind of nickname (the plural *movies* corresponds to the plural pictures). Films were later called *motion pictures*, but the name *movies* stuck, and we still have it today.

movie buff

> **(n)** informal, a fan, an enthusiast; someone who sees a lot of movies and knows a lot about movies and the movie industry ◆ *Since he began working in the theater, he's become a real* movie buff. ◆ *If you want to know when a film was released or who acted in it, ask Lani. She's a true* movie buff.

low-budget movie

> **(n)** a movie produced on a low budget, using much less money to produce than most Hollywood movies, and typically using less well-known actors. Sometimes referred to as a *B-movie*. ◆ *Recently there have been some excellent* low-budget movies *in the theaters.* ◆ *You can tell that this is a* B-movie, *but it's still good.*

feature-length film

> **(n)** the main film presentation of a theater; a film of the usual length, often averaging 1½ to 2 hours ◆ *The* feature-length film *shows every day from noon until 10 p.m.* ◆ *Now, sit back and enjoy our* feature-length film.

GOOD MOVIES AND BAD

If you *take in* (go to see) a movie and it turns out to be boring, you might say "I had to *sit through* (endure) a boring movie." However, if it's a great movie, especially one of mystery, action, or intrigue, you may say *"I was on the edge of my seat"* (with anticipation and interest). Another common way to say it is "That movie *had us on the edge of our seats."*

Here are some ways to describe good movies and bad movies:

Good Movies

> **box office hit** *or* **success:** a popular movie that makes a lot of money
> **mega box office hit (***or* **success):** a hugely popular movie that makes even more money
> **must-see:** a movie that you *must see*
> **keeper:** a great movie that movie critics recommend and audiences find memorable
> **masterpiece:** a great work created by a great artist
> **two thumbs up:** an excellent movie that movie critics recommend

Bad Movies

> **a sleeper:** a low-budget movie that gets little attention, but becomes a hit
> **a flop:** informal, a failure
> **a bomb:** (slang) a big, unexpected failure
> **not worth the price of a ticket:** poor entertainment for the price; not worth seeing

TYPES OR GENRES OF FILM

Movies often are described by genre or type. For example, an *adventure film* involves someone's quest or adventure, perhaps in the wilderness or a foreign country. A *comedy* is a humorous movie, sometimes a *spoof* or satire. It's easy to guess the general content of these types of movies by their names. But some movie types have less obvious, idiomatic names like *a thriller* — a suspense film dealing with crime and detection— or *a melodrama* — a drama with exaggerated conflicts, emotions, and characters.

Following are some other idiomatic terms for movie genres and general types:

> **whodunit:** from "who done it" — a slang variation of "Who did it?"; a mystery
> **film noir:** from French meaning "Black Film"; melodramatic movies dealing with urban crime and corruption and characterized by fatalism and cynicism, especially from the 1930s and 1940s
> **action film:** high action, often including violence, military encounters, and combat
> **Blaxploitation:** Black film productions from the 1970s characterized by exaggerated and often negative stereotypes of African-American characters, culture, and situations; a film genre featuring or promoting African-American actors
> **Bollywood:** films produced by the Hindi film industry, the Indian parallel to Hollywood
> **boy meets girl:** a love story
> **coming-of-age story:** a story of a young person's loss of innocence or personal growth

Here are a few other common expressions used to describe movies:

> **guy movie** *or* **guy film:** a film, often with action and violence, that's made to attract male audiences; a film that might appeal more to men than women
> **chick-flick:** (slang) a movie that might appeal to girls and women; sometimes called a *women's movie* or a *girl movie*
> **a romp:** a fun, lively, playful film
> **a tear jerker:** a film with sentimental or sad scenes that makes one cry

Live Entertainment

Live entertainment is any entertainment where you see and hear the performers *in person* (you are in their physical presence) rather than on a screen or a recording. There is *live theater, live concert, live broadcast,* and *live programming* (TV programs that are filmed in front of a *live audience*).

APPLAUSE

There are several idiomatic expressions for that familiar gesture of audience appreciation — applause, or *clapping*. Most of the following expressions can be used to introduce performers or speakers.

> **give someone a (big) hand** ♦ *Let's give our musicians* a big hand.
> **round of applause** ♦ *They gave a huge* round of applause *to the vocalists.*
> ♦ *Thank you for that nice* round of applause.
> **put our hands together** ♦ *Let's* put our hands together *and welcome our guest speaker.* ♦ *Everyone please* put your hands together *for Elton John!*
> **give it up for** ♦ *Let's* give it up for *the Mountain Community Singers.*

The highest form of audience appreciation and respect is a *standing ovation* — applause with the audience standing. By contrast, if a performer seriously offends the audience, they might hiss or *boo him* or *her off the stage* (shout *"Boo"* until the performer leaves the stage). Generally, however, a dissatisfied audience will either give a weak applause or *walk out* (leave before the performance is finished).

THEATER

At plays, musicals, dance concerts, and other stage performances you might encounter some of these idioms:

one act

> **(n)** a short play consisting of just one act ♦ *The poster says that the student theater group will present "An Evening of* One Acts*" on Friday night.* ♦ *I enjoy* one acts, *but I prefer a longer play.*

curtain time

(n) literally when the curtain goes up; when the show starts ♦ *At* curtain time *one of the actors hadn't arrived!* ♦ *Hurry! We don't want to miss* curtain time.

curtain call

(n) when performers come out on stage after the performance to take their bows and receive applause ♦ *It was a fabulous play. They had six* curtain calls. ♦ *Okay, everyone backstage, let's get ready for* curtain call.

take one's bow

(v) to bow to the audience at the end of a performance; to receive praise, applause, and congratulations for an excellent performance ♦ *Some of the children who acted in the school play were too shy to* take their bow. ♦ *The audience cheered wildly when the dancers* took their bow.

go on

1. (v) to have one's turn on the stage; to enter the stage to perform. Also to *come on.* ♦ *He* went on *too soon, but no one in the audience knew.*
2. (v) for a production to happen, to be performed ♦ *The play* went on *despite technical problems.*

backstage

(n) any area off the stage where performers dress, prepare themselves, or wait, and where the crew works ♦ *We waited nervously* backstage *for our turn to go on.* ♦ *After the performance, we'll go* backstage *to congratulate the performers.*

in the wings

(pp) off the stage on either side, just behind the side curtains ♦ *She waited* in the wings *for her cue to go on.* ♦ *Parents stood* in the wings *to help their children with their costumes.*

understudy

(n) a substitute performer who learns a performer's part or role in case the performer is ill or unable to perform ♦ *She is now* understudy *to one of the company's principal dancers.* ♦ *The* understudy *took the lead part on Sunday when the lead actress was sick.*

LIVE CONCERT

Some common idioms, especially for bands and solo musicians, are the following:

headliner

> **(n)** the lead or main attraction. Also said as the verb *headlining.* ♦ *It should be a great concert with The Chieftains as the* headliner. ♦ *The African musician Habib Koite is* headlining *at the Rio Theater tonight.*

opening act

> **(n)** the band that performs before the main attraction. Sometimes called *the warmup act* or *the supporting act.* ♦ *Let's go to the concert a little later; I don't care about seeing the* opening act. ♦ *We thought the* opening act *was better than the headliner. What did you think?*

lineup

> **(n)** the list of different performers for one show ♦ *You have to get tickets to this show. You should see the fantastic* lineup! ♦ *We're featuring a great* lineup *of jazz musicians for our New Year's Eve program. So, don't miss it.*

sit-down show

> **(n)** a show, usually at a small venue, where the audience sits and does not stand and dance ♦ *I wonder why it's a* sit-down show; *they're a great dance band.* ♦ *At our age, we prefer* sit-down shows.

open seating

> **(n)** means "seats are not reserved"; people can choose any seat that is available ♦ *It's* open seating *for this event, so sit wherever you like.* ♦ *It's not our policy to reserve seats in this club; it's always* open seating.

scalper

> **(n)** someone who tries to make a quick profit by reselling tickets at a higher price than the box office price, especially when an event is sold out or tickets are hard to get. Also used as a verb, *to scalp.* ♦ *Naturally, there were plenty of* scalpers *outside the Faith Hill concert.* ♦ Scalpers *were asking four times the ticket price, but people paid it.*

COMEDY

Comedy clubs and other nightspots feature comedy teams and *stand-up comedy* acts (a performance, often by a solo comedian, involving jokes, satire, and humorous monologues). Comedians often start a joke by saying *"Have you heard the one about. . . ."* Comedians, funny people, and anyone else who wants to share humor might *tell a joke* (tell a funny story with a *punch line*) or *crack a joke* (make a spontaneous funny comment). For example:

- ♦ *I want to* tell you a funny joke.
- ♦ *She's so funny. She's always* cracking jokes.

A comedian (or *comedienne,* a term sometimes used for a female comedian) might be called one of these names:

funny girl
funny man
joker
jokester

The *straight man* or *straight woman* is the person in a comedy team who stays serious and gives lines to the comedian or serves as the object of the joke.

The following idioms and expressions relate to comedy, humor, and laughing:

punch line

(n) the surprise last line of a joke that carries the point of the joke ♦ *Hmm. I didn't get that* punch line. *Why is it funny?* ♦ *I couldn't tell jokes, because I always forgot the* punch line.

the butt of jokes

(n) the object (or the topic) of a joke that ridicules or makes fun of someone or something ♦ *An unpopular politician is often* the butt of jokes. ♦ *A comedian may frequently be* the butt of *his or her own* jokes.

make fun of

(v) to tease or make jokes about someone or something ♦ *Don't* make fun of *me. I hate it!* ♦ *That stand-up comedian* made fun of *everybody in the audience; no one was safe from his jokes.*

poke fun at

(v) to tease or to playfully *make fun of* someone or something ♦ *Comedians sometimes* poke fun at *people sitting in the front row of the audience.* ♦ *My friends* poke fun at *me for liking the old music from the 1940s, but I don't care.*

razz

(v) (slang) to tease, ridicule, heckle ♦ *The comedian* razzed *John when he got up to go to the bathroom.* ♦ *If someone* razzes *you too much, it stops being funny.*

play a joke on (someone)

> (v) to trick someone in a funny or lighthearted manner, though the object of the joke might not think it's funny ♦ *On the last day of school, the kids* played a joke on *their teacher.* ♦ *The guys* played a joke on *their housemate and put all his underwear in the refrigerator.* **Note:** People often play jokes on others on April Fool's Day, which is the first day of April.

take a joke

> (v) to accept teasing and joking when one is the object of it; to allow teasing at one's own expense. Often put in the negative, *can't take a joke.* ♦ *He's so serious. He just can't* take a joke. ♦ *Ha! You played a good joke on me. Lucky for you, I can* take a joke.

Types of Jokes

Some jokes fall into one of these categories:

> **a practical joke:** a trick or joke played on someone, especially one designed to cause embarrassment or discomfort
> **a dirty joke:** an obscene or vulgar joke
> **a sick joke:** a joke that is in very bad taste or socially inappropriate
> **an ethnic/racial/sexist joke:** a joke aimed at a specific ethnic, racial, social or gender group, considered disrespectful and inappropriate unless aimed at one's one group
> **a standing joke:** an established joke among friends or family members that continues to be funny long after the initial funny situation
> **an inside joke:** a private or secret joke among friends, family, or peers

Just Plain Funny

These expressions are commonly used in place of the words *funny* and *humorous*. They can be used to describe people, movies, events, and so on.

Verb forms

> **make you laugh** ♦ *That joke really* made me laugh.
> **crack you up** ♦ *When I told him what you said, it* cracked him up.
> **tickle your funny bone** ♦ *The funny things little kids say can* tickle your funny bone.

Noun forms

> **a riot** ♦ *Have you seen Rowen Atkinson's new movie? It's* a riot.
> **a scream** ♦ *Amy Chu's stand-up routine is* a scream.

a crack up ♦ *It's really* a crack up *watching their new kitten playing.*
a knee slapper (an old expression) ♦ *That's a great joke! A* real *knee slapper.*
a laugh a minute ♦ *That guy is* a laugh a minute; *he's always cracking jokes.*

[See to *crack up,* later in this chapter.]

Comparative forms

funnier than heck (also said as *funny as heck*) ♦ *This author is* funnier than heck, *you should read this book.*
funnier than all get out (also said as *funny as all get out*) ♦ *He's* funnier than all get out, *always making people laugh.*

Ha Ha Ha! — Laughing

Everyone loves to laugh, and an old adage says *Laughter is the best medicine* — the best way to feel better and stay healthy. Perhaps that's why laughing has inspired so many idioms and expressions. The following verbs are often used to add emphasis and color to the word *laugh* and the concept of laughter:

burst out laughing ♦ *When she told the punch line, everyone* burst out laughing.
fall out laughing ♦ *When we saw his impersonation of the mayor, we* fell out laughing.
fall out of our seats ♦ *The kids' comedy act was so funny we nearly* fell out of our seats.
roll in the aisles ♦ *Everyone was* rolling in the aisles *by the time he finished his act.*
laugh till one's sides ache/burst ♦ *We* laughed till our sides ached *watching that movie.*
laugh one's head off ♦ *He was so mean to the waitress, I* laughed my head off *when they made him leave the restaurant in the middle of his meal.*
split a gut or **bust a gut** ♦ *She's going to* split a gut *when you tell her that story.*
can't stop laughing ♦ *I* can't stop laughing *about the funny incident that happened at work yesterday.*
die laughing ♦ *We just about* died laughing *when we heard the story.*
crack up ♦ *You'll* crack up *when you read the comics in today's paper.*
bust up ♦ *He* busted *everyone* up *at the party with his funny antics.*

Here are a few expressions to describe lots of laughter:

fits of laughter ♦ *We were in* fits of laughter *over that funny article.*
peals of laughter ♦ *She's such a funny teacher,* peals of laughter *are always coming from her classroom.*

There's even an expression for artificial laughter. The slang term *canned laughter* refers to recorded laughter used on radio and TV programs.

The Bar and Club Scene

Bars and nightclubs (or clubs) are popular weekend *nightspots.* Most cities have lots of clubs and several different types of bars. There are *wine bars* that serve wine and appetizers; *sports bars* that offer a sports theme and usually big screen TVs for watching sports events; *gay bars* that cater to *gay and lesbian* (homosexual) clients, but often attract *straight* (heterosexual) clients, also; and *microbreweries* that serve their own locally brewed beer.

For many people, especially *singles* (unmarried or unattached individuals) the main attraction at bars and clubs is the *social scene* (social environment and the opportunity to meet people). Groups of male or female friends may go to a bar or club hoping to meet someone or even *pick up* someone (find a romantic or sexual partner for the evening). This sexual motive has inspired the following nicknames for some bars and clubs:

> **a pick-up place (*or* joint):** (informal) a place where one can easily *pick up* someone or find a casual date for possible sexual activity
>
> **a meat market:** (slang) a bar or club characterized by patrons conducting an active search for casual sex

Of course, *couples* (people in a romantic relationship) also frequent bars and clubs, but some nightspots cater mainly to singles and may even be called *singles' bars.*

[See many more idioms on *dating, romance,* and *sex* in Chapter 8.]

Following are some common idioms and expressions related to bars, clubs, and *nightlife:*

bar hopping

> **(n, adj)** to go from bar to bar in one evening to check the social scene and possibly have a drink at each place. Sometimes said as *do some bar hopping* or *go bar hopping.* Also used as an adjective (*bar-hopping days*) to describe a period of one's life, usually one's youth, when *bar hopping* was a regular activity. ◆ *On her 21st birthday Jesse's friends took her* bar hopping. ◆ *My* bar-hopping *days are over. I'm a family man now.*

club (*or* pub) crawling

> **(n)** to go from nightclub to nightclub or from bar to bar in one evening to check the social scene and enjoy the music ◆ *After a night of* club crawling, *I usually sleep till noon.* ◆ *There are some great pubs in this town. Let's go* pub crawling, *and I'll show you.* **Grammar Note:** The expressions *bar hopping, club crawling,* and *pub crawling* are adjective/noun combinations. The nouns *hopping* and *crawling* are in the gerund (*-ing*) form.

disco

(n) (slang) short for *discotheque*, a nightclub or public place for dancing where the dance music is prerecorded and played by a *deejay*. ♦ *Are there some good* discos *in this town?* ♦ *You can find us at the* disco *every Friday night.*

[see *deejay* later in this list of terms.]

cover charge

(n) a charge to enter the bar or club, usually when there is live music, but no ticket being sold. Also called *the cover*. ♦ *You pay a $5.00* cover charge *at the door.* ♦ *There is no* cover *at this club, and they always have good bands!*

bouncer

(n) the person (usually large and muscular) hired to control and/or remove any unruly patrons, and also to checks patrons' ID at the door ♦ *My friend is the* bouncer, *so he'll let you in even though you lost your ID.* ♦ *The man was drunk and causing trouble, so the* bouncer *kicked him out.*

deejay

(n, v) (informal) short for *disc jockey* or *disk jockey,* the person who plays pre-recorded music at a disco or club (also radio or a party) when there is no live music. ♦ *He worked as a* deejay *at a popular nightclub while he was in college.* ♦ *There's no live music at this club, but there's a great* deejay.

lounge lizard

(n) (slang) a person, usually an idle, pleasure-seeking man who frequently goes to nightclubs and *cocktail lounges* (rooms in a hotel or restaurant that serve alcoholic beverages) ♦ *There are too many* lounge lizards *in this place. Let's go to a different bar.* ♦ *After his divorce, he turned into a* lounge lizard.

Leisure

Taking time off from work (taking a vacation or break from work) has inspired plenty of idioms that mean to do no work or have no schedule or obligations.

Relaxing, or *taking it easy,* is usually a good thing, but too much *taking it easy* can sometimes make a person bored, lazy, unmotivated, or uninspired. The following common expressions can be used in a positive or negative way, and they are generally used as verbs:

kick back ♦ *On the weekend we like to just* kick back *and relax.*

chill (out) ♦ *I usually just* chill out *with my friends after school.*

do nothing ♦ *After* doing nothing *for two days, it's hard to go back to work on Monday.*

goof off (often means not working when one should be) ♦ *I've been* goofing off *all day and loving it!*

hang out ♦ *Come on over and* hang out *with us.*

hang around ♦ *I don't want to* hang around *the house all day; let's go do something!*

take it easy ♦ *Let's just* take it easy *today and do the yard work tomorrow.*

lie around or **laze around** or **sit around** ♦ *I just want to* lie around *and do nothing today.* ♦ *We* lazed around *until noon.* ♦ *He* sat around *for two months before he finally decided to get a job.* **Note:** *Lying around* or *lazing around* might include napping or sleeping, but be careful not to say *sleeping around,* which means to be having sex with more than one person during the same time period.

Here are some idioms to describe a person who lies around all day doing nothing. People often use these terms to joke about themselves:

a couch potato ♦ *I work hard during the week, but on the weekend, I'm* a couch potato.

lazybones ♦ *Come on,* lazybones. *Get up and help me do some housework.*

Chillin'

Chill, a slang word from the '70s, has come to have a number of uses, particularly among young people. As slang for to relax, *chill* might be heard as "I'm just *chilling* with my friends today" (often said as *chillin',* dropping the final *-g*). *Chill* also means to wait, as in "Well, let's just *chill* here for awhile until our friends arrive," or to preoccupy oneself while one is waiting, as in "Take your time; I'll just *chill* in the bookstore until you're ready." People might say *Chill out!* to people who need to cool their anger or frustration, or they might use this slangy expression: "You need to *take a chill pill.*"

A *TV junkie* (someone addicted to TV) spends many long hours watching TV — a pastime that requires little or no mental energy. Consequently, the television set is nicknamed *the idiot box* or *the boob tube* (*boob* meaning dummy or idiot). People often sit in front of the TV and *channel surf* (mindlessly flip through the channels with the TV remote).

GETTING AWAY FROM IT ALL

In American English, people don't *go on holiday*, as they do in British English; they *go on vacation* or *take a vacation*. A holiday can be a day of freedom from work or a nationally recognized day to honor an event. So, one does not *go on it*, but one can *have* a holiday, *celebrate* a holiday, or go on vacation *during* the holidays.

A vacation often implies a planned trip or an extended time away from work. Whether a trip is planned or not, people often use the following expressions to refer in general to taking a vacation:

get away from it all (implies escaping the stress and busyness of every day life) ♦ *Going backpacking helps me* get away from it all.
get (*or* go) out of town ♦ *He's been trying to* get out of town *for months, but he's too busy.*

The expressions that follow, *be away, go away,* and *get away,* are often followed by *for* and a duration of time or a specific occasion:

be away ♦ *Would you feed my cat while I'm* away?
go away ♦ *We often* go away *for the weekend.*
get away ♦ *We hope that we can* get away *for the holidays.*

Two other similar expressions follow:

take off (to leave, go somewhere) ♦ *Let's* take off *and go camping this weekend.*
take time off (take a leave from work) ♦ *I'm going to* take *some* time off *next month.*

Transportation

Getting away from home always involves some mode of transportation. People frequently use the verbs *take, catch,* and *go by* to speak generally about transportation. *Take* and *catch* are used for commercial or public transportation, such as planes, trains, and buses. *Go by* is used to talk about all modes of travel, including car and boat. Here are some examples:

♦ *You can* take a plane, *but if you* go by car, *it's only a three-hour drive.*
♦ *We'll* catch a morning flight *out of Chicago.*
♦ *I've* taken the bus *across country, but I've never* taken the train.
♦ *There are no roads to Yalapa; you have to* go by boat.

AIR TRAVEL

A number of idiomatic expressions are specific to air travel. Taking a flight generally requires *making a reservation* or *booking a ticket* (getting a ticket), unless you plan to fly *standby* (have no reservation, and wait for an available seat on a flight). Tickets are referred to as either *one-way* or *round-trip*, depending on whether you are just going to a destination, or you plan to go and return. If your flight is *overbooked* (not enough seats for the number of tickets sold), you may get *bumped* (meaning you're required to give up your seat), and be forced to wait for the next flight.

Here are a few idioms related to air travel:

> **carry-on (n, adj):** the small bag or bags that passengers can keep with them inside the plane
> **leg room (n):** space for legs between one's seat and the seat ahead
> **jet lag (n):** the feeling of exhaustion after flying across different time zones

A few types of flights with unusual nicknames are the following:

> **red-eye flight:** flights that leave late at night; refers to red eyes from lack of sleep
> **island hopper:** short flight in a small plane that goes from island to island
> **puddle jumper:** short flight in a small plane, usually in outback areas

DRIVING

Whether one takes a *road trip* (a vacation by car) or drives for necessity, driving requires knowing the *rules of the road* (the traffic laws). If you break them, it might result in being *pulled over*, or stopped, by a *cop* (police officer).

The terms for many traffic violations, like failure to stop or making an illegal turn, are easy to understand, but some violations, like those that follow, are expressed idiomatically:

cut someone off

> to pull too closely in front of someone, requiring him or her to brake quickly
> ♦ *He caused an accident when he* cut someone off. ♦ *When someone* cut him off, *he honked and yelled at the person for the next mile.*

drive under the influence *or* **DUI**

> to drive while drunk or drugged; the citation for driving under the influence. Generally expressed in the progressive tense (verb + -ing). ♦ *You can lose your license for* driving under the influence. ♦ *After getting three* DUIs, *they finally took his license away from him.*

ride someone's bumper (*or* tail) *or* tailgate

> to drive too close to the car ahead, often carelessly or deliberately ♦ *You should slow down, you're* riding that woman's bumper. ♦ *The car behind me is* tailgating. *I wish he'd move back!*

run a light (*or* stop sign)

> to fail to stop at a red light or stop sign ♦ *Hey, that car just* ran a *red* light! ♦ *Drivers talking on cell phones are more likely to* run stop signs *and* red lights.

run (*or* drive) someone off the road

> to force someone to drive off the road by pulling into his or her lane ♦ *That big rig* ran me *right* off the road. ♦ *No one was hurt when their car was* driven off the road *by a reckless driver.*

TRAFFIC

Heavy traffic (a lot of cars on the road) always occurs at *rush hour* (the hour of the day when people are going to or from work). *Rush-hour* traffic moves slowly or *comes to a standstill* (stops completely). Traffic accidents and roadwork can also cause traffic to move slowly, which can be described by these idioms, all of which are verbs:

> **to creep along**
> **to inch along**
> **to move at a snail's pace**

Slow-moving traffic and too many cars on the road cause these traffic situations, expressed as nouns:

> **a traffic jam**
> **a (traffic) snarl**
> **a tie up**
> **bumper-to-bumper traffic**

The expressions *to tie up* traffic and *to hold up* traffic mean to cause traffic to be slow or stopped, as shown in these examples:

> ♦ *Road construction has* tied up *traffic all week.*
> ♦ *Traffic was* held up *because of an accident.*

Watching the Road

Keeping one's eyes on the road (watching and paying attention to the road and traffic while driving) is basic advice to all drivers. *Watch the road* is another way to say "Pay attention to your driving."

Using cell phones, looking at maps, and having other distractions cause drivers to *take their eyes off the road* (not watch or pay attention to the road). *Not looking where one is going* (not watching the roadway) is a risky but common road hazard. When traffic ahead slows or stops, one may have to *slam on one's brakes* or *hit the brakes* (apply the brakes hard and suddenly) to avoid an accident.

Following are some common idioms to describe types of accidents:

fender bender

> **(n)** a small accident, usually with no injuries, where the cars may receive minor dents or scratches (literally where only the car fenders are bent or damaged) ♦ *It was just a* fender bender, *but I was pretty upset anyway.* ♦ *There were a lot of* fender benders *out there on the road today during rush hour.*

head-on collision

> **(n)** a serious accident where two cars crash into each other while going in opposite directions, where two cars hit head on, or front to front ♦ *Sadly, both drivers died in the* head-on collision. ♦ *We had to drive off the road to avoid a* head-on collision!

hit and run

> **(n, adj)** an accident where the driver who caused the accident leaves the scene of the accident, to escape punishment (literally to *hit* someone and *run* away) ♦ *They caught the* hit-and-run *driver because someone saw his license number and called the police.* ♦ *He went to prison for* hit and run.

rear-end

> **(v)** to crash into the back of the car ahead; often put in the passive form, *to be rear-ended.* ♦ *She had to wear a neckbrace after being* rear-ended. ♦ *Don't follow too closely, you might* rear-end *that car ahead.*

run into

> **(v)** to hit another car or an object with one's car ♦ *His car* ran into *a tree when he drifted off the road.* ♦ *Watch out! You almost* ran into *that car!*

sideswipe

> **(v)** to drive so close to another car that one causes an accident or denting and scratching of the car ♦ *We were* sideswiped *today, but luckily no one was hurt.* ♦ *He* sideswiped *a number of cars before the cops pulled him over.*

CHAPTER 8

LOVE MAKES THE WORLD GO 'ROUND: ROMANCE

Does "Love make the world go 'round?" Yes, according to the vast number of romance novels sold each year, the popularity and box-office success of love stories in film, and the prevalence of love themes in all genres of music. Love is a hot topic, and almost everyone is interested in finding love. As you might expect, there are hundreds of idioms that relate to the topic of love. This chapter includes over 200 common idioms and expressions, both old and new, that are used to talk about love and lovers.

Is It Really Love?

In the English language there is only one small word to describe all varieties of affectionate feelings of the heart, and that word is simply *love*. There is mother's love (and father's), brotherly love (and sisterly), self-love, puppy love, first love, true love, love at first sight, unrequited love, tough love, and more. The following are lots of words—idioms and expressions—that people use to express the love they may be feeling.

INFATUATION

These idioms and expressions mean to like someone romantically, or to like someone a lot.

be interested (in)

> (adj) to want to know someone better, to want to date or have a relationship with someone ♦ *Are you* interested in *anyone right now?* ♦ *He's interested in her, but I think she just wants to be friends, nothing more.*

be attracted to

> (adj) to feel a physical or emotional attraction to someone ♦ *I'm really attracted to a guy in my class.* ♦ *What kind of men are you attracted to?* ♦ *She's a nice person, but I'm not very attracted to her.*

have chemistry

> **(v)** to feel a strong attraction, to get along very well from the start; usually refers to an inner feeling people have about someone they've just met ♦ *We* had *strong* chemistry *right away.* ♦ *We dated a few times, but there* was no chemistry.

have a thing for

> **(v)** to be attracted to, to care a lot about; sometimes used to express more serious or romantic feelings ♦ *I definitely* have a thing for *her. She's great!* ♦ *We've* had a thing for *each other for a long time.*

hit it off

> **(v)** to get along well, to have fun together. Refers to one's experience when first meeting someone or on the first few dates; often phrased *hit it off well* or *didn't hit it off well.* ♦ *They* hit it off *immediately.* ♦ *We e-mailed each other for a month, but when we finally met, we didn't* hit it off *very well.* ♦ *I'm surprised how well they* hit if off; *they're very different.*

GETTING SERIOUS

When two people begin to *get serious* (get more romantic; begin a relationship), they may not be ready to say *the L word* — love. Instead, people often say one of these:

sweet on

> **(adj)** to be enamored, to care about a lot ♦ *I think you're* sweet on *him. Am I right?* ♦ *He must* be sweet on *you; he's always calling.*

crazy about (*or* **for**)

> **(adj)** to be enamored, to think another person is wonderful ♦ *They argue a lot, but you can see that they're* crazy about *each other.* ♦ *He's* been crazy for *her since the day he met her.*

have a crush on

> **(v)** to be infatuated or enamored with. *A crush* may be short-lived, and one may have a crush on a pop star, actor, or teacher. The term is associated with teenagers, but it is also used playfully with people of all ages. ♦ *I had a big* crush on *you in high school.* ♦ *The guys all* have a crush on *their cute new science teacher, Ms. Webber.* ♦ *My dad likes to tease. He tells my mom, "I think I* have a crush on *you."*

dig someone

> **(v)** to like a lot, to be enamored ◆ *We're not in love, but we really* dig *each other.* ◆ *I* dig *you. You're totally cool!*

A FOOL FOR LOVE

If you're a *fool for love,* you'll do anything for the person you love. When love becomes an obsession, one might be *lovesick* (so much in love that one feels sick or is unable to act in a normal way). Here are a few other expressions for this condition:

be hung up on

> **(adj)** to be obsessed with another person; to be lovesick ◆ *She's so* hung up on *him that she can't see his faults.* ◆ *I don't like his new girlfriend very much, but he's really* hung up on *her.*

have it bad for

> **(v)** to be seriously obsessed with someone; to think about someone and want to be with her or him all of the time; to be lovesick ◆ *I really* had it bad for *him until he lied to me.* ◆ *Those two really* have it bad for *each other. They're so dependent, it's unhealthy.*

sprung

> **(adj)** to be totally infatuated with someone, to be smitten ◆ *Man, she's so cute. I'm totally* sprung! ◆ *You say that you don't care about him, but you're* sprung. *I can tell.*

whipped *or* **whupped**

> **(adj)** literally to be beaten or to badly lose a competition, to be submissive or controlled by one's love interest, to be willing to do anything for one's love. This idiom is generally used by men to imply that another man is controlled by his girlfriend or wife, but can be said by and about women. Usually said playfully; slang. ◆ *Looks like you're* whipped. *You'll do anything he wants.* ◆ *Okay, I admit it. I'm in love and completely* whupped.

THE REAL THING

When it's truly love, people say "it's *serious,* it's *the real thing.*" The most common thing to say is, "I'm *in love,*" or more passionately "I'm *madly in love!*" The following are a number of other ways to describe *being in love.*

These expressions use the verb *fall,* implying that one has lost one's balance; that it has happened accidentally:

fall in love

(v) to begin to feel love for someone. This expression is often used with the preposition *with* as in the first example. ◆ *I think I'm* falling in love *with you.* ◆ *I like her, but I'm not going to* fall in love.

fall (for)

(v) to fall in love, to be very enamored with someone ◆ *You always* fall *for people who aren't good for you.* ◆ *She's a great gal. A lot of men have* fallen for *her.* **Grammar Note:** When this idiom is used without the preposition *for,* it's generally put in a past tense, and may be used with the adverb *hard* as in this example: "He's *fallen hard* this time."

These idioms refer to finding the perfect match, the one person who is right for you:

be the one

the right partner, the one to marry ◆ *After the first few dates, she knew he* was the one. ◆ *He believes that she's* the one, *but I think she's going to break his heart.*

find the one

(v) to find the right partner, the one to marry ◆ *I haven't* found the one *yet.* ◆ *Well, guys, my bachelor days are almost over; I've* found the one.

find Mr. Right

(v) to find the right or perfect person ◆ *She thinks she's* found Mr. Right, *but I don't trust Internet romance.* ◆ *I've spent half my life trying to* find Mr. Right. **Note:** Typically, this idiom is said as *Mr. Right,* but one could also say *Ms. Right.*

Here are a few other expressions that mean it's love:

steal someone's heart

(v) to cause someone to fall in love ◆ *He's smart, handsome, and funny, and he's* stolen my heart. ◆ *I'm going to do everything I can to* steal her heart.

be head over heels in love

(adj) to be completely enamored, to be madly in love, to fall in love suddenly; often phrased to *fall head over heels.* ◆ *They just met and already they're* head over heels in love. ◆ *Sounds like he's* fallen head over heels.

TYPES OF LOVE

Because there is only one word in English for love, adjectives are added to specify the type of love. The following expressions all refer to romantic love:

puppy love

(n) infatuation between school-age kids or teens, or, jokingly, a similar type of infatuation between older people ♦ *They're too young to be serious; it's just* puppy love.

young love

(n) said of one's first boyfriend or girlfriend or very young people who think they are in love; implies innocence and wonder ♦ *Those two look so happy together. Ah,* young love *is wonderful!*

first love

(n) the first person one falls in love with ♦ *People say that you never forget your* first love.

love at first sight

(n) the act of falling in love the first time one sees someone ♦ *It was* love at first sight, *and we're still in love 50 years later.* **Note:** This idiom is also used to express a strong liking for a material object such as a car or house when one sees it for the first time, for example: "When we saw the house, it was *love at first sight.* We knew that we would buy it."

true love

(n) a genuine feeling of romantic love; often said playfully ♦ *Ah,* true love. *It makes everything seem perfect.* ♦ *I'm telling you, this isn't a little fling! This is* true love!

unrequited love

(n) love that is not reciprocated, not returned; a one-way love ♦ *Many songs and poems are written about* unrequited love. ♦ *She called her friends to talk because she was suffering from a case of* unrequited love.

WORDS OF LOVE

Following are a few expressions for *love talk* — saying romantic things to someone:

those three little words

the phrase "I love you" ♦ *I'm waiting for her to say* those three little words.

sweet nothings (in one's ear)

romantic, intimate talk; usually phrased to *whisper sweet nothings* ♦ *They whispered* sweet nothings *to each other as they sat in the corner of a cozy restaurant.* ♦ *When they hugged, she whispered* sweet nothings *in his ear*.

THE ONE YOU LOVE

What to call the one you love? There are plenty of endearments to choose from. The most common terms are simply *girlfriend* and *boyfriend*, though some older adults use *man friend* and *lady friend*. **Note:** Female friends often call each other *girlfriend*, but male friends don't call each other *boyfriend*, which is only used for a romantic partner. To avoid any confusion, platonic friends often say *my female friend* or *my male friend*.

Terms of endearment often suggest sweetness, such as *Sugar, Honey, Honey Bun, Sweetheart, Sweetie,* and *Sweetie Pie*. Other terms make the love object into an infant or heavenly being: *Baby, Babe, Darling,* and *Angel*.

Sometimes people describe or introduce their romantic partner as *my man* or *my woman, my guy* or *my girl*. Here are some idioms used to describe or introduce one's love interest.

Grammar Note: These terms are generally preceded by a word that shows possession, such as: *my, your, John's, his sister's,* and so on.

old man *and* **old lady**

(n) working-class slang for boyfriend or girlfriend, husband or wife. This idiom was more common in the '60s and '70s than it is today. ♦ *My* old man *drives a truck.* ♦ *Get your* old lady *and come on over to our house on Sunday.* **Note:** *My* old man *is also a common slang reference for father.*

main squeeze

(n) one's romantic partner. Here, *squeeze* alludes to hugging and cuddling. ♦ *You're my* main squeeze; *the only one for me.* ♦ *I like him a lot. He may even become my* main squeeze.

soul mate

(n) the person with whom one has a deeply personal or spiritual relationship, a person with whom one feels deeply that he or she belongs; also used to mean a person who views the world the same way you do, as in the third example that follows ♦ *My world fell apart when my wife died. She was my* soul mate. ♦ *They're* soul mates; *they have a very deep connection.* ♦ *My Uncle and I are* soul mates. *We think alike.*

partner

(n) one's husband or wife; either of two people who are not married but living together in a spouselike situation; often used by gay and lesbian couples ♦ *I'd like you to meet my* partner, *Tom.* ♦ *She and her* partner *just bought a house in the country.*

lover

(n) one's sexual partner, one's romantic love ♦ *They've been* lovers *for years but have never married.* ♦ *He's feeling pretty sad right now; his* lover *just left him.* ***Note:*** Introducing someone as *my lover* is equal to saying "This is my sex partner — and possibly the person I love." So, don't say this unless you are among friends or you want to share information about your sex life.

[See information on the term *lovers* later in this chapter.]

The following are a few more idiomatic expressions for one's love. These terms are often used in advertising for romantic vacations or gifts one might give a sweetheart:

one and only

(n) the only person that one loves; said about a partner in a serious relationship, including marriage ♦ *She's my* one and only; *the only girl for me!* ♦ *Give your* one and only *a moonlight cruise. Call for information.*

heartthrob

(n) the person one loves or wishes to have as a romantic partner. This idiom is often said teasingly and is most often used to refer to celebrities. ♦ *He doesn't know that he's my* heartthrob. ♦ Heartthrob *Leonardo DiCaprio stars in a new movie to be released next month.*

Dating

Dating (spending time and going places with someone one is interested in) is part of social life and one way to look for love.

Dating or *going out* can be expressed a number of different ways:

    date someone ♦ I dated him *when I was in college.*
    have a date ♦ *I've only* had one date *with him so far.*
    go (*or* be) on a date ♦ *We're* going on a date *Saturday night.*
    go out (together) ♦ *Would you like to* go out *together sometime?*

Some unusual or memorable dating situations are best described by handy idioms.

Grammar Note: The following idioms are usually said as *to go on* a (type of date) or *to have* a (type of date).

blind date

(**n**) a date, often arranged by a friend, where the two people have never met before. Dates arranged by people who meet through personal ads are a kind of *blind date.* ♦ *Can you believe, I met my wife on a* blind date. ♦ *My friends arranged a* blind date *for me.* **Note:** *Blind* alludes to the expression *going in blind,* meaning doing something on trust without having any background information or previous experience.

double date

(**n, v**) a date where two couples get together to do something. This term is generally used when the couples are single, not married, but sometimes married couples use it too. ♦ *We'd love to go on a* double date *with you two sometime.* ♦ *My sister and I used to* double date *a lot back in high school.*

third date

(**n**) the third time the same two people have a date; considered significant as the date that determines if two people will continue dating; also the date where people might kiss, neck, or possibly have sex for the first time ♦ *You'll know by the* third date *if you want to keep seeing him.* ♦ *If she doesn't want to kiss you after the* third date, *she's probably not very interested.* **Note:** There's no established social rule about the third date, but three dates is generally enough to know if you like someone or not.

hot date

(n) a date with someone whom one finds sexually attractive, a date with potential for sexual activity. This idiom is often used playfully for a date with a good friend, a sweetheart, or spouse; slang. ♦ *So, tell me about your* hot date *last night.* ♦ *Grampa said, "I've got to go. Your grandma and I have a* hot date *tonight."*

going dutch

(v) a date where each person pays his or her share of the expense for dinner, entertainment, transportation, and so on. This idiom is also used when friends share the bill at a restaurant. ♦ *We usually* go dutch. *It's easier that way.* ♦ *He expected me to* go dutch *on the first date. Forget it!* ♦ *My girlfriend and I generally take turns paying. It seems nicer than* going dutch. ***Note:*** Traditionally, a man *treated* a woman, and paid for all of the expenses on a date. This is often still true. But today, many couples split the expense, or even take turns paying.

In a Relationship

Whether two people are dating or married, the following expressions can be used to describe them if their relationship is good, or as people sometimes say, the relationship is *working.*

made for each other ♦ *My parents say they were* made for each other. *They have so much in common.*
a match made in heaven ♦ *Their marriage is not exactly* a match made in heaven. *They have some problems, but they seem to do okay together.*
the perfect couple ♦ *They seem like* the perfect couple. *I hope they continue to be happy together.*
good together ♦ *I think we're really* good together; *our personalities complement each other.*

Some idioms refer to how two people look together more than how well matched they really are. The following idioms imply that the couple looks good, cute, or perfect together and may also imply that they seem to have the perfect relationship or perfect life together.

poster couple ♦ *They're the new* poster couple, *but I wonder if it will last.*
classic couple ♦ *Some people said that John Kennedy, Jr. and his wife, Carolyn Bessette, were the* classic couple.

When dating evolves into a romantic or sexual involvement, people might call it *a love affair*. This expression can sometimes imply an intimate relationship without long term commitment. Here are some examples of this idiom:

- *When* a love affair ends, *some people continue to be friends.*
- *He had* a love affair *with a French girl while he was studying in France.*

People typically talk about serious romantic involvement and commitment, or dating one person exclusively, with one of these expressions:

in a relationship

dating one person regularly and exclusively, having a romantic involvement; often phrased *having a relationship,* which can also imply a secret romantic affair ♦ *Being* in a relationship *takes a lot of work and commitment.* ♦ *She was* having a relationship *with a man in her office.*

seeing someone

(v) dating someone regularly; usually put in a continuous tense (verb + *-ing*). The expression *seeing anyone* is used to ask a question, as the second example shows. ♦ *We've been* seeing each other *for a long time.* ♦ *Are you* seeing anyone *now?*

going steady

(v) dating regularly and exclusively. This expression is less popular today and was used mainly by younger teens or playfully by adults. ♦ *We're kind of* going steady. ♦ *I don't want to* go steady *with anyone. I want to meet lots of different people.*

getting serious

(v) possibly thinking about a long-term relationship or marriage ♦ *It's definitely* getting serious. *He wants me to meet his family.* ♦ *Do you think you might ever* get serious *with him?*

People in a committed relationship are often referred to by one of these idioms:

a couple

(n) two people who have been dating exclusively for awhile or are in a romantic relationship ♦ *I think they're* a couple *now.* ♦ *We enjoy having them over for dinner. They're* a *really nice* couple.

Lovers

The world is full of *lovers* — *nature lovers, sports lovers, music lovers, art lovers, dog lovers, cat lovers,* and many more! In these contexts, the word *lovers* refers to someone who has a great appreciation, love, or passion for something.

Describing two people as *lovers* generally implies that they are sexual partners, so don't say *lovers* about a couple unless you know it's okay to share that personal information. But also, the term *lovers* can mean a couple who seems very much in love or is very affectionate. For example: "Hey, you two *lovers*, stop kissing and join the conversation" or "Cities like Florence and Venice are said to be the perfect romantic place for *lovers*."

a pair

(n) two people who have been dating exclusively for awhile or are in a romantic relationship ♦ *Ben and Amelia have been* a pair *for a long time.* ♦ *We've been* a pair *for about 10 years.*

an item

(n) a couple who is the topic of gossip or interest, often said about a new couple or a new celebrity couple ♦ *I never thought those two would get together. They're* an item *now.* ♦ *So, are you two* an item *now?*

sweethearts

(n) girlfriend and boyfriend; implies a sweet, loving relationship; also said of married couples who seem very much in love ♦ *Her parents are still* sweethearts *after 35 years together.* ♦ *This necklace is the perfect gift for your* sweetheart. ♦ *He married his childhood* sweetheart.

lovebirds

(n) lovers, a couple who show their affection openly. This idiom is sometimes said of a newly married couple. ♦ *The two* lovebirds *are in Hawaii on their honeymoon.* ♦ *You should see those* lovebirds. *They're so happy to have found each other.*

"JoshandAmy"

Couples who spend all their time together, don't like being apart, and are often seen clinging to each other are sometimes called by one joined name, like "JoshandAmy" or "MattandLisa." This "nickname" is said quickly, as "Josh'n'Amy," and implies that they are no longer two separate people but one unit. Married couples are often described this way.

Tying the Knot

When people decide that they want to spend their lives together — either in a permanent relationship or marriage — they might use one of the following terms to describe their intentions.

share one's life with someone

to be life partners, to be married ♦ *I want to* share my life with you. ♦ *I do love her, but I'm not sure I want to* share my life with her. *We are too different.*

(have) a future together

to be life partners, to be married; also phrased *have a life together.* ♦ *Do you think you two* have a future together? ♦ *My boyfriend and I have been talking about* a life together.

grow old together

(v) to stay together through old age ♦ *We're very much in love, and we want to* grow old together. ♦ *If we decide we want to* grow old together, *you'll be the first one to know.*

get engaged

(v) to promise to marry someone ♦ *She wants to* get engaged, *but I'm not ready.* ♦ *My daughter and her boyfriend just* got engaged. **Note:** *Getting engaged* often includes giving a ring. So, "He gave me a ring" is sometimes used to mean "we *got engaged.*"

set a date

> **(v)** to decide on a wedding date, usually after an engagement; can also mean to get engaged ♦ *Well, have you* set a date, *yet?* ♦ *We're talking about marriage, but we're not* setting any dates *yet* (*in other words, not getting officially engaged yet*).

settle down

> **(v)** to stop being single; to get married or live together as a permanent couple ♦ *I'm not ready to* settle down *with anyone yet.* ♦ *Well mom, looks like I'm finally going to* settle down. *Tim and I are getting married.*

THE PROPOSAL

"Will you marry me?" is the classic question for a marriage proposal. To propose marriage, someone might say "I want to spend the rest of my life with you." Someone else might ask "Will you be my wife?" or "Will you be my husband?" People refer to these important questions as *the proposal*. To *propose* means to ask the marriage question, as in these examples:

> ♦ *The time has come. I'm going to* propose *to her this weekend.*
> ♦ *He* proposed *last night, and I said, "Yes!"*

Here are some other expressions that mean to propose marriage:

pop the question

> **(v)** to ask the question "Will you marry me?" ♦ *He* popped the question *while we were watching the sunset on the beach.* ♦ *If he doesn't* pop the question *soon, I'm going to do it.*

ask for one's hand (in marriage)

> **(v)** to ask someone to be one's marriage or life partner ♦ *Her father is old-fashioned and wants me to* ask him for her hand. ♦ *You two have been together for a long time. When are you going to* ask for her hand? **Note:** This idiom alludes to an old custom that required a man to ask a woman's father if he could marry her. Some people still do this today as a formality.

SAYING I DO

It's customary to call a newly married couple *newlyweds* for the first year after their marriage. Most newlyweds take a vacation, *the honeymoon,* right after the wedding ceremony. While they're *on their honeymoon,* and for a short time after, they might be called *honeymooners* or *lovebirds.*

Getting married is often described with one of the following idioms. All of these verbs allude either to an old marriage ritual or a part of modern marriage ceremonies:

get hitched ♦ *Adam and Sue are* getting hitched *next Sunday.*

say *I do* ♦ *When I finally decide to say* I do, *it will be forever.* ***Note:*** "I do" is the customary response during the marriage ceremony.

take one's vows ♦ *They* took their vows *in a little chapel by the ocean.*

tie the knot ♦ *I don't think I'm ready to* tie the knot.

make it legal *or* **make it official** ♦ *We decided that it was time to* make it legal. ***Note:*** This idiom is often used when people have been living together for some time before getting married.

walk down the aisle (together) ♦ *They'll be* walking down the aisle *in a few weeks*. ***Note:*** Refers to the aisle of a church where people often get married; the ceremony begins as the bride walks down the aisle to the altar and ends as the newly married couple walks back down the aisle and out of the church.

MARRIED LIFE

Married couples who enjoy a happy relationship are called a *happily married couple.* One could say that they are living in *marital bliss.* After years of a good marriage, a couple might call themselves *an old married couple*, implying that they have achieved that comfortable — and comforting — familiarity with each other. People may use the following idioms to refer to their spouses or married people:

hubby (short for husband) ♦ *You're the best* hubby *a woman could have.*

other half ♦ *Where's your* other half? *I though he was coming with you.*

better half ♦ *Let me introduce you to my* better half. *This is my wife, Jane.*

the (little) Missus ♦ *Nice to see you, Joe. And how's* the Missus? ***Note:*** This idiom is an older term, considered today to be slightly demeaning or old-fashioned.

Getting *Lovey-Dovey*

When people are being affectionate, kissing, and hugging, you can say that they are being *lovey-dovey* (cuddling and nuzzling like doves). As in, "My parents were always *lovey-dovey* with each other." Add intimate touching, and it's called *getting physical,* as in "When they started *getting physical,* they shut the door."

Getting to First Base

References to baseball, "America's favorite pastime," are found in many American idioms, including ones for kissing, necking, and sex. The following expressions are often used among close friends to talk about their romantic and sexual adventures (or achievements, as some see it). *Getting to first base* means getting to kiss someone; *getting to second base* means sexual touching; and so on around the bases until *hitting a home run, getting to home,* or *scoring,* which mean having sex or sexual intercourse.

Two other slangy and somewhat vulgar expressions that imply sexual achievement or conquest are *getting some* (*some* meaning sex) and *getting laid* (having sex with someone).

A KISS

A kiss might be called *a peck* (a little quick kiss) or *a smooch* (a longer, possibly romantic, kiss on the cheek or lips).

Here are some different kinds of kisses:

French kiss: kiss that uses the tongue as well as lips
wet kiss: sloppy or very wet kiss, often on the cheek
air kiss: kissing the air on either side of one's cheek; a greeting in some cultures and among some Americans
butterfly kiss: fluttering one's eyelashes on someone's cheek or elsewhere

A few (slightly rude) slang words for kissing sometimes used by young people are *sucking face* (sucking on each other's faces) or *swapping spit* (exchanging saliva).

NECKING

Necking means kissing passionately and possibly touching or *petting*. The following expressions are similar to *necking,* but can imply that there is even more sexual activity:

fooling around

(v) kissing, touching, possibly having sex ♦ *I was furious when I caught my daughter and her boyfriend* fooling around. ♦ *My daughter said, "Everybody fools around." But I certainly don't want her to do it!*

hanky-panky

(n) kissing, touching, possibly having sex; an older expression that is indirect and lighthearted ♦ *Hey, you two, no* hanky-panky *allowed in my house!* ♦ *There was a lot of* hanky-panky *going on in that movie, but no real sex scenes.*

getting frisky

> **(n)** kissing, touching, possibly having sex; an older expression that is indirect and lighthearted ♦ *He tried to* get frisky *with me on the first date, but I said, "Forget it!"* ♦ *My grandma jokes and says, "Your grandfather is always trying to* get frisky *with me!"*

GOING ALL THE WAY

Commonly, in American English, more idioms exist for situations that are personal (like using the bathroom), difficult to deal with (like death), or seem very important (like money). So, as you might imagine, loads of idioms exist for that most personal of activities, sex.

> **make love** ♦ *Old movies never show people actually* making love *like modern movies do.*
> **sleep with** ♦ *Some young people have vowed not to* sleep with *anyone until they're married.*
> **sleep together** ♦ *It's getting serious, but we haven't* slept together.
> **go to bed with** ♦ *He stopped dating her because she refused to* go to bed with *him.*
> **go to bed together** ♦ *He really felt betrayed when he found out that his girlfriend and his best friend* went to bed together.

The following slang expressions are even more indirect, using the word *it* for sex:

> **do it** ♦ *According to reports, some healthy senior citizens are still* doing it *at age 80 and even 90.*
> **get it on** ♦ *Every time my husband and I try to* get it on, *the baby wakes up.*
> **make it** ♦ *They were* making it *in the back seat of the car.*
> **make out** ♦ *They didn't want anyone to know that they had been* making out.

Some old-fashioned expressions like to *make whoopee* and *a roll in the hay* are used today to refer to sexual activity in a playful way.

SEXY PEOPLE

Of course there are plenty of idioms to describe sexy people or any person who someone else finds attractive. Most terms can be used for a woman or a man, like *a hottie, a 10,* and *a looker.* A gorgeous or sexy woman might be called a *bombshell* or a *fox,* while a sexy man might be called *a hunk* or *a stud.*

Relationship Trouble

When the relationship *isn't working* (isn't happy and harmonious) or the couple is fighting (arguing) and having other troubles, they might describe their situation with one of these expressions:

not getting along: arguing and unhappy
not doing well: having marital problems
on shaky ground: the relationship is not stable or solid
on the rocks: almost ready to end the relationship

TRUE OR FALSE

Trust and loyalty are qualities most people want their partners to have. A *faithful* partner, meaning one who is sexually intimate only with a sweetheart or spouse, might be called one of these idioms:

true ♦ *I want a woman who will* be true *to me.*
a one-woman man ♦ *I'm* a one-woman man. *I don't want other women.*
a one-man woman ♦ *She's* a one-man woman, *and luckily, that man is me!*

A person who is not faithful or who has romantic affairs with someone other than a partner might be called many things that are unfit to print in this book, but some of the more mild ones are:

untrue ♦ *She broke their engagement when she found out he* was untrue.
a cheat ♦ *Nobody wants* a cheat *for a partner.*
a two-timer (to two-time) ♦ *She was* a two-timer, *and he didn't want to believe it.*

In addition, a man who is sexually involved with or seeks sexual attention from a number of women may be called *a womanizer.* The verb form, *womanize,* is also used, typically in the form of the gerund, *womanizing*: "She finally got tired of her husband's *womanizing,* and she divorced him."

There are plenty of expressions to describe a cheating person's unfaithful activities. All of the following verbs mean to have a romantic or sexual involvement with someone other than one's partner or spouse:

cheat on ♦ *I told him if he* cheats on *me once, we're finished.*
have an affair ♦ *I would never ruin my marriage by* having an affair.
play around ♦ *Just remember, if you're going to* play around, *I will too!*
break one's (marriage) vows ♦ *She never forgave him for* breaking their marriage vows.

Grammar Note: The expression *behind someone's back* (secretly) is often added to some expressions, such as *to cheat behind someone's back* or *to play around behind someone's back.* The idioms to *cheat* and to *play around* already imply secrecy and hidden activity, so the expression *behind someone's back* isn't truly needed, but it's common.

[See *do something behind someone's back* and *do something when one's back is turned,* in chapter 13.]

Breaking Up

When the marriage or relationship is no longer *working* (functioning happily), people sometimes *break up* (end the relationship). Here are other terms that mean to *break up:*

split up ♦ *Did you hear that Chad and Emily* split up?
end it ♦ Ending it *may be the best for both of us.*
break it off ♦ *She still doesn't know why he* broke it off *with her.*
call it quits ♦ *We're not ready to* call it quits *yet, but I think it'll happen soon.*
go ones' separate ways (used with *our, your,* and *their*) ♦ *They're not together anymore. They've* gone their separate ways.

Note: To *go ones' separate ways* has the additional implication that the two people no longer have any contact with each other.

When people decide mutually to break up, they might say *it was mutual,* or they could use one of the expressions in the preceding list. But when just one person wants to end the relationship, and does so abruptly, it's best described with one of the following expressions:

dump someone

(v) to end the relationship abruptly, sometimes cruelly, and stop seeing the person ♦ *When she met someone else, she* dumped me *with no hesitation!* ♦ *He* dumped her *as soon as she started getting serious.*

split

(v) to leave abruptly ♦ *My boyfriend* split *without even saying goodbye.* ♦ *Who cares if she* split? *I don't need her.*

walk out on

(v) to leave the relationship or marriage, to abandon one's responsibilities; often refers to leaving a partner with children to take care of ♦ *She* walked out on *him because of his drinking problem.* ♦ *When he met another woman, he* walked out on *his family.*

If someone breaks up with you, you can say that the person:

left me
left me for someone else
left me for another man (*or* **woman**)

HEARTBREAK

Almost everyone knows the pain of *heartbreak* — the other side of the joys of love. If you break up with someone, that person might say "You broke my heart" or "You tore my heart out." The following are more idioms to describe one's emotional pain:

hurt (n, adj) ♦ *He left her with so much* hurt *that she never spoke to him again.*
♦ *I've been* hurt *before so I know how it feels.*
heartache (n) ♦ *So many songs are written about* heartache *and pain.*
a broken heart (n) ♦ *Some say a person can die of* a broken heart.
brokenhearted (adj) ♦ *He's been* brokenhearted *ever since she left him.*

Here's one more idiom to describe a difficult end to a relationship:

be kicked to the curb

(**v**) to be deeply hurt, to feel discarded or thrown away; also *to kick someone to the curb*. The word curb means the edge of the sidewalk along the street. ♦ *When she found someone else, she just* kicked me to the curb.

If a person's broken heart doesn't heal, the person might say, *"I'll never get over him/her."* But when a broken heart is *mended* (repaired, no longer in the pain) and a person doesn't care about the other person anymore, he or she might say, *"I'm over her"* or *"I've gotten over him."* When people are recovering from the end of a love affair or start dating again too soon after breaking up from a relationship, they're often said to be *on the rebound,* as in "She got engaged shortly after her marriage broke up. I guess she's really *on the rebound.*"

TRYING AGAIN

If *breaking up* was a mistake or two people feel that they can *make it work* (have a successful relationship), they might try again. Here are some expressions for this situation:

make up

(**v**) to apologize, forgive, and possibly forget the problem. This idiom can be used when two people get back together after breaking up, or it can be used when two people forgive each other after an argument. ♦ *He wants to* make up, *but I'm not sure that I do.* ♦ *She was really hurt when I forgot our anniversary, but we* made up.

patch it up

(v) to repair the broken relationship, to forgive and forget; sometimes phrased *patch things up*. This idiom is also used for repairing the damage after a serious argument. ♦ *They've broken up before, but they've always* patched it up. ♦ *I want to try to* patch things up *between us. How about you?*

get back together

(v) to return to the relationship or marriage after breaking up ♦ *They'll* get back together *again because they're both miserable being apart.* ♦ *His parents divorced and* got back together *again a few years later.*

go back

(v) to return to the relationship after breaking up ♦ *Do you think I should* go back *with him?* ♦ *I think he'll just hurt her again if she* goes back *to him.*

give it a second chance

(v) to try the relationship or marriage again; to work to save the relationship or marriage ♦ *Let's* give it a second chance. *I know we can make it work.* ♦ *Neither of us wants a divorce, so we're going to* give it a second chance.

CHAPTER 9

COMMON AMERICAN PHRASES AND SLANG EXPRESSIONS

The idiomatic phrases and slang expressions in this section are some of the more common expressions used every day, again and again, in casual conversation. They can be heard in a wide range of contexts and anywhere in the country. (Of course, there are hundreds of regional expressions that also exist, though they are not included here.)

Explanations are given where they are needed to clarify the idiom. Examples are also included where they are needed to help show the correct usage.

Common Greetings

Polite greetings are among the most basic, yet essential, forms of communication in any language. In some areas it's common for people to greet even strangers as they pass on the street. Knowing how to use casual greetings, and how to respond to them, opens the door to friendly conversation. This section includes common greetings, common farewells, and various ways to respond.

SAYING *HELLO*

A simple hello is often said with one of the following greetings:

Hi: the most common, casual way to say hello
Hey: slang greeting, originally a regional expression from the South but now widely used. *Hey* is a general word used to start a sentence, to get someone's attention, and as a response to many different statements and situations. Tone and intonation often reveal the meaning of the word.
Hi (*or* Hey) there: casual variations of *Hi* or *Hey*

After an initial "Hi!" people generally ask "How are you?" or they use one of the following casual expressions (typical responses are shown to the right of the expression):

	Possible Reply
How are you doing?	Pretty good. How are you?
How's it going?	Great, How 'bout you?
How's things?	Things are good, thanks. What about you?
How are things?	Not bad. And you?

Here is a related, but more formal, expression:

How do you do?

> a formal greeting or response after meeting someone for the first time ♦ *Sarah, let me introduce my grandmother. Nice to meet you!* How do you do? **Note:** Non-native speakers of English sometimes confuse the expression *How do you do?* (a polite form of *How are you?*) with *What do you do?* (What is your occupation?). It's also easy to confuse *How are you doing?* (How are you?) with *What are you doing?*

WHAT'S GOING ON? AND RELATED IDIOMS

The expressions in the following list mean *What are you doing?* or *What is happening here?* But often they're used as a form of *Hello!* or general greeting. They are usually answered with a negative expression like *Not much* or *Nothing much*. In casual situations, and particularly with young people, these greetings can simply mean *Hi*. Typical responses are shown to the right of the expression.

	Possible Reply
What's up?	Not much. What's up with you?
S'up? (short for *what's up*)	Hey.
What's new?	Nothing much, and you?
What are you up to?	Not too much. How 'bout you?
What's happening?	Nothing really. What are you doing?
What's going on?	Just hanging out.

In addition to the typical responses of *Not much* and *Nothing much*, people sometimes answer these greetings with *Same old thing* or *Same old same old*, generally meaning that life is the same and nothing new is happening.

SAYING GOODBYE

Goodbye, the common thing to say when leaving or parting from someone, originated from the expression *God be with you*. *Goodbye* can be formal when it's said slowly and distinctly. Or, it can be casual when said quickly, as *G'bye.* Many other words and expressions are used for saying *goodbye,* as shown in the following list. ***Note:*** *Goodnight* is commonly said when departing at night, but *Good morning, Good afternoon,* and *Good evening* aren't generally said when departing, because they are greetings.

Bye: short for *Goodbye*
Bye-bye: familiar, often said to children
Goodnight: also *G'night;* said at night
Farewell: formal; means "be well"
So long: informal goodbye
See ya: short for *I'll see you again; later* or *around* can be added at the end
Later: short for *See you later*
(See you) later, alligator: playful and silly; sometimes answered with *After a while, crocodile*

The four expressions that follow are often used to end a conversation and signal that one needs to leave. The examples are shown in the first person (*I*) but any pronoun or person's name could be used. Often these expressions are shortened to *Got to go, Better be going,* and so on.

	Possible Reply
I've got to go.	Okay. See ya.
I've got to split.	Yeah. Me too.
I've got to take off.	Good talking to you.
I had better be going. (more formal)	Okay, nice to see you.

The next four expressions are said as a wish of goodwill as people are parting:

	Possible Reply
Have a good day.	Thanks. You too.
Have a good one.	You too.
Take care.	I will. You too.
Take it easy.	All right. Talk to you later.

Polite Expressions and Niceties

Polite expressions and interactions are sometimes referred to as *niceties,* those nice gestures of courtesy that are important in all societies.

MAKING POLITE REQUESTS

The following phrases are polite ways to begin a request. The expressions *do you mind* and *would you mind* mean "Do you object?" or "Is it a problem?" and therefore, the usual response is *No* or *Not at all*. The other expressions listed here generally require *Yes* or a similar positive response.

Example	Possible Reply
Do you mind . . .? ♦ Do you mind *if I sit here?*	No, go ahead.
Would you mind . . .? ♦ Would you mind *helping me?*	No, not at all.
Would you be so kind as to . . .? ♦ Would you be so kind as to *assist me?*	Of course.
Could/can I trouble you to . . .? ♦ Could I trouble you to *get me some water?*	Sure. No trouble at all.
Could I ask you to . . .? ♦ Could I ask you to *smoke somewhere else?*	Yes. I'm sorry.

SAYING *THANK YOU*

Thank you may be the most useful word in the English language. There are many ways to say *thank you;* this section gives you the most common. Sometimes language-learners are confused about when to use the word *thank* and when to use *thanks*. It may help to understand that *thank you* is short for *I thank you*, which uses the first person singular form of the verb *to thank*. In most other expressions, the word is *thanks*, a plural noun. There are lots of common and acceptable responses to *thanks*, shown in the next section.

Thanks a million.
Thanks a bunch.
Thanks a lot.
Thanks much (*or* loads).
Many thanks.
I can't thank you enough.

A related expression is *I owe you one*, which is an informal way to say "I must repay your kindness." Here are some examples:

♦ *Thanks for your all your help*. I owe you one.
♦ I owe you one *for loaning me your car*.

Thanks to you . . .

The versatile expression *Thanks to you . . .* may be a bit confusing to know how to use correctly. One common use of this expression is in thanking someone for causing something good to happen. Here's an example:

♦ Thanks to you, *the fund-raiser was a great success.*

However, this expression is often used to say that someone caused something bad to happen. It's similar to *It's your fault that . . .* and it's generally said in a sarcastic tone. Here are some examples:

♦ Thanks to you, *I was late for my meeting.*

♦ Thanks to you, *I spent all my money on a stock that's now worthless.*

Context and tone of voice are the only ways to tell if this idiom is being used to praise someone or to blame someone.

RESPONSES TO *THANK YOU*

When someone says *Thank you,* the standard response is *You're welcome. You're most welcome* is a more formal version. Very often, however, people use other responses to *thank you,* from the very formal *The pleasure was all mine!* to the slangy *No sweat.*

The expressions that follow are common ways of saying *You're welcome,* though each has its specific implication, as indicated:

(It was) my pleasure: means "It gave me pleasure to do it"
Anytime: means "Ask me for help anytime"
Sure: slangy, familiar
No problem: means "It caused me no problem"
Not at all: means "It's not necessary to thank me at all; it was not a problem for me at all"
No sweat: slang; means "I didn't sweat or become overworked by helping"
It's nothing: means "It was like doing nothing; it was easy"
Don't worry about it: means "Don't feel uncomfortable because you asked for help; don't worry about repaying me"
Don't mention it: means "No need to thank me; no need to even mention it"
Forget (about) it: slightly harsh; means "I don't want to be thanked"

In American culture where self-sufficiency is highly valued, saying something like *It was no trouble* may save face or possible embarrassment for the person who received something or requested help.

SAYING *I'M SORRY*

I'm sorry can be an apology for a mistake or wrongdoing, for refusing a request, for interrupting someone, or for accidentally bumping or getting too close to someone.

All of the following expressions can mean *I'm sorry.*

Sorry ♦ Sorry *I can't join you tonight.*
Excuse me ♦ Excuse me *for interrupting.*
Pardon (me) ♦ Pardon me. *I need to get by.*
Forgive me ♦ *I didn't mean to hurt your feelings. Please,* forgive me.
Oops! ♦ Oops! *I stepped on your toe. Are you okay?*

RESPONSES TO *I'M SORRY*

Saying *Sorry* requires a response. Often people say *That's okay* or *It's okay,* meaning that it's not necessary to be sorry or that everything turned out okay. Here are some other expressions that are used in response to *Sorry:*

That's all right
It's cool: in this context, *cool* is slang for *fine, good, okay*
Don't worry about it
Never mind
Forget it
(It's) No big deal: means "It's not big enough to worry about"

The following expressions are said in reply to *Sorry* when the apology is for a more serious offense, or when the offended person is still upset:

I appreciate your apology: a polite acceptance of apology without saying *It's okay*
I'll forgive you this time: means "I'll forgive you once, but not a second time"
Don't let it happen again: a strong and serious warning; but can also be said lightly

I BLEW IT AND RELATED IDIOMS

These expressions are very common and informal ways to acknowledge that one has made a mistake or a very bad choice. They also can be used to say *I'm sorry.*

I blew it ♦ *I'm sorry I forgot about our plans. I really* blew it!
I messed up ♦ I messed up *on my term paper. It wasn't very good.*
I screwed up ♦ *As a young person* I screwed up *a lot. I needed to grow up.*

My mistake ♦ *Oh,* my mistake. *I thought the meeting was today.*
What was I thinking?! ♦ *Oh no! I cut this board too short.* What was I thinking?!
I can't believe I (did something)**!** ♦ I can't believe *I forgot your birthday!*

Note: People generally do not say *I failed* when they make a mistake. *I failed* is used when one fails (does not get a passing grade) in a class or on an exam. It's also used to introduce a sentence such as *I failed to* (do something), meaning "I didn't do it" or "I was unable to do it."

Understanding

Whether you are a native English speaker or a non-native speaker, you'll often need to use the phrases *I don't understand* and *Do you understand?* They are essential for keeping a conversation going, sharing ideas, and simply enjoying clear communication. This section shows the various expressions used to check for understanding, to say that you don't understand, or that you do.

ASKING *DO YOU UNDERSTAND?*

To ask if someone understands your English you can just say *Understand?* or you can use one of the following expressions for "Do you understand?"

The expressions in the following list can be used to ask if someone understands something unfamiliar or difficult or if someone understands one's meaning or point of view. Most of these expressions may be said in a shortened version, not using the words shown in parentheses. The shorter versions of these expressions are very common, and they're more slangy and familiar.

Did you get that?
Is that clear?
Capeesh? (derived from the Italian word for understand)
(Do you) see?
(Do you) get it?
(Have you) got it?
(Do you) get the picture? (means "Do you understand the general idea?")
(Does that) make sense? (means "Is it logical?")

The following expressions can be used interchangeably with many of the ones in the preceding list, but they have some additional meanings:

(Are you) with me? can also mean "Do you share my view?"

See what I mean? can also mean "Do you understand the problem; understand my meaning or viewpoint?"

(Do you) get my drift? means "Do you understand what I'm indirectly implying?"

(Do you) see my point? means "Do you understand my opinion?"

Am I making myself clear? often said by a person of authority after giving an order or having a serious talk

SAYING *I UNDERSTAND*

You can answer any of the questions that check for understanding by turning the question into a statement (either positive or negative). Here are a few examples:

	Possible Answer
Do you get it?	I get it! *or* Got it!
Does that make sense?	That makes sense.
Is that clear?	That's clear.
See my point?	I don't see your point.

SAYING *I DIDN'T UNDERSTAND*

When one doesn't understand, there are a number of polite statements and short expressions that mean *I don't understand:*

I'm afraid I don't understand: *I'm afraid* is a polite opener like *I'm sorry to say . . .*

I'm not clear on that *or* **It's not clear:** in this context, *clear (on)* means understanding or understandable

I don't get it: *get it* is slang for understand

Huh? *or* **What?:** casual and familiar responses

Come again?: means "Say that again" or "Explain that again"

How's that?: means "Say that again" or "Explain that again"

What's that?: means "Say that again" or "Explain that again"; doesn't mean "What is that thing?"

Say (that) again?: means "Please repeat that"

Say what?: slangy and familiar; can be considered rude

That went right over my head: means "That's too difficult for me"; sometimes said along with a gesture of one's hand sweeping past the top of one's head

EXPRESSIONS FOR WHEN YOU DIDN'T HEAR WHAT WAS SAID

If you didn't hear clearly what was said, and you want the speaker to repeat you can use the expressions in the following list. Many of them are the same expressions used to say *I don't understand.*

These expressions are polite and more formal:

> **Excuse me?**
> **Pardon me?**
> **Sorry?**
> **Come again?**

The following expressions are informal, and *Huh?* and *Say what?* can be considered too casual or rude:

> **Huh?**
> **How's that?**
> **What's that?**
> **Say (that) again?**
> **Say what?**

Note: When a person uses one of these expressions, generally it's clear whether the person didn't understand or didn't hear. But if it's not clear, the speaker might say, "Did you not understand or just not hear me?"

The two following expressions are only used when one didn't hear what was said. In this context *catch* means *hear*:

> **I didn't catch that.**
> **I didn't catch what you said.**

Yes, No, Maybe

Saying *yes, no,* or *maybe* may seem like the simplest thing in the world. But in American English, as in many other languages, there are many shades or degrees of *yes,* many kinds of *no,* and innumerable levels of *maybe.* And most of this variation is expressed as idioms. This section offers more than 50 common ways to say *yes, no,* or *maybe* to fit all kinds of situations and intentions. In addition, there are expressions for saying *I don't know* and *I don't care.*

SAYING YES

The following expressions give a strong *Yes!* or affirmation. Also, they are often used to show enthusiasm or willingness to fulfill someone's request or to indicate that one is very sure about something:

Yes, indeed
Sure
Of course
Absolutely
Definitely
No doubt about it
To be sure
You bet (slang)
You betcha (slang, familiar)

The three expressions that follow could be used for any casual situation that requires a *yes* answer. But they're most often used when the *yes* doesn't need much show of enthusiasm. In more formal situations, they may be considered rude. These expressions are the opposites of *nah, nope,* and *uh-uh,* respectively:

Yeah
Yup
Uh-huh

In addition, here are two ways to say *yes* that have specific uses and implications:

Right: used to affirm what someone says ♦ *Matt: This is her house? Ario:* Right.
I'm afraid so: used when *yes* is not good news ♦ *Yash: Did your team lose the game? Dana:* I'm afraid so.

SAYING NO

The following expressions are used for a strong *no,* especially a refusal or denial.

No way
Nothing doing
Not a chance
Not if I can help it
Not on your life
In your dreams

Here are two more ways to say *no* that are more specialized:

> **(That's a) negative:** from military talk
> **. . . Not!** slangy, colloquial and with sarcasm ♦ *Sure you can copy my test . . . Not!*

The three expressions that follow can be used in any situation that requires a *no* answer. They're very informal and familiar, so in more formal situations they may be considered rude. They are the opposite of *yeah, yup,* and *uh-huh,* respectively.

> **Nah**
> **Nope**
> *Uh*-**uh**

The expressions that follow are polite ways to say *no:*

> **(I'm) afraid not** (when *no* is not good news) ♦ *Neil: Can you join us for dinner? Mark:* I'm afraid not.
> **No can do** ♦ *James: Can you get the report to me by tomorrow? Adrienne:* No can do. *I have too much other work to do.*
> **I think not** ♦ *Randy: I'm going to borrow your car for a bit. Marcy:* I think not!
> **Maybe not** ♦ *Tim: Going ice skating would be fun. Pam:* Maybe not. *I can't skate.*

SAYING MAYBE

When you aren't sure of an answer or don't want to say *no* directly, you might say one of the following forms of *maybe.* In American society, it's okay to initially say *maybe* to a request if you're not sure whether you can (or want to) do it. But it's considered very bad manners not to eventually say either *yes* or *no.* Here are some common expressions meaning *maybe:*

Possibly

The following expressions are truly noncommittal. They don't indicate whether a *yes* or *no* answer is more likely:

> **It's possible**
> **It's 50-50**
> **Could be**
> **We'll see**
> **I don't know**
> **I'm not sure**
> **There's a chance**
> **Time will tell**

Maybe Yes

The following expressions mean that the answer probably is or will be *yes:*

> **Maybe so**
> **Probably**
> **I think so**
> **I guess (so)** (weaker than *I think so*)
> **It's likely**

Maybe No

The following expressions mean that the answer probably is or will be *no:*

> **Maybe not**
> **I don't think so**
> **I guess not** (weaker than *I don't think so*)
> **Probably not**
> **I doubt it**
> **It doesn't look good**
> **It's not likely**

SAYING *I DON'T KNOW*

The following expressions are casual and familiar. Depending on the tone of voice, they could be considered a bit sarcastic or rude. But often they are said in a moderate tone, and are simply slangy (and very common) ways of saying *I don't know.*

> **(It) beats me**
> **You've got me**
> **Search me**
> **I'm stumped**
> **Your guess is as good as mine**
> **I haven't (got) a clue**
> **I'm clueless**
> **I have no idea**
> **I haven't the faintest idea**
> **I couldn't (begin to) tell you**
> **I can't say**

The expressions that follow are often said when one doesn't know something and isn't interested in finding out, or when one is disinterested and doesn't care to know. They're often said with a defensive tone of voice.

> **Who knows?**
> **Don't ask me**

How should I know?
Why ask me?

Responses That Mean
Okay or *I Don't Care*

The expressions in this section are said in response to a suggestion or to a request about one's preference. Additionally, there are phrases used to show that one is disinterested or, in some cases, that one wants to appear disinterested.

OKAY BY ME AND RELATED IDIOMS

If you have no specific preference and are agreeable to what others want, you might use one of the expressions that follow:

(That's) okay by me: means "I'm okay with that plan"
(That's) okay with me: means the same as above
(That's) fine by me: means "I'm fine with that plan"
(That's) fine with me: means the same as above
(That) works for me: slang; previously used to confirm appointments, plans, and schedules, but now is used for any situation
Sure, why not?: means "There is no reason not to do it"
(That) sounds good: means "It sounds like a good idea" but is used generally to mean "okay"
(You can) count me in: means "I'll join you; include me in the plans"
I'm in: means "I'll join; I'll be part of the plans"
I'm game: means "Sure, I'll do it"
I can go along with that: means "I'm okay with that; I'm agreeable with that"
I'm down with that: slang; means "I'm agreeable to that"

I DON'T CARE AND RELATED IDIOMS

The expressions in the following list are used when a person doesn't have a preference or choice. Depending on the tone of voice, *I don't care, It doesn't matter,* and *whatever* can show disinterest or even sarcasm. These expressions are often said as part of a larger sentence. When that occurs they are often followed by a dependent clause, as in some of the examples shown here:

I don't care ♦ I don't care *where we eat for dinner.*
I don't mind ♦ I don't mind *what we do.*
I'm open ♦ I'm open *to anything.* ♦ I'm open *to whatever you want to do.*

It doesn't matter (to me) ◆ It doesn't matter to me *what movie we see.*
Either way ◆ Either way *is fine with me.*
Whatever ◆ *We could take a hike, go to the beach, or* whatever.

The following expressions are used to give the choice or decision to someone else. They are often used when the speaker doesn't have a preference or wants to show respect or deference to someone:

It's up to you ◆ It's up to you. *You decide.*
It's your call ◆ *I don't care, really.* It's your call.
Whatever you want (*or* think) ◆ *We can do whatever* you want. ◆ Whatever you think. *It's your choice.*

WHO CARES? AND RELATED IDIOMS

The expressions that follow are generally used to show complete disinterest, indifference, or lack of caring. They're often said sarcastically, and are generally impolite. These expressions ask the question "Is there a reason to care?" These expressions are sometimes said as part of a larger sentence. When that occurs, they are often followed by an if clause, as in some of the examples shown here:

Who cares? ◆ Who cares *if it's raining? I don't mind getting wet.*
I could (couldn't) care less (both *could* and *couldn't* have the same meaning here) ◆ I couldn't care less *about her anymore. Not since she dated my best friend.*
What's it to me? ◆ *Melanie: There are some great air fares to Paris right now. Jean:* What's it to me? *I can't afford to go to Paris.*
Why should I care? ◆ *She's upset that I don't agree with her, but* why should she care?
So what? ◆ *So they didn't hire you.* So what? *You have other job offers.*
So? (short for *So what?* or *So, why do you care?*) ◆ *Ann: Hurry! We'll be late to the party! James:* So? *No one arrives exactly on time.*
I'm supposed to care? ◆ *Brian: I can't pay my rent this month. Charlie:* I'm supposed to care? *I told you two months ago to get a job.*
And your point is . . . ? ◆ *Mick: Your ex-girlfriend is moving to London. Keith:* And your point is . . . ?

Agree to Disagree

People often show agreement simply by saying *Right, Absolutely,* or *I agree.* They often show polite disagreement by saying something like, *Maybe, but . . .* or *I'm not sure that I agree.* However, there are a number of other ways to say *I agree* and even more ways to say (politely or forcefully) *I disagree.* The following expressions are some of the most common:

SAYING *I* AGREE

The following expressions mean *I share your opinion:*

> **Right on**
> **I'm with you**
> **I think so, too**
> **I couldn't agree more**
> **You said it**
> **You ('ve) got** *that* **right**
> **You can say** *that* **again**

Thinking

If you use the expression *I think so* to mean "I agree," think again; you may not always be right. *I think, I think so,* and *I think so, too,* can cause much confusion for learners of American English, who often use these expressions incorrectly. Here's how to use them correctly . . . every time. The word in *italic* should be emphasized or accented in order to get the exact meaning.

Expressing Opinion

I **think** means "It's my opinion" (use this to introduce your opinion) ♦ I think *this class is easy.*

I **think so** means "Yes, according to *my* opinion, but maybe not someone else's" (Use this in response to someone's question.) ♦ *Tom: Do you think this class is easy? Amy:* I think so, *but some people find it difficult.* **Caution:** Don't introduce your opinion or idea with *I think so.* This is incorrect! *I think so* is not followed by an object. Don't say "*I think so* that this class is easy."

I think so, *too* means "I agree; that's my thought or opinion exactly" (Use this in response to someone's comment or opinion.) ♦ *Tom: I think this class is pretty easy. Amy:* I think so, too. ♦ *Tom: I think the library should stay open every night until midnight. Amy:* I think so, too. *It usually closes too early.*

Expressing Uncertainty and Probability

I *think* often means "Maybe yes, but I'm not sure" (Use this to answer a question.) ♦ *Tom: Is the library open tonight? Amy:* I think. *But I don't know for sure.*

I think *so* often means "Probably yes, but I'm not 100 percent sure" (Use this to answer a question. Here, the word *so* means "yes" or "That is right.") ♦ *Tom: Is the library open tonight? Amy:* I think so. *It's usually open at night.*

SAYING *I DISAGREE*

These expressions are considered polite or neutral ways to show disagreement:

I can't say that I agree: a polite way to say "I don't agree"

I don't think so: means "I don't think the same way"; "I don't think that's right"

I have a different take on it: means "I see/understand it differently; I have a different viewpoint"

I'm of a different mind: means "My viewpoint is different"

I'm not sure about that: a polite challenge to someone's statement; means "I may not agree"

I question that: a polite challenge to someone's statement; means "I probably don't agree"

I wouldn't be so sure: a challenge to someone's statement; means "You might be wrong"

The following expressions show strong disagreement, and are impolite or rude. They are sometimes used for teasing, but are mostly only used in arguments:

You're wrong
You're crazy *or* **You're nuts**
You're all wet
You're not thinking straight
You don't know what you're talking about
That's B.S. (slang)
That's a bunch of bull (slang)

Believe It or Not

In casual conversation, listeners show interest in the speaker and the topic by nodding their head, giving facial expressions, and interjecting (putting in) short comments, expressions of surprise, agreement, understanding, disbelief, and so on. The following expressions are often used as quick interjections in a conversation to show surprise, verification, or disbelief. These are also direct responses to someone's statement or question.

NO KIDDING AND RELATED IDIOMS

The intonation and forcefulness of these phrases vary depending on whether they're a response to good news, bad news, shocking news, or simple information. The expressions *Really?*, *Is that so?*, and *You don't say!* can all be used as responses to information of any kind.

No kidding? ♦ No kidding? *You won the scholarship?!*
No lie? ♦ No lie? *They're getting married?!*
For real? ♦ *You quit smoking?* For real?
Really? ♦ Really? *You lost your job? I'm sorry.*
Is that so? or **Is that right?** ♦ *Hmmm.* Is that so? *I didn't know that.*
Is that a fact? ♦ Is that a fact? *She joined the Peace Corps?*
You mean it? ♦ You mean it? *You got the job?!*
You don't say? ♦ *A big storm is coming?* You don't say!

The same expressions used to show disbelief are often used to verify that something is true. But instead of questions, they're said as statements, as below:

No kidding ♦ *Yes, I won the scholarship.* No kidding.
No lie ♦ No lie. *They're finally getting married.*
For real ♦ For real. *I quit smoking three weeks ago.*
Really (and truly) ♦ *Yes, unfortunately, I* really and truly *lost my job.*
It's a fact ♦ It's a fact. *She starts Peace Corps training in June.*
Trust me ♦ Trust me. *I know it's true.*
Believe it or not ♦ *We're moving to India.* Believe it or not.
Would I lie to you? ♦ *Of course it's true.* Would I lie to you?
I know what I'm talking about ♦ *Believe me,* I know what I'm talking about. *They're going to lay off 200 workers.*
I saw it with my own eyes ♦ *I* saw it with my own eyes. *He was driving a brand new Ferrari!*

SAYING *I DON'T BELIEVE IT*

These slang expressions show strong disbelief and mean *That's nonsense, That's impossible,* or *I don't believe it at all.* They are often said with sarcasm or exasperation:

Yeah, sure ♦ Yeah, sure! *I'll never believe that!*
No way ♦ No way! *It can't be true.*
You lie ♦ You lie! *You're not in a rock band.*
Get out of here ♦ Get out of here! *That can't be true!*
Get out ♦ Get out! *Nobody believes that.*
Go on ♦ Go on! *She never said that.*
I don't buy it or **I don't buy that** ♦ *He says he's sorry, but* I don't buy it.
Don't make me laugh ♦ Don't make me laugh! *He could never win that race!*
Give me a break ♦ Give me a break! *That's total nonsense.*
You're full of it ♦ You're full of it. *You don't know anything about it.*
You're pulling my leg ♦ You're pulling my leg. *You're making that up.*
I'll believe it when I see it ♦ *John's running a marathon?! He hates sports.* I'll believe it when I see it!

Slowing Down and Speeding Up

Asking someone to *wait up* or to *hurry up* are common idiomatic ways to say *Wait for me!* and *Hurry faster.* This section offers these and other idioms for requesting that someone go more slowly or more quickly. The prepositions *up* and *down* are often part of these idioms.

EXPRESSIONS THAT MEAN *WAIT*

These expressions are generally used to ask someone to slow down or wait for you to catch up:

Hold it ♦ Hold it. *We forgot to lock the door.*
Hold up ♦ *Hey, everyone!* Hold up! *Wait for me.*
Wait up ♦ Wait up! *I'm coming with you.*
Slow down ♦ *Would you* slow down *and wait? I can't walk that fast.*
Whoa (word used to slow or stop a horse) ♦ Whoa! *What's the big hurry?*

The rest of the expressions in this section have a variety of functions. They're used to

- tell someone who has interrupted you to wait
- reply to someone who asks you to hurry
- reassure someone who is waiting for service
- ask someone to hold on the phone
- ask others for patience

Note: The expressions are shown with the word *minute,* but you can also say *second* or *sec* (short for *second*).

Just a minute ♦ Just a minute. *I'm almost ready.*
Wait a minute ♦ Wait a minute. *I'll talk to you when I finish this math problem.*
Hang on (a minute) ♦ Hang on a minute. *I'll call her to the phone.*
Hold on (a minute) ♦ *If you* hold on a minute, *then I'll be able to help you.*

The two expressions that follow also mean to wait, but they are less polite:

What's the (big) rush? *or* **What's the (big) hurry?** ♦ *Hey,* what's the big rush? *There's plenty of time.*
Hold your horses ♦ Hold your horses! *I'll be there in a minute.*

Hurry Up and Wait

The expression *hurry up and wait* is often used when someone hurries to get some-where, but after arriving, is forced to wait. An example is when someone hurries to get to the airport on time, but then must wait in the terminal because the plane is delayed, or one rushes to get to a doctor's appointment, arrives on time, but then must wait for an hour to see the doctor.

Here's another example: "I don't know why I rush to get ready for work. It's just *hurry up and wait* because when I get on the freeway, the traffic just crawls along at 10 miles per hour."

EXPRESSIONS THAT MEAN *HURRY*

These expressions are used to tell someone to go faster or to hurry, and are often used to show impatience. The tone of voice generally shows if the speaker is simply encouraging someone or is anxious or impatient.

Hurry up ♦ Hurry up! *You'll be late for school.* ♦ *I wish they'd* hurry up *and fin-ish that road construction.*

Come on ♦ Come on. *We can't wait for you any longer.*

Step on it ♦ *You'll have to* step on it *if you don't want to miss that train.*

Speed it up ♦ *Would you quit talking and* speed it up? *You're holding up the line.*

Pick up the pace ♦ *If we don't* pick up the pace *we won't finish the project on time.*

Get going ♦ *Let's* get going. *We have to be there by 6 p.m.*

Get a move on ♦ *You had better* get a move on. *It's getting late.*

Let's go ♦ Let's go! *They just announced the final boarding call.*

The following expression also means to hurry, but it is less polite and implies that the speaker is becoming impatient:

I haven't got all day ♦ *Geez! What's taking so long? I haven't got all day!*

Stop Doing That!

Mostly short and to the point, these expressions are used to demand that someone behave appropriately, act differently, or stop doing something that's annoying, abu-sive, or unacceptable.

EXPRESSIONS THAT MEAN *BE QUIET*

Some of the expressions that follow are commonly used to tell someone to speak more quietly. Others are used to stop someone from talking about something unpleasant, rude, or private. Many of these idioms can be used in either context. They are generally said as imperatives (as shown in bold) and they can be rude or harsh:

Be quiet ♦ Be quiet. *I want to hear this program.*
Quiet down ♦ *Boys, time to* quiet down *and go to sleep.*
Lower your voice ♦ *Please* lower your voice *in the library.*
Keep your voice down ♦ Keep your voice down. *The baby is sleeping.*
Keep it down (lower voices or music) ♦ *Hey, you guys,* keep it down. *I'm trying to study.*

The following expressions are considered impolite or rude, but people sometimes say them jokingly:

Shut up ♦ *She never* shuts up. *She's always talking.*
Hush (up) ♦ Hush up, *Donny! We don't want to hear about it.*
Zip it ♦ *Hey,* zip it! *We've all heard enough.*
Put a cork in it ♦ *Better* put a cork in it. *Here comes the boss.*
Give it a rest ♦ *You've complained about it for a week.* Give it a rest!

KEEP QUIET ABOUT IT AND RELATED IDIOMS

Use these expressions to request that someone *keep a secret* (not reveal or tell a secret or something private):

Be/keep quiet about it ♦ Be quiet about *the surprise party.* ♦ *I'll tell you a secret, but please* keep quiet about it.
Keep it hushed up ♦ *They just got engaged, but they want to* keep it hushed up *until their family reunion.*
Keep it to yourself ♦ *Don't tell anyone about it. Just* keep it to yourself.
Keep a lid on it ♦ *It's top secret. So,* keep a lid on it.
Keep it under your hat ♦ *I'll tell you what I got him for his birthday if you'll* keep it under your hat.
Don't give it away ♦ *It will be a great surprise if no one* gives it away.
Don't tell (a soul) ♦ Don't tell a soul *about your idea until you're ready.*

The following two expressions use colorful metaphors that mean to accidentally give clues that reveal a secret. These very common expressions are also said in the negative:

Spill the beans ♦ *We tried to keep it a secret, but our little boy* spilled the beans.
Let the cat out of the bag ♦ *She really* let the cat out of the bag *when she called to congratulate him. He didn't know that he had won the award.*

BEHAVE YOURSELF AND RELATED IDIOMS

These expressions are usually said to children, but sometimes to others, too. People also say them jokingly or humorously to others or about themselves:

Behave yourself ♦ *Calm down and* behave yourself. ♦ *Now,* behave yourself *in the car.*
Mind your manners ♦ Mind your manners *in the restaurant.* ♦ *I'll really have to* mind my manners *when I attend the Governor's dinner.*
Mind your Ps and Qs ♦ *I expect you to* mind your Ps and Qs *when you are at your friend's house.*
Act right ♦ *If you can't* act right, *I'll take you home.*

KNOCK IT OFF! AND RELATED IDIOMS

These short but efficient expressions are used to order people to stop doing something annoying or something that they shouldn't be doing. The meaning is to immediately stop some behavior or action that is in progress.

The expressions that follow can be used seriously or as a threat, and are also used lightly or even playfully. Tone of voice and context generally make the meaning clear. *Note:* The idioms are listed with the pronoun *it,* but the word *that* can also be used.

Knock it off ♦ Knock it off! *That noise is annoying me.*
Cut it out ♦ Cut it out! *It's not okay to tease the dog.*
Quit it ♦ *Mom, tell Bobby to* quit it.
Stop it ♦ *I'm not going to argue, so you can just* stop it!

The following expressions are a little more serious, and are less likely to be used jokingly:

I'm warning you

a threat; often the consequences aren't named, although sometimes they are
♦ I'm warning you! *Stop that now!* ♦ I'm warning you *that I'll have to fire you if you don't work harder.*

Enough is enough

means "Stop, I'm losing my patience" ♦ *No more arguing over the TV.* Enough is enough! ♦ *My bank is always screwing up.* Enough is enough! *I'm switching to a different one.*

GO AWAY! AND RELATED IDIOMS

These expressions can be said as a threat, a firm command, or jokingly. They all mean *Leave!* and are often rude:

Go away
Get lost (the rudest of these expressions)
Scram
Beat it
Shoo (somewhat playful; nonthreatening)
Get out of here (also said *Get outta here!*)

GET OFF MY BACK! AND RELATED IDIOMS

People use these expressions to describe being criticized or nagged about something:

on my back ♦ *My wife has been* on my back *to quit smoking.*
in my face ♦ *Laura has been* in my face *about going to church with her.*
in my business ♦ *He's always* in my business.

The expressions are sometimes said as *all up in my face* and *all up in my business:* "Hey, I said I'm sorry, so don't *get all up in my face* about it."

If someone has been *on your back* or *in your face*, you may want to use one of the expressions in the following list to tell him or her to stop. These expressions are very strong and can be considered rude, but people say them when they are tired or receiving someone's consistent anger, criticism, nagging comments, or complaints. Teenagers often say them in response to their parents' questions and authority:

Back off ♦ Back off! *You've been nagging at me all day.*
Lay off ♦ *He really should* lay off. *The boy is doing the best he can.*
Lighten up ♦ *Come on,* lighten up! *Don't be so serious.*
Chill (out) ♦ *Would you* chill out? *Why be so angry?*
Get off my back ♦ *As soon as we finish this report, we can* get our boss off our back.
Leave me alone ♦ *His son said* "Leave me alone."
Get out of my face ♦ *Hey, it's my business, so* get out of my face!

Here are a few expressions that are used to tell someone to stop interfering in someone else's personal, private matters:

Mind your own business! ♦ *His mother should* mind her own business *and stop interfering with her son and daughter-in-law's life.*
It's none of your business! ♦ It's none of your business *what she decides to do.*
Keep out of it! ♦ *You had better* keep out of it.

Another common expression, which is generally rude but can be lighthearted, is *Get a life!* It means "Get more involved and interested in your own life, and stop interfering with other people's lives; find things to interest you besides other people's business!" It's also used to imply that a person should change his or her boring and uneventful life, and go have some fun. Sometimes the expression is said as "Go get a life". Here are some examples:

♦ *He should quit bothering his son and daughter-in-law and* go get a life!
♦ *Jean: Why was your phone busy all of the time? Tom: Why do you care?* Get a life!
♦ *I just sit around watching TV every night. I need to* get a life!

Good News, Bad News

The report of good or bad news always brings an expression of joy or condolence. People might say *I'm happy to hear that* for good news or *I'm sorry to hear that* for bad news. But commonly they'll use one of the following expressions.

EXPRESSIONS FOR GREAT NEWS

People commonly say the following when they hear good or happy news. Sometimes these expressions are said sarcastically when the news is actually bad. Expressions of congratulation are included in the "Words of Encouragement" section.

All right (Awright) ♦ All right! *We get two days off next week!*
Yes ♦ Yes! *Our team won again!*
Awesome ♦ *She was accepted at Yale.* Awesome!
Fantastic ♦ *They signed the contract.* Fantastic!
Terrific ♦ *I heard that you just bought a house. That's* terrific!
Perfect ♦ *She can go with us.* Perfect!
Right on ♦ Right on! *I got the job!*
What luck ♦ What luck! *It's a sunny day for our first sailing class.*
It's our lucky day ♦ It's our lucky day! *I stood in line all night and got tickets to the Stones concert!*

That makes my day ♦ *When I heard that they had a new baby,* that made my day!
That's the best news I've heard all day ♦ *She said the operation went well.*
That's the best news I've heard all day!

EXPRESSIONS FOR BAD NEWS

People commonly say the following when they hear bad or unhappy news, when someone doesn't reach his or her goal, doesn't succeed or win, or when someone experiences bad luck. People also say these expressions to themselves:

Oh no ♦ Oh no! *I can't find my wallet!*
Too bad ♦ *He missed the deadline to apply for the grant.* Too bad!
What a shame ♦ *He died and left three young children.* What a shame!
What a pity (also phrased *It's a pity*) ♦ What a pity *to see how he's wasted his life.*
(What a) Bummer (slang) ♦ *Your dog got lost?* Bummer!
What a drag (also phrased *That's a drag*; slang) ♦ What a drag *that your parents won't let you go out during the week.*
Shoot (slang) ♦ Shoot! *I forgot to mail these letters.*
That sucks (slang) ♦ *She broke up with him to date someone else.* That sucks!
That's the pits (also phrased *It's the pits*) ♦ *You failed the final exam? Man,* that's the pits!

A related expression is *Better luck next time,* which is often said to take the attention off the failure and put it on future success: "Well, your team can't always win. *Better luck next time.*"

Way to Go!

Way to go! is a popular expression of congratulation and encouragement. It's used for any accomplishment or situation, large or small, that deserves recognition, and it's used with people of any age, from toddlers to grandmas. In this section you'll find many more ways to say *Way to go!* and offer encouragement.

WORDS OF ENCOURAGEMENT

The short expressions of encouragement that follow basically mean "I encourage you to go and do it; do it with spirit, and do it well."

Go for it!

means "Go for your goal" ♦ *You want to get a PhD? Hey,* go for it! ♦ Go for it! *You're the best person for the job.*

You go (girl)!

originally, feisty words of support and acknowledgement for women; often phrased simply as *You go!* and used with anyone ♦ *She became a top country music star at 14! You go, girl!* ♦ *Nicole: I've lost 10 pounds now that I've started exercising. Marcia: You go!*

Do it!

means **"Go for your dreams," "Don't hesitate"** ♦ *If you really want to travel, I say* do it! ♦ *You've wanted to go to law school for years. Stop talking and* do it!

Have at it!

means "Go ahead and attempt it"; often said when there's a physical task to be done, or when there's a lot of work to do ♦ *Sue wanted to try building our deck, so I said,* "Have at it!" ♦ *When I offered to help my wife organize the basement she said,* "Have at it!"

Go get 'em!

short for "Go get them," meaning go beat the competition; also used generally to mean "Go for your goals" ♦ *You're going to run in the Ironman Competition? Wonderful!* Go get 'em! ♦ *I'm so glad you were accepted to medical school.* Go get 'em!

WORDS OF CONGRATULATIONS

When the goal is reached, whether one's success is large or small, people offer some of the following expressions of praise and congratulations:

You did it
Way to go
Well done
You done good (slangy variation of *You did a very good job*)
Good for you
Good going
That's my girl/boy (often said to a child or someone younger than the speaker)
Atta girl/boy (short version of *That's my girl/boy*)
You're the man (*the man* means the top person of either gender, the one deserving of most respect)
Bravo: from Italian; a cheer of praise and congratulations

That's Life

The expressions that follow reflect the attitude that one can't control life; to live in this world, one must accept the good with the bad. These expressions are about accepting fate. They're often said after a disappointment, but also can express a carefree attitude about life. They can be said with compassion or with cynicism.

That's life ♦ *So, you weren't chosen for the team.* That's life.

Life's like that ♦ *Son, sometimes other kids can be mean.* Life's like that!

That's the way it goes ♦ *I just got a bonus, and now I have to use it to fix my leaking roof.* That's the way it goes.

That's just the way it is ♦ *Not everyone will like your artwork.* That's just the way it is.

It is what it is ♦ *That speeding ticket made my insurance rates go up.* Well, it is what it is.

You win some, you lose some ♦ Well, you win some, you lose some. *The house we wanted just sold to someone else.*

Such is life ♦ *Our cat died. We miss him, but* such is life.

C'est la vie (French for that's life) ♦ *They didn't hire me, but I have other options. So,* c'est la vie.

PART III

IDIOMS FOR EXPRESSING EMOTION, CHARACTER, SUCCESS, AND FAILURE

*A*merican English has idioms for every aspect of life: idioms for tangible things such as food and exercise, and for abstract things such as emotions, personality, and concepts like success, failure, and luck. The idioms in this part cover these less-concrete aspects of life.

CHAPTER 10

EMOTIONS

"Don't worry, be happy," the song says. That's good advice, but sometimes one does worry, or feel sad or angry. These are common human emotions. Some people *wear their hearts on their sleeves,* meaning they openly show their emotions (especially romantic ones). These types of people are sometimes called *an open book* because they're *easy to read,* meaning it's easy to see how they feel; their emotions are visible. Other people hide their feelings or *keep everything inside.* They're sometimes called *a closed book* because they are *hard to read,* meaning it's hard to know what they're feeling.

This chapter presents idioms and expressions for a variety of emotions and sentiments: joy, sadness, peacefulness, anxiety, anger, resentment, guilt, and others.

Happiness and Contentment

The idioms in this section refer to happiness, contentment, and having a positive attitude.

IN GOOD SPIRITS AND RELATED IDIOMS

Someone who is *in good spirits* is feeling good, happy, and positive. Here are two other idioms that mean the same as *in good spirits:*

> **up** ♦ *You seem* up *today. Why are you so happy?*
> **in a good mood** ♦ *I'm always* in a good mood *after getting a letter from my daughter.*
> **in good spirits** ♦ *We've* been in good spirits *here ever since the snow melted.*

Grammar Note: The last two idioms above can also be said as be *put in good spirits* or be *put in a good mood,* meaning to be made to feel happy because of something. For example, "Going to the beach always *puts me in a good mood.*"

The following expressions mean that a person is very happy. These expressions are *similes* — comparisons that use the words *as* or *like:*

> **(as) pleased as punch** ♦ *He'll be* pleased as punch *to hear that you got the promotion.*
> **(as) happy as a clam** ♦ *Give that child some paper and crayons, and she's* as happy as a clam *for hours.*
> **(as) happy as a lark** ♦ *The newlyweds are* as happy as larks *in their new home.*

Note: The first two of these similes are particularly unusual, because neither punch (a festive party drink) nor a clam seems particularly pleased or happy.

STAY POSITIVE AND RELATED IDIOMS

The following expressions mean to be carefree, have a positive attitude, and not worry about things:

be positive *or* **stay positive**

> to keep a positive, good, hopeful attitude or outlook; can imply that a person faces adversity or is in a difficult position ♦ *I know you're going through some hard times, but try to* stay positive. *Everything will be resolved in time.* ♦ *I like to work with Stephanie because she* is *always so* positive.

happy-go-lucky

> carefree and happy; often used to describe people's personalities, rather than their mood ♦ *You're so* happy-go-lucky. *Did you win the lottery or something?* ♦ *Jimmy is a* happy-go-lucky *guy. No matter what happens, he's smiling.*

upbeat

> very positive; implies that a person is energetic and optimistic ♦ *If you can keep an* upbeat *attitude, you'll heal much faster from injury and illness.* ♦ *Whenever he faces a deadline, Brian stays* upbeat *and focused.*

JUMPING FOR JOY AND RELATED IDIOMS

The following idioms mean very happy, blissfully happy, ecstatic. Almost all of the idioms that express great happiness and joy allude to being off the ground, up in the air:

jumping for joy ♦ *Everyone was* jumping for joy *when the missing girl was found.*
walking on air ♦ *Ever since those two became engaged they've been* walking on air.
walking two feet off the ground ♦ *After winning the election, I was* walking two feet off the ground *for days.* **Note:** You may also hear people say *walking 6 or 10 feet off the ground* instead of just *two feet.*

Seeing the Glass Half Full or Half Empty

Some people *see the glass half full* and others *see the glass half empty*. These expressions refer to the belief that, if you take a glass of water and fill it halfway, an optimist will see the glass as half full and a pessimist will see the glass as half empty. Here are some examples:

♦ *She has a great attitude. She always* sees the glass as half full.

♦ *He tends to* see the glass half empty, *and criticizes everything.*

Here's another expression to describe someone who is extremely happy and is smiling widely: "He was *grinning from ear to ear*," meaning that the smile is so wide it extends from one ear to the other.

[See *on cloud nine* and *in seventh heaven* in Chapter 15; see idioms for humor and laughter in Chapter 7.]

Sadness and Melancholy

The idioms in this section describe sadness, melancholy, depression, and having a bad or negative attitude.

IN A MOOD AND RELATED IDIOMS

When people are irritable, impatient, or grouchy, they may be in a bad mood for no apparent reason. Following are some common idioms to describe this feeling:

in a mood ♦ *Be careful! The boss is* in a mood *today.*
in a bad mood ♦ *When she's* in a bad mood, *it's best just to leave her alone.*
in a foul mood ♦ *You're* in a foul mood. *What's the problem?*
in a rotten mood ♦ *I don't know why I'm* in *such a* rotten mood.

Grammar Note: These idioms can also be said as to *put* someone *in a bad mood, put* someone *in a foul mood,* and so on. These forms are used to convey that something or someone caused a person to be in a bad mood.

A related idiom is *moody,* which means to alternate from a good mood to a bad mood for no reason. For example, "He's always so *moody.* That's why our relationship didn't last."

All of the following adjectives mean irritable and impatient:

cranky
grouchy
grumpy
bitchy (a strong insult and slightly vulgar)
short-tempered

All of these words except *short-tempered* have noun forms: *crank, grouch, grump,* and *bitch.*

FEELING LOW AND RELATED IDIOMS

In contrast to being "off the ground" (blissfully happy), someone who's feeling *low* or *down* is in a sad or depressed mood. Many idioms describe this feeling:

down ♦ *She's been feeling* down *ever since her pet rabbit died.*
low ♦ *His girlfriend just left him, so he's pretty* low.
bummed (out) (can also mean annoyed or a little angry) ♦ *I'm really* bummed *about failing that exam. I thought I had passed it.*
in a funk ♦ *Sometimes, thinking about the troubles in the world puts me* in a funk.
down in the mouth ♦ *You look* down in the mouth. *Is something wrong?* **Note:** This idiom is generally said of other people, not oneself.

When someone is *in a bad mood* and feeling irritable, people might say "He *got up on the wrong side of the bed.*" This expression alludes to an old belief that it's bad luck to put one's left foot out of bed first. Here's an example:

Sidney: Why are you so grumpy today?
Lynn: I don't know. I guess I just *got up on the wrong side of the bed* this morning.

I've Got *the Blues*

If you say, "I've *got the blues,*" then you feel sad and depressed. You can also say, "I'm *blue*" or "I'm *feeling blue.*" The use of the word "blue" to describe sadness is very old, and the origin of the word isn't clear. But the expression is familiar to the world in the form of *blues music* or simply *the blues,* which is a form of African-American folk music (and the basis for jazz music), characterized by a slow tempo and melancholy words. **Grammar Note:** In American English, "I've got . . ." is a common way of saying "I have . . ."

CHEER UP! AND RELATED IDIOMS

When people are *down in the dumps* or feeling depressed, there are a number of expressions used to encourage them to feel better. The idioms *Cheer up!* and *Lighten up!* mean to try to be more cheerful, less depressed. Here are some other idioms that mean the same:

let it go

> to release whatever is bothering you; means "Forget about it" ♦ *I know you're upset that your team lost the championship, but you should* let it go. ♦ *I didn't mean it as an insult, so* let it go.

look on the bright side

> to see the positive part of a problem, to see the benefit in the situation ♦ *Hey,* look on the bright side: *Not getting that job means that you're available for something better.* ♦ *My car broke down, but I'm* looking on the bright side: *I finally have an excuse to buy a new car.*

it could be worse

> means "This situation isn't so bad, compared to a worse situation" ♦ *Well,* it could always be worse. *You could have failed two classes instead of just one.* ♦ *I have the flu, but* it could be worse. *My friend has the flu and a rash.* **Note:** The adjective *always* is often placed after the word *could,* as shown in the first example.

[See *"Get over it!"* in Part V; see more on *cheer up* and *lighten up* in Part V.]

TORN UP AND RELATED IDIOMS

When one is very sad, grieving, or deeply disappointed, his or her feelings might be described by one of the following idioms:

> **torn up (adj)** ♦ *He's really* torn up *over the death of his best friend.*
> **beside oneself (adj)** ♦ *She was* beside herself *when her husband was so ill.*
> **heartbroken** *or* **brokenhearted (adj)** ♦ *I'm* heartbroken *over that relationship.*
> **crushed (adj)** ♦ *She was* crushed *that she wasn't chosen for the softball team.*
> **a heavy heart (n)** ♦ *Seeing so many AIDS orphans gave her* a heavy heart.

[See *out of one's head* in Chapter 13.]

If you're *torn up* or *beside yourself,* you may want to cry. All of the following idioms mean to cry a lot:

> **cry one's eyes out** ♦ *Timmy* cried his eyes out *when his dog died.*
> **cry like a baby** ♦ *I* cried like a baby *watching that sad film.*
> **burst into tears** ♦ *When she was scolded, she* burst into tears.
> **break down** ♦ *He* broke down *after hearing the news of his mother's death.*

BEING NEGATIVE AND RELATED IDIOMS

The following expressions are used to describe someone with a bad or negative attitude, someone who discourages the enjoyment of others and is unenthusiastic.

negative

> having a bad or hopeless attitude about something, pessimistic, unhappy ♦ *Your financial situation isn't hopeless, so you should stop being so* negative *about it and start taking some positive action.*

a sourpuss

> one who discourages enjoyment ♦ *There's no use trying to cheer him up; he's just* a sourpuss.

a wet blanket

> a person who spoils others' fun, discourages enjoyment. Alludes to using a wet blanket to smother a fire. ♦ *Don't be such* a wet blanket. *Have a little fun.* ♦ *Let's not invite him. He's really* a wet blanket.

Staying Calm and Cool

Idioms in this section mean to feel calm, at peace, without worry, anxiety, or anger. Many of these idioms use the word *cool* (calm and relaxed) as the opposite of *hot* (angry, or sweating from anxiety).

> **keep one's cool (v)** ♦ *You have to know how to* keep your cool *if you want to teach high school.*
> **play it cool (v)** ♦ Play it cool, *man. Don't let anyone see your anger.*
> **(as) cool as a cucumber (adj)** ♦ *She's great in an emergency. She can stay* as cool as a cucumber, *and do what needs to be done.*
> **laid back (adj)** ♦ *I didn't get into too much trouble for staying out late. My parents were pretty* laid back *about it, and only said, "Next time, call us!"*

[See *laid back* in Chapter 7; see *keeping one's head* and *keeping a level head* in Chapter 13.]

Nervousness and Anxiety

The idioms in this section describe feelings of worry, anxiousness, or nervousness. A more serious level of anxiety, fear, is discussed in the next section.

A CASE OF THE NERVES AND RELATED IDIOMS

If you have *a case of the nerves,* then you feel nervous about something that you did or must do. Here are some other idioms that mean to feel nervous:

have the jitters *or* **get the jitters** ♦ *Good luck in your interview. And don't* get the jitters; *you're very qualified for that position.*

be jittery *or* **feel jittery** ♦ *Drinking too much coffee makes me* feel jittery.

be on edge ♦ *We* were on edge *all week, waiting to hear the results of the biopsy.*

be edgy *or* **feel edgy** ♦ *That industrial music really* puts me on edge.

When nervousness or anxiety (nervousness and fear combined) become more severe, you might use one of the following idioms:

a bundle of nerves ♦ *I was* a bundle of nerves *before my audition.*

bite one's nails ♦ *While the judges decided the winner, we all sat there* biting our nails. ***Note:*** This idiom refers to the nervous habit of biting the ends of one's fingernails. It can be used even when people aren't literally biting their nails.

on pins and needles ♦ *We were* on pins and needles *waiting for our son to come out of surgery.*

sweating bullets ♦ *I was* sweating bullets *over that presentation, but it went well.* ***Note:*** This idiom also implies that the person is sweating a lot from nerves.

worried sick ♦ *Where have you been?! We were* worried sick.

[See *have butterflies in one's stomach* in Chapter 13.]

DRIVING SOMEONE UP A WALL AND RELATED IDIOMS

If someone is making you nervous or annoyed with something he or she is doing, then you might say, "Stop that noise! You're *driving me up a wall!*" or "I'm *climbing the walls!*" Here are some other similar expressions:

drive someone nuts *or* **drive someone crazy** ♦ *On rainy days, the kids just* drive me crazy.

get on someone's nerves ♦ *His constant gum chewing is starting to* get on my nerves.

be in someone's hair ♦ *The kids have* been in my hair *all day, wanting me to do one thing or another.*

[See *breathe down someone's neck* in Chapter 13.]

When a person can no longer tolerate an annoyance, one of the following expressions might describe how he or she feels:

at the end of one's patience ♦ *I'm at the end of my patience with your messy habits.*

reach one's limit ♦ *She loaned money to her grown kids many times, but finally she reached her limit.*

When you have *reached your limit,* you might say one of the following:

I'm fed up!
I've had it!
I'm over it!
That's it!

Anger

There are varying degrees of anger, and American idioms can express them all. Idioms can describe angry feelings from frustration and slight annoyance to rage. This section includes many of the most common expressions.

TICKED OFF AND RELATED IDIOMS

When one is annoyed, infuriated, or angry about something, one of the following adjectives can describe the feeling well:

ticked (off) ♦ *I just broke my reading glasses. Boy, that* ticks *me* off! **Note:** Also said as *tick someone off.*

teed off ♦ *His rude comment really* teed me off.

pissed (off) (vulgar, but common) ♦ *My parents were so* pissed *when they found out that I lied to them.* **Note:** Also said as *piss someone off.*

miffed ♦ *He's* miffed *that I didn't return his call.*

The following adjectives are also used to mean that a person is angry. They all refer to things that are hot.

steamed (up) ♦ *I'm* steamed! *I waited all afternoon for the repairman to come and he never showed up or called to reschedule.*

burned up also *burn one up* ♦ *It* burns me up *to think that those criminals might get off without punishment.*

hot under the collar ♦ *There's no use getting* hot under the collar. *Your anger won't make this line go any faster.*

Another idiom that uses a heat metaphor to talk about anger is the verb *see red*, which means to be extremely angry: "If you want to *see red*, just read this article on how the big corporations avoid paying taxes."

ON THE WARPATH AND RELATED IDIOMS

When anger intensifies, it's often described with idioms that allude to war or gestures of threat:

> **on the warpath** ♦ *If the company tries to reduce our health benefits, we'll be* on the warpath.
> **up in arms** ♦ *The neighborhood is* up in arms *over the plan to build a freeway nearby.* **Note:** *Arms* is used here to refer to weapons.
> **foam at the mouth** ♦ *John was* foaming at the mouth *when the guy insulted his wife.*

The following similes also mean that one is very mad or furious:

> **(as) mad as hell**
> **madder than a wet hen**

BLOW ONE'S TOP AND RELATED IDIOMS

Some idioms that mean to express one's anger verbally allude to things *blowing up*, meaning to explode:

> **blow one's top (*or* stack)** ♦ *He's going to* blow his top *when he finds out that you destroyed the lab sample.*
> **blow a fuse** ♦ *Don't* blow a fuse *just because he broke your CD case. He'll buy you another one.*
> **hit the ceiling (*or* roof)** ♦ *Dad* hit the roof *when he saw the dent I made in his car.*

A similar idiom is *blow up at someone,* which means to yell at someone in anger: "Why are you *blowing up at me?* I didn't do it."

A few other idioms refer to losing control of oneself or one's senses:

> **have a fit** *or* **throw a fit** ♦ *Boy, she* threw a fit *when she saw the broken lamp.*
> **lose one's cool** ♦ *Don't* lose your cool *just because someone is rude.*
> **lose it** ♦ *I really* lost it *when the coach yelled at my daughter and made her cry.*
> **get worked up** ♦ *He used to* get worked up *over little things, but now he's more easygoing.*
> **come unglued** ♦ *When the store called to say that my 12-year-old son was caught shoplifting, I* came unglued.
> **fly off the handle** ♦ *People will avoid you if you are always* flying off the handle.

A SHORT FUSE AND RELATED IDIOMS

Here are some ways to describe a person who gets angry easily and quickly:

quick to anger ♦ *He's* quick to anger, *so I am always careful around him.*
has a quick temper ♦ *I know I* have a quick temper, *but I'll try to control it.*
has a short fuse ♦ *She* has a short fuse. *It doesn't take much to anger her.*
hot-headed ♦ *You are so* hot-headed; *you always get mad so easily.*

Fear

The following expressions mean to be fearful, to be afraid. Some idioms refer to the physical expression of fear, such as shaking or trembling, tingly skin, and even wetting or soiling one's pants.

These idioms mean to be very fearful, and they refer to trembling or shaking with fear:

shake like a leaf ♦ *I wasn't hurt in the accident, but I* shook like a leaf *for an hour afterward.*
shake in one's boots ♦ *He'll be* shaking in his boots *if he ever tries to start a fight with me.*
scare the crap out of someone ♦ *It* scared the crap out of me *when the hospital called. I thought you had been in an accident.*
have one's teeth chatter ♦ *Listening to ghost stories late at night* made our teeth chatter.
scared out of one's wits ♦ *We were all* scared out of our wits *by the tornado.*
have one's hair stand on end ♦ *Seeing the face of the murderer on the TV news* made my hair stand on end.

Another expression is *jump out of one's skin,* which is used when people actually jump a little because they are so scared: "We nearly *jumped out of our skin* when someone banged on the door during the scary movie."

People use these expressions when something is fearsome and disgusting:

give one the creeps ♦ *Spiders* give me the creeps. *I hate them.* ♦ *That guy* gives me the creeps. *He's always watching me.*
give one the willies ♦ *I can't watch horror movies. They* give me the willies.
make one's skin crawl ♦ *It* made my skin crawl *to touch that snake.*

Envy and Jealousy

Envy (the desire for a possession or advantage that someone else has) is often expressed with one of the following idioms, which can be used seriously or lightly:

green with envy ♦ *Everyone will be* green with envy *when they see your new sports car.*

eat one's heart out ♦ *Gwen: That's your new boyfriend?! He's so handsome! Sharon: I know.* Eat your heart out, *honey!*

Jealousy (resentment and bad feelings toward someone because of his or her possession or good fortune) is sometimes expressed with the following idioms:

shoot daggers at someone ♦ *His old girlfriend was* shooting daggers at me *all evening.*

be eaten up with jealousy ♦ *She left him for another man and he's just* eaten up with jealousy.

Resentment and Revenge

An eye for an eye means "if you hurt me, I'll hurt you back." This is revenge, or *getting back at* someone for doing something hurtful to you. Even if you don't *get back at* someone, you may feel resentful and *hang on to* your anger (stay angry for an extended period of time). This section presents other expressions for conveying resentment and revenge.

HOLD A GRUDGE AND RELATED IDIOMS

Resentment — a feeling of anger and indignation from being hurt, injured, or offended by someone — is generally expressed with one of these idioms:

hold a grudge

to remember a past offense and continue to be resentful about it. Also said as *bear a grudge* ♦ *She's still* holding a grudge *for something that happened years ago? She should forget it.* ♦ *The thing I like most about Rebecca is that she never* holds a grudge.

hold something against someone

to be resentful about something ♦ *I was a better athlete than my brother, and he's always* held it against me. ♦ *I have apologized for offending you. Please don't continue to* hold it against me.

GETTING REVENGE AND RELATED IDIOMS

Getting revenge and *taking revenge* mean to punish someone or make someone suffer for a past offense or hurt. This can also be expressed with one of these idioms:

get back at someone

to get revenge. This idiom can also be said as *get someone back*. ♦ *I was given the promotion instead of Jim, and now he's trying to* get back at me *by being cold and unpleasant.* ♦ *He insulted my team in the meeting, but I'll* get him back *when he needs help from my department.*

make someone pay

to get revenge. In this expression, "pay" doesn't mean to pay money; it means to suffer. ♦ *I'm going to* make him pay *for the rotten way he treated me.* ♦ *She's determined to* make me pay *for forgetting her birthday.* **Note:** A variation of this idiom is *someone is going to pay*, which you can say when you're not sure who is responsible. For example, "I don't know who broke the vase, but *someone is going to pay*."

teach someone a lesson

to get revenge; implies to make someone remorseful ♦ *He tried to cheat us, but we* taught him a lesson *by telling everyone about it. Now, no one will do business with him.* ♦ *I'm going to* teach him a lesson. *He'll never steal from me again!*

Shame and Guilt

Shame and guilt are powerful, and painful, emotions. They can make a person feel regret or feel very bad about him- or herself. The expressions in this section are used to convey these feelings.

PUTTING SOMEONE TO SHAME AND RELATED IDIOMS

Putting someone to shame means causing someone to feel shame, which is intense embarrassment or a mixture of embarrassment, guilt, and remorse for something one has done. The classic statement to make someone feel ashamed is *Shame on you!* Today, this expression is typically said jokingly.

Someone who looks ashamed is said to be *shame-faced*. To feel shame is also expressed with one of the following idioms. These idioms refer to the ways that people react to shame—lowering their head, covering their face, or hiding:

hang one's head ♦ *Those boys were* hanging their heads *after they got caught eating the cake for Grandpa's party.*

hide one's face ♦ *I wanted to* hide my face *when she told everyone at the table about my surgery. That's private!*

not show one's face ♦ *Ever since the scandal was discovered, he* hasn't shown his face.

When people feel that their shame will last for a long time, they might say *"I'll never live it down!"* It's also put as *never going to live it down,* and here's an example:

♦ *My sister told everyone at school that I sleep with a stuffed toy. I'm* never going to live that down!

[See *losing face* in Chapter 13.]

LOOK SHEEPISH AND RELATED IDIOMS

Feeling guilty means feeling remorseful, feeling bad for having done something wrong. When people suffer from extreme feelings of guilt, they are said to be *guilt-ridden* or *consumed with guilt.* People can also feel just a little guilty for doing something that is bad for their health or costs too much money. Here are a few more expressions that mean someone looks guilty:

look sheepish ♦ *When he came home* looking sheepish, *I knew that he had bought another expensive power tool.*

have guilt written all over one's face ♦ *I know he's seeing another woman. He* has guilt written all over his face.

Note: One difference between shame and guilt is that people can feel shame, or be made to feel shamed, even when they haven't done anything wrong. For example, one could feel shame about living in poverty, or about a physical feature that he or she is embarrassed about, such as large ears or excess weight. But feeling guilty generally means that the person has done something wrong, either deliberately or accidentally.

CHAPTER 11

CHARACTER TRAITS

Some people say you are born with your personality or character. Others say that you develop it during your life and that your environment or home life helps to shape it. This argument is part of a larger debate called the *nature-nurture argument* (is your character *natural*, inborn, or is it *nurtured*, learned and acquired in life?).

Whatever the answer, people are often described by their character or personality traits, such as generosity, honesty, and patience or selfishness, dishonesty, and impatience. Character affects how we act or behave, so idioms that describe character traits often describe specific behaviors too. This chapter is filled with idioms and expressions describing people's character and behavior.

Idioms That Express Generosity

To convey that a person is extremely generous you can say "She would *give you her last dime*" or "He would *give you the shirt off his back.*" Here are some other idioms that express generosity:

a giving person

> **(n)** a person who gives his or her time or attention to others; this idiom does not necessarily refer to giving any material object ♦ *He's a very kind and giving person; he does a lot of charity work.*

generous to a fault

> **(adj)** be too generous; overgenerous, giving more than one should ♦ *She's generous to a fault. Because of her generous nature, people are always asking her for money and other favors.*

put others first

> **(v)** to think of the needs of other people before oneself; often said as *put one's family first, put one's kids first,* and so on. ♦ *My mother always puts her family first, ignoring her own needs.* ♦ *I can be very selfish, but I'm trying to learn to put others first.*
>
> *Note:* This idiom can also have an opposite meaning when said as *put oneself first* or as *put (something) first,* in which case it means to make something the highest priority: "Their marriage suffered because he had to *put his work first,* and his personal life second."

do for others

> **(v)** to help others; have a helping, generous attitude ♦ *He was a very generous man, and spent his life* doing for others.

give of oneself

> **(v)** to give generously of time, skill, or whatever is needed ♦ Giving of yourself *is the best way to forget your own troubles.* ♦ Give of yourself, *and you'll be amazed at what you get back.*

[For idioms that describe generosity with money, see Chapter 6; also see *do a good deed* in Appendix I.]

Idioms That Express Selfishness

People who are *self-centered* are often too focused on themselves; they can also be called *wrapped up in themselves* or described as *thinking only of themselves*. People who are *self-serving* are always looking out for their own best interests. Here are some more idioms that express selfishness:

look out for number one

> to be concerned only with one's own needs and interests. In American culture *looking out for number one* is not always considered an act of selfishness. It can also represent independence and self-sufficiency, which are respected character traits. ♦ *He* looks out for number one *and no one else!* ♦ *If I don't* look out for number one, *who will?*

into oneself

> conceited, thinking of oneself as the best ♦ *I don't like him. He's too* into himself. **Note:** *Into* can be followed by any noun to express what a person is devoted to, as the following example shows: "Joe is really *into* baseball; it's all he thinks about."

it's all about someone

> when a person's thoughts and actions are self-centered. Put as *all about you, all about him and so on.* ♦ *You don't care about my feelings.* It's all about you. **Note:** The expression *all about . . .* can also mean that whatever follows it is extremely important. For example: "I'm not a doctor because of the money—it's *all about* helping people."

Me, Me, Me

Someone who thinks only of himself and rarely considers the needs or feelings of other people might be described like this:

"With him it's always *me, me, me.*"

In other words, the selfish person thinks "It's me who's most important."

This self-centered attitude is reflected in the expression the *Me Generation,* which is intended to describe people born in the 1950s to the 1970s, who live in an era characterized by materialism and self-advancement.

in it for oneself

involved in something for personal gain; to not have the best interest of the group in mind ♦ *She volunteers with a charity only when she's going to run for public office. Basically she's just* in it for herself.

out for oneself

involved in something for personal gain at the expense of others; this idiom is similar to *in it for oneself,* but is even stronger and has a more negative connotation ♦ *He acts like he's part of the team, but in truth he's just* out for himself. ♦ *Students in this graduate program won't help you; they're all very competitive and* out for themselves.

Idioms That Express Compassion

A compassionate, caring or sentimental person is sometimes called one of these nouns:

a softy ♦ *My dad is just* a softy. *He always cries at sad movies.*
a marshmallow ♦ *Don't be such* a marshmallow; *you don't have to give money to every person who asks you on the street.*
an angel of mercy ♦ *Mother Teresa was considered* an angel of mercy.
a bleeding heart ♦ *Just because I support social programs doesn't mean I'm* a bleeding heart.

In addition to the preceding nouns, there are plenty of other idioms that make reference to compassion.

HAVING A HEART AND RELATED IDIOMS

The heart is often considered the center of compassion, so it's no surprise that a number of idioms for compassion and caring use the word *heart:*

have a heart

>to show compassion or kindness; often said to a person who is hesitant or unwilling to give help, kindness, or charity ♦ *He wouldn't even speak to the homeless man, but I said, "*Have a heart. *How would you feel if people treated you so unkindly?"*

have a heart of gold

>to be compassionate and generous ♦ *That woman* has a heart of gold. *She's so kind to people.* ♦ *My grandmother* has a heart of gold.

warm-hearted

>**(adj)** to have warm, caring feelings for people ♦ *She is very* warm-hearted. *People always feel welcome in her house.* ♦ *Jerry is one of the most* warm-hearted *people I know.*

soft-hearted

>**(adj)** to easily feel sympathy and compassion ♦ *She so* soft-hearted; *she's always bringing home lost animals.* ♦ *He acts tough, but he's really very* soft-hearted *and kind.*

[See *cold-hearted, hard-hearted,* and a *heart of stone* later in this chapter.]

Your *Good Deed* for the Day

Nice things that are done for other people are often called *good deeds.* Many people believe that you should do a good deed every day. Doing a good deed, a simple kind or helpful act, is thought to develop character and compassion. A person might say, "I did my good deed for the day, I helped an elderly lady cross a busy street." People also may ask, "Have you done your good deed for the day?" A good deed can also be called one of these idioms:

selfless act ♦ *She received praise for her many* selfless acts *of charity.*

act of kindness ♦ *It was truly an* act of kindness *to help that old man.*

You're Not Alone

People often use the following short expressions to show support and understanding for someone who is having troubles. Sometimes two or more of these expressions may be said together:

You're not alone.

I've been there.

We've all been there.

I feel for you.

I hear you (ya).

Here are some examples:

♦ *If you have ever been heartbroken,* you're not alone. We've all been there.

♦ *When you say that raising kids is challenging , believe me,* I hear you!

A related expression is *I feel sorry for you,* which can also be used to show support. It is slightly different from the expressions above in that it shows stronger sympathy or pity. Also, it is generally used to refer to someone who is not part of the conversation. For example:

♦ *Joe: Did you hear that Amy was laid off from her job? Amber: Yes. And* I feel sorry for her *because she just bought a house.*

one's heart goes out to someone

to feel sorry for or sympathy for someone because of his or her unfortunate situation ♦ My heart really goes out to them *with their daughter in the hospital.* ♦ Our hearts go out to all of you *who lost your homes in the fire.*

one's heart bleeds for someone

to feel very sorry and sad for someone's misfortune; often said sarcastically ♦ My heart *just* bleeds for her. *She has had so much grief in her life.* ♦ *Kelly: I wanted a BMW, but my parents bought me a Honda. Trish: Oh, gee!* My heart really bleeds for you. *I don't even own a bicycle!*

IN THE SAME BOAT AND RELATED IDIOMS

The following expressions show empathy, which is understanding and sympathy for situations or hardships that the speaker has also experienced.

in the same boat

experiencing the same challenge, difficult situation, or circumstance; often said as *be in the same boat* ♦ *I have no family in this country either. I guess we're* in the same boat. ♦ *Well, we're now* in the same boat. *I just lost my job, too.*

be in someone's shoes

to have the same experience as someone else. In this expression *shoes* means situation or circumstance. ♦ *I remember* being in your shoes *when I was studying for my PhD. Just keep going!* ♦ *The manager doesn't know who stole from the cash register, so she may have to fire everyone. I wouldn't want* to be in her shoes.

Idioms That Express Cold-Heartedness

In contrast to being compassionate, some people are *cold* (unfeeling, with no warmth or compassion for others). A person may also feel cold or uncaring about a specific situation.

Most idioms that express lack of compassion include the word *heart*. These idioms are often used as exaggeration or teasing, as are many idioms that describe negative traits. The following idioms have the same general meaning: to be unfeeling, uncompassionate.

heartless (adj) ♦ *It was* heartless *of you to throw away her favorite toy as a punishment.*
have no heart ♦ *He didn't even call his elderly mother on her birthday. Some people just* have no heart.
cold-hearted (adj) ♦ *He was a* cold-hearted *man and showed no affection or kindness to anyone.*
hard-hearted (adj) ♦ *Her difficult childhood left her* hard-hearted *and unable to love.* ♦ *Let's forget our argument and forgive each other. Come on, don't be* hard-hearted.
a heart of stone (n) ♦ *Don't even try asking mom if we can keep this snake. She has* a heart of stone *about keeping lost pets.*

[See *warm-hearted, soft-hearted,* and *have a heart of gold* earlier in this chapter.]

The follow two expressions mean that a person doesn't care or is indifferent. These expressions are less harsh and insulting than idioms like *cold-hearted, heartless* and others in the previous group.

couldn't (*or* could) care less

> to not care at all; to be indifferent or unfeeling. *I could care less* is a common variation of *I couldn't care less,* and means the same thing. ♦ *They* couldn't care less *about the employees.* ♦ *I could care less if he's dating someone. I have no feelings for him anymore.*

not give a hoot (*or* darn *or* damn)

> to not care; be indifferent or unfeeling. The word *damn* is a swear word and considered offensive by some people. ♦ *It's clear that those land developers* don't give a hoot *about preserving the beauty of the meadow.* ♦ *It's sad that some old people in nursing homes never have visitors. Nobody seems* to give a damn about them.

[See *I don't care, who cares, who gives a damn* and similar slang expressions in Chapter 9.]

Idioms That Express Honesty

Honesty can show itself in various ways. Honest people will *tell the truth* (not lie or hide the truth). They will *be true to their word* (always do what they say they will do). One can be honest and ethical in business and in every other aspect of life. This section includes idioms for all types of honesty and truthfulness.

Many idioms that have to do with honesty are synonyms; that is, different idioms have identical or nearly identical meanings. These idioms are presented below, followed by idioms that require longer definitions.

- Here are some idioms to describe an honest person:
  - **honest as the day is long (adj)** ♦ *Mike would never lie to you. He's as* honest as the day is long.
  - **an honest Joe** (usually said of men) **(n)** ♦ *My father was* an honest Joe; *he believed in being truthful and trustworthy.*
- If you are *true to your word,* that means you always do what you promise to do. Here are some other expressions that mean the same:
  - **keep one's word** ♦ *She promised not to tell anyone about my illness, but she didn't* keep her word. *Now everyone knows.*
  - **be as good as one's word** ♦ *If Jane said she would drive you to the airport, she'll do it. She's* as good as her word.
  - **a man of his word** (a woman of her word is rarely used) ♦ *My dad said, "Be* a man of your word. *If you make an agreement, keep it!"*

- Confessing the truth is another form of honesty. A confession can be for a mistake or wrongdoing, or even about a secret act of generosity. Here are some idioms commonly used for confessing:
  - **come clean** ♦ *I finally* came clean *to Laura and told her that I was the one who sent her the love letter.*
  - **'fess up** (a slang version of confess) ♦ *Come on, 'fess up. You arranged this party for me, didn't you?*
- To encourage or demand someone to confess or tell the truth, you might say one of the following, which are typically said as exclamations:
  - **Out with it!**
  - **Let's hear it!**
- *Honesty is the best policy* is a popular saying meaning it's always best to be honest and truthful. Speaking truthfully can mean to not lie, to speak frankly, or to express a universal or personal truth. Each of these meanings is expressed with one of the following idioms:
  - **tell the truth** (to not lie)♦ *Tell the truth! How did the window get broken?*
  - **speak the truth** (to express a universal truth; say what is true in one's heart)♦ *You* spoke the truth *when you said that no one succeeds without the help of others.*

Honest to God

People often use expressions like the following to begin a statement of fact or a sentence that reveals their true feelings. These expressions mean the same as "In fact" or "Honestly":

to tell (you) the truth

in all honesty

if the truth be known

honest to God

Here are some examples:

- ♦ To tell you the truth, *I don't like the new logo.*
- ♦ In all honesty, *I think we need more time for this project.*
- ♦ If the truth be known, *she has always wanted to quit that job.*
- ♦ Honest to God, *these two children have more energy than a dozen ponies!*

The expression *honest to God* is also used when trying to convince someone of the truth. In this context it is said as a vow of honesty to God. "*Honest to God*, I'm telling you the truth!"

Following are other idioms that mean to be frank and honest, and to not hide, distort, or avoid the truth:

straightforward

(adj) be honest, without altering or avoiding the truth ◆ *I'll be* straightforward *with you about the demands of this job, so that you can decide if it's what you want.* ◆ *I wish you had told me the whole truth. You weren't very* straightforward *about it.*

straight with someone

(adj) be straightforward; be honest, not hiding or distorting the truth ◆ *Be* straight with me. *Do you want to end this relationship?* ◆ *During the interview, he wasn't* straight with us *about his job qualifications. Later, we discovered that he had lied.*

straight up

(adv) (slang) truthfully, honestly. Often said as a question, meaning "Really?" ◆ *I told him* straight up *that he can't afford a new car, but he doesn't want to accept it.* ◆ *Jane: You got accepted to Stanford? Straight up? Rita: Straight up.* **Grammar Note:** The expression *straight up* typically appears right before the statement of truth in a sentence, but it can also appear at the beginning or the end of the sentence.

tell it like it is

to be frank and straightforward; to speak the truth, not hide the truth, no matter how unpleasant the truth may be. Sometimes said as *tell you like it is.* ◆ *The management should* tell it like it is. *This company is in serious financial trouble.* ◆ *It's a great class, but I warn you, it's the hardest class the engineering program. Just* telling you like it is.

lay it on the line

to be straightforward about a problem or serious matter, no matter how unpleasant the truth may be; implies that what is being said is important or has serious implications ◆ *Let me* lay it on the line. *If you don't improve your grades, you'll be suspended from this school.* ◆ *His doctor* laid it on the line: *"Quit drinking or you'll die."*

level with someone

to be straightforward or frank about a problem or serious matter, no matter how unpleasant the truth may be; implies that in the past the truth has not always been told ◆ *Let me* level with you: *I haven't always been the best boyfriend.* ◆ *His bad-smelling breath is preventing him from getting a date. Should I* level with him *about it?*

ABOVE BOARD AND RELATED IDIOMS

The following expressions are most often used to describe openness and honesty in business dealings:

above board

> completely open and honest; not at all secretive. Said most often of business transactions ♦ *I like dealing with her company, everything is very* above board. ♦ *I was suspicious about buying something on eBay, but it seems to be all* above board.

out in the open

> open and honest representation of something; nothing hidden or secretive. Often said of business dealings and personal relationships. ♦ *He wasn't* out in the open *about the extra costs, so we voided the contract.* ♦ *Quarterly financial reports are designed to keep companies' financial gains and losses* out in the open. ♦ *Occasionally my wife and I have a big argument, but it always helps bring our frustrations* out in the open *where we can talk about them.*

on the level

> honest and ethical. Most often said of organizations, businesses, and their dealings and operations; truthful no matter how unpleasant the truth may be. ♦ *This charity organization is definitely* on the level, *and their monies go directly to the recipients.* ♦ *I have to be* on the level *with you about the risks of this surgery.*

on the up and up

> legal and ethical ♦ *Never buy things from a phone solicitor. Their business may not be* on the up and up. ♦ *The investigation proved that his financial dealings were all* on the up and up.

pull no punches

> to be honest, typically about unpleasant facts. Alludes to not hitting as hard as possible in a boxing match. ♦ *I voted for her for senator, because she* pulls no punches. *You know exactly what she supports and stands for.*

lay (*or* put) one's cards on the table

> to expose one's true motives or intentions; to be completely open and honest, typically after a period of not being completely open. Alludes to revealing one's cards in a game such as poker. ♦ *I'm going to* lay my cards on the table. *I want to buy the cheapest car you sell.* ♦ *She finally* put all her cards on the table: *She admitted that she had been looking for a new job, and said that she would only stay with the company if she got a 15% raise.*

Idioms That Express Dishonesty and Deception

A dishonest person is one who can't be trusted or does not tell the truth. A person may be dishonest or deceptive in a number of ways: by lying, hiding or distorting the truth, cheating in business, love, or other areas of life. Here are some idioms to describe such a person:

a cheat

> **(n)** someone who cheats, usually in love ♦ *Don't get involved with her. Everyone knows she's* a cheat.

a scammer

> **(n)** someone who cheats or tries to take advantage of people ♦ *The guy is* a scammer. *He's always looking for ways to cheat people out of their money.*

a phony

> **(n)** someone who presents himself or herself falsely ♦ *I've never done business with him. He seems like* a phony *to me.*

Two-Timer and Related Idioms

One type of dishonesty is duplicity (having two sides; being deceptive or hypocritical). The following expressions use *two* or *double* to refer to a dishonest person:

a two-timer

> **(n)** someone having two girlfriends or boyfriends at one time; dating someone while in a serious romantic relationship with someone else ♦ *Justin is such* a two-timer! *He's dating Julia but he's already seriously involved with Katherine.*

two-faced

> **(adj)** someone who says one thing, but does the opposite ♦ *Bill is so* two-faced; *he tells me that he likes my house, but then he tells other people it's ugly.*

double-crosser

> **(n)** someone who cheats people, often used to refer to business dealings ♦ *Judy proved to be a* double-crosser. *She was working for us but sharing information with another company.*

double talker

> **(n)** speaks deceptively; speaks in a confusing way to hide the truth ♦ *Many people feel that politicians are* double talkers.

[See also to *two-time* and to *double cross* earlier in this section.]

The following sentences illustrate another interesting way of expressing the idea that a person can't be trusted because he or she talks deceptively or doesn't tell the truth:

> *He talks from both sides of his mouth.*
> *He talks out of both sides of his mouth.*

TELLING A LIE AND RELATED IDIOMS

Saying something that isn't true is called *telling a lie*. Here are other idioms that mean to lie.

These idioms describe lying that is generally done to exaggerate or to avoid getting into trouble. The lies are usually not meant to injure anyone else.

> **fib** ♦ *He* fibbed *to his teacher about why his essay wasn't finished.*
> **stretch (*or* bend) the truth** ♦ *Sometimes she* stretches the truth *a little when she talks about the accomplishments of her children.*
> **make something up** ♦ *He didn't have a good excuse for missing work, so he* made up a story *about his car breaking down.*

The following expressions have a very similar meaning to idioms such as *fib* and *stretch the truth*, but they are harsher and more critical:

> **feed (*or* hand) someone a line** ♦ *He was trying to* feed me a line *about why he was so late, but I didn't believe him.*
> **speak falsely** ♦ *If you* speak falsely *about him in public, he could sue you in court for slander.*
> **lie through one's teeth** ♦ *He was* lying through his teeth *about his education and background. In truth he never finished high school.*

LITTLE WHITE LIE AND RELATED IDIOMS

The following idioms are commonly used to describe different types of lies and deceptions:

(little) white lie

> a lie told to avoid hurting someone ♦ *I had to tell a* little white lie *when she asked if I liked her painting. Actually I don't like it, but I wouldn't hurt her feelings by saying so.*

bare-faced lie

> a bold, shameless lie ♦ *Saying that he supports education was a* bare-faced lie. *Everyone knows that he voted to cut school funds.*

vicious lie

> a lie intended to injure someone ♦ *The tabloid was sued for printing* vicious lies *about my favorite actress.*

pack of lies

> a lot of lies ♦ *He says his book is the true account, but some people say it's just a* pack of lies. ♦ *She told everyone a sad story about why she had no money, but it was* just a pack of lies. *In truth, she was a drug user.*

A less-serious type of deception is the following:

hidden agenda

> **(n)** hidden motives or interests; typically, more selfish or self-serving motives than those publicly acknowledged. Also put as the opposite, *have no hidden agenda.* ♦ *I have a* hidden agenda *in helping Emily with her homework: I have a crush on her!* ♦ *We have no* hidden agenda. *Our intentions are simply to help build the community.*

The following idioms generally refer to false stories and excuses that are told to deceive someone. All are nouns:

> **a cock-and-bull story:** an unbelievable tale intended to deceive; may allude to the two animals that often appeared in folk tales
> **a fish tale (*or* story):** an exaggerated or false story; alludes to exaggerating about the size of the fish that one caught
> **a tall tale:** usually said of legends, but also can be said of any unbelievable story

SCAM AND RELATED IDIOMS

Business dealings that are dishonest and deceptive are often called one of the following idioms:

> **a scam**
> **a dirty deal**
> **a shady deal**
> **a snow job**
> **a rip-off**

Acting secretly in order to deceive or cheat someone (or sometimes to give a nice surprise to someone) can be described with one of these idioms:

> **on the sly** ♦ *She was stealing drugs from the pharmacy* on the sly.
> **on the down low** (*or* **D.L.**) also said as *keep it on the down low* ♦ *His business was all* on the down low *and totally illegal.* ♦ *Danny is going to be promoted to manager soon, but* keep it on the D.L. *We want to surprise him.*

The following idioms describe deliberately injuring someone with deception, especially in business dealings:

sell someone down the river

> to betray someone. Alludes to the days of slavery when slaves were sold and sent down the Mississippi River to work. ♦ *He was really* sold down the river *when the company laid him off right before his retirement. They made it impossible for him to collect a pension.*

rip someone off

> to steal from or cheat someone ♦ *Don't buy anything from that used electronics dealer. He'll* rip you off *with his products that look good, but they break down after you buy them.*

[See *stab someone in the back* in Chapter 13.]

BE SNOWED AND RELATED IDIOMS

If you've *been snowed* someone was successful in fooling or deceiving you. For example:

> *We were really* snowed *by that insurance representative. The policy does not cover many of the things he said it would!*

Following are other idioms that mean to be deceived, tricked, or cheated. **Grammar Note:** The idioms *be snowed*, *be had*, *be taken*, and *be ripped off* are presented in passive voice, as they are commonly said in this form. The idiom *be ripped off* is also often put in active voice: to *rip someone off*.

be had

> (**v**) to be fooled, tricked, or cheated in financial dealings ♦ *Dave was* had *by his own financial manager, who lied about his accounts and stole money from him.*

be taken

(v) to be tricked and cheated, especially in financial dealings ♦ *We've* been taken! *We paid for the roof repair, and now the workers have disappeared without finishing the job.*

be ripped off

(v) to be deceived, typically in the sense of not getting a fair price for something ♦ *Hey, this stereo I bought at the yard sale doesn't work. I've* been ripped off.

fall for something

(v) to accept a dishonest person's words as true ♦ *Don't* fall for *his sales talk about what a great deal it is. Believe me, there are a lot of hidden costs.*

[See idioms for expressing belief and disbelief in Chapter 9; see *pull someone's leg* and *pull the wool over someone's eyes* in Chapter 13.]

Idioms That Express Independence and Self-Sufficiency

Independence and self-sufficiency are valued traits in American society. The idioms in this section refer to leaving the security of one's parents' or guardians' home and becoming an independent adult. The idiom to *leave home* means to move away from one's family home and become independent.

The following two idioms allude to a bird learning to fly:

leave the nest

to move out of one's parents' house ♦ *She wants to get her own apartment, but I think she's too young to* leave the nest. ♦ *American kids are* leaving the nest *a little later than they did in the past.*

try (*or* test) one's wings

to experience for the first time independence from one's family ♦ *Some young people* test their wings *out in the world, and then come home to live with their family again.* ♦ *Once I had* tried my wings, *I never went back to the nest.*

The following two expressions are metaphors for ending one's dependence on family. These expressions are generally used to describe young people:

cut the apron strings

> to end one's financial dependence or childish emotional dependence on family, especially the emotional dependence on one's mother. Alludes to the habit of little children holding on to their mother's apron strings or ties for security. ♦ *At some point everyone has to* cut the apron strings *and become independent.*

cut the umbilical cord

> to end the dependence on one's family, especially financial dependence. Alludes to cutting the cord that attaches an infant to his or her mother's womb. Sometimes used in reference to any source of financial or emotional support. ♦ *He's 27 years old and still living at home. His parents should* cut the umbilical cord!

Note: In both expressions above, either the parent or the child can do the cutting of the apron strings or umbilical cord.

The following idioms mean to be independent and able to support one's self financially:

be (*or* live) on one's own

> to live independently without the financial support of parents or others; also put as *out on one's own* ♦ *All of our children are grown up and out* on their own *now.*

stand on one's own

> to be financially and emotionally independent; also put as *stand on one's own two feet* ♦ *His emotional problems made it impossible for him to* stand on his own.

[See other idioms for financial independence in Chapter 6.]

Idioms That Express Dependency

No one can live without the help of others, but some people never learn to be responsible and independent. They expect others to take care of them, and they don't give anything back in repayment. A person who tries to live off the charity of others and gives nothing back in return is sometimes called one of these names:

> **a mooch**
> **a leech**
> **a parasite**

The following idioms are also used to describe living selfishly off the charity of others.

mooch off of someone

> to expect someone else to pay one's way; to borrow or use other people's possessions; also can be said *be a mooch* ◆ *He* mooches *as much as he can* off of you *and never pays you back.* ◆ *I can't stand Tim;* he's a mooch.

leech off of someone

> to let others pay all your expenses and provide all one's needs; to cling to the support of others like a parasite (a leech). *Leeching off of someone is a more serious form of mooching off of someone.* Also can be said *be a leech.* ◆ *He'll* leech off of them *as long as they allow it.* ◆ *She* leeched off her family *for years until they finally stopped giving her money.*

lean on someone

> to rely heavily on the support of another person ◆ *Her brother was always* leaning on her *for something, either money, a place to stay, or help with his problems.* ◆ *It's great to have* friends to lean on *when you need it, but if you* lean on them *too much and too often, they may get tired of you.*

look (*or* ask) for a handout

> to expect others to pay one's way; to ask for money or other things with no intention of repaying ◆ *He never has a job for very long, so he's always* looking for a handout *from someone.* ◆ *If you're* asking for a handout, *forget it! I've already helped you plenty of times.*

Idioms That Express Sociability

People who are very sociable and who are comfortable talking with others are said to be *outgoing.* Here are some other idioms to describe such people:

a people person

> a person who likes people ◆ *Social work is a perfect job for her; she's really* a people person.

a social butterfly

> a person who loves social gatherings and socializing; alludes to the way a butterfly flits from flower to flower. Usually said of women but can be said of men too. ◆ *Jane is such* a social butterfly. *Whenever an event is happening, she's there chatting with people.*

Someone who makes other people laugh and enjoy themselves in a social setting might be called one of these idioms:

a ham

> a person who likes to perform and have people's attention ♦ *What a ham! He loves to be the center of attention.*

a character

> a person who is eccentric but lovable ♦ *You're a character. It's fun to be around you.*

the life of the party

> a person who makes the party fun and energetic ♦ *We have to invite her. She's always the life of the party.*

Idioms That Express Shyness and Introversion

Someone who is introverted and prefers to spend time alone is sometimes called *a loner*. Here are some other expressions that mean to be introverted. **Note:** These idioms are fairly polite and imply that a person is not sociable by choice:

keep to oneself

> to not socialize; to prefer or tend to be alone ♦ *We rarely see Ross. He likes to keep to himself.* ♦ *I've been* keeping to myself *lately just enjoying my own company.*

like one's privacy

> to prefer to be alone and have private space ♦ *We don't invite people over to our house very often. We like our privacy.* ♦ *I like my privacy, but I don't always want to be alone.*

prefer one's own company

> to prefer to be with oneself rather than with other people ♦ *He has a few friends, but he seems to prefer his own company.* ♦ *She probably won't come to the party. She prefers her own company.*

The following idioms are somewhat impolite or rude and are used to describe people who are shy or socially awkward:

a wallflower

> a person who remains quiet at social gatherings; often said of women. Alludes to sitting against the wall at a social gathering, refusing to dance or socialize. ♦ *Come on, don't be* a wallflower. *Get up and socialize.*

a shrinking violet

> a person who reacts nervously to social contact; often said of women. Alludes to a flower receding when touched or approached. ♦ *My sister was such* a shrinking violet. *I tried to get her to talk to people and be less shy.*

mousy

> timid and shy, with mouselike qualities ♦ *He's kind of* mousy, *so don't expect him to say much at the meeting.*

a nerd

> (slang) a person who is socially awkward or dull, preoccupied with schoolwork or intellectual hobbies; often said of men ♦ *Come on, you* nerd! *Put down those books and let's go to a club.* ♦ *He's kind of* a nerd, *and awkward around people, but he's really fun when he's with just one person.*

a geek

> (slang) socially awkward; different from others in a bizarre way; often said of men ♦ *He used to be* a real geek *and afraid to talk to people, but not anymore.* ♦ *The kids laughed at him and called him* a geek *just because he was awkward and shy.*

Someone who is too serious in a social setting or ruins others' fun might be called one of these idioms:

a wet blanket *or* **a party pooper**

> a person who tries to spoil other people's fun, refuses to join the fun or show enthusiasm ♦ *What* a wet blanket! *He never wants to do anything fun.*

a stick-in-the-mud

> a person who refuses to have fun, doesn't want to go out, is dull. Alludes to being caught unhappily in mud, unable to move. ♦ *My ex-boyfriend was such* a stick-in-the-mud. *That's why he's my ex, and not my boyfriend anymore!* ♦ *Why be* a stick-in-the-mud *when there are so many fun things to do?*

no fun

> not fun, boring ♦ *You don't want to go camping? Well, you're* no fun. ♦ *He's* no fun *to be around when he's thinking about a work project.*

CHAPTER 12

SUCCESS, FAILURE, AND LUCK

What are the *keys to success?* In other words, what criteria, actions, personal qualities, or characteristics lead one to success? Some might say hard work and determination, others might say that a lot depends on luck or opportunity. In this chapter, you'll find idioms that describe all of these things: hard work, determination, opportunity, and luck, as well as idioms related to a lack of success and failure.

Success

The idioms and expressions in this section are used to talk about success and the various skills, talents, and conditions that contribute to success.

HAVE MADE IT AND RELATED IDIOMS

If someone *has made it,* the person has become successful financially, professionally, personally, or maybe all three. This idiom usually implies that one has worked hard and has made a success of life.

A similar expression with a slightly different connotation is *have it made.* This expression often implies that the help and influence of others or good fortune has put one in a successful position. It's sometimes said as *have it made in the shade* using the word *shade* for a rhyme, and to imply having the luxury to relax in the shade. This idea can also be expressed by saying that a person *is set* (established successfully in life).

Here are some examples:

- *She was honored as the top businesswoman in America. She's* made it!
- *His parents set up a big trust fund for him. He certainly* has it made!
- *Man,* you're set! *You have a great wife, nice kids, and your business is a success.*

Grammar Note: The expressions *have made it* and *have it made* are technically the same idiom with one small grammatical difference: In the first expression, the direct object, *it*, comes at the end; in the second expression, *it* comes in the middle, separating the two verbs. Generally the placement of the direct object doesn't affect the meaning of an idiom, but in this case it can give the idiom a very different connotation.

Here are some other ways to describe someone who is, or will be, successful in life:

make a success of oneself

> to have become successful as a result of one's own hard work and talent ♦ *He has so many talents, I'm sure he'll* make a success of himself. ♦ *Jane has* made a success of herself *as a scientist for NASA's space program.*

[See also *make something of oneself* later in this chapter.]

sitting pretty

> in an advantageous position; financially successful. This idiom is always said in the continuous tense (verb + *-ing*). ♦ *I would be* sitting pretty *if I could win the lottery!* ♦ *She's* sitting pretty *since her promotion to CEO.*

sitting on top of the world

> at the top, in the most advantageous position; financially successful; very happy, pleased with one's own success or recognition. This idiom is always said in the continuous tense (verb + *-ing*). ♦ *We'll be* sitting on top of the world *if this product is a success.* ♦ *When you're* sitting on top of the world, *don't forget to give credit to the people who helped you get there.*

have the world by its tail

> to have every opportunity; to be in a good position, very successful. Alludes to controlling a wild animal by holding on to its tail. ♦ *With her intelligence and talent, she'll* have the world by its tail. ♦ *You* have the world by its tail. *Why do you want to throw it all away and quit your job?*

AMOUNT TO SOMETHING AND RELATED IDIOMS

The following expressions mean to do well in life and improve one's status, though not necessarily by being rich or famous:

amount to something

> to develop into a self-sufficient, successful person ♦ *His dad told him, "If you ever want to* amount to something, *then you have to stay in school and get an education."* ♦ *I never thought he'd* amount to anything, *but look at what a success he is!*

Note: The opposite *of amount to something* is often expressed as *never amount to anything,* meaning never develop one's potential, never improve oneself or succeed. For example, "He had potential, but he was lazy and *never amounted to anything.*"

make something of oneself

to improve oneself, become self-sufficient; to develop a career ♦ *Every one of her daughters* made something of herself. *One is a musician, one is a history professor, and the other is vice-president of a large company.* ♦ *He came from a very poor family, but he was determined to* make something of himself.

come up in the world

to improve one's financial, social, and professional status from a lesser beginning; often used lightly ♦ *You published a book of poetry? Hey, you've really* come up in the world! ♦ *He was an immigrant who came here with nothing, but he's* come up in the world *as a result of his hard work.*

get ahead

to succeed socially and financially; to make good progress ♦ *Without a good education it's difficult to* get ahead *in life.* ♦ *He worked hard to* get ahead *in his profession, and now he's highly respected in the field of geophysics.*

[For more idioms on financial success see Chapter 6.]

HAS WHAT IT TAKES AND RELATED IDIOMS

A person who has the skill, talent, personality, and determination, or whatever else is necessary to succeed, is often described like this:

> **has what it takes** ♦ *She* has what it takes *to organize an event of any size.*
> **has the right stuff** ♦ *He* has the right stuff *to run this youth outreach program.*

A related expression is *has a lot going for him* or *her.* This is typically said in admiration for someone, and means that a person has a lot of great skills, characteristics, and potential. It differs from *has what it takes* and *the right stuff* in that it's not quite as high a compliment. For example, you could say either of the following:

> ♦ *Ray* has a lot going for him. *He will be promoted soon.*
> ♦ *Even though Ray* has a lot going for him, *he won't be promoted soon.*

Small Town Boy (or Girl) Makes Good

When a person from a modest family background or a small town becomes famous or very successful, people often say "Small-town boy makes good" or "Small-town girl makes good." This expression is not said about people from rich or privileged families, but people from more *humble beginnings* (a low- or middle-income family), or someone who, literally, came from a small town where there were few professional opportunities.

People vary this expression to fit the situation. For example, if a person who didn't finish high school becomes the company president, he might say "High-school dropout *makes good!*"

The following idioms refer to meeting certain requirements, qualifications, standards, or expectations.

measure up

to prove equal to a high standard or to succeed in a demanding situation; compares to the quality or standard of something or someone else ♦ *The standards at this university are very high, but I know you'll* measure up. ♦ *This job is demanding. If you don't* measure up, *you'll be asked to leave.* ♦ *How do the new engineers* measure up *to the others?*

make the grade

to be successful or very successful. Alludes to a high academic score or a rank or grade in the military. ♦ *There's a lot of competition in this business, so if you can't* make the grade *you'll never survive.* ♦ *His managerial skills were tested when they opened the new theater, and he definitely* made the grade.

15 MINUTES OF FAME AND RELATED IDIOMS

Getting one's *15 minutes of fame* is an expression that means having a brief, temporary period of fame. It is also used jokingly when an ordinary person is recognized for an accomplishment. Here are some examples:

♦ *The winner of the game show enjoyed his* 15 minutes of fame.
♦ *Look! I finally got my* 15 minutes of fame. *Here's my picture in the newspaper.*

A similar but slightly sarcastic expression is *every dog has its day,* meaning that even the lowest creature will have occasional success, perhaps by chance. This expression is also used humorously. Here are a few examples:

♦ *I didn't think he had a chance to win, but I guess* every dog has its day.

♦ *When I finally beat Jim at chess he said, "Well,* every dog has its day."

PULL SOMETHING OFF AND RELATED IDIOMS

The following idioms mean to succeed even when there are obstacles and difficulties:

pull something off

to accomplish something impressive or unexpected; to succeed despite obstacles ♦ *We didn't think we could start our business in time for tourist season, but we managed to* pull it off. ♦ *They* pulled off *several bank robberies before finally being caught.*

make it (*or* things) happen

to accomplish something; implies special skills or the ability to get past a bureaucracy ♦ *It won't be easy getting approval for this project, but Adam can* make it happen. ♦ *If you want to learn how to succeed in business, watch Elise. She really knows how to* make things happen.

come through

to do what is required, needed or expected, often in a time of particular need or difficulty; to succeed after appearing likely to fail ♦ *I didn't think that anyone could do so much work in so little time, but she always* comes through. ♦ *Whenever the team needs to score, Jack* comes through. ♦ *She'll* come through *in the end, though her method appears disorganized.*

[See *with flying colors* in Chapter 14.]

against all odds

despite overwhelming obstacles. This idiom is almost always placed at the beginning or end of a sentence. ♦ Against all odds, *they found a way to immigrate to this country and start a successful business.* ♦ Against all odds, *he passed the other runners and won the marathon.* ♦ *He had many debilitating physical challenges, but he became self-sufficient* against all odds.

When you are successful in accomplishing something or reaching a specific goal, you might say:

I did it!
I made it!

Grammar Note: *I did it* is usually said after successfully completing a task; *I made it* is usually said when one is accepted into something or has passed a test. Here are some examples:

♦ You did it, *Liza. You learned to tie your own shoe!*
♦ I made it! *I got accepted on the varsity swim team.*

[See slang expressions for congratulating someone's success in Chapter 9.]

BUSINESS IS BOOMING AND RELATED IDIOMS

When *business is booming*, it is thriving and making a profit; it's very successful. Following are some other expressions that mean the same thing, and can be used for business and personal success:

going great guns ♦ *His construction business is* going great guns! *He never expected it to be so profitable.*
going like gangbusters ♦ *That taco bar is* going like gangbusters *all of the time. They've got the best tacos and a great price. There's always a crowd there.*
on a roll ♦ *Her music career is definitely* on a roll; *she recorded three CDs last year and will soon release another one.*

A related expression to the three above is *taking off. Taking off* has the added implication that the business or endeavor was previously stagnant, or has just started to succeed for the first time: "When he started his business, it didn't do well, but now it's really *taking off.*"

If a product is very popular and the company is selling it as fast as it can be made, someone might say the product is selling:

like crazy
like mad
like hotcakes
like nobody's business
like there's no tomorrow

Here's an example:

♦ *Now that we've cut the price, these cell phones are selling* like crazy.

Note: The expressions *like gangbusters, like crazy,* and so on can be applied to any activity that is done with great energy, enthusiasm, or speed. For example, "We worked *like crazy* to finish the house painting before the storm."

Hard Work and Determination

The ideal of *The American Dream* is that no matter how poor or disadvantaged you are, you can achieve material success through hard work and determination. Of course, in reality, the opportunity to reach this dream is greatly helped or hindered by economic and societal factors.

MAKE AN HONEST EFFORT AND RELATED IDIOMS

To *make an effort* means to try and to *make an honest effort* means to try very hard with earnest intentions. Here are some examples:

♦ *Anyone who* makes an honest effort *in this class will get a passing grade.*
♦ *He's our newest employee, but he's* making an honest effort *to learn the business, and the boss is very pleased.*

Here are some other idioms that mean to make an honest or good effort, even if one is not successful in the end:

give it the old college try
give it one's best (shot)
do one's best

Here are a few examples:

♦ *I don't know yet if I passed the bar exam, but I sure* gave it the old college try.
♦ *I can't promise that the report will be finished by tomorrow, but I'll* give it my best shot!

[See also *do one's best* in Appendix I.]

SWEAT BLOOD AND RELATED IDIOMS

Here are a number of expressions that mean to work very hard to accomplish something:

sweat blood (over something)

to work extremely hard, often with a lot of anxiety ♦ *The work crews were* sweating blood *to clean up the mess from the hurricane before tourist season began.* ♦ *I've* sweated blood *over this doctoral dissertation, and it's finally finished.*

work like a dog

to work very hard doing difficult physical labor or menial work ♦ *You'll* work like a dog *if you open a restaurant.* ♦ *He* worked like a dog *to finish the new roof before the winter storms came.* **Grammar Note:** *Work like a dog is a simile (a comparison using the word* like *or* as*).*

work one's hardest

to work very hard and to do one's best job. This expression is often followed by a verb in the infinitive form. ♦ *We're* working our hardest *to complete the construction before the holidays.* ♦ *I don't think that he's* working his hardest *to find a job. He should have found one by now.*

work one's butt off

a slang expression meaning to exhaust oneself working very hard. Sometimes used when one's work was not appreciated or successful. This expression is often followed by a verb in the gerund form (verb + -*ing*). ♦ *Those kids* worked their butts off *getting ready for their drama production.* ♦ *He* worked his butt off *for the election campaign, and never received any thanks.*

knock oneself out

to exhaust oneself working very hard; to do one's very best work. This expression is often followed by a verb in the gerund form (verb + -*ing*). ♦ *We* knocked ourselves out *getting ready for our big family reunion.* ♦ *This meal is fabulous. You really* knocked yourself out.

pull out all the stops

to use every effort and resource to accomplish something; to not hold back. Alludes to pulling out all the stops on an organ, that is, opening up all the organ pipes, to create the largest sound. ♦ *The city* pulled out all the stops *in planning for the winter Olympic Games.* ♦ *This is the biggest and most important contract the company has ever had, so we're* pulling out all the stops *to get the job done.*

[See *work one's fingers to the bone* and *have one's nose to the grindstone* in Chapter 13.]

BURNING THE MIDNIGHT OIL AND RELATED IDIOMS

Here are some expressions that mean to work long hours:

burn the midnight oil

to work late at night; work past midnight. Alludes to an oil lamp that is still lit at midnight so that one can continue working. ♦ *When I was in law school, I would* burn the midnight oil *every night.*

burn the candle at both ends

to work at a pace that is impossible to sustain; to work so hard that physical or mental health suffers. ♦ *You're going to get sick if you continue* burning the candle at both ends. *You need some rest.*

work 24/7

to work most of the time or a lot of overtime; implies working 24 hours a day, 7 days a week ♦ *We've been working* 24/7 *to finish making the costumes in time for the show.* ♦ *This new job has him* working 24/7. *When he's not at work, he's home on the computer or on his cell phone doing business.*

[Also see *24/7* in Chapter 15.]

DOGGED DETERMINATION AND RELATED IDIOMS

Many things are accomplished by *dogged determination* (stubborn determination, firm purpose, or resolve). A person's strong determination can be described with one of these expressions that use the word *set*. Here, *set* means to be firmly fixed on, unmoving.

be dead set on

to be determined to do something or determined that something will happen. This expression is often followed by a verb in the gerund form (verb + -*ing*). ♦ *She* is dead set on *getting into medical school, and she's working hard to make it happen.* ♦ *They* are dead set on *taking that bicycle trip, even though George has arthritis.*

set one's sights on

> to establish a goal or have a firm goal ♦ *He has* set his sights on *New York University, and he says that he won't go to any other college.* ♦ *Once she's* set her sights on *something, she goes out and gets it. Nothing stops her from reaching her goal.*

set (*or*** put) one's mind to**

> to put all of one's concentration and effort toward something; to have a focused determination ♦ *Whatever he* sets his mind to, *he can accomplish.*
> ♦ *I can pass the TOEFL exam if I* set my mind to *it and prepare myself.*

NO MATTER WHAT AND RELATED IDIOMS

The following expressions, which can all be used interchangeably, show solid determination when faced with some obstacles or temptation:

> **no matter what** ♦ *I quit smoking last month, and* no matter what, *I'm not going to start again.*
> **one way or another** ♦ One way or another *we're going to take a vacation this year.*
> **come what may** ♦ Come what may, *I'll find a way to finish my education.*
> **come hell or high water** ♦ Come hell or high water, *this project must be finished before the end of the fiscal year.*

Opportunity

When *opportunity knocks* or *comes along* (presents itself), you should take it—or *answer the door*. Sometimes people say that an opportunity *landed* or *fell into their lap*, meaning that they did not have to look for it or try to cultivate the opportunity. It simply came unexpectedly, by chance. Here's an example:

> ♦ *The opportunity to become theater director just* fell into my lap *when the former director quit.*

Another way to describe this situation is to say that you *were in the right place at the right time*, meaning that you just happened to be there and available when an opportunity presented itself. This expression is sometimes used when people are modest about their accomplishments, as the following example shows:

> ♦ *Many of my co-workers were qualified for the position, but I was just* in the right place at the right time, *and I got the job.*

It can also be used to imply that a person was lucky to get an opportunity, or that he or she may be underqualified:

♦ *We needed to hire a manager right away, and Brian was* in the right place at the right time.

GET A CHANCE AND RELATED IDIOMS

If you *get a chance* at something, that means that you have an opportunity. When an opportunity, an advantage, or special consideration is offered by someone, you might use a passive form, saying "I was *given the chance.*" Here are some examples of *get a chance* showing the active and the passive form:

♦ *I hope I* get a chance *at that management position.*
♦ *We've* given *him three* chances, *but he continues to come to work late. Now we have to fire him.*

Note: *Get a chance* can also mean to find the time to do something, as in, "When I *get a chance*, I'll put these photos into a scrapbook."

Following are more expressions that mean to give someone an opportunity or introduce someone to a situation that might be advantageous:

hand something on a silver platter

to give an opportunity or reward that a person hasn't had to work for. This expression is often phrased passively as to *be handed something on a silver platter,* meaning to receive or obtain something very easily or by special privilege. Alludes to the silver platter that a servant uses to pass something to a wealthy employer. ♦ *They* handed *him the CEO position* on a silver platter *because his uncle is president of the company* ♦ *Don't expect opportunities to be* handed *to you* on a silver platter. *You have to work hard and be prepared.*

get someone into something

to introduce someone to and involve someone in something; to get someone accepted or admitted ♦ *She* got him into *rock climbing, and now he's a climbing instructor.* ♦ *My dad* got me into *the company that I work for because he knows the owner.* **Grammar Note:** Saying *I got into (something)* means that one became interested or involved in something, but it does not imply that one was offered or received a special opportunity.

turn someone on to something

to introduce someone to or influence someone's interest in something. Sometimes phrased passively as to *be turned on to something,* but the expression is usually put in the active form when the meaning is "given an opportunity."

♦ *My instructor* turned me on to *the archaeological project, and I've worked there ever since.* ♦ *I want to* turn you on to *an organization that may be willing to give you a grant for your research.*

TYPES OF OPPORTUNITIES

The following are a few idioms that are all used to describe an opportunity that is rare, may not come again, and is fantastic:

golden opportunity ♦ *This new job is my* golden opportunity *to travel, take photographs, and get paid for it!*

once-in-a-lifetime opportunity ♦ *To visit the gorillas deep in the jungles of Africa is a* once-in-a-lifetime opportunity.

the opportunity of a lifetime ♦ *She's been offered a position with the Bolshoi Ballet. It's the* opportunity of a lifetime, *and something she's dreamt of.*

JUMP AT THE CHANCE AND RELATED IDIOMS

Seeing an opportunity and quickly taking it is often described with one of the following expressions:

jump at the chance ♦ *If I get an opportunity to work overseas,* I'll jump at the chance.

go after it ♦ *When you see an opportunity, you have to* go after it. *Don't wait until it's gone.*

go for it ♦ *You like the house, and it's a good price. If I were you, I'd* go for it.

take (*or* grab) it ♦ *It's a great opportunity.* Grab it *before someone else does!*

Note: In the expressions above, the preposition *it* is substituted for a previously mentioned noun. If the noun has not been mentioned, one would say, for example, "You should *go after* the management position" or "I'd *grab* the opportunity if I were you."

LOSE THE CHANCE AND RELATED IDIOMS

In contrast to *jumping at the chance*, if you wait too long, or aren't ready when an opportunity comes along, you'll *lose* or *miss the chance* or *opportunity*. Here are some examples:

♦ *He submitted his application after the deadline, so he* lost the opportunity *to get financial aid this semester.*

♦ *Darn! We* missed the chance *to buy concert tickets to see Jewel. They sold out yesterday.*

Here are a few more idioms that mean to miss a chance or an opportunity:

miss out (on something)

> to not be aware of an opportunity; to not be physically present when an opportunity arises; to not take advantage of an opportunity ♦ *I'm sorry I* missed out *on the party, but I was getting my car repaired.* ♦ *This sale runs for two days only, so don't* miss out!

lose out (on something)

> to miss an opportunity, often to lose an opportunity to a rival or competitor ♦ *If you don't register for classes on the first day of registration, you'll* lose out; *all your classes will be taken.* ♦ *I* lost out on *the chance to be promoted when Bob got the promotion instead.*

let something get away

> to not take advantage of an opportunity that may never come again ♦ *I had the opportunity to travel and work in Egypt, and I* let it get away. *At the time I thought I was too busy to go, but I should have found the time.* ♦ *Don't* let this opportunity get away! *Go to graduate school while you have the chance.*

[See *slip through one's fingers* in Chapter 13.]

Creativity

Thinking creatively in order to form ideas and solve problems is often talked about with these interchangeable idioms that use the preposition *up:*

> **think up** ♦ *Whoever* thought up *the idea of a fast-food restaurant would be surprised to see how internationally popular fast food is today.*
> **come up with** ♦ *His job is to* come up with *an exciting logo for their business.*

A very similar idiom is *dream up,* but *dream up* suggests that the ideas may be unusual or impractical.

When someone thinks of a good idea, he or she might say one of these expressions, all of which have basically the same meaning:

> **Here's a thought** ♦ Here's a thought: *We could send some of our camping equipment by mail before we leave so that we'll have less luggage to carry on the plane.*
> **I've hit on an idea** ♦ I've hit on an idea *for improving the sales of this product.*
> **I have a brainstorm** ♦ *Last night* I had a brainstorm *about how to work part time and still have enough money for our expenses.*

If you're part of a group that's trying to come up with ideas or that's discussing the pros and cons of an idea, you might use one of these expressions (followed by *idea* or *ideas*) to describe what you're doing:

toss around ♦ *We tossed around a lot of ideas before deciding on a marketing strategy for the new laptop.*
throw around ♦ *Let's get together and throw around some ideas for the new brochure design.*
kick around ♦ *We kicked the idea around a bit, but didn't make a final decision.*

Grammar Note: Toss around, throw around, and *kick around* are separable phrasal verbs.

[For information on separable phrasal verbs, see Part V.]

The following idioms also refer to discussing ideas and to creative thinking:

a think tank

a group or center organized to do extensive research and problem solving
♦ *Many ideas that eventually affect how the government works come from* think tanks. ♦ *When the Senator lost his reelection attempt, he joined a* think tank.

brainstorm

1. (n) a sudden idea, inspiration, or plan ♦ *He had a* brainstorm: *He would ask Marty to be his new secretary.*
2. (v) to spontaneously and quickly come up with thoughts and ideas, typically in a group setting ♦ *Why don't we all* brainstorm *some ideas to find a good title for this book?* ♦ *When I worked in marketing, we would spend all day* brainstorming *good slogans.*

Failure

American English has many idioms meaning to fail, in part because people rarely say "I failed," unless they are talking about failing (not getting a passing grade in) an academic course. To say "I failed" implies defeat and shame—attitudes that are not encouraged in the American psyche. Instead, people use a variety of idioms that allude to falling down, to losing a game, making a mistake, and other such situations.

BITE THE DUST AND RELATED IDIOMS

bite the dust

> to end; to fail; to be defeated. Alludes to eating dirt or dust when one crashes to the ground, and can mean literally to hit the ground. ♦ *Our vacation* bit the dust *when our car broke down; we spent the week waiting for it to be repaired.* ♦ *The company finally* bit the dust *and sold all its assets.*

fall flat (on one's face)

> to fail completely ♦ *The deal* fell flat *because the two companies could not agree on the terms of the contract.* ♦ *It will be hard for you to succeed in the restaurant business with no experience; you might* fall flat on your face.

crash and burn

> to fail completely and disastrously ♦ *My relationship with Jenny just* crashed and burned. *I hope I never see her again.* ♦ *His business started out well, but eventually it* crashed and burned *because of his drug habit.*

bomb

> to fail to attract interest; to fail a test; often used to describe failed movies and plays. ♦ *The movie Formula 51* bombed *at the movie theaters. What a disappointment for the producers!* ♦ *Man, I know I* bombed *that test. I didn't study at all.*

strike out

> to fail in an attempt. Alludes to a strikeout in baseball when a batter misses the ball after three tries and loses a turn. ♦ *We tried to get the contract for the construction of the new mall, but we* struck out. *Another company won the contract.* ♦ *I always* strike out *with women; they never want to date me.*

The following idioms are used specifically for failed businesses:

> **fold:** to stop operating a business, typically because of financial troubles
> **close** *or* **shut down:** to stop operating a business, not necessarily because of financial reasons
> **go under:** to stop operating a business, specifically due to financial troubles; typically used in the passive form as in "The steel mill finally *went under.*"
> **go bust:** to stop operating a business, specifically due to financial troubles; implies that the business was once successful or large. It is typically used in the past tense, as in "Most railroad companies have *gone bust.*"

GETTING NOWHERE FAST AND RELATED IDIOMS

When people say, "We're *getting nowhere fast*," they mean "We are not making any progress; we're not being successful." Often people simply say *"We're getting nowhere!"* Here's an example:

> ♦ *We're* getting nowhere fast *on this crime investigation. We just don't have enough evidence.*
> ♦ *I've been looking on the Internet for information on this disease, but I'm getting nowhere. Maybe I don't know how to do a search.*

Here are some other idioms that also mean to make no progress or to go backward:

lose ground

> to fall behind, to fail to hold one's position, to deteriorate; often followed by the preposition *to* or *on* depending on the context ♦ *I think we're* losing ground *to our competition. Their sales were much higher than ours last year.* ♦ *If we don't get more money for this study, our research will* lose ground. **Note:** The opposite is *to gain ground*. **Grammar Note:** The idiom *lose ground* is followed by the preposition *to* when the direct object refers to a competitor: "We *lost ground* to the opposing team in the first part of the game." The preposition *on* is generally used when the direct object is not a competitor: "We're *losing ground* on this project because of technical problems."

go downhill

> to deteriorate; to fail to hold one's position ♦ *Consumers' trust in the economy continues to* go downhill. ♦ *The deal* went downhill *when both parties refused to compromise.*

take a nosedive

> to quickly deteriorate or fail to hold one's position; generally refers to economic situations. Alludes to a plane falling nose first to the ground. ♦ *The stock market* took a nosedive *and still hasn't improved.* ♦ *Our profits have* taken a nosedive *during this economic crisis.*

go bad (*or* sour)

> to become negative, unsuccessful, disappointing; usually said of business deals and contracts, also said of relationships ♦ *Their relationship* went bad *because he was dating other women.* ♦ *When the actor's drinking problem began to interfere with his work, his movie career* went sour.

go to the dogs

> to deteriorate, to decrease in quality or value; to fail to progress ♦ *There's no way for our team to win now. We've* gone to the dogs *ever since our best player was injured.* ♦ *That used to be my favorite restaurant, but it's* gone to the dogs *since new management took over and changed everything.*

COME TO NOTHING AND RELATED IDIOMS

The following idioms are often used to describe a situation that never develops or doesn't materialize as one hopes or expects:

come to nothing

> to fail to develop; to have one's efforts be in vain, to not produce any results ♦ *All of our hard work on this project has* come to nothing *because the company has decided not to complete it.* ♦ *He tried very hard to keep their marriage together, but all his effort* came to nothing *because she still wanted a divorce.*

fall through

> to not develop as one expected or hoped; to fail to happen; often used for business deals, contracts, and important plans ♦ *We were expecting a big contract, but the deal* fell through, *and they hired another company to do their advertising.* ♦ *All of our vacation plans* fell through *when the school board changed the starting date of the school term to a week earlier.*

not work out

> to fail to happen in the end; to fail to develop as one hoped; often used for personal plans and situations ♦ *We dated for a few years, but in the end the relationship didn't* work out, *and we separated.* ♦ *Let's plan to meet on Monday, but if that doesn't* work out *for any reason, we can reschedule.*

MISS BY A MILE AND RELATED IDIOMS

When something *misses by a mile,* it fails to come close to the goal; it is inadequate and doesn't meet expectations. The idioms that follow are similar in meaning, but don't have quite as strong a tone:

> **come up short** ♦ *His qualifications* come up short. *They don't meet our requirements.*
> **fall short** ♦ *The conclusions of this research* fall short *of our expectations. Either our hypothesis or our data is wrong.*

You can modify either of these idioms by including the word *just,* in which case they mean to barely miss, or to miss by a very small margin: "His proposal almost won the contract, but it *came up just short."*

BLOW IT AND RELATED IDIOMS

Sometimes people contribute to the failure of an endeavor by making poor decisions, procrastinating, or failing to work hard enough. The following expressions are often used when people cause something to fail:

> **blow it** ♦ *This job is a fantastic opportunity for me. I don't want to* blow it *by demanding too much.*
> **mess up** ♦ *I really* messed up *by lying to her. She found out that I lied and now she doesn't trust me at all.*

PUT THINGS OFF AND RELATED IDIOMS

Procrastinating, or *putting things off* until later, means to delay doing something that should be done immediately. A wise saying about avoiding procrastination is the following:

> ♦ *Don't* put off *until tomorrow what you can do today.*

Sometimes procrastinators (people who procrastinate) jokingly turn this advice around, saying *Don't do today what you can* put off *until tomorrow!*

Grammar Note: Put off is a separable phrasal verb (it can be separated by its direct object). When *put off* is followed by a verb, that verb is in the gerund form (verb +-ing). Here are some more examples of the expression *put off:*

> ♦ *He* put off *paying his bills because he didn't have enough money.*
> ♦ *You should start that book report now. Don't* put it off *until the night before it's due.*

The following idioms also mean to procrastinate or delay:

drag one's feet

> to delay; implies hesitancy or bureaucratic delay ♦ *The city government is* dragging its feet *on a pay raise for sanitation workers.* ♦ *The company always* drags its feet *when it comes to responding to complaints.*

take one's (own sweet) time

> to delay; implies thoughtless or leisurely delay ♦ *I don't like to shop with my wife because she always* takes her time *and must look at every item.* ♦ *She borrowed my camera and she's* taking her own sweet time *returning it.*

ON THE BACK BURNER AND RELATED IDIOMS

Traditionally, the back burner of the stove was the warming burner. It kept cooked food warm while other food was being prepared on the front burners. So, when something is *put on the back burner,* it means that it is kept or held until a later time. Something that's *on the back burner* may be a low priority, but it's not forgotten. People sometimes say that they *have something on the back burner,* meaning that they are thinking about doing it in the distant future. Here's an example:

♦ *Let's* put that idea on the back burner *until next semester.*
♦ *We have plans for a trip to Peru* on the back burner. *Maybe we'll go within the next year or so.*

Here are some related idioms:

on hold (adj)

delayed until a later time; often used with the verb *to put* ♦ *The meeting is* on hold *because the foreign representatives have not arrived yet.* ♦ *Please* put *your questions* on hold *until Dr. Coltrain finishes her presentation.*

on ice (adj)

delayed until a much later time or indefinitely; often used with the verb *to put.* Alludes to keeping something frozen. ♦ *The project is* on ice *until we can get government approval.* ♦ *We need a new car, but we have to* put *that purchase* on ice *because of unexpected medical bills.*

hold off (n)

to temporarily delay; often followed by the preposition *on* when the idiom has a direct object, as in the first example that follows ♦ *I'm* holding off *on planting those tulips until November.* ♦ *I don't want to buy my ticket yet, but if I* hold off *too long, it will cost more.* **Grammar Note:** When *hold off on* is followed by a verb, the verb is in the gerund form (verb + *-ing*).

DILLY-DALLY AND RELATED IDIOMS

The following idioms also mean to purposely and leisurely delay. They imply that one is being unproductive:

waste time

to be unproductive when one needs to be productive ♦ *He* wastes *a lot of* time *answering personal e-mails while he's at work.* ♦ *Don't* waste *so much* time *in front of the TV when you have work to do.*

dilly-dally

> to go very slowly, waste time, and be unproductive ♦ *While the administrators are* dilly-dallying *over expensive lunches, the rest of us are hard at work.* ♦ *We can't* dilly-dally. *We have to be ready to go in 20 minutes.*

fuss (*or* mess *or* fart) around

> to be unproductive, do nothing of value ♦ *Employees waste a lot of time* fussing around *at their desks for the first hours of the day.* ♦ *Stop* messing around *and eat your dinner.* **Note:** *Fart around* is considered crude, but people say it occasionally.

Good Luck and Bad Luck

Some people say that success is simply a matter of good luck, and failure is the result of bad luck. Whether or not this is true, plenty of idioms use the word *luck*. Here is an example:

be in luck

> to be fortunate; to be lucky regarding a specific effort or interest ♦ *You're* in luck! *We have one more ticket for that concert.*

The direct opposite is this:

be out of luck

> to be unfortunate, unlucky regarding a specific effort or interest ♦ *You're* out of luck. *We just sold the last ticket for that concert.*

TYPES OF LUCK

Here are some idioms that describe different types of luck:

> **beginner's luck:** said when a person has success in his or her first try at something
> **dumb luck:** unexpected luck; luck that a person is extremely fortunate to have

Here are two examples:

> ♦ *What a great shot! And this is your first time on the golf course. It must be* beginner's luck.
> ♦ *What* dumb luck. *His flight was cancelled, but he was the only one to get a seat on the next flight because he was standing next to the ticketing agent!*

LUCK OUT AND RELATED IDIOMS

To *be out of luck* means that one is not lucky, but to *luck out* means just the opposite—to be very lucky. When a person experiences unexpected good luck, someone might say, "How did you *luck out?!*" meaning, "What did you do to bring such good luck?" Here's another example:

- ♦ *We* lucked out *finding a parking space so close to the theater.*
- ♦ *I have a terrific dormmate this year at college. I guess I just* lucked out.

The following expressions also refer to good luck and being lucky:

as luck would have it

luckily, fortunately ♦ *I thought I had missed my bus, but* as luck would have it, *the bus was late.* ♦ *Our car broke down, but* as luck would have it, *the man who stopped to help us was an auto mechanic!*

get a lucky break

to have an unexpected opportunity ♦ *We* got a lucky break *on the price of this house. The owners wanted to sell it fast, and they accepted our first offer.* ♦ *It was just* a lucky break *that the film director was at our school play with his granddaughter. He saw me on stage and hired me for a part in his film.*

A RUN OF BAD LUCK AND RELATED IDIOMS

People often refer to occasional misfortune as *bad luck,* even if there is a logical reason for the trouble. For example, if you have an old car and it finally breaks down, you could still use *bad luck* to describe this event. But when one *has a run of bad luck* (a number of troubles over a short period of time), it may truly seem like fate. Here are some examples of this expression:

- ♦ *Poor Danny. His dog died recently, his car was stolen, and then his girlfriend broke up with him. He sure is* having a run of bad luck!
- ♦ *This building project* has had a run of bad luck: *First there were delays getting the permits, and then a worker was injured, and now the project manager has quit.*

The following idioms also refer to bad luck:

be down on one's luck

to be experiencing misfortune and difficult times, especially financially ♦ *The welfare agency helps people who* are down on their luck. ♦ *You gave me a loan when I* was down on my luck. *Now it's my turn to help you.*

Good Luck!

Saying, "Good Luck!" is a common way to wish someone success in any endeavor or effort. For example, a person might say "Good luck on your exam" or "Good luck in your new job." In some cultures, wishing people good luck is a bit insulting because it implies that their skills or intelligence are not adequate, and therefore they need luck to succeed. But in American English, saying *good luck* is like saying, "I wish you much success; I wish you well."

♦ *Jack: I'm on my way to ask the boss for a raise. Marty:* Good luck!

Sometimes people wish someone good luck when a situation seems hopeless, and the person really does need luck to succeed. In this case, *good luck* is said in a sarcastic or cautious tone. Sometimes the speaker adds "You're going to need it."

♦ *Mary: I'm asking dad if I can borrow the car Saturday night. Rebecca:* Good luck! *You're going to need it.*

When people are going to try something new or make an effort, no matter how small, they might say, "Wish me luck!" Sometimes people add "I'm going to need it!" Here are a few examples:

♦ *I start my first teaching job tomorrow.* Wish me luck. *I think I'm going to need it!*

♦ *Okay. I'm going to ask her for a date.* Wish me luck!

Grammar Note: When the idiom *good luck* is followed by a verb, the verb is in the gerund form (verb + *-ing*).

one's luck run out

to stop being lucky, or having an advantage, or avoiding consequences; often used to describe someone who has previously avoided being punished for a crime or offense ♦ *He escaped from prison and was hiding in another country for years. But finally* his luck ran out *and he was caught.* ♦ *I've always been able to get a flight without a reservation on Wednesday nights, but* my luck *finally* ran out. *This time the flights were full.*

the cards stacked against one

to have a disadvantage that makes it difficult to succeed ♦ *They were already in debt when they opened the new business, so* the cards were stacked against them *from the start.* ♦ *If you don't have a good education, then* the cards are stacked against you *when you go out into the job market.*

PART IV

IDIOMS BY KEY WORDS

*M*ost idioms and idiomatic expressions have a key word or main word (often a noun or verb) that carries much of the inference or meaning. The key word could be almost anything, but some very common key words that are included in this part are body parts (get cold feet), colors (blue collar), numbers (two timer), negative words (not a chance), and question words (who knew). Using key words is also a good way to organize and think about idioms. Some people find it easier or more interesting to learn a group of idioms that have the same key word.

CHAPTER 13

BODY IDIOMS

Nearly every part of the body, inside and out, has been used in idioms. This is no surprise, as the body is with us all of the time. It can be our closest ally (and sometimes our worst enemy). With its many functions, capabilities, and frailties, it becomes a handy metaphor for expressing our thoughts, feelings, and ideas.

An idiom that includes the name of a body part is often related in meaning to the function, capability, inadequacy, appearance, or location of that part. For example, saying that someone is *all thumbs* (clumsy, awkward with one's hands) alludes to the awkwardness of trying to manage with a hand that has five thumbs. Or having *butterflies in one's stomach* (feeling nervous anticipation) is a very good description of that fluttery sensation one gets in the stomach when feeling a little nervous or excited.

There are enough idioms that use the names of body parts to fill a book the size of the entire *Webster's New World American Idiom Handbook*. This chapter focuses on idioms that are related to the face and to the main appendages, with some common stomach and gut idioms also included.

Idioms with Head, Neck and Shoulders

In this section, you'll find expressions with *head, neck,* and *shoulders*. In most cases, the meaning of the expression alludes to the function, capabilities, and vulnerabilities of the body part.

THE HEAD

The head houses the brain and it rests at the very top of the body. So it's not surprising that a number of idioms with *head* refer to intelligence, knowledge, and being at the top. Some idioms that use the word *head* refer to a sense of mental stability, or instability, while others make a completely different reference — to the head under the guillotine!

Heads That Are First or Better

As the head is situated at the top of the body, idioms using the word *head* often refer to the top, the best, or the first.

at the head of the class

> to be the best student in the class or the best in a particular field ♦ *She's a great student, always* at the head of the class. ♦ *They are definitely* at the head of the class *in animation technology.*

head and shoulders above

> clearly superior to all others. Alludes to the height of the head and shoulders. Often said as *head and shoulders above the rest.* ♦ *This organic brand of coffee is* head and shoulders above *the rest.* ♦ *As a pediatric surgeon, Dr. Carr is* head and shoulders above *the other doctors at the hospital.*

a head start

> to begin something before it is necessary, so that one can get ahead, be early or first; to have an advantage ♦ *I decided to get* a head start *and begin my Christmas shopping early.* ♦ *Children whose parents read to them have* a head start *when they begin school.* **Note:** Head Start is the name of a federal program that provides early schooling to low-income children.

Heads That Are Intelligent

The head is the place of intellect—the location of the brain. So, some idioms with *head* refer to thinking, having intelligence, and using one's brain.

have a good head on one's shoulders

> to have good sense, to be intelligent and make good choices ♦ *I don't worry about my son; he* has a good head on his shoulders. ♦ *You've* got a good head on your shoulders, *but you don't always use it.*

off the top of one's head

> to say something spontaneously without much thinking; to give a quick guess or estimate ♦ Off the top of my head, *I'd say it takes about 12 hours to get to Denver by car.* ♦ *Sorry, I can't think of anyone,* off the top of my head, *who has a room for rent.*

put ones' heads together

> to discuss a problem in order to find a solution, or to work together to make or formulate a plan ♦ *I'm sure if we* put our heads together, *we can figure this out.* ♦ *We* put our heads together *and came up with a great idea for our drama project.*

use one's head

to think about something; to use logic and common sense ♦ *Rock climbing takes skill, but you also have to* use your head. ♦ Use your head, *Allen. You can't repair that water leak with tape!*

[See also *keeping one's head (about oneself)* later in this chapter.]

Heads That Are Confused

The head, or brain, can also be the place of confusion, or the place where there's a lack of understanding. The following idioms relate to being confused.

make one's head spin

to get confused or dazed ♦ *Hearing about all the extra college costs* made my head spin. ♦ *It* makes my head spin *to think about planning my daughter's wedding.*

over one's head

too difficult or complex to understand ♦ *That math lesson today went right* over my head. ♦ *Keep the poetry reading simple for the kids. Otherwise it will go* over their heads. ***Note:*** To *go over one's head* also means to skip over rather than to follow the normal chain of command or authority, as in "The manager was angry that we *went over his head* with our complaint."

scratch one's head

to be confused or unable to figure something out. This idiom comes from the actual gesture of scratching one's head, which indicates that a person is trying to think or figure something out; the idiom is often used without one literally scratching one's head. This idiom is almost always put in the continuous form (verb + *-ing*) ♦ *The school board plans to end the after-school program, and we are all* scratching our heads *wondering why.* ♦ *I was* scratching my head *trying to figure out these tax forms.*

Heads That Stay in Control (or Lose Control)

Keeping a level head and *keeping one's head (about oneself)* mean to stay calm, rational, and in control, especially when it's hard to do so. Here are some examples:

- ♦ *Despite the emergency, she was able to* keep a level head.
- ♦ *You've got to* keep a level head *during a boat race, or you'll be in trouble.*
- ♦ *When you travel,* keep your head about you.

The following idiomatic expressions mean to lose control, to be mentally unstable, or to act in a crazy or foolish way.

head over heels

> to lose control, typically because of love. This idiom is often stated as *head over heels in love.* ♦ *He is* head over heels *for your sister.* ♦ *They've been* head over heels *in love since the day they met.*

lose one's head

> to be irrational, illogical, or to lose control of one's senses or mental faculties, usually temporarily, over love, money, a problem, or a misfortune ♦ *The coach* lost his head *and started yelling at his players.* ♦ *Be careful when traveling. Don't* lose your head *and become too trusting.*

out of one's head

> to act very irrationally, to be crazy; also put as to be *out of one's mind* ♦ *You've been driving without insurance?! Are you* out of your head? ♦ *You're* out of your head *if you think I'm going to give you money again.* **Note:** People can be *out of their heads with grief* or *worry,* as this example shows: "They were *out of their heads with worry,* until they their son finally called."

soft in the head

> to be mentally deficient, foolish, irrational ♦ *Maybe he's a little* soft in the head, *but he's a loyal dog.* ♦ *You're driving with an expired license? Are you* soft in the head!?

Heads That Fall Off

The unpleasant notion of literally losing one's head appears in idioms. The following expressions refer to having one's head separated from one's body.

heads will roll

> means "people will get into trouble," "people will be punished or reprimanded"; it can also mean that employees may be fired. Alludes to the use of the guillotine to chop off someone's head as a punishment. ♦ *When they discover the accounting error,* heads will roll. ♦ Heads will roll *if the project is not completed by June.*

talk someone's head off

> to talk incessantly; to talk until others are tired of listening ♦ *She's an interesting person, but she'll* talk your head off. ♦ *We* talked our heads off *catching up on old times.*

laugh someone's head off

> to laugh hysterically, to be very amused; to laugh sarcastically or out of spite
> ♦ *Oh man, we* laughed our heads off *watching that comedy.* ♦ *If that team is disqualified,* I'll laugh my head off *because they always try to bend the rules.*

Heads That Describe People

A number of idioms using *head* are adjectives that describe personality and intelligence (or the lack of intelligence). Here are some of the most common expressions. All of these are adjectives:

> **hard-headed:** stubborn
> **thick-headed:** not able to understand things quickly
> **hot-headed:** easily or quickly angered
> **cool-headed:** always calm and in control

Other idioms that describe people are nouns:

> **knucklehead:** foolish, silly, not very smart
> **bonehead:** not intelligent (if the head is hard as a bone, nothing can go in)
> **sleepyhead:** someone who is very sleepy, groggy with sleep
> **pothead:** habitual marijuana smoker

Heads That Are Arrogant

The expressions *go to one's head, get a big head,* and *get a swelled head* mean to think oneself very important or overly important. When people *get a big head,* they often act arrogant and prideful. Here are some examples:

> ♦ *All the attention he received for his success* went to his head.
> ♦ *You're a fantastic artist. But hey, don't let it* go to your head!
> ♦ *Now that she's famous, I hope she doesn't* get a big head *and act like a snob.*
> ♦ *Since he was voted most valuable player, he's* gotten a swelled head.

Indicating Direction with *Head*

The word *head* also means to go in a specific direction or to leave. A number of idioms use *head* plus a preposition in this context. Here are the most common ones:

> **head off:** to go, leave on a journey or errand ♦ *We* headed off *toward the city.*
> **head on:** to continue to go ♦ *We'll stop for gas and then* head on.
> **head in:** to turn to go back in to home or shore ♦ *We should* head in. *It's getting dark.*

head out: to start on a journey ♦ *We'll head out at 6 a.m., so be ready.*
head to *or* **head for:** to go in the direction of ♦ *When school is out, we* head to *the beach.*

A Few Other *Head* Idioms

Following are a few other idioms with *head* that are unrelated to any of the preceding categories.

turn heads

> to catch people's attention; to make people turn their heads and look. Usually used when referring to an attractive, sexy, or famous person. ♦ *If you wear that red sweater, you'll* turn heads. ♦ *They're such an attractive couple that they* turn heads *wherever they go.*

keep one's head above water

> to handle financial and other demands, often with great stress or difficulty. Alludes to not drowning. ♦ *He works two jobs just* to keep his head above water. ♦ *My workload has increased, but I'm keeping* my head above water.

THE NECK

Though the neck is essential in holding up the head, it's also vulnerable. Most idioms with *neck* refer to this vulnerability, but there are a few exceptions. To *go for the neck* means to attack, often verbally or legally, the weakest area with the intent to overpower or destroy. This expression, as well as to *get it in the neck,* allude to the behavior of animal predators that overcome and kill their prey by biting the jugular vein in the neck.

Necks That Are Vulnerable

The neck is a somewhat vulnerable part of the body. It's easy to injure, it becomes stiff, sore, and gets kinks. In the past, one's neck could meet up with the guillotine. A number of *neck* idioms refer to this vulnerable aspect of the neck. Here are some of the most common ones:

a pain in the neck

> someone or something that is annoying or irritating; a lot of bother ♦ *It was* a pain in the neck *getting all the permits to remodel our house.* ♦ *My little brother is* a pain in the neck, *but I love him.*

break one's neck

to try very hard to accomplish something; to make a huge effort ♦ *He practically* broke his neck *to get tickets to the concert.* ♦ I broke my neck *trying to get here in time for the meeting.*

at breakneck speed

to go very fast, excessively fast ♦ *We'll have to work* at breakneck speed *to be ready for the conference.* ♦ *The poor guy was running* at breakneck speed *to catch the bus.*

risk one's neck

to risk physical harm; to risk something like a job or money in order to accomplish something ♦ *I'll never* risk my neck *going mountain climbing.* ♦ *They* risked their necks *trying to save their business.*

stick one's neck out

to risk something in order to help someone or for some gain ♦ *We* stuck our necks out *buying a new house before our old house sold.* ♦ *He* stuck his neck out *for me at the meeting, and I appreciate that.*

save one's neck

to rescue one from a problem situation ♦ *You can help* save my neck. *Just tell my parents that I was at your house last night.* ♦ *You* saved my neck *by finishing this project for me.*

A Few Other *Neck* Idioms

be up to one's neck (in something)

to have a large excess of something or be very occupied with something, usually work or a demanding project ♦ *After the harvest, we were* up to our necks *in squash!* ♦ *I am* up to my neck *in work. I can't get together this week.*

breathe down someone's neck

to watch over someone's activities very closely; to supervise and observe closely, possibly looking over someone's shoulder ♦ *The manager kept* breathing down my neck *today, making me nervous.* ♦ *You kids have been* breathing down my neck *all afternoon. Go outside and play.*

neck of the woods

> a region or general area ♦ *Please come visit next time you're in our* neck of the woods. ♦ *I really like this little* neck of the woods. *It's a great place to live.*

be neck-and-neck

> to be exactly even; to be tied in a race or contest or election. Alludes to horse racing. ♦ *The two runners* were neck-and-neck *to the finish line.* ♦ *The candidates* were neck-and-neck *until the absentee ballots were counted.*

[See *necking* in Chapter 8.]

THE SHOULDERS

The following idioms use *shoulder* or *shoulders,* often to imply responsibility.

Shoulders That Are Responsible

The shoulders are sturdy, capable of carrying heavy loads or weights. A number of idioms with *shoulder* mean to carry the weight of responsibility, blame, or troubles. The following idioms have this meaning:

shoulder

> to carry or take on responsibility, blame, or troubles ♦ *He* shouldered *the blame for the mistake, though it wasn't totally his fault.* ♦ *He has a lot of responsibility* to shoulder, *with five kids and his elderly parents to care for.* ♦ *When I was on vacation, Jill* shouldered *the load at work.*

on one's shoulders

> to bear the responsibility of something ♦ *The success of this deal is* on his shoulders. ♦ *She has a lot* on her shoulders *right now, with a new job and new baby.*

carry the weight of the world on one's shoulders

> to appear to be burdened with excess responsibility ♦ *She seems to be* carrying the weight of the world on her shoulders; *maybe we can help her.* ♦ *He always looks like he's* carrying the weight of the world on his shoulders. *He needs a vacation!*

a shoulder to cry on

> sympathetic support; a friend who listens to one's problems. Often said as *to be* or *have a shoulder to cry on.* ♦ *If you need* a shoulder to cry on, *I'm here.*
> ♦ *Thanks for always being* a shoulder that I can cry on.

A Few Other Shoulder Idioms

If you *rub shoulders with someone,* it means that you associate with them, especially if they are well known, influential, or a celebrity. For example

> ♦ *In her work as a reporter she* rubs shoulders with *some very interesting people.*

On the other hand if you *give someone the cold shoulder,* then you refuse to associate with him or her. You are cold and unfriendly, often because of something unacceptable that the person has done. For example

> ♦ *When I first came to the new school, some kids* gave me the cold shoulder.
> ♦ *They've* given him the cold shoulder *ever since he tried to cheat them.*

If you say "He *has a chip on his shoulder,*" that means the person is carrying resentment and anger. He may want to argue for no reason, or try to challenge people to a fight. The *chip* alludes to an old practice of placing a wood chip on one's shoulder, and then daring someone to knock it off, thus starting a fight. For example

> ♦ *If you get rid of that* chip on your shoulder, *people will be friendlier to you.*
> ♦ *Ted: What's the matter with John? Ron: Oh, he's* had a chip on his shoulder *ever since he got fired from his job.*

[See *have a good head on one's shoulders* earlier in this chapter.]

Idioms with *Face, Eyes, Ears, Nose,* and *Mouth*

In this section, you'll find expressions with *face, eyes, ears, nose,* and *mouth.* In many of these idioms, the expression alludes to functions of the five senses or to the expressiveness of the face and eyes.

THE FACE

The face is one's outward identity, and it often shows what's true—or hides the truth. Most idioms using *face* allude to truth or to the expressive nature of the face.

Shows on One's Face and Related Idioms

If something *shows on your face*, then a person can tell something about you just by looking at your face. For example: "He says he's not in pain, but it *shows on his face.*" Something can also be *written all over someone's face*. For example: "Although he denied the crime, guilt was *written all over his face.*" A number of other idioms with *face* refer to the truth and reality:

tell it to one's face

> to express one's displeasure or anger at someone directly, rather than telling other people ♦ *If she really doesn't like my idea, I wish she'd* tell it to my face. ♦ *I'm so angry at him, and I need* to tell it to his face.

look someone in the face

> to be direct and honest with someone about something difficult (alludes to making direct eye contact as a show of honesty); also to *look someone in the eyes* ♦ *It will be hard* to look him in the face *and say that I want to break our engagement, but I have to.*

take something at face value

> to accept someone or something as true from its outward appearance; to accept it as it appears ♦ *We* took him at face value, *but he wasn't as honest as he appeared.* ♦ *You can't just accept the offer* at face value, *because there may be hidden conditions.*

show one's true face

> to reveal one's true feelings or character ♦ *She rarely* shows her true face *to anyone except her closest friends.* ♦ *It's hard for me not* to show my true face. *I don't hide my feelings very well.*

Face It! and Related Idioms

To *face something* or to *look something in the face* mean to accept the reality of something that is difficult to accept. The following expressions also mean to accept the truth, accept reality, although it might be unpleasant:

> **Face it!** ♦ Face it! *You're not going to get a raise unless you work harder.*
> **Let's face it!** ♦ Let's face it, *we work a third of the year just to pay our taxes.*
> **Face the facts!** ♦ Face the facts, *man. She left you because you drink too much.*

Two other expressions, *face up to something* and *face the music,* mean to accept responsibility, or to accept punishment for one's wrongdoings. The following examples show how to use these expressions:

♦ *The error is mine. I'll have to tell the boss and* face the music.
♦ *He didn't want to* face up to it, *but his parents knew that he'd broken the window.*

Plain as the Nose on One's Face and Related Idioms

When something is *as plain as the nose on one's face,* then it's very obvious and clear. For example

♦ *After he explained it, it was* as plain as the nose on my face.
♦ *The problem is* as plain as the nose on his face. *He needs to get a job!*

When something is *staring one in the face,* it's obvious, but one doesn't see it; one doesn't realize the truth about a situation, though there are many clues. Here's how to use this expression:

♦ *She never realized they were stealing from her, though it was* staring her in the face!
♦ *The solution to my problem was* staring me right in the face, *but I couldn't see it.*

Show Your Face and Related Idioms

If you don't want to *show your face* or you want to *hide your face,* then you are probably ashamed or embarrassed. For example

♦ *He was ashamed to* show his face *after the scandal was publicized.*
♦ *When I saw how the newspaper misquoted me, I wanted to* hide my face. *The mistake made me sound like a fool!*

[Also see *show one's face* (around here) later in this chapter.]

Losing face happens when one is publicly humiliated, shamed, or embarrassed, and thus loses respect or status in others' eyes. The opposite of *losing face* is *saving face,* meaning to keep from being shamed.

♦ *If he told his friends he was afraid,* he'd lose face.
♦ *In order* to save face, *the President resigned rather than being impeached.*

If you *have egg on your face,* then your embarrassment is obvious and shows clearly. People use this expression when a person has embarrassed him or herself by making a serious social mistake or doing something wrong. For example

- *Now look who has* egg on his face! *You have to admit you were wrong.*
- *He going to have* egg on his face *if he doesn't keeps talking.*

Make a Face and Related Idioms

make a face

> **(v)** to create a funny, twisted, or unpleasant gesture with one's face for fun or to show displeasure ◆ *The children* made a face *when they saw spinach on their plate.* ◆ *He can get everyone laughing by* making *funny* faces.

make a face at someone

> **(v)** to create an unpleasant face in order to communicate one's dislike or displeasure ◆ *Mom, Bobby is* making faces *at me!*

a long face

> **(n)** a sad or depressed look on one's face; often said as to *have a long face* ◆ *Hey, why the* long face? *Is something bothering you?*

keep a straight face

> **(v)** to stop oneself from laughing; to look serious ◆ *It was hard for the security guard* to keep a straight face *when he overheard a funny joke.*

screw up one's face

> **(v)** to make an unpleasant face to show displeasure or disgust ◆ *My sister and I always* screwed up our faces *when dad put worms on the fishing hook.*

Red and Blue Faces

One might *have a red face* (be embarrassed) or *talk until one is blue in the face* (talk excessively trying to persuade someone), which alludes to talking so long that one stops breathing and becomes blue from lack of oxygen. Here are some examples of these expressions:

- *Her face* turned red *when she realized her socks didn't match.*
- *You can* talk until you're blue in the face, *but I'm not going to change my mind.*

A Few Other Face Idioms

Here are two more idioms with *face:*

show one's face (around here)

> **(v)** to make an appearance, show up somewhere, often where one isn't welcome. ♦ *He's a drug dealer, and if he* shows his face *around here, I'm going to call the police.* ♦ *I've been so busy working at home that I haven't* shown my face *around the office for awhile.*

slap in the face

> **(n)** an insult, either a direct or an indirect one, that usually happens when a person is feeling taken advantage of or disregarded ♦ *After all the years you worked for this company, being laid off is* a slap in the face. ♦ *She's never even acknowledged all the help I gave her. What* a slap in the face!

THE EYES

The eyes are our *window on the world*, the lens from which we experience the world. Most idioms with *eye* or *eyes* refer to the ability to literally see or to figuratively see — understand, be aware.

Eyes That Are Amorous

The eyes are for looking and seeing. So, lots of idioms with the word *eye* refer to looking. The following idioms mean to look at someone with romantic or sexual interest:

> **make eyes at** ♦ *He was* making eyes at *her across the table.*
> **give someone the eye** ♦ *Hey, Danny, I think she likes you. I saw her* giving you the eye.
> **eye someone** ♦ *They* eyed each other *across the room, hoping someone would introduce them.* **Note:** To *eye someone* also can simply mean to look at someone with interest or attention, as in "The security guard has been *eyeing me* since I came in the store."

[See also *catch one's eye* later in this chapter.]

Eyes That Are Alert

The following expressions mean to watch for, to watch carefully, to notice, or to attract attention.

keep an eye out for

to watch for something, to be watchful ♦ Keep an eye out for *a parking space. They're hard to find here in the city.* ♦ Keep an eye out for *your ride. You don't want them to have to wait for you.*

keep an eye on

to watch something or someone carefully; sometimes put as *keep a close eye on* ♦ *Could you* keep an eye on *my bag while I go to the restroom?* ♦ *When you're working with the power saw, you have to* keep your eye on *what you're doing.* **Note:** People who seem able to *keep an eye on* everything at once, especially on things that someone is trying to hide, might be said to *have eyes in the back of their head.* For example: "Don't try to sneak out for a smoke. The boss *has eyes in the back of her head.*"

catch one's eye

to attract one's attention; to be noticeable; also put as to *catch someone's eye,* meaning to try to attract someone's attention ♦ *That red jacket* caught my eye *in the store window.* ♦ *His big beautiful smile* caught my eye *right away.* ♦ *We were trying* to catch your eye *across the room, but you didn't see us.*

[See *go in with one's eyes open* later in this chapter.]

Eyes That Are Happy

If you are happy to see someone whom you haven't seen for awhile, you might say *You're a sight for sore eyes,* meaning, "It's wonderful to see you," "It's a joy or relief to see you." For example

♦ *Rachael, come in! You're* a sight for sore eyes.

Anything that is a delight or a joy to see, and that makes you very happy, will make your *eyes light up.* For example

♦ *When she opened the gift, her* eyes lit up.

The apple of your eye is your favorite or most beloved person. For example

♦ *That granddaughter of mine is* the apple of my eye!

Eyes That Are Open

To *open one's eyes* is used in a number of expressions that have somewhat different meanings, depending on the exact wording of the idiom.

keep one's eyes open (*or* peeled)

> to be observant, watchful ♦ Keep your eyes open *and you'll see some shooting stars up there.* ♦ *You've got* to keep your eyes open *if you don't want to miss opportunities.*

go in with one's eyes open

> to do something knowing all the possibilities; to enter a situation without being naive ♦ *I lived in the house for years before I bought it, so I* went in with my eyes open. ♦ *Being from racially mixed families, they're going into this mixed marriage with their eyes open.*

open your eyes!

> means "See the truth!" or "Stop ignoring the truth!" ♦ Open your eyes! *He's just trying to take your money.* ♦ *Can't you see that she's cheating on you?* Open your eyes!

have something open one's eyes

> to be made aware; to be enlightened or to understand more deeply ♦ *The documentary really* opened my eyes *to the history of racial discrimination.* ♦ *Traveling can* open your eyes *to the world.*

A Few More Eye Idioms

see eye-to-eye

> to agree, to view something the same way ♦ *We* see eye-to-eye *on everything, except politics.* ♦ *The world leaders don't* see eye-to-eye *on the best strategy for peace.*

cry one's eyes out

> to cry very hard and for a long time ♦ *When she heard the news of her mother's death, she* cried her eyes out. ♦ *We* cried our eyes out *watching that movie.*

one's eyes are bigger than one's stomach

> said in reference to taking more food than one was able to eat ♦ *I guess* my eyes are bigger than my stomach, *because I just can't finish this.* ♦ *Your* eyes were bigger than your stomach. *You can save the rest for later.*

pull the wool over someone's eyes

> to succeed in deceiving or tricking someone ♦ *Don't believe her. She's trying to pull the wool over your eyes.* ♦ *They really pulled the wool over his eyes. He never suspected they were embezzling.*

THE EARS

Most idioms with *ear* or *ears* allude to one of the common functions of the ears — to hear other people's stories and problems.

All Ears and Related Idioms

The ears are used for listening, so some idiomatic expressions with *ears* refer to listening attentively—or not listening at all. The following expressions mean to listen closely and attentively, to pay close attention to what someone is saying:

be all ears

> to eagerly wait to hear something interesting or important ♦ *So, tell me what happened! I'm all ears.*

lend an ear

> to pay close attention to what someone will say ♦ *If you'll lend an ear, I'll tell you how to register for this program.*

prick up one's ears

> to begin to listen closely to something one hears ♦ *When I heard them say your name, I pricked up my ears.*

In One Ear and Out the Other and Related Idioms

When someone doesn't pay attention to or heed what is being said (usually advice or instructions) people say that the information *goes in one ear and out the other*. This expression implies that the information doesn't stay in the brain but simply passes through the head. Here are a few examples:

> ♦ *I continually tell my son to hang up his clothes, but it* goes in one ear and out the other.
> ♦ *His doctor has advised him to quit smoking, but it just* goes in one ear and out the other.

Advice or information that *falls on deaf ears* is ignored or disregarded as if one is deaf and doesn't hear it. Here are some examples of this expression in context:

♦ *Any advice you give him will* fall on deaf ears. *He doesn't want to hear it.*
♦ *We told them not to invest in that risky venture, but it* fell on deaf ears.

When a person chooses not to listen, or is unwilling to heed advice or instructions, people might say that he or she *turned a deaf ear.* Here are a few examples:

♦ *If you* turn a deaf ear *to the doctor's warnings, you'll end up in the hospital.*
♦ *I explained the procedure, but he* turned a deaf ear, *and consequently did it wrong.*

Bend Someone's Ear and Related Idioms

A number of idiomatic expressions with *ear* refer to talking, or rather, making someone else listen. The following two expressions mean to talk too much, to talk incessantly for a long time:

bend someone's ear ♦ *She* bent my ear *for over an hour with all her problems!*
talk someone's ear off ♦ *I've been* talking your ear off *for 20 minutes. So tell me about yourself.*

If one is hearing gossip, interesting news, or is being scolded for doing something wrong, one might say "I *got an earful*" or "I *was given an earful.*" Here are some examples:

♦ *He* gave me an earful *about Ted and Linda's divorce.*
♦ *I really* got an earful *from mom about breaking that vase.*

A Few More Ear Idioms

play something by ear

1. to play a musical instrument without looking at the music or without formal training ♦ *He can* play *almost any piece* by ear. ♦ *I* play *piano* by ear *so I never learned to read music.*
2. to act without a preset plan; to improvise as a situation demands ♦ *I'm not sure I want to go to that party tonight. Can we just* play it by ear? ♦ *We don't always have a set itinerary when we travel. Sometimes we just like* to play it by ear.

wet behind the ears

> to be young and inexperienced, naïve. Alludes to the back of the ears as the last place to dry on a newborn calf. Often said to someone younger or much less experienced. Also put as *not dry behind the ears.* ♦ *Of course he's going to make mistakes; he's still* wet behind the ears. ♦ *Hey, don't try to give me advice. You're still* wet behind the ears.

out on one's ear

> to be dismissed, thrown out, fired disgracefully or roughly ♦ *The dean said, "You'll be* out on your ear *if you fail any more classes."* ♦ *When they caught him adding extra hours to his time card he was* out on his ear.

out of earshot

> beyond hearing range; the opposite is *within earshot* ♦ *When the children are* out of earshot, *I'll tell you what I bought them for Christmas.* ♦ *It's a good thing that Paul was* out of earshot *when you said that about him.*

dog-eared

> refers to bent or turned down corners of pages in a book ♦ *I loaned him the book, but it came back to me all* dog-eared. ♦ *I've read this book so many times; that's why it's all* dog-eared.

THE NOSE

An important job of the nose is to smell things, but surprisingly few idioms allude to this function. Instead, idioms with the word *nose* allude to the nose being prominent, and therefore the body part that is closest to one's work or something that one is investigating. Being prominent, the nose is also more vulnerable to injury than other features of the face. A number of idioms allude to this fact.

The Busy Nose

The nose sticks out a lot, or a little, on the face. So the nose is sometimes used in idioms as the most present, active, or curious body part. The following idiomatic expressions have the nose as central to the action.

have one's nose in a book

> to spend a lot of time reading; to be deeply engrossed in reading ♦ *She always has her nose in a book. It's impossible to have a conversation with her!* ♦ *You can usually find him with* his nose in a book. *He's a real bookworm.*

have one's nose to the grindstone

to work intently; to work very hard on something. Alludes to a grindstone used to sharpen tools. This expression implies that one's face (nose) remains close to one's work. Also put as *keep one's nose to the grindstone.* ♦ *He* had his nose to the grindstone *for weeks trying to finish that project.* ♦ *If you* keep your nose to the grindstone, *you'll get good grades.*

poke (*or* stick) one's nose in someone's business

to be nosy, to interfere or inquire about someone's private business (private life). Also put as the opposite, to *get one's nose out of someone's business* and to *mind one's own business.* ♦ *Why do you want* to poke your nose in her business? *It will only cause trouble.* ♦ *He shouldn't* stick his nose in their business! *It doesn't concern him.*

nose around

to investigate, to look around out of curiosity or to look for something ♦ *The police* nosed around *the crime scene looking for clues.* ♦ *We like* to nose around *in antique shops.*

Noses That Can Be Hurt

The nose is more likely to get bumped or injured than the other facial features. A few *nose* idioms use this possibility to express their meaning. The following idioms suggest injury to the nose:

no skin off one's nose

it's not a bother or an inconvenience; means "It doesn't matter to me" ♦ *It's* no skin of my nose *if he doesn't wants to join my group.* ♦ *The new policy doesn't affect her, so it's really* no skin off her nose.

rub someone's nose in something

to remind people of their bad luck, misfortune, or of something they did wrong. Rubbing someone's nose in something is considered unkind or cruel. ♦ *She knows how badly I feel about forgetting her birthday; she doesn't have* to rub my nose in it. ♦ *So he made a mistake; you don't have* to rub his nose in it.

get one's nose (bent) out of shape

to get upset, agitated, or angry about something. This idiom is often said to ridicule someone's anger. Also said as to *get one's nose out of joint.* ♦ *He* got his

nose bent out of shape *just because I didn't return his call for a few days.*
♦ *Don't get your nose out of joint over such a small thing. It's not a big deal.*

cut off one's nose to spite one's face

to hurt or injure one's own interests out of anger or resentment ♦ *If you leave the job in anger, maybe you'll be* cutting off your nose to spite your face. ♦ *She destroyed her painting just because he criticized her work. She's just* cutting off her nose to spite her face.

Noses That Indicate Snobbishness

Pointing the face, and thus the nose, upward is a gesture of rejection, disapproval, or strong dislike. The following expressions mean to reject or to disapprove of something or someone that one considers inferior.

turn up one's nose

to reject or show dislike; to consider something inferior ♦ *She* turned up her nose *at two good job offers!* ♦ *We kids always* turned up our noses *when mom served broccoli.*

look down one's nose

to consider something inferior (the nose is pointed up, so one must look downward to see) ♦ *We were poor, so some people* looked down their noses *at us.*
♦ *They* look down their nose *at anyone who doesn't share their religion.*

have one's nose in the air

to consider oneself superior ♦ *Don't put* your nose in the air. *It makes you look arrogant and silly.* ♦ *When they became rich they walked around with* their noses in the air.

Thumbing One's Nose

Another expression using the nose is to *thumb one's nose,* which means to show contempt, defiance, or ridicule. This expression refers to an impolite, but somewhat silly, gesture of putting one's thumb under the nose and wiggling one's fingers. This expression can be used to refer to the actual gesture or to merely imply the intention behind the gesture. Here are some examples:

   ♦ *The kids on the winning team* thumbed their noses *at the losers.*

   ♦ *I expect that the voters will* thumb their noses *at this proposal on voting day.*

A Few Other Nose Idioms

be (right) under one's nose

> to be very obvious, to be directly in front of one, though one may not see it; also put as *right in front of you* ♦ *There's your pen. It's* right under your nose. ♦ *The solution to a problem is often* right under your nose.

keep one's nose clean

> to stay out of trouble and do the right thing ♦ *The police officer told the boy,* "You keep your nose clean. *I don't want to see you here in the detention center again."* ♦ *Dad said, "If you want me to help you buy that car, then you have to* keep your nose clean *and get good grades."*

hard-nosed

> unfeeling, tough, stubborn ♦ *He's a good coach. He tells us what we're doing wrong without being* hard-nosed *about it.* ♦ *She's really* hard-nosed *about keeping our breaks to exactly 10 minutes.*

[See *pay through the nose* in Chapter 6.]

THE MOUTH

A few idioms with *mouth* refer to the sense of taste. But it's talking or keeping quiet that are most often alluded to in *mouth* idioms, with expressions like *open one's mouth* and *shut one's mouth*. Many more idioms use *mouth* to mean talk too much or too little, talk nonsense, or gossip.

Mouths That Talk Too Much

Words come out of the mouth, so it makes sense that most idiomatic expressions with *mouth* refer to talking. Information that is passed verbally, through talking, is passed *by word of mouth* or *through word of mouth*. Here are some examples:

> ♦ *News of layoffs spread quickly* by word of mouth.
> ♦ *Cheryl: How did you hear about the Hospice Program? Diane: Just through* word of mouth. *Some of my friends have used your services.*

If the talking is incessant babbling and bragging about oneself or about nonsense, then one of the following expressions might apply:

run off at the mouth

> to babble, brag incessantly ♦ *He's always* running off at the mouth *about the famous people he knows.*

shoot off one's mouth

> to brag, or to harass others ◆ *Why did you have* to shoot off your mouth? *It nearly caused a fight.*

your mouth is open!

> means "you're talking nonsense" ◆ *Hey Dude,* your mouth is open! *You're babbling about nothing.*

If the talking is gossip, then one of these expressions might be used:

have a big mouth

> to gossip; to reveal private information ◆ *She* has such a big mouth! *Now everyone knows about my family problems.*

open one's mouth

> to give unwanted opinions; to tell secrets ◆ *I probably shouldn't have* opened my mouth *at the meeting. Next time I won't express my opinions.* ◆ *Your secret is safe with me. I won't* open my mouth.

Mouths That Don't Talk

Some expressions with *mouth* mean to not talk, to refrain from saying something, to shut up, or to stay quiet. The following expressions have these meanings:

keep one's mouth shut

> to keep a secret; refrain from saying something ◆ *You all have to promise to* keep your mouths shut *about mom's surprise party.*

shut one's mouth

> to be quiet; to stop saying something ◆ Shut your mouth! *I don't want to hear that foul talk.*

not open one's mouth

> to remain silent; to keep a secret ◆ *Is something wrong? You* haven't opened your mouth *all evening.*

Mouths That Have Something Inside

Some expressions with *mouth* refer to putting things in or taking things out. Here are some interesting examples.

Saying a Mouthful

When someone *says a mouthful* it means that he or she has said something small that is profound, important, or meaningful. For example: "Whoever said, 'Love conquers all' definitely *said a mouthful*."

The expression *a mouthful* without the word *say* is also an idiom that refers to any name that is very long and difficult to pronounce. For example: "They named her Leah-Ann Elizabeth Leilani Masterson. Now that's *a mouthful!*"

put one's foot in one's mouth

to say the wrong thing; to embarrass oneself by making a social mistake
♦ *Boy, I sure* put my foot in my mouth *when I asked if his wife was his mother!*
♦ *Oops, I should shut up before I* put my foot in my mouth. **Note:** A funny expression that is used when a person always says the wrong thing is "He only opens his mouth to change feet."

put words in someone's mouth

to tell people what they should say; to talk for someone; also, to accuse someone of misrepresenting someone else's words ♦ *You're* putting words in Timmy's mouth. *Let him explain how he feels.* ♦ *That's not what I said. Don't* put words in my mouth!

take the words right out of someone's mouth

to say exactly what someone else was thinking or going to say ♦ *I agree! You* took the words right out of my mouth. ♦ *Go out for pizza? Great idea. You* took the words right out of my mouth.

Mouths That Taste

A couple of idiomatic expressions with *mouth* allude to taste:

leave a bad taste in one's mouth

to leave one with a bad impression, bad memory, feeling, or suspicion; people use this expression when they feel uncomfortable or vaguely displeased with what someone said or did ♦ *Something about that conversation has* left a bad taste in my mouth. ♦ *I was interested in him but his attitude toward his parents* leaves a bad taste in my mouth.

make one's mouth water

> to make one hungry or think about good food; refers to one's mouth literally salivating when imagining or eating good food ♦ *When he talked about the seafood in Veracruz, it* made my mouth water. ♦ *It* makes my mouth water *already, thinking about Thanksgiving dinner.*

Idioms with *Back, Stomach,* and *Gut*

In this section, you'll find expressions that include the words *back, stomach,* and *gut.* In most cases, the meaning of the expression alludes to the function or weaknesses of the body part.

THE BACK

When the back is strong and sturdy it gives the body support, holds it up straight, and allows a person to stand. Many idioms with *back* allude to this function of the back. At the same time, the back is vulnerable because one's back is hidden from one's own view. It's hard to know if secrets or deceptions are happening *behind one's back.* Other idioms with *back* refer to this quality.

The Backbone

The *backbone* is, literally, the center of support. To be *the backbone* of something means to be the primary person or thing that supports an effort. Look at these examples:

> ♦ *Those two players have been* the backbone *of our team all year.*
> ♦ *Donations from our supporters provide* the backbone *of our organization.*

Someone with *no backbone* cannot stand up to pressure and is easily intimidated. Here are examples:

> ♦ *If you have* no backbone, *people will take advantage of you.*
> ♦ *I used to have* no backbone, *and I let others tell me what to do.*

Backing Someone Up

Some expressions with *back* refer to supporting or helping someone, taking care of someone's interests.

back someone up

to support someone's cause, argument, or explanation ♦ *If she doesn't believe you, I'll* back you up. *I know you're telling the truth.* ♦ *If you are going to tell the director about the problem, I'll* back you up *because I agree with you.*

give someone backing

to provide support, usually financial support. When this idiom does not mean financial support, it is sometimes expressed as to *give someone full backing.* ♦ *We've* given the World Children's Fund our backing *because we strongly believe in their mission.* ♦ *When we met to choose a new board member, I* gave my full backing *to Jim because he was the best for the job.*

Here are a few other expressions meaning to help someone else:

scratch someone's back

to do a favor for someone, generally with the hope that the favor will be returned ♦ *I'm happy to help you get this promotion. After all, you've* scratched my back *plenty of times.* ♦ *Politicians and big business have been* scratching each other's backs *for years.* **Note:** Often said in the expression *You scratch my back, and I'll scratch yours,* meaning "We'll help each other get something we each want."

give someone the shirt off one's back

to do anything to help, be very generous ♦ *She's my best friend. I'd* give her the shirt off my back *if she needed it.* ♦ *He just a real generous guy. He'd* give you the shirt off his back.

I've Got Your Back

When people say *I've got your back,* they mean, "I'm watching out for you and your interests." It alludes to protecting someone's back during a physical confrontation. It can still have this literal meaning, but today it's more commonly used metaphorically.

Here are some examples:

♦ *My big brother always told me, "Don't worry about anything,* I've got your back."

♦ We watch each other's backs *at the office; if one of us comes in late, the others cover for him.*

pat someone on the back

> to acknowledge someone's good work; to congratulate or to encourage some-one. Refers to literally patting someone on the shoulder or back to say "Good job." Also said as *give someone a pat on the back.* ♦ *You really deserve* a pat on the back *for the way you handled that contract.* ♦ *They* gave us all a pat on the back *for increasing sales by 20 percent, but none of us got a raise or bonus.* **Note:** Sometimes said sarcastically, when one believes that one should receive more than just a thank you and a pat.

Behind One's Back

While the back provides support, it can also be something to hide behind. You can't see what's going on behind you. So, if people want to deceive you, they'll do so *behind your back.* The following expressions refer to deception:

do something behind someone's back

> to act secretly or deceptively, often in violation of someone else's expectations, wishes, or authority. This idiom implies betrayal. ♦ *He was seeing other women* behind her back. ♦ *I told my son not to get a body piercing, but he went* behind my back *and did it anyway.*

do something when one's back is turned

> to do something secretly when one isn't paying attention, isn't looking. This expression is not as strong as the preceding expression, and is sometimes used to refer to positive secrets or surprises. ♦ *The girls grabbed a handful of cookies* when their mom's back was turned. ♦ While my back was turned, *he planned the whole surprise party for me.*

stab someone in the back

> to betray someone's trust. Alludes to the most cowardly kind of attack, literally, stabbing someone in the back. ♦ *Don't become too friendly with Ted. He'll* stab you in the back *if you don't watch him.* ♦ *I can't believe* he stabbed me in the back *after I trusted him.* **Note:** A *back stabber* is a person who stabs someone in the back: "What a *back stabber!* She offered to help with my project, and then sold the idea as her own."

A Few More Unpleasant Things

have one's back to (*or* against) the wall

> to be trapped in a hard-pressed situation with no way to escape. Alludes to being forced back until one has reached the wall and has no escape. ♦ *Okay,*

you win. I cannot argue any longer, my back's to the wall. ♦ *Our troop tried to retreat, but there was nowhere to go.* Our backs were up against the wall.

get one's (*or* someone's) back up

to become upset or angry; to make someone angry. Alludes to a frightened or angry cat with its back arched. ♦ *Don't* get your back up *about it. It's not a big deal.* ♦ *When you criticized his brother, you really* got his back up.

get off my back!

means "Leave me alone!" "Stop nagging me!" ♦ *I wish my parents would* get off my back *about my room. I like it messy.* ♦ *Okay,* get off my back *about it! Nagging me to quit smoking won't make me stop.*

break one's back

to work very hard; to put out much effort to accomplish something ♦ *We've been* breaking our backs *trying to put our three kids through college.* ♦ *This project is going to* break my back. *I'm already exhausted, and I'm nowhere near the end.* **Note:** *Back-breaking* is the adjective: "Harvesting the fields is *back-breaking* work. I want to find another job."

A Few Other Back Idioms

back to back

1. with backs touching ♦ *Stand* back to back *so we can see who is taller.* ♦ *We put the bookshelves* back to back *and created two small office spaces.*
2. things happening one right after another, in very close succession ♦ *We had three weeks of rain,* back to back. ♦ *They played Beatles songs* back to back *all afternoon on KUSP.*

with one hand tied behind one's back

very easily, seemingly effortlessly. Refers to doing a job with only one hand that normally requires two. ♦ *I've been doing the same job for so long that I could do it* with one hand tied behind my back. ♦ *Felix says that he's built so many clocks, he could probably do it* with one hand tied behind his back. **Note:** a similar expression is *with one's eyes closed.*

THE STOMACH

The stomach is the place where digestion happens. If one is sick, or specifically, *sick to one's stomach,* it's the stomach that feels bad, upset, or nauseous. A number of expressions with *stomach* allude to digestion and how the stomach feels. They often mean to tolerate or not tolerate something unpleasant.

stomach something

> to tolerate something unpleasant or unacceptable, often used in the negative
> ♦ *He couldn't* stomach the filthy conditions *in some of the field hospitals.* ♦ *I don't know how you* stomach that person; *he's dishonest and rude to everyone.*

have a strong stomach

> to have a high tolerance for something distasteful ♦ *You need* to have a strong stomach *to watch all the violence on the news.* ♦ *Only those of us with* strong stomachs *were able to dissect frogs in biology class.*

have no stomach for (*or* **have a weak stomach**)

> to have low tolerance for something distasteful ♦ *He wanted to be a surgeon, but he* had no stomach for *blood.* ♦ *I* have a weak stomach for *such violent movies.*

turn one's stomach

> to make someone feel nauseated or disgusted ♦ *It* turns my stomach *to think of how cruelly some animals are treated.* ♦ *I'm disgusted by the constant talk of war to solve every world problem. It just* turns my stomach.

have butterflies in one's stomach

> to be nervous or anxious about something ♦ *The first day in front of a class, new teachers always* have butterflies in their stomachs. ♦ *Before I went on stage, I* had butterflies in my stomach.

[See *one's eyes are bigger than one's stomach* earlier in this chapter.]

THE GUTS

Guts are literally a person's entrails and stomach, the center of the body. The gut is often a metaphor for one's innermost feelings or intuition. The following expressions allude to this idea:

> **gut reaction**
> **have a gut feeling**
> **feel something in one's gut**

These idioms all mean to know something by instinct or feeling. Here are some examples:

> ♦ *I knew right away that she'd be perfect for the job. It was just a* gut reaction.
> ♦ *We can't just rely on* gut feelings; *we also have to do some research to find evidence to prove we're right.*
> ♦ *Somehow I just know that he was hiding some serious problems. I just* felt it in my gut.

Guts are also a metaphor for courage. The following idioms allude to this:

have the guts

> to have the courage to do something; to not be afraid to do something ♦ *I didn't think she'd* have the guts *to go skydiving and jump from an airplane, but she did.* ♦ *If you don't* have the guts *to confront him and tell him he's wrong, then I will. I'm not afraid of him.*

be gutsy

> to be courageous and daring, unafraid ♦ *It was very* gutsy *to just walk right into the president's office and give her your opinion. And she listened, too!* ♦ *My grandmother was so* gutsy. *She went bungee jumping at the age of 75!*

be gutless

> to be afraid, cowardly, without courage ♦ *It was* gutless *of me to hide the truth about what happened, and I'm sorry.* ♦ *Don't* be gutless. *You'll never get a date if you're afraid to talk to girls.* **Note:** *Spineless* means the same thing.

Here is one other idiom with *gut:*

hate someone's guts

> to loathe or detest someone; also said as an exaggeration or in jealousy over someone's good fortune ♦ *Mommy, that girl was so mean to me. I* hate her guts! ♦ *What?! You got on the team and I didn't? Man, I* hate your guts!

Idioms with *Arms, Hands, and Fingers*

In this section, you'll find expressions that relate to the arms, hands, and fingers, including the thumbs. Almost all of the following expressions allude to the function and capabilities of these body parts, or the disadvantage of having any of these parts restrained.

THE ARMS

Arms are good for reaching or keeping things at a distance, and also for holding and hugging. The following few expressions with *arm* allude to these uses of the arms.

The Length of an Arm

Keeping someone *at arm's length* means keeping him or her at an emotional or social distance to avoid intimacy or interaction. One might also keep people at arm's length to avoid appearing to favor one person over another. Here are some examples:

- *The boss keeps everyone* at arm's length. *It's hard to get close to the guy.*
- *I like him, but he's a married man, so I'm keeping him* at arm's length.

Even longer than arm's length is *the long arm of the law.* This expression refers to the ability of the police and other law enforcement agencies to capture criminals, no matter how far they run or where they hide. The following are some examples:

- The long arm of the law *finally caught up with him in Argentina.*
- *He escaped from jail, but* the long arm of the law *will get him eventually.*

Just the Right Arm

These expressions refer to the right arm as the essential arm, because most people are right-handed (they write, eat, and have more control with their right hand):

be someone's right arm

be someone's main supporter or helper, especially during difficulties. ♦ *My assistant* has become my right arm. *I couldn't function without him.* ♦ *Since I have a disability and use a wheelchair, my guide dog* is really my right arm.

give one's right arm

to sacrifice something of value to alter a situation or to achieve something; typically said when something is unattainable ♦ *He'd* give his right arm *for a chance to play in that band.* ♦ *I'd* give my right arm *to see her again, but she died last summer.*

A Few Other Arm Idioms

arm in arm

> **(adj, adv)** literally to walk with arms joined; also to be supportive of one another; often said as *walk arm in arm* ♦ *It's nice to see the old folks walking* arm in arm *through the park.* ♦ *My parents went through life* arm and arm; *they were always there for each other.*

twist someone's arm

> **(v)** to try very hard to convince or persuade someone; to talk someone into something. ♦ *We see you're busy, but we'd like you to join us for dinner. Can we* twist your arm? ♦ *I didn't have to* twist his arm *very hard to convince him that we should take a vacation.*

with open arms

> with warmth and welcome, in a very friendly way; gratefully embracing an idea or plan. Literally, to open one's arms to welcome and hug someone. ♦ *We met her at the airport* with open arms. ♦ *The decision to reduce class size was greeted* with open arms *by everyone involved with the school.* **Note:** *To greet* and *to meet* are the verbs most often placed in front of *with open arms.*

arm candy

> an attractive-looking individual who accompanies someone else just to make that person look better ♦ *I think her new boyfriend is just* arm candy *to her.* ♦ *Some celebrities never appear in public without their* arm candy.

[See also *cost an arm and a leg* in Chapter 6.]

THE HANDS

There are many idioms and expressions that use *hand* or *hands*. Most of these idioms refer to the basic function of the hands and their usefulness in working, helping, protecting, and creating things. Others refer to having responsibility or letting it go. The following idioms are organized by topic.

Hands That Help

A common saying, "Many hands make light work," means that work is easier when many people help. Hands are often a metaphor for helping. So, it's logical that some idiomatic expressions with *hand* refer to helping or supporting others. Both of the following expressions mean to help someone:

lend someone a hand ♦ *Hey! Could you* lend *me a hand* with this heavy box?
give someone a hand ♦ *Let me* give you a hand. *You shouldn't do all that work*
by yourself.

These expressions are often said to *lend a helping hand* or *give a helping hand:* "Bob is so kind. He's always there to *lend a helping hand.*"

Grammar Note: An indirect object (in the form or a noun or pronoun) almost always comes before *a hand*, as in the above expressions.

Two similar idioms are used when a person needs help:

could use a hand ♦ *I could* use a hand *with this.*
need a hand ♦ *I* need a hand *moving this furniture.*

To inquire if someone needs help, you can ask one of the following:

♦ *Could you* use a hand *with that repair job?*
♦ *Do you* need a hand *with the groceries?*

In addition, here are some idioms to describe people whose occupation it is to *lend a hand*:

a hired hand: one who is hired to work around a farm, ranch, or estate
right-hand man: one's assistant and most valuable helper

[See also *give someone a hand* (to applaud and show appreciation) later in this chapter.]

Hands That Control

Holding something in one's hands can be a metaphor for holding responsibility or having control, as in the following expressions:

be in good hands

(adj) be in a secure, safe position; often used to assure someone that a person or service is responsible, trustworthy, and capable ♦ *With Dr. Mozayan, you're in very good hands. He's an excellent surgeon.* ♦ *When you insure your home through us, your investment* is in good hands.

in someone's hands

be made someone's responsibility to safeguard; implies that the fate or outcome of something is in someone's power; often used to refer to God or other deities ♦ *The doctors have done all they can for the girl. Now* it's in God's hands. ♦ *Thank you for offering to take over this troublesome project. We're putting it* in your hands.

put one's life in someone's hands

to trust someone with one's life, safety, or well-being; also phrased *to have someone's life in one's hands* ♦ *Drive with that drunk?! No way! I'm not* putting my life in his hands. ♦ *As a commercial pilot she has the* lives of hundreds of people in her hands *every day.*

have one's hands full

to have too much or a lot of responsibility; to be very busy ♦ *Wow, with six children and two jobs, she really* has her hands full! ♦ *I'm sorry, but I can't take on any new assignments right now.* My hands are totally full.

get (*or* have *or* gain) the upper hand

to take control from someone who once had control over you, or exceed someone who was previously ahead of you ♦ *For years, the older brothers bullied him, but now he* has the upper hand *because he's much bigger.* ♦ *Our team was losing until the last quarter, when we* gained the upper hand.

Hands That Don't Have Control

When something is *out of one's hands* one is no longer in control or responsible for it; one can do nothing more to help or influence a situation. Here are some examples:

♦ *I recommended her for the job, but the decision to hire her is* out of my hands.
♦ *He asked us to help him get a visa, but that kind of thing is totally* out of our hands.

Taking Your Life In Your Hands

When you do something that is potentially life threatening, you *take your life in your hands*. This expression means that you risk your life, or take risks with serious consequences. This expression is often used to exaggerate a situation. Here are some examples:

♦ *I warn you,* you take your life in your hands *crossing that busy street!*

♦ *If you want to* take your life in your hands, *just drive with grandpa! He's a terrible driver, and he can't see very well.*

♦ *Why is she* taking her life in her hands *traveling in that dangerous area at night?!*

The following expressions also relate to being unable to help, or to release responsibility or have no control.

one's hands are tied

be unable to help someone because of policy, rules, or other factors ♦ *I'd like to help you out, but* my hands are tied. *Our policy doesn't permit it.* ♦ *Son,* my hands are tied. *I would let you buy a motorcycle, but mom says no. And you know she's the boss!*

wash one's hands of

to no longer want to associate with or be responsible for something or someone; to renounce something or someone. Alludes to washing something dirty off one's hands. ♦ *If you are going to disregard safety regulations,* I wash my hands of *the whole project!* ♦ *We've tried to help him many times without success. So we've* washed our hands of *him.*

be (*or* get) out of hand

be out of control; uncontrollable; unable to stop a thing or person from doing harm to someone or something else ♦ *When the children start* getting out of hand, *I make them play outside.* ♦ *You can't let that dog* get out of hand. *Bruno is big, and he could hurt someone.* ♦ *A small brush fire can* get out of hand *quickly.*

throw up one's hands

to give up trying to control, influence, or understand something ♦ *I was about to* throw up my hands *and call a plumber when I finally figured out how to repair those pipes.* ♦ *Before you* throw up your hands, *let me try to help you.* ♦ *After they made a big mess, she* threw up her hands *and stopped trying to get her kids to eat squash.*

Hands That Make Things

Some *hand* idioms relate to working with the hands. Something *made by hand, hand-made,* or *hand-done* is made by a person, not a machine. The expression *hand-done* often refers to decoration or added details. The expression *hand-crafted* often refers to something that involves detailed craftsmanship, such as furniture or jewelry. Here are some examples:

- ♦ *She's an excellent seamstress. She* makes *all her clothes* by hand.
- ♦ *This store sells only* hand-made *goods.*
- ♦ *The carving on this table was all* hand-done *by my father.*
- ♦ *She* hand-crafted *many of these beautiful gold rings.*

Hands That Hold

To *take one's hand* means to hold on to someone's hand or to put someone's hand in yours. Someone might say to a small child, "Susie, *take my hand*" just before crossing a street together. A person can also take someone's hand romantically, compassionately, or to check someone's health, as in these examples:

- *He* took her hand *and said, "I love you."*
- *The nurse* took my hand *and checked my pulse.*

When two people are *holding hands* or are *hand in hand,* one person's hand is in the others. Here are some examples of these expressions:

- *They* held hands *through the entire movie.*
- *You can see sweethearts walking* hand in hand *along the beach.*
- *He* held my hand *when I was sick.*

A similar expression, at least on the surface, is *give someone your hand.* If you *give someone your hand* (in marriage), then you accept that person's marriage proposal. And to *ask for someone's hand* means to ask someone to marry you. Here are some examples:

- *My father* asked for my mother's hand *after knowing her for only two weeks.*
- *She accepted and* gave him her hand.

Hand + Prepositions

The verb *to hand* generally means to pass something from one to another. Idioms with the verb *to hand* plus a preposition refer to various types of passing something from one person to another. Here are the idioms:

hand in (to submit something) ♦ Hand in *your homework at the beginning of class.*
hand out (to distribute something) ♦ *The professor* handed out *the syllabus.*
hand off (to pass to someone else) ♦ *Next week we'll* hand off *the project to the manufacturer.*
hand over (to give unwillingly) ♦ *The thief yelled,* "Hand over *your wallet!"*
hand down (to pass to the next generation) ♦ *Native American traditions have been* handed down *from generation to generation.*

Grammar Note: These idioms are separable phrasal verbs. They require a direct object, which can come between the two words of the idiom. For example: "The professor *handed* the syllabus *out.*" (In casual speech and writing, it is okay to end a sentence with a preposition.)

[For more information on separable phrasal verbs, see Part V.]

The plural noun *hands* is combined with the prepositions *up*, *down*, *on*, and *off* to form the following idioms:

Hands up!

means "Put your hands above your head"; usually said by a criminal or a law-enforcement officer with a weapon ♦ *"Hands up! You're under arrest!" the police shouted.*

hands down

(adv) easily, without effort; without doubt or question ♦ *They won every game* hands down. *The other team was no competition.* ♦ *She's the hottest new rapper,* hands down.

hands on

(adj) refers to an activity or training where one actively participates ♦ *The kids love the experiments they get to do in their science class. It's all* hands on. ♦ *This museum for kids is very* hands on. *Look at all the interactive exhibits!*

hands off

a request to not touch or take something or someone ♦ Hands off *those cookies until after dinner.* ♦ Hands off, *girl! That's my boyfriend.*

Hands That Lay On

Three different expressions use *hand* or *hands* with the words *lay on*. Here they are:

lay a hand on someone

to hurt physically; to attempt to take; to touch sexually; this expression is often used in the negative ♦ *I scold my kids, but I never* lay a hand on them *in anger. I don't believe in spanking.* ♦ *She warned her housemates, "Don't anyone* lay a hand *on that cake. It's for the party tonight."* ♦ My father told every guy I dated, *"If you* lay a hand on my daughter, *I'll have you arrested!"*

lay one's hands on something

to find or locate something that is missing or that one is interested in discovering ♦ *I've finally* laid my hands on *a good idiom book,* The American Idiom Handbook. ♦ *I know his business card is here somewhere, but I can't* lay my hands on it *right now.*

laying on of hands

> a healing method that involves laying or putting one's hands on the injured part ♦ *She was greatly respected for her skill in healing by the* laying on of hands.

Hands That Give Credit

The following expressions mean to show appreciation and to give credit to one who has earned it:

hand it to someone

> to give credit to or acknowledge people for something they have managed to do, usually in spite of difficulty. Usually said as *have to hand it to (someone)* ♦ *I've got to* hand it to him. *He managed to get his law degree while working full time.* ♦ *Boy, I* have to hand it to you. *You dealt with that rude customer a lot better than I would have.*

give someone a hand

> to applaud, clap; also to *get a big hand* ♦ *Wasn't that a great show? Let's* give the performers a hand. ♦ *When her speech was finished, everyone* gave her a big hand.

Firsthand and Secondhand

The expressions *firsthand* and *secondhand* have the following meanings:

firsthand

> refers to information that comes directly from the source ♦ *Believe me. I heard it* firsthand *from people who were there and saw what happened.* ♦ *You should call her and get the information* firsthand *rather than trusting what someone else says.* ♦ *As a newspaper reporter, I'm interested in* firsthand *reports, not hearsay.*

secondhand

> **1.** refers to information that comes from someone who heard it from the source, in other words, the information has come through two people. This idiom can imply that the information is less reliable because it didn't come directly from the source. ♦ *I heard it* secondhand *from Jane, but she wouldn't lie, so I believe it.* ♦ *Check with the manager on the details. I just have* secondhand information.
>
> ***Note:*** If the information comes through three people before you hear it, then it's referred to as *thirdhand. Thirdhand* information is considered unreliable. It's also possible to say *fourth hand* or *fifth hand,* but people rarely do.

2. refers to used items that are sold or given away by their original owners ♦ *There's a good* secondhand *shop downtown. They have some great deals on clothes and household items.* ♦ *I bought all my furniture* secondhand *at yard sales.*

Grammar Note: The expressions *firsthand, secondhand,* and so on can function as adjectives, as in "It's secondhand information" or adverbs, as in "I heard it secondhand."

A Few Other Hand Idioms

an old hand at

(n) a person who has a lot of experience doing something ♦ *Of course I can make you an apple pie. I'm* an old hand at *making pies.* ♦ *He's* an old hand at *playing poker, so you'll probably lose if you play with him.*

at hand

handy, nearby, where one can easily reach or get something; often phrased *close at hand* ♦ *When I'm working on an art project, I need all my supplies close* at hand. ♦ *I don't live with either of my children, but they're close* at hand *if I get sick or need something.*

empty-handed

(adj) having nothing in one's hands or carrying nothing when one arrives or leaves; often implies that one leaves without the thing he or she came to get or that one has arrived without bringing a customary gift ♦ *Please take some of these oranges from our tree. I don't want you leave* empty-handed. ♦ *My mother told me that when you visit someone's home, you should never arrive* empty-handed. *Always bring a small gift.*

on hand

available when one needs it; in stock; often used with the verbs *to have* and *to keep* ♦ *Do we have enough soda* on hand *for the party, or do we need to buy some more?* ♦ *We keep a number of different brands of paint* on hand, *but not the one you're looking for.*

wait on someone hand and foot

to attend to someone's every need, to attentively serve someone ♦ *She* waits on *her son hand and foot. It's time he started taking care of himself.* ♦ *On Mother's Day, everyone* waits on *me hand and foot. It's wonderful!*

THE FINGERS

Fingers are used to touch and hold things, to gesture, and also to work. The following expressions refer to these uses of the fingers.

Fingers That Gesture and Touch

To *finger* something means to handle and touch it with one's fingers, to experience how it feels. Here are some examples:

> ♦ *Kids, don't* finger *all the candies; just take one.*
> ♦ *I like to* finger *and feel all the different textures of fabric in the fabric shop.*

The following idioms refer to actual gestures make with the fingers:

cross one's fingers

> to wish or hope for good luck, success; literally and figuratively crossing the middle finger over the index finger; often put as *to keep one's fingers crossed*
> ♦ *He doesn't know if he got the job yet. We're* keeping our fingers crossed *for him.* ♦ *Keep* your fingers crossed; *we're going to start the car and see if I was able to fix it.*

give someone the finger

> to make a vulgar gesture of anger and contempt; literally and figuratively holding up the middle finger with fist clenched ♦ *When the car zoomed past us, the driver* gave us the finger. ♦ *We really laughed when we saw grandma* give that rude guy the finger! ***Note:*** This gesture is also called *flipping the bird* or *flipping someone off.*

point the finger at

> to blame or accuse someone of something. Alludes to the actual gesture of pointing at someone or something; also said with a plural noun as *point fingers at.* ♦ *Don't* point the finger at *me. It isn't my fault.* ♦ *Now scientists are* pointing the finger at *environmental pollution as a major cause of cancer.*

A Few Other Finger Idioms

at one's fingertips

> handy, accessible, easy to find, reach, or get; usually said as *have* or *keep something at one's fingertips* ♦ *I keep my reading glasses in my shirt pocket so that I have them* at my fingertips *when I need them.* ♦ *The Internet keeps the world* at our fingertips.

finger food

>food that one typically eats with one's fingers, for example, pizza, fried chicken, chips, and most appetizers ♦ *I'm not going to serve a meal at my party, I'll just have some* finger food. ♦ *Come over and watch the game at my house. Bring some* finger food!

lay a finger on

>**1.** to touch with the intent to harm someone or something; to attempt to take something that one shouldn't take. Often said in the negative, and used in a threat. ♦ *Don't you kids* lay a finger on *those hors d'oeuvres until the guests arrive.* ♦ *Don't worry. I won't let those mean boys* lay a finger on *my little brother.*
>**2.** to touch someone sexually ♦ *If he* lays a finger on *my sister, I'm going to break his neck!*

[See also *lay a hand on someone* earlier in this chapter.]

lift a finger

>to make the slightest effort; to do the least amount of work possible. Almost always used in the negative, as in *didn't lift a finger.* ♦ *On my birthday, my kids do everything for me. I don't have to* lift a finger. ♦ *What jerks! They didn't* lift a finger *to help while she was sick.*

put one's finger on something

>to be able to identify, remember, or figure out something; often used in the negative to mean that someone can't quite remember something ♦ *I've met that man before, but I can't* put my finger on where. ♦ *What's the name of that song they're playing? I can't quite* put my finger on it.

slip through one's fingers

>to miss an opportunity, to let something get away by not paying attention or acting on it in time ♦ *She could have gotten the scholarship but she missed the deadline and the chance* slipped through her fingers. ♦ *He had a wonderful girl-friend, but he let her* slip through his fingers *by not proposing.*

work one's fingers to the bone

>to work very hard with one's hands; usually refers to cleaning and housework ♦ *I worked my fingers to the bone getting the house ready for our guests.* ♦ *You* work your fingers to the bone *in this job, and the pay is bad.* ♦ *All her life, she was* working her fingers to the bone *trying to support her kids.*

wrap (*or* twist) someone around one's (little) finger

> to have someone in one's control; to create a situation where a person will do anything one wants them to do; also *to have someone wrapped* or *twisted around someone's finger* ♦ *He's so in love that his girlfriend could* wrap *him* around her little finger *if she wanted to.* ♦ *Face the facts; the boss has you* twisted around his finger *and he's taking advantage of you.*

The Thumb

The thumb is perhaps the most essential finger on the hand. Without it, many normal everyday activities would be difficult or impossible. But despite the importance of the thumb, there are only a few expressions that refer to the thumb. This section includes the most common ones.

The following expressions refer to gestures made with the thumb. The idioms are often used figuratively, but can be used to describe the actual gesture.

thumb a ride

> to hitchhike, literally to stick out one's thumb toward traffic in an effort to get a ride from a passing motorist; figuratively to ask an acquaintance or friend for a ride ♦ *We* thumbed rides *all the way across the country. What at trip!* ♦ *We used to* thumb rides, *but it's not safe anymore.* ♦ *Hey John, can I* thumb a ride *to work with you tomorrow?*

twiddle one's thumbs

> to sit idle and bored, usually while waiting for something; to do nothing. Refers to the habit of folding one's hands together and circling one's thumbs around each other; usually said as *sit twiddling one's thumbs.* ♦ *The speaker was late, so we just sat there* twiddling our thumbs *for a half hour.* ♦ *Don't just sit* twiddling your thumbs. *Help me clean up this mess!*

thumbs up *and* thumbs down

> very good/not good. These expressions are said as a way of showing approval or disapproval, or reporting good news or bad news; refers to the literal gesture of the thumb pointing up (good) or down (not good) with the fist clenched.
> ♦ *After she read my report, she gave it a* thumbs up. ♦ *When he came out of the audition, he gave us a* thumbs up, *and we knew he got the part.* ♦ *Man, I give that movie a* thumbs down. *Don't waste your money going to see it.*

[See also *thumb through* in Part V; see *Thumbing One's Nose* earlier in this chapter.]

Here are some more idioms with *thumb:*

all thumbs

clumsy with one's hands, not good with handling or fixing things ♦ *Don't ask mom to make your costume. She's* all thumbs *around a sewing machine.* ♦ *I could never be a brain surgeon;* I'm all thumbs.

have a green thumb

to be very good at growing plants, to be an expert gardener ♦ *Richard* really has a green thumb. *Have you ever seen his beautiful garden?!* ♦ *I don't* have a green thumb. *Every time I plant something, it dies.*

stick out like a sore thumb

to be highly visible and obvious because of some peculiar feature; to be conspicuous ♦ *With his hair dyed green, he* sticks out like a sore thumb. ♦ *We won't have trouble finding her in this crowd. She's so tall, she* sticks out like a sore thumb.

Idioms with *Legs, Feet,* and *Toes*

This section includes expressions that relate to the legs, feet, and toes. Some of these expressions allude to standing, stepping, and putting one's foot somewhere. Others refer to being quick or alert. Still others seem to have no connection to the functions or frailties of these body parts.

THE LEGS

The legs are designed for standing and walking, so most idioms that use the word *leg* refer to those functions. Following are a few idioms with the word *leg*.

not have a leg to stand on

to have no support or justification for one's case ♦ *He was drunk when the accident happened, so he* doesn't have a leg to stand on *in court.* ♦ *You* don't have a leg to stand on, *Buddy. We already know the real story because your partner confessed.*

on one's last leg

almost worn out; ready to collapse; close to dying ♦ *This old refrigerator is* on its last leg. *We'll need to buy a new one soon.* ♦ *He is 92 years old and* on his last leg, *but he still has a great attitude.*

pull someone's leg

> to tease, trick, or joke with someone in a harmless way; also used to ask if someone is joking; always used with the singular *leg* ♦ *Don't believe him; he's just* pulling your leg. ♦ *I'm just* pulling your leg. *I don't really own a Ferrari.*

shake a leg

> to hurry up, to get up and get going and not dawdle ♦ *Tom, you'd better* shake a leg *or you'll be late for school.* ♦ *Oops. I've got to* shake a leg *if I want to be home in time for dinner.*

THE FEET

The feet are featured in many idioms and expressions that have a variety of meanings. The following idioms use *foot* or *feet*, and are organized by similar wording or similar meaning.

Feet That Touch (or Don't Touch) the Ground

The feet give one something to stand on, and when both feet are firmly on the ground, one is stable and isn't going to fall over. If one has *both feet on the ground*, one is stable emotionally and mentally, one is solid and self-sufficient. Here are some other expressions that imply standing firm:

be back on one's feet

> to be physically well or economically stable again ♦ *I was really sick for awhile, but* I'm back on my feet *now.* ♦ *Their business nearly went bankrupt after the fire, but they're beginning to get* back on their feet *again.*

land on one's feet

> to come out of any difficult situation successfully. Alludes to a common misconception regarding a cat's ability to land on its feet no matter how far it falls. ♦ *Just as her company was going bankrupt, she was offered a much better position elsewhere. She always seems to* land on her feet. ♦ *You may have hard times in life, but you'll do fine if you learn how to* land on your feet.

stand on one's own two feet

> to be independent and self-sufficient, both economically and emotionally; to support oneself without help ♦ *Becoming an adult means* standing on your own two feet. ♦ *Your son will never learn to* stand on his own two feet *if you keep paying his bills.*

In contrast to having one's feet on the ground, if one's *feet haven't touched the ground* for a while, it means that one is very happy, elated. This usually happens because of love or joyous news. People also say that one is *walking on air.* Here are some examples:

* *Since they met their* feet haven't touched the ground.
* *When I heard that our sons were coming home from the war my* feet didn't touch the ground *for weeks.*

Another idiom that refers to one's feet not being on the ground is *swept off one's feet*, meaning that a person has been overwhelmed by something wonderful or awesome. Again, it's often love that can sweep one off one's feet, but other passionate things can too. This expression is also put in the active voice, *to sweep someone off his* (or *her*) *feet.*

* *She was* swept off her feet *by his charm and good looks.*
* *The stark beauty of the glaciers just* swept me off my feet.

On and Off One's Feet

The idiom *on foot* simply means to walk, as opposed to using other means of transportation. See the following examples:

* *You can get there* on foot, *but it's a long walk.*
* *I had to come* on foot *because my car is in the repair shop.*

To *be on one's feet* means to be standing or walking, and not able to sit down or rest, for example, while at work or shopping and running errands. People don't commonly use this expression to talk about hiking or walking for pleasure. Here are some examples:

* *He's* on his feet *all day in his job as a mail carrier.*
* *Boy, I'm tired. I've been* on my feet *all day running errands.*

To *get off one's feet* is the opposite of being on one's feet. It means to be able to sit down, to stop standing or walking. Sometimes people say *take a load off (one's feet).* Here are some examples:

* *I need to* get off my feet. *I've been on them all day long shopping.*
* *Welcome home. Come sit down and* take a load off your feet.

Putting Feet Up and Down

To *put one's feet up* and to *put one's feet down* have two completely different meanings:

put one's feet up

> to sit or lie down and elevate one's feet; to relax ♦ Put your feet up *for awhile. It might help you feel better.* ♦ *I am so tired I just can't wait to get home and* put my feet up.

put one's foot down

> to disallow or stop some action; to assert one's authority by saying no; always said with the singular *foot* ♦ *We give our teenage daughter a lot of freedom, but when she wanted to get a tattoo we* put our foot down. ♦ *I had a lot of pets when I was a kid, but my parents* put their foot down *when I brought home a goat.*

The Right Foot and the Wrong Foot

If you *start on the right foot,* you begin something well prepared and with the right attitude; you start in a way that is likely to bring success. Here is an example:

> ♦ *Start the school year* on the right foot: *Have your supplies and your books, and arrive on time to class.*

On the other hand, if you *start on the wrong foot,* you begin something unprepared, or you start something that already has problems; you start in a way that is likely to fail. See the following example:

> ♦ *Don't start your marriage* on the wrong foot. *See a counselor and work out your problems before you take your vows.*

Either *out* or *off* can be inserted between *start* and *on* in these two idioms. Here are some examples:

> ♦ *We started* off *our vacation* on the right foot *by spending a night in New York City.*
> ♦ *The trip started* out on the wrong foot *when we missed our plane, and our luggage ended up in Spain.*

Cold Feet and Hot Footing It

Here are some idioms using *cold* and *hot* in conjunction with feet:

get cold feet

> to become hesitant and apprehensive, and decide at the last minute not to do something. This expression is generally used to talk about marriage and business deals. ♦ *She* got cold feet *and cancelled her wedding just one week before the ceremony.* ♦ *We almost bought that house, but we* got cold feet *when we saw the home inspector's report.*

hotfoot it

> to leave in a hurry, usually to escape or avoid being caught ♦ *When the graffiti writers saw the police car pull up, they* hotfooted it. ♦ *I'm not ashamed to* hotfoot it *if some big guy on the street wants to start a fight.*

Putting One Foot Somewhere

The following idioms refer to using one foot only:

put one's best foot forward

> to present or show the very best of oneself; to act or do one's very best ♦ *In a job interview, you have to* put your best foot forward. ♦ *On a first date, always* put your best foot forward *and dress to impress.*

get one's foot in the door

> to succeed in the first small step toward a larger opportunity or success; often used in a business context. Alludes to a door-to-door salesman putting his foot in the doorway to prevent the door from being closed before he or she can make a sales pitch. ♦ *He's tried three times to meet with the director, but he hasn't* gotten his foot in the door *yet.* ♦ *The only way to* get your foot in the door *with that company is to know someone who works there.*

have one foot in the grave

> to be close to death ♦ *She already* had one foot in the grave *when, miraculously, she got better.* ♦ *I won't stop dancing and performing until I* have one foot in the grave!

set foot somewhere

> to appear somewhere or be in a specific place; often put in the negative as *not to set one's foot somewhere* ♦ *I told him that if he* sets foot in here *again I'll have*

him arrested. ♦ Don't set foot in my kitchen! *Last time you did, you made a huge mess.*

[See *put one's foot in one's mouth* earlier in this chapter.]

A Few Other Foot Idioms

These following idioms are presented in alphabetical order:

foot the bill

to pay the bill or tab, to cover the expenses of others or pay for damage caused by others ♦ *Go ahead and order anything on the menu. I'm* footing the bill. ♦ *When store windows were broken on New Year's Eve, the city had to* foot the bill.

footloose and fancy free

to be carefree, having no responsibilities or commitments ♦ *Youth is a time to be* footloose and fancy free. ♦ *They felt* footloose and fancy free *with their children away at summer camp for two weeks.*

have a foot in both camps

to support or have an interest in two opposing sides ♦ *He won't argue with you because he* has a foot in both camps. ♦ *When you* have a foot in both camps, *it's hard to be strongly committed to either one.* **Note:** An expression with a similar meaning is *riding the fence.*

jump in with both feet

to commit oneself completely to something with no hesitation; to act without much forethought ♦ *When I decide to do something, I usually* jump in with both feet. ♦ *She was ready to* jump in with both feet *and buy the house when the inspector found cracks in the foundation.*

my foot!

means "Nonsense!" "That's ridiculous" "I don't believe that" ♦ *He was sick last week?* My foot! *I saw him on the beach playing volleyball.* ♦ *Budget problems,* my foot! *Administrators just gave themselves a big raise!*

[See *wait on someone hand and foot* earlier in this chapter.]

the shoe is on the other foot

the situation has reversed; people have changed places and they now know how the other feels ♦ *Someday, when you have your own children and* the shoe is on the other foot, *you'll understand why we have rules in this house.* ♦ *He laughed when he broke my heart, but now his girlfriend has left him and* the shoe is on the other foot.

shoot oneself in the foot

to carelessly or foolishly damage one's own interests or causes ♦ *Don't* shoot yourself in the foot *by refusing to work the shifts they ask you to. You'll be fired.* ♦ *You'll be* shooting yourself in the foot *if you push her to marry you before she's ready.*

[See also *cut off one's nose to spite one's face* earlier in this chapter.]

think on one's feet

to be able to respond quickly and spontaneously to unexpected questions ♦ *He's often interviewed by reporters and has to be able* to think on his feet. ♦ *I'm no good at* thinking on my feet. *I need time to formulate my ideas.* **Note:** An idiom similar in meaning is *to be quick on one's feet.*

THE TOES

Though there are 10 toes on the human foot, there are only a few expressions using the word *toes* and most of them include the words *on one's toes.*

To be *on one's toes* means to be alert, attentive, and ready for anything that might happen. Here are some examples:

♦ *I have to be* on my toes *every minute working with toddlers in the preschool.*
♦ *If you're* on your toes, *you can make money in this business.*

To *keep people on their toes* means to make people stay alert, attentive, prepared, and ready for anything. This expression often refers to a training or classroom situation. Here are some examples:

♦ *Our teacher often gives an unexpected quiz, just to* keep us on our toes.
♦ *As a lifeguard, knowing that I'm responsible for people's lives really keeps me* on my toes.

walk on tiptoes

to walk or tread very quietly and carefully so as not to upset anyone; to avoid controversial issues. This expression refers to literally and figuratively walking softly on the very tips of one's toes; also *to tiptoe (around).* ♦ *Please* walk on tiptoes *so that you don't wake up the baby.* ♦ *I'm not going to* tiptoe around *the board members. If I have an opinion, I'll give it.*

step on someone's toes

> to offend someone or get involved where one doesn't belong; to step uninvited into someone else's place or get involved in someone else's responsibility ♦ *I would offer to help them, but I don't want to* step on anyone's toes. ♦ *He* stepped on a lot of toes *when he tried to redesign an already excellent program.*

One more expression with *toes* alludes to keeping one's toes along a prescribed line, as one is ordered to do:

toe the line

> to do what one is told and expected to do, to obey the rules; to stop ignoring or challenging the rules ♦ *If you don't* toe the line, *you'll be looking for a new job!* ♦ *Our father was strict; we always had to* toe the line.

CHAPTER 14

COLOR IDIOMS

Some idioms with color words refer to an actual color. For example *to turn red* (to become embarrassed) refers to the reddening or flushed color of the face when one feels embarrassed or self-conscious. The idiom *a gray hair* (an elderly person) refers to an older person's gray hair.

Other idioms are metaphors for color. For example, to have *a green thumb* (to be able to grow plants easily) uses the color green as a metaphor for healthy plants.

The idioms in this chapter are listed by color: first the primary colors, *red, blue,* and *yellow;* then other colors; then multicolors; and finally a few expressions that use the word *color.*

Red

Some idioms that use *red* can be traced back to skin color. If a person becomes extremely mad or extremely embarrassed, his or her facial skin may turn red or deepen in color—hence *red* idioms relating to anger or embarrassment. *Red* is also a color that is associated with excitement and good times, as in the idioms *paint the town red* and *red carpet.*

turn red

> **1. (v)** to become extremely embarrassed and blush; depending on context, can also mean to become extremely angry ♦ *She* turned *bright* red *when she opened the package with lacy underwear in front of her coworkers.* ♦ *My dad was so mad when I wrecked the car that he* turned red *in the face.*
> **2. (adj)** blushing as a result of extreme embarrassment; often used with the verbs to *be, become, get,* and *turn* ♦ *He* got red *in the face when I asked about the broken window, so I know he did it.* ♦ *My boss* became red *in the face when I criticized her.*

see red

> **(v)** to be extremely angry ♦ *I* saw red *when I came home and found the house such a mess after I'd cleaned it yesterday.*

paint the town red

to go out and have a fantastic evening of fun and entertainment; enjoy nightlife
♦ *On my 40th birthday, we went out and* painted the town red.

red carpet

(n, adj) special or royal welcome and attention. Alludes to the red carpet that is rolled out for royalty or dignitaries to walk on at special events; often phrased as *the red carpet treatment* or *roll out the red carpet.* ♦ *You sure gave us the* red carpet *treatment when we came to visit. Thank you.* ♦ *I'm not expecting you to roll out the* red carpet; *I just need a place to sleep for the night.*

red tape

(adj) excessive bureaucratic rules and regulations that often cause long delays; often expressed as *to get caught up in red tape* ♦ *There was so much* red tape *involved in trying to get our business loan, we thought we'd never get it.*

in the red

to have a negative balance in one's account; refers to red ink used to show a negative balance or money that is owed ♦ *Your account is* in the red. *You need to pay the balance due.*

[See also *in the black* later in this chapter.]

catch someone red-handed

to catch someone in an illicit act, like committing a crime or being sneaky and deceptive ♦ *Ah ha! I* caught you red-handed *taking my favorite shirt. Put it back; you didn't ask, and you can't borrow it!*

Blue

While some idioms with *red* imply getting more blood to the face, some idioms that use *blue* imply just the opposite — less blood to the face or a lack of oxygen. Sometimes the word *blue* means sad, melancholy, or depressed. The following idioms express some of these conditions, or have other meanings.

turn blue

(v) to be extremely cold; to have extreme difficulty breathing as a result of choking or coughing, or have trouble catching one's breath because of laughter. This may literally refer to becoming blue from cold temperatures, lack of

circulation, or lack of oxygen. ♦ *It's so cold outside today. I'm* turning blue!
♦ *That comedian made us laugh so hard we were* turning blue.

talk until one is blue in the face

to talk without ceasing; to talk a lot, often in an effort to convince someone of something. Alludes to passing out from a lack of oxygen; often linked with the verb *argue.* ♦ I talked until I was blue in the face, *but she refuses to listen to my advice.* ♦ *You can* argue until you're blue in the face, *but we're not going to buy you a car.*

blue

(adj) sad, melancholy, or depressed; often phrased as *feel blue* ♦ *Why do you look so* blue? *What's wrong?* ♦ *He's been* feeling *pretty* blue *since his relationship ended.*

the blues

(n) sadness, melancholy, or depression; often phrased *have the blues or get the blues* ♦ *I don't know why, but I just* have the blues *today.* ♦ *Cold weather always gives me* the blues.

sing the blues

(v) to feel sad, melancholy, or regretful, often about lost love, but also other situations that cause regret; usually said in the continuous form (*singing*) ♦ *Man, since my girlfriend left, I've been* singing the blues. ♦ *Chris, if you don't start studying for your exams you're going to be* singing the blues. ***Note:*** This idiom alludes to *blues music,* also called *the blues*—a type of African-American folk music and jazz that's characterized by a melancholy beat and a focus on mournful events.

talk a blue streak

to talk without ceasing, to talk a lot. Alludes to creating a streak of lightning from talking so fast and continuously. ♦ *That woman can* talk a blue streak. *Once she starts it's impossible to get her to stop.*

blue hair

(n) an elderly woman whose hair dye makes her hair turn a blue shade ♦ *Did you see all the* blue hairs *playing the slot machines in Las Vegas?* ♦ *Everyone came to the reunion, from infants to the* blue hairs.

blue-collar

> **(adj)** describes a person who does factory work or manual labor and traditionally wears a blue work shirt or blue coveralls with a blue collar; also *blue-collar job* and *blue-collar neighborhood* ♦ *Our neighborhood was all* blue-collar *workers.* ♦ Blue-collar *jobs are declining while public service jobs are on the increase.*

[See *white-collar* and *pink-collar* later in this chapter.]

true blue

> **(adj)** very loyal, staunch, and trustworthy ♦ *As a friend, she's* true blue. *You can always depend on her.*

once in a blue moon

> very rarely, not often. Refers to the rare second full moon in a month, called a *blue moon.* ♦ *They see her only* once in a blue moon; *they wish it were more often.* ♦ *My family rarely took vacations — only* once in a blue moon.

out of the blue

> comes completely unexpectedly and often suddenly. Alludes to something dropping suddenly out of the sky; also phrased *out of the clear blue sky* and *out of nowhere* ♦ *We got a call* out of the blue *from an old college friend. It was a wonderful and unexpected surprise.* ♦ *I don't know where I got that idea — it just came out of the clear blue sky.*

Yellow

Yellow isn't used often in idioms. The idiom below is the only usage:

yellow *or* yellow-bellied

> cowardly and afraid. This idiom has a slightly outdated feel to it, as it's often associated with old cowboy movies. ♦ *Are you going to fight me or are you* yellow? ♦ *He's a* yellow-bellied *coward to leave her with three kids.*

Green

The color green, of course, is associated with nature. This leads to some of its idiomatic uses.

have a green thumb

to have a skill or talent for growing plants easily and successfully ♦ *My mother has such a green thumb. Her plants always look so healthy.*

a green

(n) an environmentalist; more specifically, a member of the political party called the Green Party, which champions environmental causes ♦ *We greens want to see an environmental president elected.*

green

(adj) naive, inexperienced ♦ *These first-year students are still green. They hardly know their way around the campus.*

get the green light

to get approval to go ahead with a plan or project. Refers to the color green on a traffic light signaling one to go. ♦ *We finally got the green light on our home loan, so we can buy the house.*

green around the gills

sick; nauseated ♦ *After an hour on the boat I was really green around the gills.* **Note:** Gills is an old word for the area around the mouth.

green with envy

envious, desiring someone else's possessions or good fortune; often said lightly as a way of congratulations ♦ *Man, I'm green with envy about your trip to Europe.* ♦ *You got a huge raise?! Everyone will be green with envy.*

Pink

Idioms that use *pink* tend to be positive.

in the pink

in good physical condition and healthy. Refers to the healthy pink skin tone of light-skinned people. ♦ *He was sick for awhile, but he's back in the pink again.*

tickled pink

pleased; delighted ♦ *She was tickled pink to get a cell phone for her birthday.*

pink-collar

> **(adj)** describes jobs such as secretary or salesclerk that are typically held by women. Refers to pink as a feminine color; also *pink-collar job* and *pink-collar worker.* ♦ *When we were young the only jobs available to women were* pink-collar jobs.

[See also *blue-collar* and *white-collar* in other parts of this chapter.]

Brown

There are just a few idioms that use the color brown.

brown-bag it

> to bring one's lunch from home to eat at work. Refers to the standard brown paper lunch bag. Someone who brings such a lunch is a *brown-bagger.* ♦ *Until I get my paycheck, I'm* brown-bagging it; *no expensive lunches out for me.* ♦ *You can save money if you* brown-bag it *every day.*

brown-nose

> **(v)** to seek favor or approval by showing too great a willingness to obey or serve someone ♦ *I'm not going to* brown-nose *the boss, though some people in the office do.* ♦ *He* brown-nosed *his way into a better position.* **Note:** This is considered a very crude expression.

brownie points

> credit for doing good deeds. Refers to points or credit earned for achievements by girls in the Brownies, the youngest group of Girl Scouts; often phrased *to earn brownie points.* ♦ *You definitely got some* brownie points *for helping me yesterday.* ♦ *She's just trying to* earn brownie points *with the teacher by helping to straighten the classroom.*

[See the opposite of *brownie points*, *black mark*, later in this chapter.]

Black

Although many idioms with *black* have a negative connotation, others simply allude to darkness or have a positive meaning.

go black

1. to become unconscious ♦ *The last thing I remember was bumping my head, then everything* went black.
2. to lose electrical power, specifically the lights ♦ *When the earthquake hit, the whole town* went black.

black hole

a place where lost things go. Alludes to a region in the universe of such intense gravitational pull, not even light can escape. ♦ *Well, we lost another sock in the* black hole *of the dryer.* ♦ *This car keeps breaking down. Repairing it is like pouring money down a* black hole!

in the black

to be financially sound, owing no money; to have a positive, not a negative balance on one's accounts. Refers to the black ink used to show a positive balance. ♦ *We've managed to keep this company* in the black *even during difficult economic times.*

[See *in the red* earlier in this chapter.]

black eye

1. an eye that is bruised black (and blue or purple) from being hit or injured ♦ *Hey, you have a* black eye. *Who hit you?* ♦ *I got a* black eye *from running into a door.*
2. a disgrace or discredit; something that attracts unwanted negative attention ♦ *When our vice president was arrested for drunken driving, it was a* black eye *for the whole company.* ♦ *Missing the important meeting because he was playing golf gave him a* black eye *in the view of management.*

little black book

a book of phone numbers, particularly numbers of women or men one might call for a date. Refers to a small black address book. ♦ *She's got a* little black book *full of guys' names.* ♦ *Hey man, you got any girls in your little* black book *for me?*

black gold

oil. Refers to the black color and the high value (like gold) of oil. ♦ *Tankers carrying millions of tons of* black gold *go in and out of this port every day.*

black mark

an unfavorable comment or item on one's record, an indication of wrongdoing or failure; can be used jokingly ♦ *If you don't want any* black marks, *then don't be late to work.* ♦ *Oh, you forgot to put some milk in my coffee. That's one* black mark *against you!*

[See the opposite of *black mark, brownie points,* earlier in this chapter.]

black mood

a bad or depressed mood; an irritable mood ♦ *Gee, you're in a* black mood. *What's the problem?* ♦ *I don't even try to talk to her when she's in such a* black mood.

the black sheep

the least-respectable member of a family or group; a family member who does not meet with the family's expectations. This expression can be used seriously or lightly. ♦ *Jim was called* the black sheep *of the family because he hadn't become a doctor like his brothers.* ♦ *In our family, I was considered* the black sheep *because I never had a steady job.* **Note:** This idiom alludes to the wool of black sheep being less valuable.

Gray

gray area

(n) something that is not clearly defined, where room exists for ambivalence or disagreement ♦ *How to handle teenage criminals is really a* gray area. *The laws are unclear.* ♦ *Education theory may seem black and white, but there are a lot of variables and* gray areas.

[See the opposite of *gray area, black and white,* later in this chapter.]

gray matter

(n) the brain. Refers to the gray color of brain tissue. ♦ *You have to use your* gray matter *if you want to succeed in life.* ♦ *Okay everyone, use your* gray matter *and try to figure out the answer to this question.*

gray hairs

(n) elderly people, old people with gray hair; can be impolite if said in a derogatory context ♦ *This charity is owned and operated totally by* gray hairs. ♦ *I go to the Senior Center to enjoy the company of all the old* gray hairs *like myself.*

White

White is often used as a metaphor for goodness and innocence, or for appearing to be good or innocent, though not necessarily being good in reality.

lily white (adj)

1. to be very innocent, pure, and delicate; to act as if one is innocent ♦ *She's not as* lily white *as she seems. Away from work she's pretty wild.*
2. to be predominately composed of people of Anglo-Saxon or northern European descent ♦ *This town is just too* lily white *for me; I prefer a more cultural and ethnic mix of people.*

whitewash

(adj) to cover up and hide faults; to make something falsely appear favorable. Alludes to using a light watery coat of white paint to cover something. ♦ *Don't* whitewash *the story. Tell me the truth.* ♦ *The government tried to* whitewash *their involvement in the scandal, but we all know what really happened.*

white-collar

(adj) refers to professionals and office personnel who traditionally wear a white dress shirt to work; also *white-collar job* and *white-collar neighborhood*
♦ *I'm looking for a* white-collar job. *I don't want to do manual labor forever.*
♦ White-color jobs *have decreased by 5% this year.*

white as a ghost (*or* sheet)

1. having a very pale complexion from fright or illness; generally used to describe people with light skin tone ♦ *You kids were* white as ghosts *after watching that horror film.* ♦ *I can see that you're sick. You're* white as a sheet.
2. very light or pale skin tone ♦ *Look at me, I'm as* white as a sheet! *I need to get some sun.*

white lie

(n) a small "harmless" lie that is told to avoid hurting or offending someone; often called *a little white lie* ♦ *I didn't want to hurt her feelings so I told a little* white lie *and said I liked her new hair style.* ♦ *Admit it. Everyone tells* white lies *sometimes.*

Golden

Idioms that use *gold* tend to refer to things that are of tremendous value.

golden anniversary

the 50th anniversary of one's wedding day ♦ *We celebrated my grandparents'* golden *wedding* anniversary *with all the relatives.*

golden handcuffs

refers to the financial benefits that an employee will lose if he or she resigns; the benefits are like handcuffs keeping the employee from leaving ♦ *I can't afford to leave the company. The* golden handcuffs *are keeping me there.*

golden handshake

a big or generous retirement package; sometimes offered to encourage employees to retire early ♦ *Our company is offering* golden handshakes *to some of us. I may accept and retire early.*

golden parachute

a big or generous severance package to executives in the event that a merger or other situation causes dismissal ♦ *He has a* golden parachute, *so he's not worried about the mergers.*

golden opportunity

a valuable opportunity; an opportunity that may not come again ♦ *This job is a* golden opportunity *to do what you've always wanted to do.*

the golden rule

(n) any fundamental or primary rule; also the golden rule from the Bible, Matthew 7:12, Luke 6:31 "do unto others as you would have them do unto you" ♦ *The* golden rule *of teaching is always stay calm and in control.* ♦ *If you live by the* golden rule *you will never need to feel guilty about mistreating someone.*

Silver

silver anniversary

the 25th anniversary of one's wedding day ♦ *We'd like you to help us celebrate our* silver anniversary *next month.*

silver lining

> a positive or hopeful side to an otherwise bad situation; short for "every cloud has its *silver lining*" ♦ *Being laid off may have a* silver lining. *You could find a more interesting job.*

born with a silver spoon in one's mouth

> born into a wealthy family; being accustomed to having wealth and privilege ♦ *He has no understanding of poverty or struggle. He was* born with a silver spoon in his mouth.

Multicolored

black and white

> very clearly defined; not vague; seen as right or wrong; also *get it down in black and white,* meaning to get something confirmed on paper, in writing ♦ *He's very opinionated and sees everything in* black and white. ♦ *It's not a* black-and-white *issue. I really don't know what to do!* ♦ *Don't rely on a verbal contract. Get it all down in* black and white.

black and blue

> badly bruised, referring to the dark blue and purple color of bruises ♦ *After I fell off the horse, I was* black and blue *for weeks.*

the red, white, and blue

> the American flag; refers to the colors of the American flag and implies patriotism ♦ *Many war veterans display* the red, white, and blue *in front of their homes on Veterans' Day.*

Color

While this use isn't strictly idiomatic, you should know that *colorful* can mean lively or even scandalous, as in "My Uncle Harry has been a professional baseball player, a bartender, and a lawyer — and he's been married eight times! He's had a *colorful* life." *Colorful* can also be a polite way of saying that someone's language is foul: "When she gets mad, watch out! She can use some pretty *colorful* language."

Here are some expressions with the word *color:*

local color

(n) attractions and points of interest, including unique individuals of a specific local area ♦ *We like to drive into small towns and walk down the main street to see some* local color. ♦ *Tom Scribner, the old guy who played music on a saw, was part of that town's* local color.

off color

(adj) slightly crude or vulgar ♦ *She doesn't like to hear* off-color *jokes.* ♦ *It was an interesting story, but too* off color *for the kids to hear.*

show one's true colors

to reveal one's true character and loyalties ♦ *In a crisis, people often* show their true colors.

with flying colors

with easy and great success; with honors or distinction; generally said about tests ♦ *She passed her exams* with flying colors!

CHAPTER 15

NUMBER IDIOMS

Some idiomatic expressions use numbers to convey meaning. The expressions in this chapter use numbers from one to ten; also one hundred, one thousand, and one million; the ordinal numbers, first, second, and so on; and a few imaginary numbers, such as "umpteenth."

One, Two, Three

The cardinal numbers from one to ten are commonly used in idioms, as are numbers that can be divided by ten — twenty, thirty, and so on. *Zero* is also used.

ZERO

Zero is used to mean none or no, and is often followed by a noun, as in "We've had *zero* rain this winter." Here are some common *zero* idioms:

zero in

> to focus or concentrate hard on something; to identify specifically ♦ *Now that we have* zeroed in *on the problem, we can figure out how to solve it.* ♦ *Great athletes know how to* zero in *when they need to.*

zero tolerance

> to have no patience for an issue or problem or wrongdoing; to refuse to tolerate or accept ♦ *The new laws reflect* zero tolerance *for drunken driving.* ♦ *I have* zero tolerance *for insults or teasing in my classroom.*

ONE

The number *one* is used more often in idioms than any other number.

The Best

These expressions mean the best, the top; top quality:

>**number one** ♦ *Our team is* number one. ♦ *Dad, You're* number one!
>**A-one** ♦ *This car is in* A-one *condition.* ♦ *The fruits and vegetables in that market are always* A-one *quality.*

One and *One Together*

These expressions both use the number *one* twice:

one to one

>**(adv)** describes direct communication between two people, often to resolve a conflict. Almost always used with the verbs *talk* or *discuss*. ♦ *Let's talk* one to one *about this problem.* ♦ *I'm sure that we can resolve our disagreement if we sit down and talk* one to one.

one on one

>**(adj, adv)** describes a direct competition between two people. Often used to talk about competition that generally has more than just two people, or that begins with more than two people. ♦ *This volleyball game is just* one on one, *you and me.* ♦ *My brother and I used to play a lot of basketball* one on one.

One at a Time

The following two expressions mean to follow in succession:

one by one

>**(adv)** to go individually, one after the other; this idiom can imply tedium or slowness ♦ *They recounted the ballots* one by one. ♦ *One by one, the graduates went up to the podium to receive their diplomas.*

one at a time

>**(adv)** used when people or things are taking turns or waiting in line; implies that something must be finished before another similar thing can be started ♦ *I can't understand any of you when you all talk at once. Please speak* one at a time. ♦ *I read just* one *book* at a time, *but my wife is usually reading several books at any given time.*

From the Beginning

When you use the expression *from day one,* that means that a condition or situation has existed right from the start, from the first day or beginning. Here are some examples:

- *I've loved this class* from day one.
- *She was uncomfortable with that doctor* from day one, *so she found a different doctor.*
- *He's done exceptionally well on this job* from day one.

Grammar Note: If the condition or situation still exists at the time of speaking, use the present perfect tense with this expression. If the condition or situation is finished, use the simple past tense.

The expression *back to square one* means that one is back to the starting point of a project, task, or enterprise, and must begin again; one must start over because of a problem. It implies that any progress that was made has been lost. It can also mean that one needs to rethink how to do or solve something.

- *The experiment didn't work, so we're* back to square one.
- *After two weeks at his new job, the company closed down, so he's* back to square one *looking for work.*

Totally Unique

The following expressions say that something or someone is unique, rare, and unmatched in quality:

one of a kind

unique, individual, nothing else like it; special, of rare value ♦ *This native basket design is* one of a kind. *You won't ever find another like it.* ♦ *She's* one of a kind. *There will never be another woman like her.*

one in a million

very rare and exceptional, extraordinary; the very best ♦ *Mom, you're* one in a million. *You're the best!* ♦ *This pearl is* one in a million. *It's huge.*

Just One

The following idioms are all two-word adjectives that are connected with a hyphen. They are used to convey that there is only one aspect or possibility:

one-sided

to favor one side or one person and not the other; to be unfair or prejudiced. Said of an argument that is unfair or has only one point. ◆ *The new tax cuts are very* one-sided *in favor of big business.* ◆ *This seems to be a* one-sided *argument; there's really no opposition to it.*

one-track mind

a mind that is focused on only one line of thought or action. Often said of a person who thinks constantly of sex. ◆ *Man, you have a* one-track mind. *Do you ever think of anything besides sex?* ◆ *When she gets interested in something, she has a* one-track *mind. She puts all her attention on it.*

one-way ticket

1. a plane, bus, or train ticket for one direction only, not for the return trip ◆ *I bought a* one-way ticket *because I'm not sure when I'll be returning.*
2. an action or situation guaranteed to bring a certain outcome or consequence ◆ *Taking drugs is a* one-way ticket *to nowhere, except trouble.* ◆ *Her exceptional musical talent was her* one-way ticket *to success.*

[See *round-trip ticket* in Chapter 7.]

A Few Other Idioms with *One*

one too many

a polite way to say that someone is drunk; implies that the last drink was the one that caused the person to become drunk ◆ *Hey, you've had* one too many. *You can't drive home; I'll take you.* ◆ *Man, I feel terrible. I had* one too many *last night.*

one up

1. (v) to have an advantage or lead over someone; to defeat or embarrass someone by being faster or better. Often put in the passive form, *to be one-upped by someone.* The noun form is *one-upmanship.* ◆ *The two brothers tried to* one up *each other in everything.* ◆ *I have some pretty flowers in my garden, but you've definitely* one-upped *me with your beautiful tulips.*

2. (adj) to be a little better, faster; to be ahead by a small but important amount ◆ *Hey, I'm* one up *on you. I finished all my homework, and I can go play. You still have some to do.* **Note:** This expression can also be used sarcastically to mean a negative lead over someone: "Well, I guess I'm *one up on you.* I've been married three times, and you've been married only twice!"

[See *have one foot in the grave* in Chapter 13.]

Two

If you *put two and two together,* you can see the obvious and logical conclusion by looking at the facts. For example

- ♦ *If he* put two and two together, *he'd see that his bad attitude prevented him from getting the promotion.*
- ♦ *She's engaged to Shawn, but I've seen her kissing Tom. It's not hard to* put two and two together.

Two Faces

These expressions are used to describe a person who deceives or lies:

two-faced

> **(adj)** deceitful, hypocritical ♦ *What a* two-faced *liar! He asked me to help him pay his rent, and now I find out that he has plenty of money in the bank.*

two-timer

> **(adj)** a person who has two lovers or has two boyfriends or girlfriends at the same time. The verb form is *to two-time someone.* ♦ *She's a* two-timer, *man. Can't you see that?* ♦ *Don't get involved with him. He'll* two-time *you like he has all his other girlfriends.*

Two People

These expressions almost always refer to two people:

two of a kind

> two very similar individuals; two people who are very much alike; a pair. Also used to describe things. ♦ *My aunt and uncle are really* two of a kind. *They're perfect together.* ♦ *You guys are* two of a kind. *You both love Jamaican Dub poetry.*

two's company, three's a crowd

> a saying that means a third person ruins the privacy of a romantic couple; that three people is too many; or that a third person spoils the quality interaction that two people can have together. Often just shortened to *two's company* or just *three's a crowd.* ♦ *Let's just have a private dinner tonight.* Two's company. . . .
> ♦ *Thanks for the invitation, but you two go ahead without me.* Three's a crowd.

it takes two (to tango)

> a saying that means that one person alone can't have a disagreement; that generally both sides or people have fault in a disagreement or argument; that two people or both sides must be willing to cooperate to resolve a disagreement or work out a compromise ♦ *You can't blame everything on him.* It takes two to tango, *you know.* ♦ *When I broke up with my girlfriend, I told her* "It takes two."

Two Things

The following expressions refer literally or figuratively to two things:

two bits

> **(n)** (slang) 25 cents; a small sum ♦ *When I was a kid we could see a movie for* two bits. ♦ *This rake is not worth* two bits; *I just bought it and it's already falling apart.*

two-bit

> **(adj)** of inferior or cheap quality ♦ *What kind of* two-bit *restaurant is this? I'm leaving.* ♦ *No thanks! I don't want to buy that old* two-bit *stereo of yours. I want a quality sound system.*

two left feet

> clumsy on one's feet ♦ *I can't dance at all. I have* two left feet.

feel like two cents

> to feel worthless, ashamed, or of little value, usually because of a wrongdoing or an embarrassment ♦ *I'm sorry that I hurt your feelings; I really* feel like two cents. ♦ *The kids teased him constantly and made him* feel like two cents.

one's two cents

> one's opinion or thoughts on a matter ♦ *If you want* my two cents, *I think you should take the job.* ♦ *Nobody asked for* your two cents, *so keep quiet!*

in two shakes (of a lamb's tail)

> very soon, very quickly. Alludes to the way lambs quickly flick their tails. Often said to someone who is waiting for something. ♦ *I'll be with you to take your order* in two shakes of a lamb's tail. ♦ *When I said, "There's homemade ice cream," the kids were here* in two shakes.

THREE

Here are a few expressions with the word *three:*

the three R's

the basics of education; literally refers to reading, 'riting, and 'rithmetic (reading, writing, and arithmetic) ♦ *Schools offer* the three R's, *but other classes like art and language have been cut due to lack of funds.*

three-ring circus

complete confusion and chaos. Alludes to the three separate circus acts happening at the same time in a circus show that features three rings or stages. ♦ *Growing up with eight brothers and sisters was like living in a* three-ring circus.

three strikes and you're out

means "You have only three chances to succeed. If you fail the third time, you can't try again." Alludes to a rule in baseball. ♦ *You only have three chances to pass the qualifying exam.* Three strikes and you're out.

[See *three sheets to the wind* in Chapter 7.]

FOUR

The following expressions use the number *four:*

the four corners of the earth

the farthest points on the earth; all over the entire earth ♦ *People came from* the four corners of the earth *to participate in the World Peace Conference.* ♦ *He's traveled to* the four corners of the earth, *but he loves his hometown best.*

four-letter word

a vulgar or obscene word, often four letters long in American English. Also called a *bad* or *dirty word.* ♦ *Her speech is filled with* four-letter words; *it's obnoxious!* ♦ *He taught his little brother to say all the worst* four-letter words.

on all fours

down on one's hands and knees. Refers to having four limbs on the floor. Often put as *down on all fours.* ♦ *He likes to get down* on all fours *and play with his grandkids.* ♦ *We were down* on all fours *looking for his lost contact lens.*

FIVE

The following slang expressions with the number five refer to a hand-slapping gesture used in greeting, congratulations, and celebration. *Five* makes reference to the five fingers of the hand.

> **give me five (gimme five)**
> **high five**

Give me five (often pronounced *gimme five*) is a request to slap the hand of another person, and is usually accompanied by holding one's hand out, palm up, to be slapped. When you *high-five* someone, you slap his or her raised palm (with your hand held high). Here are some examples of these two common expressions:

- ♦ *Hey, we fixed the computer!* Gimme five, *buddy!*
- ♦ *Janie, you got 100% on your spelling test?!* Gimme five!
- ♦ *It's tradition to* high-five *all the members of the opposing team after a game.*

SIX

six of one, half a dozen of the other

> means "It doesn't matter, there is no difference between two choices." Refers to the fact that six and a half dozen are the same quantity. ♦ *Well, it's really* six of one, half dozen of the other. *We can leave today and return on Saturday, or leave tomorrow and return on Sunday.*

at sixes and sevens

> chaotic, disorganized, confused ♦ *Everything was* at sixes and sevens *on registration day. No one knew where to go or how to register.* ♦ *Our flight was so delayed that we were all* at sixes and sevens *trying to get connecting flights and find our luggage.*

six feet under

> dead and buried. Alludes to the traditional depth of a buried coffin. ♦ *He won't quit drinking until he's* six feet under.

EIGHT AND NINE

behind the eight ball

> in a difficult, awkward, or unlucky situation; to be stuck or in trouble. Alludes to a difficult situation in the game of billiards. ♦ *They've got me* behind the

eight ball. *I don't approve of the project, but if I don't agree to do it, I may lose my job.*

on cloud nine

happy, blissfully content ♦ *When all their children and grandchildren came for the holidays, they were* on cloud nine. ♦ *I'm* on cloud nine! *I've just been accepted to acting school.*

dressed to the nines

dressed elegantly, dressed up for a special occasion ♦ *Everyone at the opera is* dressed to the nines.

the whole nine yards

the whole, complete thing, everything that is relevant. May have once referred to the total yards of fabric needed to make a suit or complete set of sails. ♦ *We gave her the biggest birthday party you could imagine: a huge cake, flowers, decorations, a hundred guests, music, speeches,* the whole nine yards. ♦ *Before they hired him, they put him through* the whole nine yards — *physical exam, blood test, drug test, background check, and more.*

TEN

ten to one

a very high probability that something will (or won't) happen. The statement "Ten to one that I get a date with her" is similar to "I bet a get a date with her" or "I think I will get a date with her." ♦ *You've studied so hard for that class,* ten to one *you'll get an A.* ♦ *Those kids are so spoiled.* Ten to one *they won't even thank us for the gifts we sent.*

top-ten

the ten best, most popular, most important things. Often used by radio stations to announce the ten most frequently requested songs. Also popularized by talk show host Dave Letterman with his humorous top ten lists. ♦ *The computer company created a list of the* top-ten *reasons to buy a new computer.* ♦ *He's one of the* top-ten *baseball players of all time.* ♦ *Coming up next, we count down the* top-ten *songs in the country.*

TWENTY

Everyone seems to have *twenty-twenty hindsight.* That means that we can often see clearly and perfectly (with 20/20 vision) what we should have done or said in the past (in hindsight or looking back). We may be muddled, confused, and unclear about our present condition, but *hindsight is always 20/20. 20/20* can also be written *twenty-twenty.* Here are some examples:

♦ *I should have listened to my parents when I was younger, but* hindsight is always 20/20.
♦ *Don't be so hard on yourself about it. We all have* twenty-twenty hindsight.

FORTY AND FIFTY

forty winks

> (n) a short nap ♦ *If I can get* forty winks, *I'll feel refreshed.*

fifty-fifty

> (adv, adj) shared evenly; equal. Also said as *go fifty-fifty on. 50-50* is an acceptable way to write this idiom. ♦ *My housemate and I share the housework* fifty-fifty. ♦ *We always go* fifty-fifty *on the household expenses.* ♦ *We agreed on a* 50-50 *split of the profits.*

ONE HUNDRED, ONE THOUSAND, ONE MILLION

Expressions with one hundred, one thousand, and one million are always used as exaggerations and hyperbole.

One Hundred

one hundred and one reasons

> a lot of reasons or excuses, either good or bad; also said *a hundred and one*
> ♦ *He'll give you* one hundred and one reasons *why he can't find a job, but the truth is, he's just lazy.* ♦ *There are* a hundred and one reasons *why you should avoid getting into debt.*

if I live to be a hundred

> an expression used to indicate surprise or resignation, meaning "I'll never do or understand something." Often said without completing the idea. ♦ *Why do*

kids have piercing all over their faces? If I live to be a hundred, *I'll never under-stand it.* ♦ *Richard: Did you see that person with the pink hair? Jim:* If I live to be a hundred. . . .

One Thousand

a thousand apologies

means "I'm very sorry." Formal, or sometimes said sarcastically. ♦ A thousand apologies. *I didn't mean to bump into you. Are you all right?*

if I've told you once, I've told you a thousand times

an expression showing exasperation at having to repeatedly remind or advise someone of the obvious. Often said simply as *I've told you a thousand times.*
♦ If I've told him once, I've told him a thousand times *not to leave his wet towels on the floor.* ♦ I've told those kids a thousand times *to wipe their feet before coming in.*

A Million

thanks a million

means "Thanks very much" ♦ Thanks a million *for all of your help.*

look like a million dollars (*or* bucks)

to look fantastic, beautiful, sexy ♦ *Wow! You* look like a million bucks!

a (*or* one) chance in a million

a very small chance or no chance at all that something will happen ♦ *Getting a part in the movie was* a chance in a million, *and she got it!* ♦ *I know it's* one chance in a million, *but it's no chance at all if I don't try.*

never in a million years

means "absolutely never!" Sometimes said without finishing the sentence.
♦ Never in a million years *will I understand why anyone would want a tattoo.*
Grammar Note: Because this expression begins with the negative *never,* the subject and verb are reversed in the main clause of the sentence, as in the example.

[See *one in a million* earlier in this chapter under "One"; see also *feel like a million* in Chapter 4.]

First, Second, Third . . .

The ordinal numbers, *first*, *second*, and so on, are commonly used in idioms. Idioms with *first* and *second* are most frequently used.

FIRST

The word *first* in idioms generally refers to either the beginning or the first one.

First Things First

These expressions refer to the first or initial thing:

at first

> initially, before something changed. This expression is almost always followed or preceded by a clause beginning with *but, however, although,* and so on. ♦ *At first we thought he had the flu, but it was a more serious virus.* ♦ *I was really nervous around horses* at first, *but now I love them and I ride everyday.*

first things first

> a saying that means to take care of the important things first before doing other things; to do things in a logical sequence ♦ *We'll read a bedtime story, but* first things first. *Go brush your teeth.* ♦ *I want to get a car, but* first things first. *I need a driver's license.*

first come, first served

> a saying that means whoever arrives first will get the first choice or service. Often said to mean "I advise you to come early." ♦ *There is no reserve seating for this event. So if you want a good seat, it's* first come, first served.

Primarily, Most Important

These expressions are used to introduce the first or primary item of discussion. The idiom *first and foremost* means the primary and most important thing.

> **first off** ♦ First off, *let me thank everyone for joining our forum tonight.*
> **first of all** ♦ First of all, *we'll discuss your grades and then your attendance problem.*
> **first and foremost** ♦ First and foremost, *your job is to help customers.*

[See *first base* in Chapter 8; see also *firsthand* in Chapter 13.]

SECOND

Idioms using *second* can be about good things . . . or not-so-good things.

When Second Is Very Good

second to none

> the best, not second best; means "nothing is better" ♦ *Her artistry is* second to none. *She's the best choreographer of this era.* ♦ *We want our product to be* second to none.

second nature

> a skill, behavior, or habit that seems innate because one has practiced for a long time or has a natural talent for it ♦ *Snowboarding is* second nature *to Dana. She's been doing it since she was four years old.* ♦ *Managing all the kids in the classroom is just* second nature *to an experienced teacher.*

second wind

> a second burst of energy or renewed ability to finish a task or effort; generally put as *get a second wind* ♦ *I was getting tired, but then I got a* second wind *and stayed up until midnight.* ♦ *The team was playing badly, but they got their* second wind *and scored a goal.*

When Second Is Not Very Good

second rate

> of poor quality, less than satisfactory ♦ *I never do business with that* second-rate *operation.* ♦ *Don't buy that brand. It's really* second rate. **Note:** This idiom doesn't mean the same thing as *second best,* which is often a compliment meaning literally the second in quality or skill, right after the first or best: "Out of a thousand competitors, he was *second best.*"

second-class citizen

> a member of society who is treated as an inferior, and often denied full rights and privileges ♦ *When I arrived in Utah with my Southern accent, I was treated like a* second-class citizen. ♦ *Women in many parts of the world are fighting to change laws and social attitudes that treat them as* second-class citizens.

play second fiddle

> to accept a less important or a subordinate role to someone. Alludes to the position of second violin in an orchestra. ♦ *Being the eldest child in the family,*

Tom wasn't used to playing second fiddle *to anyone.* ♦ *It's hard to* play second fiddle *to someone who is less competent than you are.*

Second Thoughts

The following expressions are used when people change their decision about something or have a different idea after their initial idea:

have second thoughts

> have doubts about a prior decision ♦ *I'm* having second thoughts *about buying that used car.* ♦ *After her first year in college, she started* having second thoughts *about whether she belonged in school.*

on second thought

> said when one changes one's mind ♦ *I was going to order the lasagna, but* on second thought, *I'll have the spaghetti.* ♦ *I thought I knew how to get there, but* on second thought, *maybe I should look at a map.*

[See *seconds* in Chapter 3; see also *secondhand* in Chapter 13.]

THIRD

Three seems to be the key number for luck. The expression *third time's a charm* means that on the third try, one is often lucky. Here are some examples of this expression:

> ♦ *He's running for governor again. He didn't win the last two times, but* third time's a charm.
> ♦ *Okay, try to start this car again. Let's hope that* third time's a charm.

[See *three strikes and you're out* earlier in this chapter.]

Here are two more idioms with *third:*

the third degree

> interrogation; harsh questioning and possibly rough treatment to obtain information; usually put as *give someone the third degree* ♦ *My parents will give me* the third degree *if I come home too late.*

third world

> **(n, adj)** refers to undeveloped or developing countries; conditions or groups resembling the poverty and rural nature of third-world countries ♦ *Riding on* third-world *buses with goats and chickens is a unique experience.* ♦ *Many people seldom think of the* third world.

[See *third base* in Chapter 8.]

FIFTH, SIXTH, AND SEVENTH

A few idioms use the ordinal numbers *fifth*, *sixth*, and *seventh*:

fifth wheel

> the odd numbered or extra person, the single person in a group of couples. Often the *fifth wheel* is actually a third person, not a fifth person. ♦ *They always invite me to join them, but since I don't have a partner, I feel like a* fifth wheel.

sixth sense

> intuition, an innate or supernatural knowing; considered by some as another sense like sight, hearing, touch, taste, and smell ♦ *She has a* sixth sense *about people and knows who to trust or not trust.*

in seventh heaven

> delighted, overjoyed; very content ♦ *I'll be* in seventh heaven *if my photos are selected for publication in the book.* ♦ *Just give him a good book and a hot cup of tea, and he's* in seventh heaven.

[For other idioms with similar meaning to *in seventh heaven*, see *on cloud nine* earlier in this chapter.]

ELEVENTH

at the eleventh hour

> at the very last possible moment; almost too late; with very little time left ♦ *He finally started his science project* at the eleventh hour, *but there wasn't time to finish it.* ♦ *A lot of people mail their yearly tax returns* at the eleventh hour — *literally a few minutes before midnight on April 15.*

Nonsense Numbers

A few idioms use make-believe or invented numbers to imply a vast amount:

umpteen

> a great number of, very many; too numerous to count. Also said like an ordinal number, *umteenth*. ♦ *We have* umpteen *things to do to before we can leave on vacation.* ♦ *For the* umpteenth *time, no, you can't have a pet iguana.*

a gazillion

> a very large indefinite number ♦ *There were* a gazillion *little kids at the children's fair.* ♦ *There must have been* a gazillion *mosquitoes out today. I've got bites all over me!*

to the nth degree

> to the extreme; to a large degree ♦ *I don't like her. She's self-serving to the* nth *degree.* ♦ *The reception was elaborate to the nth degree. I've never seen such elegant decorations and gourmet food.*

Number Combinations

The idioms in this section use more than one number:

9 to 5 *or* **nine to five**

> the standard work day; a regular day job; a monotonous, humdrum job. Does not necessarily mean that a person works from 9:00 a.m. to 5:00 p.m. ♦ *Working* nine to five *was my father's life for 50 years.* ♦ *I like working for myself and setting my own hours. I'd go crazy in a* 9-to-5 *job.*

24-7 *or* **24/7**

> literally 24 hours a day, 7 days a week; all the time; for a very long amount of time ♦ *The main campus library is open* 24-7 *during final exam week.* ♦ *We've got to work* 24/7 *to finish these blueprints in time.*

CHAPTER 16

NEGATIVE WORD IDIOMS

Idioms that begin with negative words *no, none, not,* and *nothing* are very common in everyday speech. Some of them have similar meanings, like *no way, not a chance,* and *nothing doing,* which mean "Absolutely no!" Negative word phrases like *no problem, not at all,* and *think nothing of it* can be used in response to a thank you. Most of the expressions in this section, however, have their own unique meaning and usage.

No

The word *no* at the beginning of an idiom generally means not, as in *no fair* (not fair), or without, as in *no doubt* (without a doubt). The word *no* is used in most idioms before nouns (*no fool*) and adjectives (*no fair*). The following common idiomatic expressions are listed in alphabetical order:

(it's) no big deal

it's not important, not serious; it's nothing to worry about. Sometimes said in response to a request. ♦ *I cut my finger, but it's* no big deal. ♦ *Todd: Mom, I just spilled milk all over the floor. Mom:* No big deal; *just clean it up.* ♦ *Sure, I can help you move. It's* no big deal.

[See *no problem* later in this chapter.]

(it's) a no-brainer

it's easy, not hard to understand or figure out; it's the obvious solution; it doesn't take a lot of intelligence to understand ♦ *It's* a no-brainer: *More cars mean more pollution.* ♦ *Set your alarm earlier, and you won't be late to work. It's really* a no-brainer.

no buts about it

there is no doubt; it's decided; it is going to happen; you can't object or refuse the offer. Usually said when one offers a favor or gives a command and wants to stop the other person from objecting. This expression is similar to saying "I won't take no for an answer." ♦ No buts about it; *he should get the award. He has earned it.* ♦ *I said that I'm paying for everyone's dinner.* No buts about it, *so put away your money.* ♦ *You have no choice — you have to improve your grades.* No buts about it.

no can do

means "it's not possible"; "I can't (or won't) do it"; "I can't (or won't) make it happen" ♦ *He wants the report tomorrow, but* no can do. *I don't have all the data yet.* ♦ *Jan: Can you take care of my dog while I'm on vacation? Don: Sorry.* No can do. *I'll be gone that week too.*

no dice

it's not going to happen; it's been refused ♦ *We asked for an extension on our loan, but* no dice; *the bank won't give us an extension.* ♦ *I tried to buy some batteries for our flashlights, but* no dice. *The stores were sold out because of the storm.*

[See *no go* later in this chapter.]

no doubt

there is no doubt about it, very probably. Often used to introduce a news-worthy or controversial topic. Also said as a reply meaning "You are undoubt-edly right." ♦ No doubt *you've already heard the good news.* ♦ *Mary: They went surfing, but I heard that the waves are flat today, so they'll probably be back soon. Dan:* No doubt.

no end

1. (adv) a lot, a great deal ♦ *It rained* no end *last week.* ♦ *He loves that little dog* no end.
2. seemingly without limit, too large an amount to count or calculate. Said as *no end of; no end to.* ♦ *There's* no end *to the benefits of regular exercise.* ♦ *We've had* no end *of problems with our new car.*

(it's) no fair

it's not fair; not equitable; a complaint that something doesn't seem equitable or that someone has an advantage over another ♦ *It's* no fair! *She never has to do as many chores as I do.* ♦ *Hey* no fair! *You can't use the encyclopedia to find the answer!*

no go

it won't or can't happen. Also put as a *no go.* ♦ *After all of our preparation, the project is a* no go. ♦ *It's* no go. *The bad weather has forced us to cancel our plans.*

I'm No Angel!

The word *no* can be placed in front of a noun to mean what a person is not. For example, "I'm *no angel!*" means that a person has a side that's less than perfect. "I'm *no angel"* is similar to saying "I'm good, but I'm not perfect." "I'm *no fool"* is another common expression. The word *no,* in this context, basically means *not equal to.* The noun or pronoun doesn't have to be *I,* as the following expressions show:

♦ *She's* no fool; *she knows how to invest her money.*

♦ *Her son may be polite, but he's* no angel.

While *fool* and *angel* are the words most often used in this expression, the possibilities are almost endless. For example, you could convey that you don't cook especially well by saying "I'm *no chef."*

It's common to place the name of a famous person who is known for being excellent in a particular area after *no.* Here are some more examples:

♦ *I'm* no Tiger Woods, *but I like to play golf.* (This means "I'm not an expert golfer, but I like to play anyway.")

♦ *I can't believe they promoted him. He's* no Einstein. (This means "I'm surprised they promoted him, because he's not particularly smart.")

no good

1. spoiled or rotten; not good quality or character, said about a thing or a person ♦ *Someone forgot to put the milk away, and now it's* no good. ♦ *That movie was* no good; *a complete waste of money.* ♦ *He was* no good *and often spent time in jail.*
2. inadequate, unsatisfactory; unsuccessful. Often put as *to do no good.* ♦ *We complained to the supervisor about the problem, but it did* no good; *nothing has changed.* ♦ *It's* no good *trying to write a research paper in one night. You won't have enough time to do an adequate job.*

[See also *(it's) no use* later in this chapter.]

no hard feelings

there's no anger, resentment, or regret. Usually said as a way to forgive someone after resolving a problem or to let someone know that you don't feel any resentment. ♦ *Hey,* no hard feelings. *Okay? It was just a misunderstanding.* ♦ *I hope there will be* no hard feelings *if we don't invite everyone.*

No Fooling?

The expressions *no fooling, no kidding,* and *no lie* mean that the statement is indeed, a fact. Alternatively, they can also mean that the person isn't joking or lying. The expressions are often added to a statement or question that is surprising or possibly unbelievable. For example, "*No lie,* I won the scholarship!" or "I heard that they're getting married. *No fooling.*" Another common way to say that you are not lying or kidding is by saying *Would I lie to you?*

When said as a question, these expressions ask "Is it true?" or "Is it real?" They're often said to emphasize surprise. For example, "*No kidding?* You really won the scholarship? Congratulations!" or "*No lie?* They're getting married?"

Another use of these expressions is as a scornful acknowledgment of something obvious. For example, when discussing a test, Matt says "Man, that was a hard test!" and Lisa replies "*No kidding!* I probably failed it!"

no need

it's not necessary; it's useless; it won't change anything. Sometimes said as a polite response to someone's generosity, similar to "You shouldn't have (done it)." ♦ No need *to call me back tonight; I'll talk to you tomorrow.* ♦ *He brought a nice gift to our party, but there was* no need. ♦ *There's* no need *to get angry about it. That won't change the situation.*

no pain, no gain

without hard work or sacrifice, there won't be any rewards or success ♦ *I don't like to exercise, but I want to stay healthy, so* no pain, no gain. ♦ *Come on, you kids.* No pain, no gain. *Get back to your homework.*

(it's) no picnic

not fun; very unpleasant, but possibly necessary ♦ *Going to the dentist* is no picnic, *but it's necessary.* ♦ *Those long hot bus rides were* no picnic, *but it was a cheap way to travel.*

no problem *or* no sweat

it's no trouble; it causes no problems; it's easy. Often said in response to "Thank you" or to brag about one's abilities, as in the last example that follows. ♦ *Ann: Thanks for helping me. Sarah: Hey,* no problem. ♦ *Jack: I'm sorry to dump all my work on you, but I have to leave early today for a dental appointment. Elliot:* No problem, *I owe you a favor anyway.* ♦ *I can do 50 push-ups —* no sweat!

no question

there is no doubt about it; it's certain ♦ No question. *This is the best meal I've ever had.* ♦ *Son, I'll always be here for you,* no question *about it.*

no show

someone or something didn't come or arrive as expected. Usually said as *a no show.* ♦ *We waited for the speaker, but he was* a no show. ♦ *If we have any* no shows, *we can sell the tickets right before the performance.*

no siree

an emphasized no; absolutely no. Sometimes said as *no siree Bob.* ♦ No siree, *Eric. You're not going to use your father's car.* ♦ *Tim: Do you want to sell some of your old blues records? Forrest:* No siree, Bob. *I'm keeping those.*

(it's) no skin off my nose

it won't affect, bother, or embarrass me; I don't care ♦ *Devon: Hey, I saw your ex-girlfriend with Tom. Matt: I don't care who she sees. It's* no skin off my nose. ♦ *Lynn: They're thinking about relocating the district office. Joyce: Well, it's* no skin off my nose. *I work at home now.*

no sooner said than done

it happened (or will happen) soon after the request or suggestion. Often said as a response to a request, meaning "I'll do it immediately." ♦ *The kids are particularly helpful during the holidays. I asked them to clean their room, and it was* no sooner said than done. ♦ *Patricia: Could you help me put away the groceries? Jacob:* No sooner said than done!

no spring chicken

no longer young. Said about women more often than men. Generally intended to be slightly humorous, but may be considered impolite. ♦ *She's* no spring chicken, *but she sure can dance!* ♦ *We were* no spring chickens *when we met and fell in love.*

no strings attached

there are no conditions, restrictions, or obligations connected with the item or event in discussion ♦ *They're giving away CDs at the music store.* No strings attached. ♦ *He offered to help her buy a car,* no strings attached, *but she felt uncomfortable about accepting his money.*

No Such Animal and No Such Thing

Both *no such animal* and *no such thing* mean that there is nothing like the item that is mentioned; that there is nothing of that kind; that nothing similar exists. For example, "My grandmother wants to buy a manual typewriter not an electric one, but there's *no such animal* anymore." *No such thing* can also mean on the contrary, no, or absolutely not, as in "My 14-year-old daughter wants to go to an all-night party. I said, 'You'll do *no such thing!*'"

(it's) no use

1. it's impossible; it can't or didn't succeed ♦ It's no use! *I'll never figure out how to program this stupid remote control!* ♦ *With sandbags, they tried to stop the water from coming into their house, but* it was no use. *Their house flooded anyway.*
2. it's pointless; it serves no useful purpose ♦ It's no use *worrying about the economy. Worrying won't change anything.* ♦ It's no use *trying to talk to him when he's in a bad mood. Wait until later.*
Grammar Note: When the idiom *no use* is followed by a verb, the verb is in the gerund form (verb + -*ing*).

no way

absolutely no; it's not going to happen; it's not possible. This is sometimes said as *no way José*. ♦ No way! *You can't use my toothbrush. Are you crazy?* ♦ *My husband wants to rent out one of our bedrooms, but I said* "No way! *I like my privacy."*

(it's) no wonder

it's not a surprise; it's not at all unexpected. Also sometimes said as *small wonder*. ♦ No wonder *you're so tired, you've been rehearsing for the play every day for a month.* ♦ *James: Ted says his kids aren't getting any of his money when he dies. Felix: Well, it's no wonder. They never call him or come to visit.* ♦ *Jan: Did you know that Joyce sold five of her paintings? Lynn: It's no wonder, she's an excellent artist.*

no worries

there is nothing to worry about; don't worry; it doesn't cause problems
♦ *There's a lot of traffic, but* no worries; *we'll get to the concert in plenty of time.*
♦ *Annie: Thanks so much for your help — I'm sorry to bother you. Jake: No worries. I'm happy to help.*

None

The word *none* at the beginning of an idiom generally means not or not any, as in *none too soon.*

bar none

> without exception. Generally used with a superlative (the superlatives in the following sentences are in bold). ♦ Bar none, *that was the* **worst** *movie I've ever seen.* ♦ *She was* bar none *the* **most** *influential folk singer of the '60s.*

have none of it

> to not accept something; to disregard advice; to disallow or not permit something ♦ *Her kids tried to blame the dog for the mess, but she would* have none of it. ♦ *I warned him about investing his money in that company, but he would* have none of it. *Now he's lost everything.*

(it's) none of your business

> it doesn't concern you; it's private. Also sometimes said as *none of your concern.* Sometimes jokingly said as *none of your beeswax.* It is somewhat impolite. ♦ *He wanted to know where I live, but I said* "None of your business!" ♦ *I know it's* none of my business, *but I'm curious to know what they were arguing about.*

(it's) none other than

> specifically the person or thing being discussed; often someone notable or of interest, but also said jokingly about a friend or one's self ♦ *Hey look! It's* none other than *our old friend Jim.* ♦ *Guess who I saw at the event last night?* None other than *Faith Hill.*

none but the best

> only the best. Usually said of people. Also sometimes said as *none but the brightest* or *the smartest.* ♦ None but the *very* best *get into that university.* ♦ *They hire* none but the best *in genetic research.*

none the wiser

> unaware of something that is happening; unaware of something one should have learned ♦ *He was stealing from the company, and his boss was* none the wiser. ♦ *She seems to be* none the wiser *after her car accident; she's still driving too fast.*

None Too . . .

The words *none too* followed by an adjective mean not at all or not very, as in *none too happy, none too warm, none too friendly,* and so on.

♦ *They were* none too *happy to see their son's poor grades.*

♦ *It's* none too *warm outside. You might want to take a coat.*

♦ *That dog is* none too *friendly. Don't try to pet it.*

None too is also followed by some adverbs, for example, *none too soon, none too well,* and *none too happily.*

♦ *The ambulance came* none too *soon. He needed help fast.*

♦ *She's been* none too *well in the past few months.*

♦ *He finally went in to clean his room, but* none too *happily.*

none the worse for wear

still in good condition; not very worn or harmed after much use or abuse
♦ *You seem to be* none the worse for wear *after that long flight.* ♦ *This comfy old chair has been in the family a long time, but it's* none the worse for wear.

second to none

the best; not the second best ♦ *My mom's apple pies are* second to none. ♦ *He's won prizes for his hand-crafted furniture. His work is* second to none.

Not

The word *not* at the beginning of an idiom simply means not and is usually followed by a noun (*not a chance*), a prepositional phrase (*not on your life*), or an adverb (*not now*). The following idiomatic expressions are listed in alphabetical order:

not again

an expression of surprise that something has happened again; also said as a weary acceptance of a continuing problem or complaint ♦ *Aaron: Mom, the dog got out of the yard. Mom:* Not again! ♦ *When he told me about getting fired, I just said,* "Not again."

not all there

not mentally present or competent; not having one's wits or common sense
♦ *Sometimes David seems* not all there, *but he's a skilled worker.* ♦ *I don't know how I burned this food. I'm just* not all there *these days.*

not at all

no problem; it was no trouble at all. A somewhat formal response to a thank you. ♦ *Ellen: Thank you for everything. Sue:* Not at all. *It was my pleasure.*

not bad

okay or satisfactory (said with dropping intonation); pretty good or very good (said with raising intonation). This idiom is also used in the slang expressions *not half bad* and *not too shabby,* meaning pretty good. ♦ *Your essay is* not bad *(said with dropping intonation), but it needs some work.* ♦ *This essay is* not bad *(said with rising intonation). You should enter it in the essay contest.*

not a chance

it's impossible; it's not going to happen; absolutely no. Also sometimes said as *not a chance in hell.* ♦ *Sally: Are you going to retire early? Bob:* Not a chance. *I'm going to work as long as I can.* ♦ *There's* not a chance *in hell that we'll get that contract.*

not a day goes by

no day passes without doing or thinking something; a thought or event recurs everyday. Used primarily to emphasize the frequency of something, usually thoughts concerning memories or regrets. ♦ Not a day goes by *that we don't think of you.* ♦ *Since my father's death last week,* not a day goes by *without someone calling to offer sympathy.*

not for love or money

it absolutely will not happen; nothing, not even love or money, will make me do it ♦ *I wouldn't leave my kids* for love or money! ♦ *He wants her to get back together with him, but she said "*not for love or money!"

not in the least

not at all; not in the slightest degree. Sometimes said as *not the least bit.*
♦ *Mitch: I think it would be cool to have a snake for a pet, don't you? Ellen:* Not in the least! ♦ *He's* not the least bit *interested in running for public office.*

not on your life

absolutely not ♦ *You want me to go bungee jumping with you?* Not on your life! ♦ *Cheat on her?* Not on your life! *I'm not going to ruin a great relationship.*

not one's cup of tea

not something that one is interested in or likes ♦ *Well, staying in youth hostels is* not my cup of tea, *but they're great for budget traveling.* ♦ *Thanks for the invitation, but opera is* not my cup of tea.

not one's day

not a good day for someone; a day in which things have gone wrong ♦ *Ouch, now I bumped my head. This is just* not my day! ♦ *Sorry you're having a bad day. I guess this is just* not your day.

not one's self

not feeling 100 percent well; feeling a little sick or troubled ♦ *I'm sorry that I yelled at you. I'm just* not myself *today.* ♦ *Is something wrong? You* haven't been yourself *all day.*

not that I care

not concerned; means "I do not care." Sometimes said to hide genuine caring or hurt. ♦ *I heard that she's got a new boyfriend now. . . not that I care.* ♦ *Did you borrow my skirt? Not that I care; it's okay. I was just wondering.*

Not If I Can Help It

The expressions *not if I can help it, not on my watch,* and *not if I have anything to do with it* mean "It won't happen if I can stop it" or "I will do everything possible to prevent it." These expressions also mean that it won't be allowed. People also say "*not if I'm around.*" Here are some examples of how these expressions are used:

♦ *I can guarantee that there won't be any trouble —* not on my watch!

♦ *Jennifer: Mom, I'm going to an all-night concert with Mike. Mom:* Not if I can help it!

♦ *Worker: I heard that the company wants to cut everyone's' hours. Manager:* Not if I have anything to say about it.

... *Not!*

Adding *not!* to the end a statement is a modern cliché to emphasize that you mean exactly the opposite of what you said. Saying, "I like this band... *not!*" means "I definitely don't like this band at all." Here are some examples:

♦ *Well, that was an interesting lecture* ... not!

♦ *Bush seems to have won the election* ... not!

♦ *Everyone is in favor of widening the highway* ... not!

♦ *Of course I'm going to date her* ... not! *Are you crazy? She's my best friend's girl.*

not to worry

don't worry; no problem; nothing to be concerned about ♦ *Johnny had a bike accident, but* not to worry, *Mom. He didn't get hurt.* ♦ *It's an important exam, but* not to worry. *You already know this material.*

Never

The word *never* at the beginning of idioms often means don't, as in *never fear.* The word *never* is generally followed by a verb (*never say* die) or an adjective (*never better*). The following idiomatic expressions are listed in alphabetical order.

never again

to never let something happen again; a strong confirmation of a conviction ♦ *He hurt me once, but* never again! ♦ *Never again will I lend him something. He always loses things.* **Grammar Note:** When *never again* begins a sentence, the subject of the sentence and the auxiliary verb are reversed, as in the second example above. When an auxiliary verb would not normally be present, the verb *do* or *did* is used as an auxiliary verb, as in "*Never again* do I want to be in the hospital."

never better

> this is the best that someone or something has been. It's short for "It has *never been better,*" "I have *never felt better,*" and so on. Also said as *better than ever.*
> ♦ *Robin: How are you feeling after running your first race? Adam:* Never better!
> ♦ *I feel* better than ever *now that I gave up smoking.*

never a dull moment

> something is always happening or changing ♦ *There was* never a dull moment *growing up with my five brothers and sisters.* ♦ *Oh no. The cat is stuck in the tree again. Well, at least there's* never a dull moment.

never fear

> don't worry; don't be concerned. Often said lightly or with exaggerated serious-ness. ♦ Never fear. *I'll have this problem fixed in a minute.* ♦ *Mom: Oh no. I just spilled juice all over the floor. Son:* Never fear! *I'm here with the sponge to help you!*

never hear the end of it

> that blame or reprisals, typically for doing something wrong or not doing something, will last for an extended period of time ♦ *If we don't attend their daughter's wedding we'll* never hear the end of it. ♦ *I thought I'd* never hear the end of it *from my parents when I dropped out of school.*

You Never Know!

The expressions *you never know* and *you never can tell* mean that one can't be certain that something will or won't happen. These expressions are often used to encourage someone just in case something good happens.

> ♦ *You should go to that singles dance.* You never know. *You might meet someone.*

> ♦ *I told her, "Go to that audition,* you never know." *And sure enough, she got the part!*

> ♦ *We might get some sunshine today, but* you never can tell.

> ♦ You never can tell *about him; he's unpredictable.*

never hurts to ask

> that one should ask for what one wants, even if the answer might be no because the request or wish will definitely not happen if the request is not made ♦ *I'm going to call and find out if this bill is right. It* never hurts to ask. ♦ *She might say no to your request, but it* never hurts to ask.

I never!

> an exclamation to show disgust or insult. This is short for "I've never heard" or "I've never experienced anything like this." ♦ *Well* I never! *That's the most ridiculous thing I've ever heard.* ♦ *How insulting!* I never!

never mind

> forget it; it's not important; don't trouble yourself ♦ *If you didn't hear me,* never mind. *It wasn't important.* ♦ Never mind *about the dishes. I'll do them later.*

never say die

> keep trying; keep hoping; don't give up. Usually said with mock seriousness. ♦ *If you can't figure something out,* never say die. *Try it again.* ♦ *We're stuck in a ditch, but* never say die. *We'll get out.*

never too late

> some opportunities are always there. This expression is usually said as encouragement for people to do something that perhaps they should have done sooner. ♦ *You can go back to school at any age now. It's* never too late. ♦ *It's* never too late *to build a closer relationship with your family.*

Nothing

The word *nothing* within an idiom generally means not anything, as in *nothing short of,* or implies zero, as in *count for nothing. Nothing* is generally followed by a prepositional phrase (*nothing to it*) or an adjective (*nothing flat*). The following idiomatic expressions are listed in alphabetical order:

come to nothing

be unsuccessful or unfruitful. Also sometimes said as *come to naught.* ♦ *All of our efforts to advise him have* come to nothing. *He's going to do what he wants to do.* ♦ *Our work on this project has* come to nothing. *They cancelled the contract.*

count for nothing

worthless; of no value ♦ *His medical license from his country* counted for nothing *when he came here. So he had to start over again in medical school.* ♦ *He thinks I never help him. Does it* count for nothing *that I often loan him money?*

get by on nothing

to manage to live on very little money ♦ *We* got by on nothing, *but we had a lot of love.* ♦ *Many elderly people are trying to* get by on nothing.

here goes nothing

said before trying something that one is anxious about or doesn't expect to be successful. This expression is an extension of *here goes!* ♦ *Well,* here goes nothing. *I'm going to call her for a date.* ♦ *I've never tried surfing before, so* here goes nothing.

in nothing flat

instantly, immediately, and without delay; with no problem ♦ *Don't worry. I can fix your tire in* nothing flat. ♦ *She can fix a delicious meal in* nothing flat. *How does she do it?*

Nothing but . . .

The expression *nothing but* followed by a superlative, like *nothing but the best,* or by a noun, like *nothing but trouble, nothing but work,* and so on, means "only" or "exclusively." So, saying that something was *nothing but trouble* means that it was a lot of trouble. *Nothing but the best* means only the best and nothing else. Here are some examples:

   ♦ *All parents want* nothing but *the best for their children.*

   ♦ *That car has been* nothing but *trouble since we bought it!*

   ♦ *You've done* nothing but *work all weekend. Take a break.*

   ♦ *That café serves* nothing but *salads and sandwiches.*

nothing doing

definitely no; not a chance; I won't do it; I won't let you do that ♦ Nothing doing! *I'm not loaning you my car.* ♦ *She wanted to do all of the party preparations, but I said,* "Nothing doing! *We're going to help you."*

nothing like it

unusual; extraordinary; the best. Literally, *nothing like it* means that nothing is similar, but the idiom *nothing like it* means "it's great," "it's the best." ♦ *If you've never tried river rafting, you should. There's* nothing like it! ♦ *"Being in love is great," he said. "There's* nothing like it!"

nothing short of

equal to; the same as; not less than ♦ *Her recovery is* nothing short of *a miracle.* ♦ *His speech was* nothing short of *political propaganda.*

nothing to do with

to not associate with; to ignore. Usually said as to *have nothing to do with* or to *want nothing to do with.* ♦ *They'll* have nothing to do with *him since he kicked their dog.* ♦ *I* want nothing to do with *your crazy money-making schemes.*

nothing to it

it's easy; simple to do; not difficult ♦ *My grandkids say there's* nothing to it, *but I still can't work a computer.* ♦ *Sewing is easy. There's really* nothing to it *if you just follow the pattern.*

nothing to write home about

not very interesting, exciting, or newsworthy. Literally, it's not interesting enough to tell the family about. ♦ *The new job is okay, but it's* nothing to write home about. ♦ *We've dated a few times, but it's* nothing to write home about. *We're just casual friends.*

stop at nothing

will not be stopped; will do everything necessary to reach one's goals. Sometimes implies doing something illegal or unethical to get what one wants. ♦ *The police say they will* stop at nothing *to catch the kidnapper.* ♦ *If he wants the position, he'll* stop at nothing *to get it.*

sweet nothings

words of love between sweethearts ♦ *Their letters were filled with* sweet nothings. ♦ *He whispered* sweet nothings *to her in front of the fire.*

[See *sweet nothings* and other love words in Chapter 8.]

think nothing of it

> don't worry about it; said when something was or can be done easily without giving it much thought or concern. Often said in response to "Thank you."
> ♦ *Adrian: How can I thank you? Jerry:* Think nothing of it. *It's my pleasure.*
> ♦ *They* think nothing of *spending $200 for a meal.* ♦ *At 60 she's so healthy, she* thinks nothing of *hiking all day.*

[See Chapter 16 for more expressions using negative words.]

CHAPTER 17

QUESTION WORD IDIOMS

A number of common idiomatic expressions begin with or include the question words *what, when, where, why, who,* and *how.* Most of these expressions are said as questions or mock questions, such as *Who knew? Why not?* and *What's it to you?* Others are exclamations, like *How nice!* or *That's why!* *Where* and *when* are often used in longer phrases, such as *when all is said and done.* You'll find all of these expressions within this chapter, along with many more, all of which are organized by question word.

Idioms That Use *What*

Many idiomatic expressions with *what* have similar meanings and uses. The sections that follow group together those idioms with similar meanings.

USING *WHAT* TO ASK WHAT'S HAPPENING

When people ask *What's cooking?* they may not be inquiring about dinner. The idiom *What's cooking?* and the ones in the following list mean "What is happening?" or "What are you doing?"

What's up?
What's going on?
What's new?

People use these expressions as greetings when they get together or meet casually. The typical response to one of these expressions is something like "Not much," "Nothing much," or "Nothing," followed by some information on what's happening at the moment or what has been happening lately. Occasionally people start right in talking about what's happening without the usual "Nothing" or "Not much."

Here are some examples of these expressions in context:

Hi Janie. Nice to see you. *What's new?*
Nothing much. How about you?

Hey Chuck. *What's cooking?*
Not much. Just waiting for Joanne.

What's up with you guys?
We're here looking for a gift for my brother's birthday.

USING *WHAT* TO MEAN *WHY* DO YOU CARE?

A number of expressions with *what* mean "Why do you care about it?" or "Why are you concerned or interested?" They are used to imply "It's not your concern or business," and they are often said rudely, as a challenge. The expressions are as follows:

What's it to you?
What do you care?
What about it?
What of it?

The following conversation shows the expressions *what's it to somebody?* and *what does somebody care?* in context:

Dan: Ted wants to know how we spent our bonus.
Alice: That's our business. *What's it to him?*
Dan: Exactly! *What does he care?*

Whatever

Whatever has become a versatile idiom with a number of handy uses. It's often used as a reply meaning "It doesn't matter to me" when someone asks for your preference. It's also put at the end of a list of choices to mean "or something else." Here are a few examples:

Emily: Which of these movies do you want to see? Bev: *Whatever.*

We can go for a hike, go down to the beach, *or whatever.*

If you want we can use my car, *or whatever.*

Whatever is also used as a scornful way of dismissing something a person says or does. It can mean "forget it" or "you're hopeless." For example:

Damian: Hey, don't mess around with my car!

Paul: *Whatever.*

Here is another example:

Todd: No! I don't want to wash the dishes!

Dad: *Whatever*, but you won't get your allowance this week.

The next conversation shows *what's it to you?* and *what of it?* in context:

> Rachael: Hey, did Mom buy you that CD?
> Claire: Yeah, *what's it to you?*
> Rachael: So, I didn't get one.
> Claire: *What of it?* She bought you the book you wanted.

The expression *what about it?* has two common meanings: In addition to meaning "Why do you care?" it can also mean "Okay? Are you agreeable?" The following examples show these meanings in context:

> Kristin: Dad gave you $5?
> Adam: So? *What about it?* I earned it.

> Leslie: Let's go to Mexico for our vacation. Okay? *What about it?*
> Jessica: Great idea!

So what? is an idiom that is related to *what's it to you?* and the other idioms meaning "Why do you care?" *So what* means "Why should I care?" This expression is very common, and can be rude or just conversational, depending on the context and how it's said.

> Larry: I spent a lot of money on this tie.
> Rebecca: *So what?* It's ugly. Don't wear it.

> Carmelita: Hey, you're using my pen!
> Stephen: *So what?* You weren't using it.

People often just say *so?* as a shortened form of *so what?*

> Emily: I want to watch *Friends*.
> Alice: *So?* I hate that show.

WHAT THE HECK . . .!? AND RELATED IDIOMS

A number of idiomatic expressions with *what* mean "What's the problem?", "What's happening here?", or "What is this?!" The following expressions can show surprise, curiosity, or annoyance, depending on the context:

What gives?
What in the world . . .?
What in the heck . . .? (the word *in* is optional: "What the heck?")
What in the hell . . .? (the word *in* is optional: "What the hell?")
What the . . .?

Here are some examples:

♦ What in the world *happened to you?! You're all scratched up!*
♦ What in the heck *did I do with my car keys? I can't find them, and I have to leave for work.*
♦ What the hell?! *You can't do that!*
♦ *Tiffany:* What the . . .? *What is that? Sarah: It's a huge bug! Gross!*

Note: *What in the hell . . .?* is often used to show frustration or anger. The word "hell" is offensive to some people and too informal for many situations, so it is often shortened to the odd, *What the . . .?* which is acceptable in any context.

What gives? is sometimes used to express suspicion that something secretive is happening. The following examples show this idiom in context:

♦ *Hey,* what gives *with her? Why is she so angry?*
♦ *Come on,* what gives? *I know there's something you're not telling me.*

OTHER *WHAT* EXPRESSIONS

The following are some other very common idiomatic expressions with *what:*

What do you know!

means "That's surprising!" or "That's good news"; also used to show mock surprise ♦ *Well,* what do you know! *You're on time for once.* ♦ *Hey,* what do you know. *Someone found my lost wallet with all the money and credit cards still inside!*

What for?

means "Why?" Used as a response to a statement or request ♦ *Chad: Hey, come here a minute. Lisa:* What for? ♦ *Sam: Dad, could I borrow some money from you? Dad:* What for?

what not (*or* what have you)

said at the end of a list of things (or just one thing) to mean "and things like that" or "and related activities" ♦ *On the holidays we'll visit the relatives and* what not. ♦ *He needs to buy some school supplies: a notebook, paper, and* what have you.

What's up with that?!

means "What is the reason or purpose of that?!" or "That's no good!" Usually said in frustration or to show displeasure. ♦ *She won't give you back your photographs?* What's up with that?! ♦ *Hey, the bank is closed already!* What's up with that?! *They must have changed their hours.*

What's up with . . .?

means "What is the problem with something?" or "What is the reason for something?"; can also mean "What's happening with something?" or "What's the progress?" Generally said to express interest, curiosity, or to get information. ♦ *Shawn: Hey,* what's up with *your arm? Darrell: I hurt it playing basketball, and I have to wear this sling for a few days.* ♦ *What's up with that funny hat? It's not Halloween!* ♦ What's up with *the beach party? Is it still going to happen?*

What's with someone?

means "What is the problem with someone?" or "What's wrong with someone?" Used to ask why someone is upset, irritable, or angry; also *what's up with someone.* ♦ What's with him? *Why is he so upset?* ♦ What's with you? *You've been irritable all day.*

what's what

the important facts about a thing; the way that things truly are; usually said as to *know* what's what, which means to fully understand or know what's happening, or to be savvy and informed about something ♦ *Please explain the problem to me. I need to know* what's what *before I take any action.* ♦ *It will take awhile to learn* what's what *in your new position.*

Idioms That Use *When*

Most idiomatic expressions with *when* either introduce an adverb clause, as in *when all is said and done,* or are shortened versions of adverb clauses, as in *say when* (say when I should stop).

say when

means "Tell me when to stop." Said when serving someone food or drink, but also used in other contexts. ♦ *I don't know how much wine you want, so* say when. ♦ *Here. Let me put some sunscreen in your hand.* Say when.

Note: In response to *say when,* people often say, playfully, "When!"

Since when?

1. means "How long has it been happening?" or "When did it happen?" ♦ *Jesse: The old art theater closed. Allen: Really?* Since when?
2. "I don't believe it." Used to show disagreement or surprise, or to challenge someone's statement ♦ *Ken: I'm a very serious student. Ross: Ha!* Since when? *You nearly failed last semester.*

when all is said and done

in the end, ultimately; in spite of everything ♦ When all is said and done, *we have a lot to be thankful for in our lives.* ♦ *We had some bad weather, but* when all was said and done, *it was a fantastic trip.*

when in Rome . . .

the beginning of a saying that means to follow local customs or trends; to follow what others in the group are doing ♦ *When I went to Iran with my friend, she didn't want to eat any of the local food, but I said* "When in Rome . . ." *and she was willing to try it.* ♦ *I wouldn't normally go to a public bath, but* when in Rome. . . .

Note: This idiom is short for "When in Rome, do as the Romans do." This saying is so well known that it is usually shortened to simply *when in Rome.*

when it comes to

regarding, concerning ♦ When it comes to *good cooking, my dad's the best!* ♦ *You can't be apathetic* when it comes to *your health.*

when it comes down to it

in the end, ultimately; "If you want to know my true feelings. . . ."; used in a similar way to *when it comes to;* often said as *when it comes right down to it.* ♦ When it comes down to it, *I'll probably lend him the money if he needs it.* ♦ When it comes *right* down to it, *I'd really rather stay home for the holidays.*

when the dust settles

when things return to normal, when everything calms down. Also said as *until* or *after* or *before the dust settles.* ♦ *They've just moved into their new home. So,* when the dust settles, *we'll go visit them.* ♦ When the dust settles *from the merger, you can take some time off.*

Idioms That Use *Where*

Idiomatic expressions that begin with *where* either form a complete question, such as *Where's the fire?,* or introduce an adverb clause, as in *where one stands.*

Where's the fire?

means "Why are you in such a hurry?"; implies that the person is running to put out a fire ♦ *Hey,* where's the fire? *There's no need to run.* ♦ *Ben:* Where's the fire? *Chris: I'm late to work!*

Where have *you* been?

> means "Why don't you know about this?" or "Everyone else knows. Why are you so uninformed?" Implies that one has been gone while things continue to happen; also can be phrased *where have I been?* or *where has he* or *she been?* and so on. ♦ *Rene: Michael Jackson has children?! Ellie: Geez,* where have you been? ♦ *Joan: They closed that restaurant a year ago. Didn't you know? Gail: Well,* where have I been? **Note:** To convey the correct meaning, emphasize the pronoun: *you, I,* and so on.

where someone (*or* something) is concerned

> anything concerning or regarding someone or something ♦ *She's always responsible* where money is concerned. ♦ Where my children are concerned, *I don't compromise.*

where it counts

> where it will have the most influence or value; usually said of time, energy, and money ♦ *Put your time* where it counts. *Volunteer for a charity organization.* ♦ *They put their money* where it counts—*into their children's education.*

where it's at

> the center of activity, where important or trendy things are happening; the ultimate of what's "cool" ♦ *He really thinks he's* where it's at *with that new sports car.* ♦ *The Harbor Club is definitely* where it's at *for good jazz music.*

where one is coming from

> one's perspective, beliefs, or underlying motives ♦ *It's hard to know* where he's coming from. *His campaign message is so vague.* ♦ *Now that I understand* where she's coming from, *her behavior makes more sense.*

where one stands

> one's position or status relative to others; how one is viewed by others ♦ *When I get a copy of my evaluation, I'll know better* where I stand. ♦ *I like her a lot, but I'm not sure* where I stand *with her.*

Idioms That Use *Who*

Most idiomatic expressions that begin with *who* are followed by a verb, as in *who cares* or *who can say.*

Who can say?

means "I don't know" or "Nobody knows" ♦ *A lot of people think they know which stocks will perform well, but* who can *really* say? ♦ Who can say *why some TV shows are popular?* **Note:** This expression is similar to *who knows* but is slightly more polite.

Who cares?

means "I don't care" or "It's not important enough to care about" ♦ Who cares *about school? I just want to have fun!* ♦ *She made a big deal about which waste-basket to use, but* who cares?

Who gives . . .

typically followed by an obscenity or by *darn, rap,* or *straw* to mean "I don't care." Similar to *who cares,* but can be stronger. ♦ *Brooke: I saw Brian with your ex-girlfriend yesterday. Chris:* Who gives *a darn? I'm through with that relationship.*

Who knew?

means "None of us knew about this," or "How could we have known?" This idiom is often said with real or mock surprise, and sometimes as light ridicule. ♦ *Our guest left early because she is allergic to cats.* Who knew? *She never said so, and she knows we have cats.* ♦ *Her new husband turned out to be a gambler.* Who knew?

Who knows?

means "I don't know" or "Nobody knows for sure" ♦ Who knows *when we'll get our bonuses?* ♦ Who knows *how he got lost so easily?* **Note:** This expression is similar to *who can say* but is slightly more sarcastic and less polite.

Who says . . .?

a show of disbelief or challenge to a statement, a rule, or a common belief; often said as *Who says?* or *Says who?* ♦ *Dean: You can't wear a nose ring at work. Kylie:* Who says *I can't?* ♦ *Krista: Our team is going to beat your pathetic team today! Megan: Oh really?* Says who?

Who's there?

a question that's asked after someone knocks on the door; also phrased *Who is it?* ♦ *Cindy:* Who's there? *Is that you, Elly? Elly: Yes, it's me.*

Knock-Knock Jokes

Knock-knock jokes use "who's there" as the standard response to "knock, knock," such as in the following example:

Robin: Here's a joke. Knock, knock.

Sandy: *Who's there?*

Robin: Orange.

Sandy: Orange who?

Robin: Orange you glad to see me? (Aren't you glad to see me?)

who's who

who each person is, each person's name; who is important and influential; often phrased as *know who's who* ♦ *After a few days, I usually learn* who's who *in the classroom.* ♦ *Aunt Dorothy is listed in* "Who's Who *in American Business."*

Idioms That Use *Why*

Idiomatic expressions that begin with *why* generally introduce questions, such as *Why don't you . . .?* However, in a few cases *why* has other functions.

Why . . .!

a sentence opener that expresses surprise; similar to "hey!" ♦ Why, *look who's here! It's our old friend Cindy.* ♦ Why, *you've done very well with your business, haven't you?*

Why don't . . .

1. used to introduce advice or a suggestion. *Why don't* (or *why doesn't*) is usually followed by a pronoun, as the examples show. ♦ *Look, if you're worried about your brother, then* why don't *you call him?* ♦ *Why don't* we go get some ice cream after dinner? ♦ *If he wants to get in shape,* why doesn't *he join a gym?*
2. used sarcastically to emphasize one's anger ♦ *Tell everyone about my problems,* why don't *you!* ♦ *Why don't* we just wake up the whole neighborhood?!

Why in the world . . .?

> used for emphasis when one is surprised or confused ♦ *Why in the world did you quit your job? Now what are you going to do?* ♦ *Why in the world would anyone have loaded guns around children?* ♦ *I don't know* why in the world *he wants to buy that old car, but he does.*

Why not . . .?

> **1.** used to introduce advice or a suggestion; similar in usage to *why don't. . . .* In this context, *why not* is followed by a verb in the base form (the infinitive form without *to*). ♦ *If we have some free time,* why not *go to a movie?*
> **2.** an affirmative response to an invitation or suggestion ♦ *Phil: Will you go to lunch with me? Kristy:* Why not? ♦ *Elizabeth: Maybe you should go for a walk around the park to get some exercise. Leonard:* Why not? *That's a good idea.*

that's why

> used as emphasis at the end of an answer to the question "why?" ♦ *Rita: Why did you stop dating him? Jane: Because he had too many other dates,* that's why!

Idioms That Use *How*

Idioms that begin with *how* often function as greetings, to show surprise or interest, or to ask why.

USING *HOW* AS A GREETING

A number of idiomatic expressions with *how* are used as casual greetings that mean "How are you?" or "How has your life been lately?" Sometimes they're said instead of *hello*. Here are some of the most common:

> **How goes it?**
> **How's it going?**
> **How's life?**
> **How's life been treating you?**
> **How're things? (How's things?)**
> **How's everything?**

The typical responses to these greetings are *good, great, not bad, fine, okay, nothing to complain about,* and other similar replies.

Here are a few examples:

> Bob: *How goes it?*
> Jane: Great!
>
> Cindy: *How is everything?*
> Pam: Things are going well. I love my new job.
>
> Tina: *How are things?*
> Patricia: Okay, but I can't wait for this week to be over!

[See more greeting expressions and responses in Chapter 9.]

OTHER *HOW* IDIOMS

How . . .

used before an adjective to emphasize or intensify the adjective; also expresses surprise. ♦ *Your wife bought you that tie?* How *sweet of her!* ♦ *Ellen's mother passed away?* How *sad.* ♦ How *stupid of me! I forgot to call her on her birthday.*

How about that?

means "That's surprising", "That's remarkable", or "What do you think of that?" Also, "That's great!" ♦ *Well,* how about that! *Sy and Rachael are going to have a baby.* ♦ *Lilly: Mom, I won an award for my art project. Mom: Wow!* How about that!

How come?

means "Why?" or "Why is it so?" ♦ *Dana: I've got to go to court today. Scott:* How come?! ♦ *Lou: My feet are killing me! Lynn:* How come *you don't sit down for a minute?*

How so?

means "Why?" or "Why is it so?" ♦ *Josh: Whew! What a stressful day it was at work today! Lynn:* How so?

Note: *How so?* and *how come?* are very similar, with one difference: *How so* can only serve as a response to a statement; it cannot introduce a longer question. If someone feels sick, you can say, "*How come* you don't go to the doctor?" but you can't say "*How so* you don't go to the doctor?"

How could you?

an expression of shock or anger at someone's actions; similar to "Why did you do such a thing?!" This idiom is often meant to cause shame or remorse.
♦ How could you *be so mean to your little brother?! You should apologize.*
♦ *Jeremy: I decided to sell that ring Dad gave me. Ellen: Jeremy,* how could you? *That belonged to our grandfather and was very special.*

How do I know?

means "I don't know," or "Why do you think I would know?"; also, "There is no way to know." Often said somewhat scornfully about something that one is unhappy about or not interested in. ♦ *Pete: Do you think you're going to get that promotion? Dan: How do I know? They haven't said anything.* ♦ How do we know *what the government is really planning to do?*

How do you do?

a very formal "How are you?" generally used when someone is introduced or as a formal greeting ♦ How do you do, *Dr. Coltrain? It's very nice to meet you.*
♦ How do you do? *I've heard so much about you.*

How in the world . . .?!

means "How did that happen?" or "How can it be done?" This idiom is used as an emphasized "how" when one is surprised, amazed, angry at someone's actions, or completely confused about how to do something; also phrased *how in the heck?* or *how in the hell?* ♦ How in the world *do those skydivers get the courage to jump out of a plane?* ♦ How in the heck *do you work this paint sprayer?! I can't figure it out.*

How . . . is that!?

a modern expression used as an exclamation of surprise, disgust, or other strong emotion; usually said at the end of a statement. A comment such as "How good is that!?" is similar in meaning to "That's very good!" ♦ *Her dad bought her a new car. Man,* how cool is that! ♦ *You partied all weekend before the final exam?* How dumb is that!

PART V

PHRASAL VERBS

*E*veryday conversation is full of phrasal verbs. And though they may seem difficult to you at first, phrasal verbs and idioms often simplify communication. In fact, many idioms developed naturally as shortcuts to longer, more descriptive, and more laborious language.

CHAPTER 18

USING PHRASAL VERBS

Before you get very far in your study of idioms, you'll encounter a large category of idioms called *phrasal verbs*. The term *phrasal verb* may sound intimidating, but it simply means a phrase that typically consists of a verb plus one or two prepositions. Phrasal verbs are often called *two-word verbs* or *three-word verbs*.

The two or three words together form a unit that has a different meaning than the literal meaning of the words individually. Sometimes the phrasal verb merely extends or makes more specific the literal meaning of the verb, as in the phrasal verbs *sleep in* (to sleep later than usual in the morning) or *eat out* (to eat outside the home in a restaurant). Other times the phrasal verb has its own unique meaning that is completely unrelated to the literal meaning of the verb, as in the phrasal verbs *call off* (to cancel) or *stand for* (to represent).

Following are some sentences that include phrasal verbs, shown in *italics*:

♦ Hand in *your essays at the end of the week.*
♦ *I need to buy more milk, before we* run out.
♦ *I* came down with *a cold yesterday.*

In the sentences above, the words *hand, run,* and *come* have nothing to do with a hand or with literally running or coming. The meanings of the phrasal verbs is given below:

hand in: to submit homework or some other work project
run out: to deplete the supply of something
come down with: become sick with

More than 4,000 common phrasal verbs exist in American English, with new ones appearing regularly. Phrasal verbs are some of the most frequently used verbs in both casual and formal communication. Without them, it's often difficult and cumbersome to communicate naturally and effectively.

What Is a Phrasal Verb . . . and What Isn't

A phrasal verb is different from a simple verb and preposition in three specific ways:

- In a phrasal verb, the verb and preposition go together as a unit to form the verb.
- A different preposition with the verb creates either an error or a new phrasal verb with a completely different meaning.
- A phrasal verb functions like a single word, even though it is composed of more than one word.

For example, the phrasal verb *run into* is an idiom meaning to meet someone or something unexpectedly. Of course, you can also literally *run into* someone or something — to be running or moving quickly and accidentally bump into a person or thing. In that case, *run into* is not an idiom; it means exactly what it says. The following sentences show the difference between the phrasal verb *run into* and the simple verb *run* plus the preposition *into*:

> **Phrasal verb:** I *ran into* (met unexpectedly) an old friend of mine yesterday. It was nice to see her again.
>
> **Simple verb and preposition:** I was in a hurry, and I accidentally *ran into* (bumped) someone on the sidewalk. How embarrassing!

Mastering Phrasal Verbs

The good news is that some phrasal verbs are easy to learn. Here's why:

- Some verb-preposition combinations make sense. They're somewhat logical, so you can easily guess the meaning. For example:
  - **go out:** to go outside the home for entertainment or other activities; to date
- Many phrasal verbs have almost the same meaning as the verb alone. This is often the case with idioms that include the prepositions *up* or *down*:
  - **finish up:** to complete or finish the last of something
  - **quiet down:** to become quieter

Of course, learning phrasal verbs has its challenges. First, there are so many commonly used phrasal verbs to learn. Second, phrasal verbs have some specific traits that can make them tricky to master — but also fun to learn:

- With most phrasal verbs, it's difficult or even impossible to guess the meaning from the individual words. For example, the idiom *egg on* has nothing at all to do with eggs, breakfast, chickens, food, or any other egg-related thing. Curiously, *egg on* means to urge or provoke, to encourage someone to act wrongfully: "The older boys *egged on* the younger ones to throw stones at the window."
- While you're learning idioms, it's easy to make a mistake by choosing the wrong verb or preposition, and accidentally saying something embarrassing. For example, if you go to the gym to *work out* (exercise), don't make the mistake that one language learner made of telling your spouse that you are going to the gym to *make out* (kiss passionately and possibly have sex).
- Most phrasal verbs have more than one meaning. Take *make out,* for example. In addition to meaning to kiss passionately, this idiom has six other very common meanings. Here are a few of them:
  - see or discern with difficulty
  - manage, handle a situation
  - write as a reminder or a record

The Big Role of Little Prepositions

By definition, a *preposition* is a word, or in some cases a group of words, that links one element of the sentence to another and shows a relationship between the two elements. Prepositions, such as *of, in, up, down, with, over,* and so on, function in a sentence as connectors or to show location or direction. They typically do not serve as content words or elements that help carry the main meaning of the sentence.

However, in phrasal verbs, prepositions are essential to the meaning of the sentence. They help to convey the content of the sentence, though they may act as connectors, too. The following three examples show the preposition *in* as a simple connector, as a word of location, and as part of a phrasal verb:

> **Preposition as connector:** Are you interested *in* classical music?
> **Preposition of location:** The book is *in* my school bag.
> **Preposition as part of an phrasal verb:** I'm tired. I'm going to *turn in* (go to bed).

The preposition that is used most frequently in phrasal verbs is the preposition *up,* but all of the following prepositions commonly appear in phrasal verbs:

around	out
away	over
down	through
for	up
in	under
off	with
on	without

Almost any common one-syllable verb can be joined with one of these prepositions to form a phrasal verb and create an idiom. For example, in the following list the preposition *up* forms a phrasal verb when combined with *sit, stand, look, talk,* and *write.* The phrasal verbs have an idiomatic meaning that is shown after the bolded phrasal verb:

sit up: stay awake, generally through the night, with a sick or troubled person ♦ *He* sat up *with his daughter, who had the flu.*

stand up: remain strong, durable, or valid ♦ *This old furniture has* stood up *well over the years.*

look up: check a reference book for information ♦ *Will you* look up *the phone number for The Lakeshore Hotel?*

talk up: promote someone or something ♦ *Rebecca can't stop* talking up *this sales opportunity.*

write up: write a citation for; report on one's findings ♦ *I'll* write up *my research results and give you a copy.*

Other prepositions can be combined with these simple verbs to create even more idioms. For example, the preposition *for* with *stand* gives you *stand for* (to represent). The preposition *out* gives you *stand out* (to protrude or be very obvious). *In* gives you *stand in* (to substitute for someone or something), and so on.

Although prepositions play a very big role in phrasal verbs, they are often used incorrectly or neglected altogether. They can be the most difficult part of the phrasal verb to remember and to use accurately. Here's why:

- Prepositions generally are not emphasized or accented in speaking, so you don't always hear them clearly — or hear them at all.
- One verb might combine with different prepositions to form different idioms, so if you choose the wrong preposition you may create a different idiom with a completely different meaning.
- There is no rule to tell you which prepositions join with which verbs, and usually there is no logic to the choice of preposition. For example, why do people say "*Write down* this phone number" (meaning record this information on paper), when in fact you are writing *across* the page, not down!

Transitive and Intransitive Phrasal Verbs

Phrasal verbs fall into two distinct categories:

Transitive: Transitive verbs require a direct object.
Intransitive: Intransitive verbs do not require a direct object.

Transitive verbs require a direct object to form a complete sentence. Intransitive verbs do not require a direct object to form a complete sentence. It's important to know whether the phrasal verb is transitive or intransitive in order to use it correctly. And many phrasal verbs can be either transitive or intransitive depending on their meaning in the sentence. Sound a bit challenging? Don't worry — it's not necessary for you to name each verb as transitive or intransitive; it's only important to know how these two types function in a sentence.

The following sections on transitive and intransitive verbs explain the differences in greater detail and give examples of each type.

TRANSITIVE VERBS

Webster's New World Dictionary defines transitive verbs as "expressing an action [that is] thought of as passing over to or having an effect on some person or thing." That person or thing is the direct object, and with transitive verbs, it is needed to form a complete sentence. For example, the phrasal verb *look up* (to check a dictionary or reference for information) is a transitive verb, and therefore must have a direct object — you must *look up* **something.** As an idiom, *look up* is not complete without its object. In the following sentence, the direct object of the phrasal verb *look up* is the phone number:

I *looked up* **the phone number** in the phone book.

Without an object, the phrase *look up* isn't an idiom, it's a simple verb with a literal meaning, to look in an upward direction. For example, "*Look up* in the sky."

Here's another example of a transitive verb: The idiom *look for* (to search, hoping to find something or someone) requires a direct object. You must *look for* **someone** or **something.** In the following sentence, the direct object of *look for* is you:

We were *looking for* **you** all morning! Where were you?

INTRANSITIVE VERBS

Intransitive verbs are verbs that don't require a direct object to form a complete sentence. They do not transfer or pass on their action to a person or thing. For example, the phrasal verb *come back* (return to a starting point) is an intransitive verb and, therefore, it does not require a direct object. You don't *come back* (something) or *come back* (someone); you simply *come back!* Here are some examples of this intransitive verb in context:

> My dog ran away, but eventually he *came back.*
> They went to Hawaii on vacation, and they're *coming back* next week.

PHRASAL VERBS WITH BOTH TRANSITIVE AND INTRANSITIVE FORMS

Some phrasal verbs can be transitive in some situations and intransitive in others. Here's why:

- When a phrasal verb has multiple meanings, one meaning may require a transitive verb, while another meaning uses an intransitive verb. The idiom *drop off* provides a good example. When *drop off* means to unload or deliver, it is transitive and has a direct object; you must *drop off* **something**:
  - **Transitive:** I have to *drop off* **this package** at the post office.

- When *drop off* means to fall asleep or to decrease, it is intransitive and doesn't have a direct object:
  - **Intransitive:** I often *drop off* (fall asleep) while watching TV in the evening.
  - **Intransitive:** Because of the poor economy, housing sales have *dropped off* (decreased).

- Some phrasal verbs require a direct object when the action of the verb is directed at someone else, but do not use a direct object when the action of the verb is directed upon oneself. One such phrasal verb is *wake up* (to awake from sleeping). You can wake up **someone else** or you can simply wake up (yourself).
  - **Requires a direct object:** I *woke up* my son.
  - **Doesn't use a direct object:** I *woke up*.

- Occasionally a reflexive pronoun is used with phrasal verbs such as *wake up*; when used, it is placed between the verb and preposition: "I woke **myself** up." This sentence implies that you caused yourself to wake up, possibly by snoring loudly or coughing.

- Some transitive phrasal verbs do not use their direct object when the direct object is implied in the meaning of the idiom. For example, with the phrasal verb *pull over* (to move a vehicle out of the flow of traffic, and slow down or stop), it's not necessary to say "I *pulled* **the car** *over*" because *the car* is implied by the idiom. You can simply say "I *pulled over*." However, like the previous example with *wake up,* a direct object is required when the action is directed at someone else. For example, when police officers direct someone to pull a vehicle off the road and stop, a direct object is required: the officer *pulls over* **someone.**
  - **Requires a direct object:** The police officer *pulled over* the speeding driver.
  - **Direct object is implied:** I got a flat tire so I *pulled over* to the side of the road.

SEPARABLE AND NON-SEPARABLE PHRASAL VERBS

Transitive phrasal verbs (verbs that require a direct object) can be either *separable* or *non-separable,* which affects the placement of the direct object. The words *separable* and *non-separable* look a lot like *separate* and *not separate,* and that's exactly what they mean:

Separable phrasal verb: The direct object can separate (go between) the two words of the phrasal verb.

Non-separable phrasal verb: The direct object cannot separate the two words of the phrasal verb; it must follow the phrasal verb.

Helpful Hints on What's Separable and What's Not

Although there are no exact rules to help you learn which phrasal verbs are separable and which are non-separable, the following tips will give you a head start and help you to make a good educated guess when you aren't sure:

- Two-word phrasal verbs with *in, out, up,* and *down* are generally separable.

- Two-word phrasal verbs with *off* and *over* are often separable.

- Two-word phrasal verbs with *on* may be separable or non-separable.

- Phrasal verbs with *catch, come, fall, go, run, speak,* and *stand* are generally non-separable.

- Two-word phrasal verbs with *for, into, of,* and *with* are generally non-separable.

- Three-word phrasal verbs are almost always non-separable.

The following examples show a separable and a non-separable phrasal verb in context. In the first example, the direct object, the party, is separating the phrasal verb *call off*. In the second example, the direct object, you, cannot separate the phrasal verb *call on*, because this phrasal verb is non-separable.

> **Separable:** We *called* the party *off*.
> **Non-Separable:** I'll *call on* you tomorrow afternoon.

PLACEMENT OF THE DIRECT OBJECT IN TRANSITIVE VERBS

In order to use phrasal verbs accurately, it's important to know where to place the direct object. The following discussions and examples explain the rules and show you a few exceptions.

Separable Phrasal Verbs

With a *separable* phrasal verb, the direct object can either go between or after the phrasal verb. For example, the idiom *look up* (check a dictionary or reference for information) is separable. The following examples show you the two possible locations for the direct object, which is shown in bold.

- ♦ *I looked up **the word** in my dictionary.*
- ♦ *I looked **the word** up in my dictionary.*

Exceptions: Here are two exceptions to the general rule above:

- When the direct object is a pronoun (me, you, him, her, it, we, they), the pronoun always separates (goes between) the two parts of the verb. Here are some examples:
  - **Correct:** He *called up* (telephoned) Jennifer for a date.
  - **Correct:** He *called* her *up* for a date.
  - **Incorrect:** He *called up* her for a date.

- This exception often applies to possessive pronouns also (myself, yourself, and so on):
  - **Correct:** The criminal *turned* himself *in* (surrendered) to the police.
  - **Incorrect:** The criminal *turned in* himself to the police.

- When the direct object is a long phrase (more than three words), it should follow the phrasal verb. Don't divide up a separable phrasal verb with a lengthy phrase. That puts the two parts of the verb too far away from each other. Here's an example:

- **Say this:** She *handed in* the fiscal report on the South Beach Water Project.
- **Avoid this:** She *handed* the fiscal report on the South Beach Water Project *in*.

Non-Separable Phrasal Verbs

A *non-separable* phrasal verb cannot be separated by its direct object. The direct object must follow the entire phrasal verb. The idiom *look for* (search, try to find) is non-separable. Its object can't go between the two parts. The following examples show you both the correct and incorrect placement of the direct object, "the book":

Correct: I *looked for* the book at the bookstore, but I didn't find it.
Incorrect: I *looked* the book *for* at the bookstore, but I didn't find it.

Even when the direct object is a pronoun, it cannot separate a non-separable verb. Here is an example in which the direct object is the pronoun, "you":

Correct: We were *looking for* you all morning!
Incorrect: We were *looking* you *for* all morning!

It may seem mind-boggling to figure out where to place the direct object, so here are a few helpful tips: When in doubt, it is almost always safe to place the direct object *after* the phrasal verb, except in the few cases discussed under "Exceptions." Also, if you separate a phrasal verb with a direct object, and it sounds very strange or wrong, it probably is!

[See Chapter 20, for three-word verbs that require both a direct and indirect object, and for information on their placement.]

Using Active and Passive Voice with Phrasal Verbs

Many transitive verbs (verbs that require a direct object) can be expressed in both active and passive voice. Most intransitive verbs can only be expressed in active voice.

Active voice exists when the subject of the sentence does the action of the verb. In the sentence, "Lynn teaches our son," Lynn (the subject) does the action (teaching). So, the verb *teaches* is in active voice. Our son (the direct object) receives the action (the teaching).

Passive voice exists when the subject of the sentence does not do the action of the verb, but receives the action of the verb; in other words, the subject is "passive." In the sentence "Our son is taught by Lynn," our son (the subject) does not do the action (he does not teach), so the verb *is taught* is in passive form. ***Note:*** Essentially, the passive voice can be created when the direct object is used as the subject of the sentence. The passive voice requires the verb *to be* and the past-participle form of the verb.

Here is another example of a phrasal verb in active and passive form:

> **Active form:** The professor *handed out* (distributed) the exams.
> **Passive form:** The exams *were handed out* by the professor.

Intransitive verbs are generally expressed only in active form because there is no direct object that can be used as the subject of the sentence. It's usually not possible to use passive form when there is no direct object, with no person or thing that is affected by the action of the verb. In the following example, the verb *take off* (to begin flight in a plane) is intransitive and therefore can only be expressed in active form:

> **Correct:** The plane *took off* an hour late.
> **Incorrect:** The plane *was taken off*. (by whom or what?)

[For more examples and information on using *come* and *go* correctly, see Chapter 19, *Two-Word Phrasal Verbs*, "Phrasal Verbs with Up and Down."]

Coming and Going

Knowing when to use *come* or *go* can have you *wondering if you're coming or going* (feeling very confused). But there are some general rules to help you decide:

1. Use *come* to refer to the place where you are (or where the person you're talking to is) at the time of speaking.

I *came* to the U.S. last year. (speaker is still in the U.S.)

Do you *come* to this bookstore often? (speakers are in the bookstore)

Hi, Mom. I called to tell you that I'm *coming* home for the holidays. (the mom is at home)

2. Use *go* to refer to any place where you aren't (or where the person you're talking to isn't) at the time of speaking:

I *went* to the U.S. last year. (speaker is no longer in the U.S.)

Do you *go* to that bookstore often? (speakers aren't in the bookstore)

I decided to *go* home and see my mom for the holidays. (speaker isn't at home)

3. Use *come* to invite someone to join you in a pre-planned activity or to meet you at a place where you will be. In this case, *come* implies *join me/us*.

Can you *come* to my house for dinner tonight? (speaker may or may not be at home at the time of speaking, but will meet the guest there)

Yes, I can *come*. Thanks.

We're going camping this weekend; do you want to *come*? (to join us)

Note: In the last example above, you can also say, "Do you want to go?" but in that case, people usually say "Do you want to go *with us?*" or "'Do you want to go *along?*"

4. Use *go* to talk about doing something that is not yet planned or to talk about going somewhere together.

Do you want to *go* to a movie later?

Sure, I want to *go*.

Let's *go* to the beach this weekend.

CHAPTER 19

TWO-WORD PHRASAL VERBS

Two-word verbs are either transitive (they require a direct object) or intransitive (they don't require a direct object). Transitive phrasal verbs are separable (they can be separated by the direct object) or non-separable (they cannot be separated by the direct object). You can learn more about this aspect of phrasal verbs in Chapter 18.

The following notations are used in this chapter: Transitive phrasal verbs are marked as either **(S)** for separable or **(NS)** for non-separable. A phrasal verb with multiple definitions may be separable or non-separable depending on the definition. In those cases, each definition is marked either **(S)** or **(NS).** Intransitive phrasal verbs are not marked.

Phrasal Verbs with *On* and *Off*

Many idioms are formed with the prepositions *on* and *off*. Phrasal verbs with the preposition *on* often mean to enter or start, acquire or hold, stay, continue, or increase. For example, *keep on* means to continue and *take on* means to assume or add responsibility. Phrasal verbs with the preposition *off* often have a meaning of to exit, stop or delay, go away from or release, leave, or decrease. For example, *hold off* means to delay, *keep off* means to stay away from, and *take off* means to leave or to deduct.

Note: Phrasal verbs using the prepositions *on* and *off* are often transitive and separable, though there are exceptions, especially when the idiom means to enter or exit, board or disembark from a mode of transportation. [For more information on transitive and intransitive, separable and non-separable verbs, see Chapter 18.]

ON/OFF OPPOSITES: PHRASAL VERBS WITH OPPOSITE MEANINGS

In some cases, the same verb can be used with either *on* or *off* to express opposite meanings. For example, *climb on* and *climb off* can mean to board and to disembark or exit a bus or other mode of transportation. This section includes phrasal verbs with *on* and *off* that are *antonyms* (opposite in meaning).

Using a Mode of Transportation

The following idioms have a general meaning of to board or exit a vehicle structure or ride, or to mount or dismount an animal like a horse or donkey. *Note: Get on* and *get off* are the most commonly used idioms in this group, and they have a number of additional meanings, as shown below.

get on/get off (NS)

1. to board or enter/exit or leave a vehicle or moving transport such as a bus, boat, plane, train, subway, bicycle, or motorcycle, but **not** a car or taxi, in which case you use the preposition *in* ♦ *Please wait until passengers* get off *the bus before you* get on.
2. to sit on or mount/get down from or dismount any structure, an amusement park ride, or an animal such as a horse ♦ *Lea* got on *a pretty painted horse on the carousel.*
3. to enter/leave a freeway or road ♦ Get on *highway 46 at Smith Road.* ♦ *After three miles,* get off *at Hill Street.*
4. to be accepted onto a team or committee/to quit a team or committee ♦ *Her experience helped her* get on *the planning committee.*

climb on/climb off (NS)

1. to board or enter/exit or leave a vehicle or moving transport such as a bus, boat, plane, train, subway, bicycle, or motorcycle, but **not** a car or taxi, in which case you use the preposition *in* ♦ *I* climbed on *my motorcycle and fastened my helmet.*
2. to sit on or mount/get down from or dismount any structure, an amusement park ride, or an animal such as a horse ♦ *My cat always tries to* climb off *the table at the veterinarian's.*

Note: If the vehicle, structure, ride, or animal is very tall or high, people often say *get up on/get down from* or *climb up on/climb down from.*

jump on/jump off (NS)

1. to board or enter/exit or leave a vehicle or moving transport such as a bus, boat, plane, train, subway, bicycle, motorcycle, but **not** a car or taxi, in which case you use the preposition *in* ♦ *To catch a trolley car in San Francisco, you often have to* jump on.
2. to sit on or mount/get down from or dismount any structure, an amusement park ride, or an animal such as a horse ♦ *Bobby was able to* jump off *his bike before it hit a tree.*

3. to enter/exit a freeway or highway when you have very easy access ♦ *My office is close to home. I just* jump on *the freeway, and I'm there in five minutes.*

Note: Use *jump on* and *jump off* when you're in a hurry to get on or off a vehicle, structure, ride, or animal, or when it is about to leave without you.

let on/let off(S)

1. to allow someone to board/exit a vehicle, structure, or amusement park ride; to mount/dismount an animal ♦ *The ride operator stopped the Ferris wheel to* let *some people* off.
2. to allow someone to enter/exit a freeway or road ♦ *When traffic is heavy, a courteous driver will signal you to* let *you* on *the freeway.*
3. to allow someone to join/quit a team or committee. ♦ *He's hoping the coach* lets *him* on *the swim team.*

Note: The idiom is also said as *let* (someone) *get on/off.*

Grammar Note: This idiom is usually separated by its direct object.

Getting Dressed and Undressed

The following idioms have a general meaning of to dress or undress in clothing, jewelry, glasses, or to apply or remove cosmetics, body products, medicine, and bandages. The idioms *put on* and *take off* have various additional meanings.

Note: Notice that the opposite of *put on* is *take off* (not *put off*). The idiom *put off* has several meanings, unrelated to the idiom *put on,* and is shown later in this section.

put on/take off(S)

1. to dress/undress in clothes, jewelry, eyeglasses, contact lenses ♦ *Some people* take *their shoes* off *when they enter the house.*
2. to use or apply/remove cosmetics and health-care products (deodorant, lotion, sunscreen, cologne, after-shave, medication, bandages, and so on) ♦ *You should* take off *that bandage and* put *more antiseptic* on *your cut.*
3. to gain/lose weight ♦ *Exercise will help me* take off *the extra pounds I* put on *during vacation.*
4. to place a music CD, cassette, or record in or on a stereo/remove a record from a stereo ♦ *Let's* take off *that blues record and* put on *this jazz CD.* **Note:** Use *take out* for removing CDs and cassettes.

throw on/throw off (S)

1. to hurriedly and maybe carelessly dress/undress in clothes, jewelry, eye-glasses (but not contact lenses, which require care and time) ♦ *We're late! Just* throw on *your shoes, and let's go!* ♦ *When I get home from work, I* throw off *my work clothes and take a shower.*

2. to hurriedly and maybe carelessly apply cosmetics and health-care products (deodorant, lotion, sunscreen, cologne, after-shave lotion, medication, band-ages, and so on) ♦ *On Saturday, I get up late,* throw on *some old clothes, and go out to my backyard.*

3. to casually put a music CD, cassette, or record in or on a stereo without much care about the choice of music ♦ Throw on *some music while I get us a drink.*

Note: People often use *throw on* when they're unconcerned about or give no thought to what they'll wear. For hurriedly applying cosmetics and health products, you can also use the idiom *slap on.*

pull on/pull off (S)

to dress/undress in clothes that are somewhat heavy, bulky, or require some effort to put on or take off ♦ *He* pulled on *his jeans and ran outside to play.* ♦ *When she got home, she* pulled off *her boots and heavy jacket.* *Note:* Slip on and *slip off* are often used when clothes are easy, quick, and comfortable to get into or out of.

Starting and Stopping the Power

The following idioms have a general meaning of to start or stop the power on electrical, mechanical, or other power-driven products; they also mean to start or stop mental, physical, or emotional energy.

turn on/turn off (S)

1. to operate electrical lights, appliances, and other electrical or gas-driven products ♦ *Let's* turn on *the air conditioner. It's too hot in here.*

2. to start or stop the power on a machine, motor, or engine ♦ Turn off *your engine when you're filling your car with gas.*

3. to consciously start or stop mental activity or emotions ♦ *It's impossible to simply* turn *your feelings* off *and* on.

4. to inspire someone's intense interest/disinterest or disgust (often used in passive form) ♦ *We were really* turned off *by the speaker's arrogant tone.*

Note: Turn (someone) *on/off* can have a sexual connotation.

When *Off* Means to Start Rather Than to Stop

The word *off* in phrasal verbs frequently means or implies to decrease, stop, or end, but in a few phrasal verbs, it means *to start.* For example, the idiom *touch off* means to start or initiate something that has far-reaching results or major consequences. Here are a few examples:

♦ *His lies* touched off (started) *a huge argument that lasted for days.*

♦ *The earthquake* touched off (started in motion) *a series of tidal waves.*

The idiom *start off* refers to beginning a presentation, project, or journey. *Set off, push off,* and *head off* mean to start a journey. And every space mission begins with the *blast off* from the launch pad. Here are a few more examples:

♦ *He* started off (began) *his speech with a joke.*

♦ *At 6 a.m. the climbers* headed off (started to go) *for the first peak.*

♦ *They* set off (start going, usually on a mission) *for the shopping mall.*

♦ *NASA reports that the Voyager 7 spacecraft* blasted off (began its flight, was launched) *on schedule.*

switch on/switch off(S)

1. to start or stop electrical lights, appliances, and other electrical or gas-driven products ♦ *In the winter, we have to* switch *the lights* on *in the afternoon.*
2. to start or stop the power on a machine, motor, or engine ♦ *Let's* switch on *the motor, and see if it works.*
3. to consciously start or stop mental activity or emotions ♦ *Sometimes it's hard to* switch off *my thoughts at night and fall asleep.*

log on/log off (*or* sign on/sign off) (S)

to enter information (like a username or password) into a computer to begin a session, and to end a computer session that requires that information ♦ *I* log on *every morning to check my e-mail.* ♦ *You can't end your session without* signing off. ♦ *My computer automatically* signed *me* off *before I was finished.*

[See *sign on* later in this chapter.]

COMMON PHRASAL VERBS WITH THE PREPOSITION *ON*

The preposition *on* is frequently used to form phrasal verbs. Two-word verbs with *on* are almost always transitive, and are often separable.

Accepting or Acquiring

The following idioms have a general meaning of to accept, assume, acquire, or cause to be acquired.

take on (S)

> **1.** to accept or undertake a project, challenge, extra work, or responsibility
> ♦ *Today, many seniors are* taking on *the responsibility of raising their grandchildren.* ♦ *We* took on *a few extra clients this month to boost our income.*
> **2.** to accept a challenge or compete against someone or something in a challenge or game ♦ *The Hornets* take on *the Fighting Tigers tonight at the arena.*
> **3.** to assume or acquire the quality or character of ♦ *My white clothes* took on *a pink hue when I washed them with red socks.*

Note: When a boat is leaking, and water is coming in, people say "The boat is *taking on* water." In some regions, people say that someone *takes on* (often followed by *so*) when they're very upset, angry, or sad. "She *took on so* over the loss of her cat." [See also *carry on* later in this section.]

sign on (S)

> **1.** to hire or be hired, usually by contract. Often used in sports. *Sign on* is often followed by the preposition *to* or *for.* ♦ *Borland Corporation* signed on *200 new employees last month.* ♦ *The New York Mets recently* signed on *three new players.*
> **2.** to engage oneself or others for a project ♦ *I'm interested in working on this project, so* sign *me* on. ♦ *Bob surprised me when he* signed on *for the new project.*

Note: *To take on* and *to sign on* both mean to acquire or accept work, responsibility, or employees, but *sign on* generally has the extra meaning of signing a contract. *Sign on* emphasizes the commitment by verbal or written contract, whereas *take on* emphasizes the additional work or people. [See *sign on/sign off* earlier and later in this section.]

bring on (S)

> **1.** to hire or assign to a project, usually a specialist in the field ♦ *They* brought on *a soil specialist to inspect the construction site.*
> **2.** to cause oneself or someone to acquire a problem ♦ *Touching the plant* brought on *a rash.* ♦ *He* brought *the problems* on *himself.*

Bring It On!

If you're ready, willing, and eager to take on a challenge or extra work, you might say (jokingly or seriously) "Okay, *bring it on!*" Are you ready to face a challenging component in a contest or game? You might announce *"Bring him on!"* or *"Bring her on!"* Are you part of a team? *"Bring 'em on!"* (shortening the word *them* to *'em*.) This expression has a slight double meaning, since *bring on* can also mean to bring or present someone or something to others.

Hang On and Related Idioms

The idioms in this section have a general meaning of to wait, persevere, maintain or keep one's grip.

hold on *or* **hang on**

> **1.** to remain on the telephone ♦ *Please* hold on. *An operator will assist you in a minute.* ♦ *After* hanging on *for 10 minutes, I finally hung up!*
> **2.** means "stop!"; to stop and wait for someone or something ♦ Hold on! *You can't enter this restricted area.* ♦ Hang on *a minute. I need to get my coat.*
> **3.** to persevere through difficulty, hardship, or challenge ♦ *My legs ached, but I tried to* hang on *for the last mile of the race.*
> **4.** to cling to, maintain one's grip, hold tightly ♦ *Okay,* hold on! *This roller coaster is really fast.* ♦ *My grandmother* hung on *to her old-fashioned ideals.*
> **5.** to stay alive (usually with *hang on*) ♦ *The injured skier* hung on *for three days without food or water until she was rescued.*

wait on (NS)

> to wait for someone or something to arrive in order to continue or proceed
> ♦ *I'm* waiting on *the survey results before I finish this report.* ♦ *We're just* waiting on *Tom. He's the only one not here yet.* **Note:** *Wait on* implies that something is being postponed or delayed while waiting.

[See also *wait on* in Chapter 3.]

Delaying a Decision

The following idioms have a general meaning of hold back, postpone, or delay a decision or action.

Read On! — When *On* Means Continue

To find out how to create a number of easy-to-remember idioms, *read on*. In other words, continue reading this paragraph. By simply adding the preposition *on* to many common verbs, you create idioms that mean to continue doing the action of the verb (often after a pause). For example, *drive on, talk on, play on, read on,* and *run on* mean to continue driving, talking, playing, reading, or running, or to continue after pausing. Here are some examples:

♦ *After stopping at the border, we* drove on.

♦ *The speaker* talked on *until late afternoon.*

♦ *The referee shouted* "Play on!" *after the timeout.*

♦ *The movie* ran on *for three hours.*

The idiom *go on* is often used as a general expression to mean continue doing whatever you were doing before an interruption or pause: "*Go on,* what where you saying?" Also, *go on* and *move on* can mean to continue going or moving, or to transfer to a new location, position, job, relationship, and so on: "After six years with the company, I *moved on* to a better job."

A number of other idioms mean to continue. To learn about them, *continue on* to the next section.

sit on (NS)

1. to postpone or delay a decision, action, or resolution, usually deliberately
♦ *The city council* sat on *the proposal for months.*
2. to hold back or suppress information ♦ *The investigation committee is* sitting on *some important evidence.*

Note: Be careful not to use "sit down on" when you mean to use the idiom *sit on.* "Sit down on" means simply to sit on a chair or another surface. So, if you say: "The city council 'sat down on' the proposal," it means that they put a copy of the proposal on their chairs, and then sat on top of it!

sleep on (NS)

to think about something for a day or two before making an important decision on it or taking action ♦ *It's a big decision. Maybe we should* sleep on *it for awhile.* *Note: Sleep on* implies that after one or two nights' sleep, a correct decision or course of action will become clearer.

Note: The important difference between *sitting on* something and *sleeping on* something is this: Saying "I'm going to *sit on* it for awhile" implies that you don't want to make a decision yet. You may even want to avoid thinking about it or making a decision. However, saying "I'm going to *sleep on* it for awhile" means that you want to think about more carefully before you decide.

Adding Something More

These idioms have a general meaning of to increase, or to add to an already existing collection of things.

add on (S)

> to add to an existing thing, often to increase the size ♦ *They* added on *an extra room to their house.* ♦ *The company* added on *several new employees.*

tack on (S)

> to add an extra item to an existing thing, often related to money ♦ *A late fee was* tacked on *to the unpaid bill.* ♦ *I* tacked *an appendix* on *to my report.*

Proceeding and Persisting

These idioms have a general meaning of continue, keep doing something, persist, or proceed. The idiom *keep on* has a number of different meanings, each requiring a slightly different construction, which is shown in parentheses before each definition.

keep on

> **1. (NS)** (keep on doing) to continue doing something, making an effort or persisting in any activity or behavior ♦ *Keep on going. Main Street is just ahead.* ♦ *She* keeps on *losing her car keys in the house.*
> **2. (NS)** (keep on about) to continue to nag or complain about someone or something. Generally put as *keep on about.* ♦ *He* kept on *about the problem until everyone was tired of hearing about it.*
> **3. (NS)** (keep on someone) to continue to urge, nag, or pressure someone ♦ *I* kept on *my sons until they finally cleaned their room.*
> **4. (S)** (keep something on) to continue to wear or stay attached ♦ *Some people* keep *their shoes* on *in the house; others take them off.* ♦ *Keep this bandage* on *the burn for a few days.*
> **5. (S)** (keep someone on) to continue to employ or be employed ♦ *They couldn't* keep *everyone* on *during the economic crisis.*

go on (*or* carry on)

> **1.** to continue or proceed ♦ *We'll* carry on *with the meeting until all the issues are discussed.* ♦ *He* went on *talking, even though half the audience had left.*

2. to continue doing or saying something after an interruption; to permit or instruct someone to proceed ♦ *Sorry to interrupt you. Please* go on. ♦ *When the inspection is finished,* carry on *with your work.*

3. to continue or proceed to the next step, level, or phase ♦ *She plans to* go on *to medical school after graduation.* ♦ *After you register for your classes,* go on *to the clerk to pay your fees.*

4. to strongly encourage or instruct someone to proceed, go, or try something ♦ Go on! *You can do it.* ♦ Go on! *You're going to be late for school if you don't hurry.*

Note: *Carry on* is often considered more formal and is more commonly used by figures of authority.

[See the index at the back of the book for the location of the many other uses of *go on*.]

move on

1. to continue or proceed to the next step, level, or phase, usually after completing the one before ♦ *Let's* move on *to the next agenda item.*

2. to continue moving or walking after a pause, or to instruct someone to do so ♦ *People stopped to see what had happened, but the police told them to* move on.

3. to continue with daily life after a bad experience; to try to leave a bad experience in the past ♦ *After the divorce, she tried to* move on *with her life.*

4. to advance or progress, often in one's personal or professional life ♦ *She wants to* move on *in her career.*

press on (*or* push on)

to continue or proceed on one's way, particularly with effort or difficulty ♦ *The trail was steep, but they* pushed on *until they reached the top.*

Life Goes On

After a bad experience or personal loss, people may say "Life *goes on*." Depending on the seriousness of the situation, they could mean any of the following:

Despite the misfortune, one must continue living.

I won't allow this misfortune to destroy or disrupt my life.

This misfortune is not so important to me.

On and On . . . Endlessly

Add *on and on* to any action verb to show that the action continued or persisted for a long time without stopping. *On and on* can imply something positive and good, such as: "They strolled happily *on and on* down the beach," or it can imply something tiresome or unpleasant, such as: "The boring speaker talked *on and on*." People often use *on and on* to express a feeling of endlessness, for example: "The qualifying exam seemed to go *on and on*." To exaggerate or emphasize the endlessness, use *on* a few more times. "The speaker went *on and on and on and on*."

COMMON PHRASAL VERBS WITH THE PREPOSITION *OFF*

Many fewer phrasal verbs include the preposition *off* than the preposition *on*. Except for a few cases, two-word verbs with *off* are transitive and separable.

Releasing or Emitting

These idioms have a general meaning of send out, emit, or release, such as light, energy, a scent, and so on.

give off (S)

> to send out or emit, usually a scent or light ◆ *Gardenias* give off *a wonderful scent.* ◆ *Halogen lamps* give off *a lot of bright light.*

let off (S)

> **1.** to release something under pressure or by explosion, such as steam, explosives, fireworks ◆ *Many cities* let off *fireworks on the Fourth of July.*
> **2.** to release from punishment or allow to escape from or be free from something ◆ *My son always washes the dishes, but today I* let *him* off *to finish his homework.* ◆ *The judge* let *him* off *with a fine, but next time he'll go to jail.*

Note: *Give off* and *let off* are similar, but *give off* is generally used for things that naturally (by their nature) release a substance or form of energy. *Let off* is generally used for things that need help or permission to be released. The expression "to *let* someone *off* the hook" also refers to releasing someone from obligation, blame, or punishment.

go off

> to release or emit sound or energy, as with an explosion or firearm ◆ *My alarm* goes off *at 6 a.m. every morning.* ◆ *The gun* went off *accidentally, but no one was hurt.*

Clearing Financial Obligation

These idioms have a general meaning of to get rid of, eliminate, or clear financial obligation. In these idioms, the preposition *off* implies an end to one's obligation or responsibility.

pay off (S)

> to eliminate a debt by paying the remaining balance ♦ *They celebrated when they finally* paid off *their house.*

sell off (S)

> to get rid of personal items or assets (usually at a low price) by selling them ♦ *He* sold off *some of his stock.*

write off (S)

> **1.** to eliminate from financial accounts as a loss ♦ *The company was never able to collect the debt, so they had to* write *it* off. ♦ *She* writes off *some of her expenses from her taxes.*
> **2.** to drop from consideration something or someone regarded as a failure or worthless ♦ *When he was a child, Einstein was* written off *as unintelligent.*

Deducting, Decreasing, or Stopping

These idioms have a general meaning of to deduct, decrease, reduce, or stop.

take off (S)

> to deduct or decrease the price, quantity, or amount of ♦ *They* took *20 percent* off *the original price.* ♦ *When I get my hair cut, I like just a little bit* taken off *the sides and back.*

[See *take off* earlier in this section and check the index to find the location of other definitions of the idiom *take off*.]

knock off (S)

> **1.** to deduct or decrease the price; to get rid of a portion of ♦ *Because the item is damaged, we'll* knock *$10* off *the price.*
> **2.** to quit an activity for the day, often some form of work or practice ♦ *We usually* knock off *work at 4:30 p.m.*

fall off (*or* drop off)

> to decrease or decline drastically; to become worse or less ♦ *Employment rates* fell off *sharply during the recession.* ♦ *Her interest in tennis really* dropped off *after she started playing golf.*

work off (S)

> **1.** to work in exchange for paying a debt directly, until the debt is paid ♦ *I was able to* work off *some of my rent by painting my apartment.*
> **2.** to eliminate or reduce weight and extra calories by exercising ♦ *He's trying to* work off *a few extra pounds.* ♦ *That was a huge meal. Let's take a walk and try to* work *some of it* off.

Holding Things Off

These idioms have a general meaning of to postpone, delay, or cancel, or to restrain, remove, or eliminate a threat.

put off (S)

> **1.** to postpone an action or decision, often out of laziness or because it is unpleasant or difficult ♦ *He* put off *going to the dentist until his toothache was unbearable.* ♦ *We had to* put off *our vacation until September.*
> **2.** to avoid or delay responding to or interacting with someone ♦ *He wanted my answer right away, but I* put *him* off *for a few days.*
> **3.** to offend or intimidate someone by being overly abrasive, assertive, or difficult ♦ *His pushy approach really* puts *people* off.

Grammar Note: When *put off* is followed by a verb, use the gerund form (verb + -*ing*).

hold off (S)

> **1.** to deliberately postpone an action or decision; to hesitate in a decision ♦ *We'll* hold off *the decision until we have more information.* ♦ *I want a new car now, but I have to* hold off *buying one until I get a raise.*
> **2.** to keep someone away, at a distance, or to deliberately delay interacting with someone ♦ *Can you* hold off *those salesmen? I don't want to see them now.* ♦ *He wanted to see her, but she was angry with him and kept* holding *him* off.

Grammar Note: When *hold off* is followed by a verb, use the gerund form (verb + -*ing*).

call off (S)

> **1.** to cancel a scheduled plan ♦ *The parade was* called off *because of rain.*
> **2.** to call away or summon an aggressive person or pet ♦ *Call off *your dog! It won't let me pass.*

Knock It Off!

Knock it off! is a strong, common expression used to order someone to be quiet or to stop behaving in a certain way. It's often said to children when they are too noisy or rowdy: "Okay, you kids, *knock it off!* Quit running in the house." But it's also used, rudely, with adults: "Hey, *knock it off!* You're making too much noise." *Knock it off* can be serious or playful depending on the situation.

fight off (S)

to defend oneself against attack; drive back an enemy; struggle to avoid being defeated or overcome. Often used to refer to illness, temptations, or sleep.
♦ *I've been* fighting off *a cold all week.* ♦ *I* fought off *the temptation to have a second piece of pie.*

Back Off and Related Idioms

These idioms have a general meaning of stay back or away from, retreat, avoid, dismiss, or reject.

back off

1. to move back a little bit, often out of caution ♦ *The dog looked friendly, but when he showed his teeth, we* backed off.
2. to lessen or stop annoying or pressuring; often used in regard to an argument, nagging, scolding, or advising ♦ *I'm not going to change my opinion, so please* back off! ***Note:*** In this context, this idiom is considered very strong and can be rude.

Don't Put Off Until Tomorrow...

A well-known saying goes "Don't put off until tomorrow what you can do today." It advises you to take advantage of the present moment or opportunities, to avoid procrastination, and not wait to do important or necessary things. Usually people shorten the expression and just say "Don't put off till tomorrow . . . ." As a humorous twist in meaning, when people are procrastinating, or feeling particularly lazy or uninspired, they may joke and excuse their inaction by saying "Don't do today what you can put off until tomorrow!"

Clean It Off!

When the preposition *off* is joined with a cleaning verb (clean, clear, dust, sweep, wash, and so on), the result is often an idiom that means to clean the top or outer surface of something, or to get the top layer of clutter or dirt off the surface. For example, to *rinse off* the plates generally means to run water over the surface to remove leftover food, (while to *rinse* the plates implies to rinse them thoroughly after washing them to remove all of the soap). These idioms are often used to refer to a light cleaning or clearing of clutter. The following sentences include the most common of these idioms:

♦ Clean off *the kitchen counter* (remove the clutter or wipe it clean).

♦ Clear off *your desk* (remove papers, books, and so on, from the top surface).

♦ Dust off *these books* (lightly dust).

♦ Rinse off *this apple before you eat it* (run water over the surface).

♦ Sweep off *the porch* (lightly sweep, often in preparation for use).

♦ Wipe off *the garden chairs before you use them* (lightly clean or wipe with a damp or dry cloth).

Note: The verbs *to vacuum*, *to mop*, and *to wax* are rarely joined with *off*, because these cleaning jobs generally take more time and effort; they can't be done lightly.

[See "*Clean It Out!*" and "*Clean It Up!*" later in this chapter.]

keep off (S)

1. to stay away from; to avoid trespassing or getting on ♦ *The sign on the stone monument read "Please* Keep Off.*"*
2. to prevent from getting on; avert ♦ *This hat will help* keep *the sun* off *your face.*

kiss off

1. means "Go away!" A strong, often rude expression of dismissal or rejection ♦ *She was so angry with him that she told him to* kiss off.
2. **(S)** to reject, dismiss, or let go of something, often that which is considered unworthy or a loss ♦ *He'll probably never pay you back, so you might as well* kiss *that money* off.

Phrasal Verbs with *In* and *Out*

The prepositions *in* and *out* are very commonly used in phrasal verbs. Phrasal verbs using *in* and *out* have a variety of meanings. In many instances, a verb with *in* and the same verb with *out* have an opposite meaning, such as *let in* and *let out*, *hand in* and *hand out*.

Note: Phrasal verbs using the prepositions *in* and *out* are often transitive and separable. But there are plenty of exceptions.

The following idiom is unique in that it has the same basic meaning whether it includes the preposition *in* or the preposition *out*.

fill in/fill out (S)

> to supply required information, often by completing a form ♦ *Choose your answer, and then* fill in *the corresponding circle with your pencil.* ♦ *When you finish* filling out *the forms, take them to the registration office.*

Note: *Fill in* and *fill out* have basically the same meaning, but *fill in* often refers to writing information in the blank spaces of a form (*fill in* the blanks), or marking the correct answer (*fill in* the answer). *Fill out* is generally used when referring to the overall process (*fill out* the form or paperwork).

[See *fill in* (substitute) later in this section.]

IN/OUT OPPOSITES: PHRASAL VERBS WITH OPPOSITE MEANINGS

Some phrasal verbs that use *in* and *out* have exactly opposite meanings; for example, *log in* and *log out* on a computer mean to begin and end a computer session. The following section includes phrasal verbs with *in* and *out* that are *antonyms* (have opposite meaning).

These idioms have the general meaning of to enter the necessary information into a computer to start a computer session, and to end the computer session. *Sign in/sign out* and *check in/check out* have a number of other meanings. **Grammar note:** The phrasal verbs in this group appear intransitive (having no direct object) when the direct object is *oneself* — myself, yourself, herself, and so on.

log in/log out

> **1. (S)** to enter a number, name, or password into a computer to begin a computer session/to quit or close the computer file or site to end a computer session ♦ *I* log in *every morning to check my e-mail.*
> **2. (S)** to record numbers or data into a record book or program; to record information into a machine to begin/end an operation ♦ *After you* log *the figures* in, *see what the data tells us.* ♦ *Don't forget to* log out *of the cash register at the end of your shift.*

[See *log on/log off* earlier in this chapter.]

sign in/sign out

> **1.** to enter a number, name, or password into a computer to begin a session/to quit or close the computer file or site to end a computer session ♦ Sign in *now by entering your password.*
> **2.** to sign your name into a register book to indicate that you have arrived or are leaving, usually at a medical office, a workplace, meeting, or conference ♦ *Please* sign in *and take a seat in the waiting room.* ♦ *Oops! I forgot to* sign out *when I took my lunch break today.*
> **3. (S)** to sign (something) in/out; to record that something has arrived or has been returned/to record that something is being removed or borrowed, often equipment or a package ♦ *We* sign *each rental car back* in *when it's returned.*
> ♦ *If you want to borrow this AV equipment, then you need to* sign *it* out.

[See *sign on/sign off* earlier in this chapter; see *sign up* later in this chapter.]

check in/check out

> **1.** to register to stay at a hotel or attend a convention; to settle the bill and leave a hotel or hospital ♦ *After we* check in, *let's go to the pool.* ♦ *You must* check out *of your room by 11:00 a.m.* **Grammar note:** To register at a hospital, use the verb *to be admitted.* You can also use the idiom *check into/check out of.*
> **2. (S)** to record that borrowed items have been returned; to borrow items, usually books and other materials, from a library or equipment room ♦ *You're allowed to* check out *five books and two videos at one time.* ♦ *It usually takes me an hour to* check in *all the returned library books.*
> **3.** to quit or leave in a hurry or out of boredom or restlessness ♦ *This movie is boring. I'm* checking out. *See you later.*

[See *check in* (report) and *check out* (investigate, look, approve) later in this section.]

These idioms have the general meaning of to enter or exit, or to allow someone or something to enter or exit.

break in/break out

> **1.** to enter or exit by force, usually through a door or window ♦ *A burglar* broke in *and stole some jewelry.* ♦ *He tried to* break out *of prison, but he didn't succeed.* **Note:** *Break out* can be separable when expressed as *breaking* someone *out* of jail, prison, or a routine.
> **2. (S)** to force oneself or someone else to change his or her regular schedule, habits, or day-to-day routine. Often put as *break out of.* ♦ *Taking a vacation helps you* break out *of your monotonous routine.* ♦ *Yoga and tennis helped* break *me* out *of my inactive lifestyle.*

These idioms have a general meaning of to submit by hand and to distribute by hand.

hand in/hand out (S)

> to submit something by hand, generally paperwork, a report, or project/to distribute something by hand, generally paper or other products or material ♦ Hand in *your project proposals next Monday.* ♦ *They* handed out *free tickets to the concert.*

pass in/pass out (S)

> to submit something by hand, generally paperwork, a report, or project/to distribute something by hand, generally paper or other products or material ♦ *I'll* pass out *the exam now.* ♦ *Please* pass *your workbooks* in, *and I'll collect them.* **Note:** *Pass in/pass out* is often used in a classroom or meeting where participants may pass the materials from one to another to distribute or return them. The idiom *pass in* can only be used in a group setting.

[See also *turn in* and *give out* later in this section.]

Coming In and Going Out

These idioms look simple at first because they can have the literal meaning of to come or go inside and to come or go outside. But they also have a number of specific uses and meanings including to visit, enter, or let someone enter a home, building, and so on; to return to one's home; or to allow something to enter or escape. ***Grammar note:*** Choose the verb *come* or the verb *go* depending on meaning and on where the speakers and listeners are when they're talking.

[For more information on how to use the verbs *come* and *go* correctly, see the sidebar in Chapter 18.]

[See *come out* (result in) and *go out* (extinguish) later in this section.]

A Few Additional *In/Out Opposites*

move in/move out

> to begin/end occupancy of a residence, office, neighborhood, or professional position ♦ *Our neighbors just* moved out, *and now some new people are* moving in. **Grammar Note:** Often put as *move into/move out of.*

tune in/tune out (S)

> **1. (S)** to be knowledgeable or aware; to pay close attention to/to turn one's attention away from (often talk, music, or noise) ♦ *She's really* tuned in *to the art world.* ♦ *I live on a noisy street, but I've learned to* tune *it* out.
> **2. (S)** to adjust a radio or TV to a particular frequency, station, or channel to receive information or a specific program/to adjust the radio or TV dial to eliminate static or interference ♦ *Tune in at 6 p.m. for the nightly news on channel 4.* ♦ *I tried to* tune out *the static on this station, but it's still there.*

butt in/butt out

> **1.** to get involved in someone else's personal business or conversation/disengage from someone else's personal business or conversation ♦ *He* butts in *everyone's business. It's annoying!* ♦ *It's their problem; I tried to help, but I think I should* butt out.
> **2.** to interrupt/enter an existing conversation ♦ *Sorry for* butting in, *but I have a quick question.*

Note: This idiom is often put as *butt into/butt out of.* *Nose in/nose out* means the same thing.

Note: *Butt out!* can mean "leave me alone!"

PHRASAL VERBS USING THE PREPOSITION *IN*

Phrasal verbs with *in* often allude to entering or being involved in something. Except for a few cases, two-word verbs with *in* are transitive and separable. [See information on transitive and separable phrasal verbs in Chapter 18.]

Visiting

These phrasal verbs are all use in reference to visiting, and inviting someone in:

drop in

> **1.** to visit a home without an invitation ♦ *I wish they wouldn't* drop in *unannounced.* ♦ *Feel free to* drop in *anytime. I'm usually home.* **Grammar note:** *Drop in* is often followed by the word *unannounced,* meaning to visit people without telling them ahead of time.
> **2.** to stop quickly at a home, shop, or office, often put as *drop in to* or *drop in at* ♦ *I need to* drop in *at the post office to get some stamps.* ♦ *Let's* drop in *to the library for a minute and return these books.*

invite in (*or* **ask in**) **(S)**

> to invite someone to enter a home, office, or other structure ♦ *She talked to him at the door, but she didn't* invite *him* in. ♦ *Tommy,* ask *our guests* in; *don't leave them standing on the front porch.*

[See *ask out* (invite for a date) later in this section.]

Sleeping

These idioms both refer to sleep. *Note:* The idiom *turn in* also has many other meanings.

sleep in

> to sleep later than usual, generally by choice, often on the weekend or during a vacation ♦ *We like to* sleep in *on Sunday morning.* ♦ *I feel well rested today because I* slept in.

[See other sleep-related idioms in Chapter 3.]

turn in

> to go to bed, ready for sleep, at the end of the evening ♦ *We usually* turn in *around 11:00 p.m.* ♦ *It's late. Let's* turn in. **Note:** Don't use *turn in* to refer to taking a nap or falling asleep unexpectedly. Also, *turn in* is rarely used when referring to children, because they are usually put to bed or sent to bed by an adult. **Grammar note:** And certainly don't say *turn* the children *in*! That means to surrender them to the police for their crimes!

Sorry for Interrupting . . .

If you've ever tried to join a conversation of American English speakers, you've probably discovered that to get a chance to speak, you have to interrupt someone, or jump in at the slightest pause. There will rarely be a long pause, or any organized taking of turns. So, it's no surprise that American English has a number of idioms that mean to interrupt a conversation. *Butt in* is just one of them. There is also *cut in, break in,* and *jump in.* They all mean to interrupt, but *break in* implies that more effort is required to enter the conversation; *jump in* suggests active participation with plenty to say; you can *cut in* with just a word or two.

[See *jump in, dive in, break in,* and *cut in* later in this section.]

Substituting

These idioms have a general meaning of to substitute or take someone's place.

fill in

> to substitute for someone, take someone's place, or fill an extra work position ♦ *They asked me to* fill in *for an employee who's out sick.* ♦ *Thanks for* filling in *during the holiday shopping rush.* **Note:** This idiom is also put *to fill in for.*

[See *fill in/fill out* (complete a form) earlier in this section.]

pitch in

> to help with a job, project, or chore ♦ *On the weekend, everyone* pitches in *to clean the house.* ♦ *Thanks for* pitching in *when we had the party.*

stand in

> to substitute for someone or take someone's place, often at an event or a ceremony ♦ *My assistant will* stand in *for me at the meeting while I'm out of town.* ♦ *Thanks for* standing in *at the reception when my brother couldn't come.* **Note:** This idiom is also put as *to stand in for.*

Getting In

These idioms often have a general meaning of to enter or interrupt a conversation, or to force oneself ahead of others in a line or traffic.

break in (*or* break into)

1. to suddenly enter or interrupt a conversation, discussion, or speech, often with some news or information ♦ *The announcer* broke in *with news of the World Cup results.* ♦ *It's hard to* break into *a discussion when everyone is talking fast.*

2. to force oneself ahead in a line ♦ *When he tried to* break in *line, people told him to go to the end.*

cut in

1. to suddenly (and often rudely) enter or interrupt a conversation, discussion, or speech ♦ *She told her son not to* cut in *when other people are talking.* ♦ *Commercials have* cut in *to this program every 10 minutes!*

2. to force oneself ahead in a line, often simply put as *to cut;* to get into a line of traffic, often abruptly or recklessly ♦ *The line was so long that I let two old ladies* cut in *front of me.* ♦ *He* cut in *traffic, nearly causing an accident.*

The following idioms have a general meaning of to begin or to get involved enthusiastically in something without hesitation or fear.

dive in (*or* jump in)

1. to start doing something with enthusiasm and without hesitation; to involve oneself completely and wholeheartedly in something ♦ *She* dove into *the project with much enthusiasm.* ♦ *If you want to learn computer skills, you just have to* jump in *and start trying.*

2. (NS) to get into an ongoing discussion or conversation (generally only with jump in) ♦ *Jump in the discussion whenever you want. Don't wait to be invited.*

Note: These idioms are sometimes put to *dive/jump into* or put as to *dive/jump in with both feet,* to emphasize the full involvement.

check in

1. to report by phone or in person about one's whereabouts or schedule ♦ *I have to* check in *at home with my parents before dark.* ♦ *Should I* check in *with the office during my vacation?*

2. to present a plane ticket or your name at the ticket counter to confirm your reservation and receive a boarding pass ♦ *You should* check in *two hours early for international.* ♦ *Wow! Look at the long line of people waiting to* check in.

3. (S) to check something in; to present your luggage or other items to be put in the cargo section of a plane or train; often put simply as *to check* ♦ *You have to* check *that bag* in; *it's too big to carry on the plane.* ♦ *We usually* check in *all our bags.*

[See *check in/check out* (register at a hotel) earlier in this section.]

Giving and Taking

give in

> to yield to someone or something; to relent or give up an argument or opposition ♦ *He finally* gave in *and let his son drive his new car.* ♦ *She refused to* give in *to her desire for sleep, and worked all night.*

take in (S)

> **1.** to observe with great interest; to visit or experience, often entertainment or tourist attractions ♦ *The baby* took in *all the sights and sounds of the fair.* ♦ *We* took in *a movie and then had dinner.* ♦ *We didn't have enough time to* take in *all the museums in Washington, D.C.*
> **2.** to understand; to absorb mentally ♦ *The speaker gave us so much information that I couldn't* take *it all* in. ♦ *I* took in *all my parents' advice — but I didn't always follow it.*
> **3.** to provide shelter for or to receive in one's home for pay ♦ *Their neighbors* took *them* in *for a few months after their house burned.* ♦ *My grandmother* took in *borders to earn extra money.*

[See *take out* later in this section.]

Fitting In and Related Idioms

These idioms have a general meaning of to make time for, insert, add into, or be in harmony with.

fit in

> **1. (S)** to make time in a schedule ♦ *We hope we can* fit in *a trip to the East Coast this summer.* ♦ *I can't* fit *another thing* into *my schedule on Tuesday. It's full.*
> **2.** to be in harmony or accord with ♦ *I think this sofa will* fit in *well with our other furniture.* ♦ *This project* fits in *well with our overall mission.*
> **3.** to be accepted and recognized as part of a group (non-separable) ♦ *All children want to* fit in *and be liked by other kids.* ♦ *It's a perfect group for you. I know you'll* fit in *well.*

figure in

> **1. (S)** to add into or include ♦ *Owning a car is expensive when you* figure in *the cost of insurance.*

2. to influence or play a part in (generally not separated) ♦ *Her experience* figured in *more than her credentials when she got the job.* ♦ *The warm climate definitely* figured in *to our decision to move to Florida.*

work in (S)

to make time in a schedule, or add into a schedule as an extra element ♦ *The doctor's schedule is booked but we'll try to* work *you* in. ♦ *I* worked in *a trip to Vancouver while I was in Canada on business.*

[See *figure out* and *work out* later in this section.]

PHRASAL VERBS USING THE PREPOSITION *OUT*

Almost all of the phrasal verbs with the preposition *out* have different meanings. Most phrasal verbs with *out* are transitive, or have some transitive forms depending on meaning. All transitive phrasal verbs listed here are separable. [For information on transitive and separable phrasal verbs, see Chapter 18.]

Caution!

These idioms have a general meaning of to be alert and or to be careful about a potential threat or danger. *Note:* Pronounce *look out* and *watch out* with a stronger accent on the word *out*, especially when the danger is immediate: *Look* **OUT!** *Watch* **OUT!**

look out (*or* watch out)

1. to beware, be careful or cautious of, be alert to or on one's guard; often used as a strong warning of immediate danger; often put *look out for/watch out for*
♦ Look out! *There's a car coming.* ♦ Look out *for the wet paint. Don't touch it.*
2. a warning to take special care in using something, said before, during, or after use; often put as *look out* or *watch out with something* ♦ Watch out *with those chemicals. They're pretty caustic.* ♦ *Hey,* watch out! *You almost hit me with your golf club.*

Dating

These idioms are all used to refer to the planning of and going on a date. *Go out* and *take out* have a number of other meanings, also.

but *figure out* is generally used when a person discovers or learns something from his or her own effort or mistakes. *Find out* can be used this way, but also can mean that something is discovered accidentally, or is learned from someone else. **Grammar Note:** Both idioms can be transitive and separable, for example, "We *figured* the game *out*" and "We *found* some things *out* about the company." But often these idioms aren't separated.

The following example sentences highlight the differences and similarities in *figure out* and *find out*.

figure out (S)

to discover, learn, understand, or determine as a result of trial and error, practice, experience, or investigation ♦ *After a few failures, they* figured out *how to put up their tent.* ♦ *He's an odd person. I can't* figure *him* out.

find out

1. (S) To discover or learn information from an inquiry, investigation, experience, or through word of mouth (usually not separated) ♦ *They read the directions to* find out *how to put up their tent.* ♦ *He's a private person, so I haven't* found out *much about him yet.*

2. (S) to learn the truth or true nature of something; to become aware of the truth ♦ *We didn't know how humid Hawaii could be, but we* found out! ♦ *He took his parents' car when they were gone, but they* found *him* out. **Note:** The previous example sentence could also read "... but they *found out*." **Grammar Note:** In this context, *find out* implies that one was previously uninformed or ignorant, and was surprised to learn the truth.

Check Out *and* Work Out

check out (S)

1. (S) to inspect, investigate, or look closely for information ♦ *I'll* check out *a few Web sites on the topic.* ♦ *Check out the appendix in the back of the book for a list of phrasal verbs.*

2. (S) to look at with curiosity or interest; to look with romantic or sexual interest ♦ *Hey,* check out *this beautiful sunset!* ♦ *She saw him* checking *her* out *from across the room.*

3. to have one's purchase totaled up and to pay a cashier, such as in a grocery store ♦ *Are you ready to* check out?

4. to pass inspection; to prove to be working or sound after examination ♦ *We had the engine* checked out *before our road trip.* ♦ *The building inspector said that everything* checked out *okay.*

work out

> **1. (S)** to discover the cause of ♦ *I haven't yet* worked out *what was wrong with my printer.*
> **2.** to exercise or train, usually in a gym; to make someone else exercise or train (separable) ♦ *I* work out *three times per week.* ♦ *Our dance instructor* works *us* out *pretty hard.*
> **3. (S)** to resolve a problem or find a solution ♦ *The counselor helped them* work out *their differences.* ♦ *Don't worry, everything will* work *itself* out *in the end.*
> **4. (S)** to solve a mathematical problem ♦ *She* worked out *all the math problems in her head.*

[See also *work out* later in this Part.]

Point Out and *Stand Out*

point out (S)

> to direct someone's attention to something, to identify, or to show ♦ *The instructor* pointed *our mistakes* out *to us.* ♦ *Our tour guide* pointed out *a number of historical buildings.*

stand out

> to be obvious, prominent, noticeable ♦ *He's so tall that he really* stands out *in a crowd.* ♦ *The pale lettering doesn't* stand out *enough. Let's make it darker.*

Extinguishing

These idioms have a general meaning of to extinguish or stop illuminating or functioning.

burn out (S)

> to stop burning, such as a flame or electrical light; to overheat (get too hot) and stop working, such as an electric motor ♦ *The candle* burned out. *I'll relight it.*
> ♦ *The kitchen light just* burned out. *Let's change it.*

go out

> to suddenly and unexpectedly extinguish, such as a flame, or to turn off, such as electricity; to stop working, such as a motor ♦ *The candle* went out *in the wind.* ♦ *During the storm, the electricity kept* going out.

turn out (S)

to turn off or shut off electrical lighting ♦ *Okay, boys, it's time to stop playing and* turn out *the lights.* ♦ *Please* turn *the lights* out *when you leave the room.* ***Note:*** This idiom sometimes means to turn off the lights and go to sleep.

[See *go out* (date) earlier in this section. See *burn out* (become exhausted) earlier in this section, and various other meanings of *turn out* that follow.]

Resulting In

These idioms often have a general meaning of to result in, end up, or eventually become. ***Note:*** *Come out* is sometimes used for short-term results, while *turn out* is sometimes used for longer-term results. The definitions that follow show a few other differences in usage. ***Grammar Note:*** *Come out* can be followed by an adverb or prepositional phrase, while *turn out* can be followed by an adverb, prepositional phrase, or by the infinitive *to be* plus an adjective.

come out

to end up, to result in the end, often after work or effort ♦ *The meal* came out *very well.* ♦ *These set designs are* coming out *well. You're doing a great job!*

turn out

1. to end up, to result in, to become in the end, sometimes by chance or luck, but also after work or effort; *turn out* can imply that the result is different from what was expected ♦ *Their children all* turned out *to be professionals.* ♦ *This party is* turning out *better than we expected.*
2. to arrive in numbers or assemble for an event ♦ *Thousands of people* turned out *for the peace march.* ♦ *All of her relatives* turned out *for her 90th birthday party.*
3. (S) to evict or expel, often from a house. Sometimes put *turn out on the streets.* ♦ *He was* turned out *on the street when he failed to pay the rent.* ♦ *Don't* turn *your rebellious teenagers* out. *They need a stable home.*
4. (S) to produce, often referring to mass production; to graduate, often individuals with specialized training ♦ *The factory* turns out *500 new cars per day.* ♦ *This university has* turned out *many of the world's top scientists.*

Call Out and *Speak Out*

call out

1. **(NS)** to call or shout loudly to get someone's attention; often put as *call out to* or *for* ♦ *She* called out *to her children who were in the yard.* ♦ *He kept* calling out *for help until the rescue team found him.*
2. **(NS)** to use a telephone to make, but not receive, calls; also *dial out* ♦ *On this line you can only* call out.
3. **(NS)** to order food by phone to be delivered ♦ *Let's* call out *for pizza.*
4. **(S)** to challenge someone to a fight ♦ *He* called *the man* out *after they had argued in the bar.* ♦ *Hey! I'm* calling *you* out!

speak out

to express one's opinions or support openly, freely, or forcefully; often put as *speak out on* or *about* (a topic) or *speak out for/against* (a cause) ♦ *Dr. Martin Luther King, Jr.* spoke out *for equal rights.* ♦ *He's afraid he'll lose his job if he* speaks out *about the long hours.*

[See *speak up* later in this chapter.]

Give Out and *Hold Out*

These idioms have somewhat opposite meanings: *hold out* can mean to last or endure, while *give out* can mean to be depleted (not last) or to stop enduring.

give out

1. **(NS)** to be depleted, as a supply of something; to stop operating, running, or moving because of poor condition or exhaustion ♦ *Their money* gave out *before the end of the trip.* ♦ *Let's sit down; I'm* giving out!
2. **(S)** to distribute ♦ *The teacher* gave out *stickers to all her students.* ♦ *Packages of food and clothing were* given out *to the refugees.*

hold out

1. to last, endure, or continue to operate or run despite being old or in poor condition ♦ *I hope this old car* holds out *for a few more years.* ♦ *Their supply of canned food* held out *through the winter.*
2. to continue to resist, to not yield, to stand firm in one's demands; often put as *hold out for* or *against* ♦ *We're* holding out *for the best offer on our house.* ♦ *The village* held out *against the rising flood waters.*
3. to withhold; to not give information on something that is expected; often put as *hold out on* ♦ *Tell me all the details; don't* hold out on *me.*

Drop Out and Other Slang Expressions with *Out*

All of the following idioms are slang expressions.

drop out

> **1.** to quit going to school, to stop participating, usually in a class or program
> ♦ *He* dropped out *of school and joined the Navy.* ♦ *She had to* drop out *of the program.*
> **2.** to stop being an active member of mainstream society ♦ *He* dropped out *and lived in a cabin in the wilderness.* ♦ *In the 1960s some young people* dropped out *and lived on communes.*

[See also *give up* later in this chapter.]

freak out (S)

> to become upset, agitated, or afraid; to make someone have these feelings
> ♦ *My dad really* freaked out *when he saw the dent in the car.* ♦ *Snakes* freak *me* out. *I'm afraid of them.*

hang out

> **1.** to relax, spend idle time, do nothing ♦ *Let's just* hang out *this weekend.*
> **2.** to spend time with friends or family, to get together, to associate with
> ♦ *Do you want to* hang out? ♦ *I usually* hang out *with my family on Sundays.*

space out (S)

> **1.** to be forgetful, not able to remember; sometimes simply put as *spaced* ♦ *I* spaced out *some of the questions on the exam.* ♦ *I'm sorry, you told me your name, but I immediately* spaced *it* out.
> **2.** to disorient, often used in the adjective form *to be spaced out* ♦ *This pain medication the doctor gave me really* spaces *me* out.

wipe out (S)

> to eliminate, destroy, make extinct, or kill ♦ *Efforts to* wipe out *world hunger have not yet succeeded.* ♦ *Smallpox has nearly been* wiped out *worldwide.* **Note:** *Wipe out often refers to disease, hunger, or other world problems, or to permanently destroying large numbers.*

Cleaning

air out (S)

to allow fresh air to remove odors or mildew, or to replace stale air ♦ *She opened a window and* aired out *the room.* ♦ *We* aired *our sleeping bags* out *after the camping trip.*

clean out (S)

1. to thoroughly clean or remove the dirt, bacteria, or clutter from the inside of something ♦ *He* cleaned out *the cut and put disinfectant on it.* ♦ *We're planning to* clean out *our garage this weekend.*

2. to completely use up, generally money or food ♦ *When our grandsons came to visit, they* cleaned out *the refrigerator!* ♦ *Those house repairs really* cleaned *me* out.

Clean It Out!

When the preposition *out* is joined with a cleaning verb (*clean, sweep, wash, wipe,* and so on), the result is often an idiom that means to clean the dirt or clutter from the inside of something. For example, to *clean out* the car generally means to remove any clutter or dirt from the inside of the car or the floor of the car (while to *clean* the car generally implies to wash the outside). These "clean out" idioms are often used to refer to a thorough and complete cleaning or removal of clutter from the *inside* of something. Some idioms, such as *sweep out* and *vacuum out*, imply to sweep or vacuum an enclosed space. **Note:** *Wash out* has two meanings: first, to wash the inside of something, concentrating on the dirt or leftover food that's on the inside, and second, to wash the dirt or stains out of cloth or clothing, or to it wash by hand in a sink. The following sentences include the most common of these idioms:

- ♦ *I* cleaned out *my desk when I quit my job.*

- ♦ Wipe out *the inside of the refrigerator with a damp cloth.*

- ♦ Sweep out *the garage.*

- ♦ Wash out *this pan.*

- ♦ *I'll try to* wash *the stains* out *of this shirt.*

- ♦ Vacuum out *the car.*

Phrasal Verbs with *Up* and *Down*

When the prepositions *up* and *down* are used with a verb, they often add emphasis or make the verb more specific. Therefore, many phrasal verbs that use *up* and *down* have a meaning similar to the verb itself. For example, *eat up* means to eat heartily or finish eating; *calm down* means to become calmer, less upset, or less angry; *close up* means to close and lock or to finalize. In these cases, the preposition extends the meaning of the verb, gives it added stress, or makes it less general. These types of idioms can be easier to learn because the basic definition of the verb isn't changed by adding *up* or *down*.

Note: Phrasal verbs using the prepositions *up* and *down* are often transitive and separable. But there are plenty of exceptions. Each transitive idiom presented in this section is marked with either **(S)** for separable or **(NS)** for non-separable.

UP/DOWN OPPOSITES: PHRASAL VERBS WITH OPPOSITE MEANINGS

Some phrasal verbs with *up* and *down* have opposite meanings. For example, *turn up* and *turn down* can mean to increase or decrease the volume of a radio, TV, your voice, and so on. The following section includes phrasal verbs with *up* and *down* that are *antonyms* (having opposite meanings).

turn up/turn down (S)

1. to increase/decrease volume, light, heat, or cooling ♦ *Please* turn down *the music. It's too loud.* ♦ *They* turned up *the lights in the theater during intermission.*
2. to turn something, like cards, so that the front side or face is showing, or so it is standing up, or to turn something so that the back side is showing ♦ Turn up *three cards and start playing.* ♦ *Your collar is* turned up *on one side. You should* turn *it* down.

[See *turn up* and *turn down* later in this section.]

go up/go down (NS)

1. to increase/decrease; generally used with prices, statistics, quantity, or quality ♦ *The price of a postage stamp just* went up *to 37 cents.* ♦ *The quality of service has* gone down *drastically.*

2. to ascend/descend, to rise/fall; generally used with the stock market or temperature ♦ *The stock market* went up *50 points today.* ♦ *At night the temperature* goes down *pretty low.*

COMMON PHRASAL VERBS WITH THE PREPOSITION *UP*

The preposition *up* is the most frequently used preposition in phrasal verbs. Often the preposition *up* adds emphasis to the meaning of the verb or makes the action of the verb more specific. For example, the idiom *look up* means to *look* for information, specifically in a reference book or source. *Write up* means to *write* an account or summary of one's research or work, as in "I'll *write up* the test results tomorrow," or "Please *write up* a bill for me showing the cost of materials and labor." Most phrasal verbs with *up* are transitive and separable, but of course there are exceptions.

The first four sections that follow include easy-to-learn idioms in which the preposition *up* extends or emphasizes the literal meaning of the verb. The remaining sections are organized into categories of idioms with similar or related meanings.

Coming Up and *Coming Down*

Use *come up* (rather than *go up*) to mean to appear or come into view from below. For example, when the sun (or moon) rises or comes into view, say "The sun *came up.*" However, when the sun or moon sets (disappears below the horizon), use the idiom *go down.* You would say "The sun *goes down* at 6 p.m.," not *comes down.* Use the idiom *go down* to talk about other things that lower and/or disappear from sight. Here are some examples with *come up* and *go down*:

♦ *Flowers* come up *in the spring* (appear above the soil).

♦ *The bath water* went down *the drain* (disappear down the drain pipe).

♦ *He put ice on the bump on his head and it* went down (got smaller or disappeared).

So when should you use *come down?* Use *come down* (or *come back down*) when you mean to return to the normal or original position, or to the preferred position.

♦ *His fever has finally* come down (return to normal or close to normal).

♦ *Will gas prices ever* come back down? (return to a more normal or preferred price)

♦ *Hey,* come down *out of that tree!* (return to the ground).

When *Up* Means into Pieces

When the preposition *up* is added to verbs like *cut, tear, slice,* and so on, the new verb means to separate into pieces (often small pieces). For example, *tear up* means to tear into small pieces (and possibly discard). If someone says "Oops! I *tore* my report," you might say "Here's some tape to repair it." But if someone says "I *tore up* my report," you'll probably be surprised and say "Why?! What was wrong with it?" The following sentences show some of the most common phrasal verbs of this type. They are all separable.

- *She* cut up *an onion for the stew* (cut into pieces).
- Chop up *some celery for the stuffing, please* (chop into small pieces).
- *She* ripped up *an old shirt for rags* (rip or tear into pieces).
- Slice up *this tomato, please* (slice into many slices).
- *He* tore *the letter* up *and threw it away* (tore into small pieces).

When *Up* Means Completely or Until Gone

When the preposition *up* is added to verbs like *drink, eat, use,* and others, the new verb means to finish or do until completed or gone. For example, *"Drink* your milk" means, in general, to take a drink of it. But *"Drink up* your milk" means specifically to finish it or drink it all. The idioms in the following examples all mean to do the action completely or until finished. They are all separable.

- *Who* ate up *the cake* (ate the last of it)?
- Drink up *your coffee, and I'll refill your cup* (drink it all).
- *She* filled up *the tank with gas* (filled it completely).
- *I* finished up *the report last night* (completed the last part).
- *We* used *all the bread* up (finished it all; it's gone).

Without the word *up*, the verbs in the preceding sentences still mean to eat, drink, fill, and so on. However, they don't necessarily imply or emphasize that the action should be finished or done completely. For example, "Who *ate* the cake?" could mean "Who had some of the cake?" but "Who *ate up* the cake?" definitely means "Who finished it?" To *fill* the tank and to *fill up* the tank have the same meaning, but strangely, you can also say, "She *filled* the tank halfway." If you want to state clearly that something is filled completely, say *"filled up."*

In some contexts, the verb alone sounds like a command or order. For example, "Drink your coffee!" sounds like a command, but "Drink up your coffee!" sounds more like a suggestion or invitation to empty your cup. To politely tell someone to finish the entire contents, say *"Drink up."*

[See also *"Clean It Up!"* later in this section.]

When *Up* Means More, Faster, Better, and So On

Sometimes, adding *up* to a verb is like adding a comparative, such as *more, better, faster, sooner,* and so on. For example, "Hurry!" means to go quickly so you won't be late or miss something. "*Hurry up!*" also means to go quickly but specifically means to hurry faster. *Hurry up* is usually used impatiently to urge someone to go faster or to quickly finish something, for example, "*Hurry up!* We're all waiting for you" or "Would you *hurry up* in the bathroom. I need to get ready for work."

Note: It would be incorrect to say "The nervous speaker *hurried up* through his speech." The correct way is "The nervous speaker *hurried* through his speech."

The following examples show some of the most common idioms of this type, all of which use *up* to imply *more.* All are separable except *speak up.*

♦ *The weather is beginning to* warm up.
♦ *She* lightened up *the skin tones in her painting.*
♦ *The sky begins to* lighten up *around 6 a.m.*
♦ *The white paint really* brightens up *this room.*
♦ *I* tightened up *those loose screws.*
♦ *It's starting to rain. I wish the bus would* hurry up.
♦ *You can't* hurry *him* up; *he goes at his own pace.*
♦ *We can't hear you.* Speak up, *please.*

[See *cheer up, speak up,* and *lighten up* later in this chapter.]

When *Up* Adds Emphasis

Using the preposition *up* with some verbs adds emphasis or subtle meaning to the verb. You might argue that these are not true idioms, but often these terms are used in a limited context or to express meaning that is more specific than the general meaning of the verb. The following are some common idioms in this category. The definitions show how the idiom's meaning or usage is slightly different form the verb alone.

♦ *They* cooked up *a delicious meal* (not just cooked, but prepared for the purpose of serving).
♦ *My aunt* mixes up *a batch of cookies whenever I visit* (mixes and bakes in order to serve).
♦ Eat up, *everyone!* (eat heartily and with enjoyment)
♦ Call *me* up *sometime* (telephone, often to socialize).

[See also *mix up* later in this section.]

Clean It Up!

Idioms that include the preposition *up* and a cleaning verb (*clean, sweep, vacuum, wipe,* or *rake*), mean specifically to remove or get rid of visible clutter or bits of dirt or debris. For example, "*Rake up* the leaves" means specifically to rake and remove the leaves. Of course you can simply say *clean, sweep, vacuum* and so on to describe general cleaning. But people tend to add the preposition *up* to imply that specific bits of debris or dirt need to be removed. For example "*Wipe up* the counter" implies that something specific like crumbs, a spill, or other mess needs to be wiped and removed. The following examples show how these idioms are used:

- ♦ *He* cleaned up *the leaves in the back yard.*
- ♦ *After woodshop class, everyone helps* sweep up.
- ♦ *Please* vacuum up *the dirt you brought in the house!*
- ♦ Wipe *that spill* up *quickly before someone slips on it.*

Note: You can say *vacuum the rug* or simply *vacuum up,* but don't say *vacuum up the rug.* That implies the entire rug will be sucked into the vacuum!

The Five Senses and Phrasal Verbs with *Up*

You can remember the following group of phrasal verbs by noting their reference to the five senses: sight (*look up*), sound (*listen up*), smell (*smell up*), taste (*spice up*), and touch (*touch up*).

look up (S)

1. to look for or check information in a dictionary or other reference source
   ♦ *You can* look up *idioms in the index of this book.*
2. to locate, call, or visit someone, especially someone you don't see regularly
   ♦ *We* looked up *our old college friends when we were in New York.* ♦ *Please* look *me* up *if you ever come to my city.*

listen up

to listen carefully or attentively to someone's announcement; usually said as a command ♦ Listen up, *everyone, I want to make an announcement.* ♦ Listen up! *Here's the schedule for tonight's game.*

smell up (*or* stink up) (S)

to cause something (usually an area) to smell bad or take on a strong odor
♦ *Cooking fish or cabbage can* smell up *the house.* ♦ *Ugh! That cigar really* stinks *the room* up. **Note:** *Stink up* is used for especially bad odors.

spice up (S)

1. to make food or drink more spicy (hot) or flavorful by adding spices ♦ *Those red peppers really* spice up *this dish.*
2. to make something more interesting or exciting, to add zest ♦ *We can* spice *this poster* up *with some colorful photos.*

touch up (S)

to repair or freshen chipped paint or nail polish, make-up, or photos ♦ *She just had time to* touch up *her make-up before going out for the evening.* ♦ *I need some special paint to* touch up *the scratch on my car.*

Speaking Out and Keeping Quiet

The idioms *speak up* and *talk up* can mean to express one's opinion or support, or to speak openly or louder. By contrast, the idiom *clam up* and the slang expression *shut up* mean to withhold one's opinion or to be quiet. *Talk up* is the only transitive and separable phrasal verb of this group.

speak up

1. to express one's opinion, desires, or support freely and openly without hesitation or fear ♦ *He finally* spoke up *about the problems at work.* ♦ *If you'd like something to eat, just* speak up.
2. to speak louder or more clearly so that you can be heard; often said as a request ♦ *You'll have to* speak up. *I don't hear very well.*

talk up (S)

to speak in strong support or in favor of something; to promote; often used to imply promoting for economic or personal gain ♦ *A sales representative's job is to* talk up *the quality of a product.* ♦ *We want this idea to be approved, so* talk *it* up *at the meeting.*

clam up

to keep silent or refuse to talk or respond; generally used informally ♦ *When he tries to chat with his teenage daughter, she often* clams up.

shut up

1. to stop or cause to stop talking; to say nothing more about a specific topic. *Shut up* is considered informal and very rude when said as a command. ♦ *This speaker should* shut up *and sit down!* ♦ *Hey,* shut up! *I'm trying to hear this program.*

2. (S) to prevent from speaking or writing freely ♦ *His government tried to* shut *him* up *by exiling him, but he continued to write.* ♦ *They paid him just to* shut *him* up *about the scandal.*

3. (S) to confine, imprison, or enclose ♦ *We usually* shut *the dog* up *in the garage at night.* ♦ *He was* shut up *in prison for 20 years.*

Thinking and Dreaming

Think up and *dream up* both mean to imagine, invent, or devise an idea or solution, but they are used in slightly different ways (as described below). *Make up* implies devising a falsehood or untruth.

think up (S)

to invent, devise, or create by thinking ♦ *Let's* think up *a good name for our club.* ♦ *She's good at* thinking up *creative projects for her students.*

dream up (S)

to invent or create usually new or unique ideas by imagining, daydreaming, or thinking creatively. ♦ *My father was always* dreaming up *new and useful inventions.* ♦ *Pet rocks were a big success! What will they* dream up *next?!* **Note:** This idiom is often used to imply that the idea is impractical, unwise, or crazy.

make up (S)

to invent or create a falsehood or fiction ♦ *She liked to* make up *stories to tell her children.* ♦ *He* made up *a good excuse about his late assignment, but his teacher knew it wasn't true.*

[See *come up with* in Chapter 20.]

Being Happy and Avoiding Worry

The idioms *loosen up, lighten up, cheer up, ease up,* and *let up* can mean to relax, be less formal or serious, less angry or depressed, or to be happier.

loosen up (S)

to become less formal, serious; to relax; to talk freely ♦ *I go for a run every evening to help me* loosen up *after work.* ♦ *People sometimes say that alcohol* loosens up *the tongue. People say crazy things when they're drunk!*

lighten up

to become less serious, depressed, worried, or angry ♦ *Come on,* lighten up! *You don't need to get so angry about it.* ♦ *You should* lighten up *and enjoy life more.*

Romance Trouble

Here's some advice and some examples on how to use four romance-related idioms. If you don't *show up* (appear) for a date or if you *stand* someone *up* (fail to appear for a planned date), your partner might *break up* with you (end the relationship). Don't try to *make up* (create or fabricate) an excuse. Just apologize, and your partner may be willing to *make up* (forgive the wrong, and continue the relationship) with you.

[See *light up* in Chapter 4.]

cheer up (S)

> to become more cheerful ♦ Cheer up. *It's not so bad.* ♦ *We tried to* cheer *her* up *in the hospital.*

ease up

> **1. (S)** to relax or reduce pressure or intensity; often phrased *ease up on* ♦ *My schedule will* ease up *after the conference* ♦ *They* eased up on *the dress code, so now we can wear jeans to work.*
> **2. (NS)** to lessen one's demands on someone; to reduce one's nagging, complaining, or anger toward someone ♦ *You should* ease up *on him. He's doing the best he can.* ♦ Ease up, *mom! I'll do my chores in a minute.*

let up

> to reduce pressure or intensity; to become less intense; often used in reference to weather conditions. This idiom is also phrased *let up on.* ♦ *I hope this rain* lets up *soon.* ♦ *During training our coaches didn't* let up on *us for a minute.*

Note: The three idioms *lighten up, ease up,* and *let up* can also be used to mean to reduce the pressure on a gas or brake pedal, the clutch, or other mechanism, as in "*Lighten up* on the gas. You're going too fast!" or "*Let up* on the clutch as you begin to accelerate."

Opening and Starting

Some idioms with *up* mean to start or open, while others mean to stop or close. *Open up, start up, strike up,* and *take up* mean to open or begin. *Hang up* and *close up* mean to end, finish, or close. The first definition and example under each idiom shows these meanings:

open up

1. (S) to start a new business ◆ *A new restaurant just* opened up *downtown*.
2. (S) to open or unlock an enclosed space ◆ *Only the manager can* open up *the supply room*.
3. to express one's feelings, thoughts, or opinions freely ◆ *I asked her what's wrong, but she won't* open up. ◆ *He finally* opened up *and told us about his life*.

start up

1. (S) to start, cause to begin, or organize a new business, academic term, or interaction ◆ *Our business has had steady profits since we* started up *in 1985*.
◆ *After vacation, school* starts up *again in September*.
2. (S) to cause an engine or other motor to begin running ◆ *They* started up *their engines and waited for the signal to begin the race*.
3. (NS) to begin expressing a strong opinion, complaint, or nagging; often phrased *start up about* or *start up with* ◆ *Please don't* start up *with your complaining*. ◆ *As soon as he came in the door, his parents* started up *on him about his messy room*.

strike up (S)

1. to initiate conversation ◆ *They* struck up *a conversation and soon became friends*.
2. to cause music to begin or a band or orchestra to begin playing ◆ *Tell him to* strike up *the band. This party needs some music!*

take up (S)

1. to become interested in and begin a hobby, occupation, study, or belief system ◆ *He* took up *the guitar three years ago*. ◆ *After many years in business, she* took up *a new career in law*.
2. to shorten or hem ◆ *These pants are too long. I need to* take *them* up.
3. to absorb (a liquid) ◆ *He used a sponge to* take up *the water*.

Closing and Quitting

close up (S)

to close and lock an enclosed space; to prepare to end business or other activity for the day ◆ *We're* closing up *soon, so please pay for your purchases now*.
◆ *Don't forget to* close up *the garage when you finish working in there*.

give up

1. to stop trying; to admit defeat or failure ♦ *This math problem is too difficult; I give up!* ♦ *The saying "Never give up!" encourages people to overcome difficulties and reach their goals.*
2. (S) to cease or stop doing something; usually a habitual or regular activity ♦ *She finally gave up smoking.* ♦ *I used to play the piano, but I gave it up years ago.*
3. to lose faith in or lose hope for, to surrender; often said in the passive voice and phrased *given up on* ♦ *She has given up on trying to get her son to keep his room neat.* ♦ *They had given up on him when he finally arrived three hours late.*

hang up (S)

to end a phone conversation, to replace the phone handset on the receiver or turn off a cell phone ♦ *It was nice talking to you, but I should hang up now and get back to work.* ♦ *She said "Hello," but no one answered, so she hung up.*

Staying on Schedule

The idioms *catch up* and *keep up* refer to becoming current or up to date with one's schedule or obligations, and to staying on one's schedule.

catch up

1. to become even, current, or on schedule by hurrying or doing extra work; often phrased *caught up to, caught up on,* or *caught up with* ♦ *I'm behind on this project, so I'll work over the weekend to catch up.* ♦ *She caught up to the lead runners in the third mile of the race.*
2. (S) to bring someone up to date with news or other information ♦ *Let me catch you up on the family news.* ♦ *When he returns from vacation, we'll need to catch him up on the status of the project.*

keep up

1. to stay even, current, or on schedule, sometimes through extra effort; often said as *keep up with* or *keep up on* ♦ *The class was too advanced for him. He couldn't keep up.* ♦ *Now that I have an assistant, I'm able to keep up with my work.*
2. (S) to continue or sustain something ♦ *You're doing a good job, so keep it up.* ♦ *The rain kept up all day.*
3. (S) to maintain in good condition ♦ *She kept up her car, so it lasted many years.*
4. (S) to cause someone to stay awake or out of bed ♦ *The noise outside kept us up all night.* ♦ *Coffee keeps me up if I drink it in the afternoon.*

A Few Other Idioms with *Up*

back up

1. (S) to go in a backward direction; to go back to an earlier position, point, or idea ♦ *She* backed *the car* up *and out of the driveway.* ♦ *Let's* back up *a minute to my original point.*

2. (S) to support or help someone or something ♦ *He* backed up *his commitment to a cleaner environment by refusing to own a car.* ♦ *I'll* back *you* up *if you decide to talk to the boss.*

look up (S)

to look for specific information in a reference book or other source ♦ *I don't know his phone number. I'll have to* look *it* up *in the phone book.* ♦ *You can use this idiom handbook to* look up *idioms that you want to learn.*

mix up (S)

to confuse one thing for another, to be wrong about a specific detail, to mix things together in a confusing way; also phrased to *get* something *mixed up.* This idiom is often phrased as an adjective, *to be mixed up.* ♦ *I often* mix up *the words "fell" and "felt."* ♦ *We missed the party because we* got *the dates* mixed up.

pay up (S)

1. to pay on time, or pay in full instead of in installments ♦ *He* paid up *his car insurance for the year.*

2. to pay the balance on a debt, often to another person; sometimes said as a demand or mock demand ♦ *You lost the bet, so come on,* pay up!

run up (S)

1. to let bills and debts accumulate ♦ *They really* ran up *their credit cards while on vacation.*

2. to quickly sew; often to complete a sewing project ♦ *She* ran up *their Halloween costumes over the weekend.*

sign up

to register, enlist, or enroll oneself or someone else in a class, an event, military service, or other commitment ♦ *I* signed up *to volunteer for the food drive.*
♦ *She plans to* sign up *with the Navy after high school.*

turn up

> to appear after having been lost or missing, or having been gone longer than expected ♦ *I hope my sunglasses* turn up. *I don't want to buy another pair.* ♦ *We were worried when our son didn't return from school, but he finally* turned up.

stay up

> to stay awake, or stay awake until a late hour; to not go to bed ♦ *I like to* stay up *late and read.* ♦ *He* stayed up *all night worrying about the problem.*

COMMON PHRASAL VERBS WITH THE PREPOSITION *DOWN*

Phrasal verbs with the preposition *down* are not as numerous as phrasal verbs with the prepositions *up, in, out,* and *off.* Still, there are plenty of them. Most phrasal verbs with *down* are transitive and separable, but there are a few exceptions. The word *down* often has a negative connotation, so many idioms with *down* have a negative meaning, for example *turn down* (reject or refuse), *let someone down* (disappoint), *bring down* (destroy), and so on. Most phrasal verbs with *down* have more than one definition, so some definitions are not negative, but neutral, like *write down* (record), or even positive, like *calm down* (become calmer, less upset or angry).

The first two sections that follow include easy-to-learn idioms in which the preposition *down* simply extends or emphasizes the literal meaning of the verb. The remaining sections are organized into categories of idioms with similar or related meaning.

When *Down* Means No Longer Standing

Idioms that include the preposition *down* and are verbs such as *cut, knock, push, pull,* and so on, mean to cause something to fall over, to no longer stand upright or collapse. The preposition *down* extends or makes more specific the meaning of the verb. For example, the verb *cut* is very general; there are many ways to cut something. However, to *cut down* is more specific, and means to cut so as to cause something to fall to the ground. To *push down* means to push hard enough to cause someone or something to fall on the ground.

The verb *fall* already means to drop, possibly to the ground, but *fall down* specifically means to drop from an upright or suspended position to the ground or floor. For example, during an earthquake things such as lamps, buildings, statues, trees, and so on might *fall down* (fall from a standing or upright position to the ground). But don't say, "A meteor *fell down*" or "The stock market *fell down*." The idioms in the following example all mean to cause something or someone to fall to the ground. They are all separable.

- *The loggers* cut down *some trees.*
- *The high winds* knocked down *the old barn.*
- *Some electrical wires* fell down *during the storm.*
- *Let's* pull down *the old fences and rebuild them.*
- *The little girl pushed her* friend down *on the grass.*
- *People eventually* tore down *the Berlin Wall.*

Note: *Tore down* is a general term that is often used for any kind of destruction that causes something to fall or collapse completely. Usually, however, *tore down* is used for buildings and other structures or for paper and fabric items that can literally be torn; for example, "After the concert, we *tore down* all the concert posters."

[See also *bring down* later in this section.]

When *Down* Means to Record for Later Use

Idioms with the preposition *down* and verbs like *write, jot, take,* and *get* mean to write or record information in order to remember it and use it later. For example, to *take* or *get* information only says that you have it (probably in your head), but to *take down* or *get down* information means to record or write it somewhere for reference or future use. The following are some common idioms of this type. The idioms in the following example all mean to record for future use. They are all separable.

- Write down *your address on this paper.*
- Jot down *my phone number.*
- Take down *the schedule so you won't forget it.*
- *Did you* get *the information* down?

[See also *put down* later in this section.]

Deny, Disappoint, and Destroy

The following phrasal verbs can have negative connotations, meaning to refuse or reject, deny, disappoint, or destroy. The first definition of each idiom shows its negative meaning; other definitions may be neutral or positive.

turn down (S)

1. to refuse or reject someone's request or offer ♦ *The offer was too low, so we* turned *it* down. ♦ *She* turned *him* down *when he asked for a date.*
2. to fold something over or in a downward position; often bedding, a collar, or page in a book ♦ *Some hotels* turn down *the covers for you in the evening.*
♦ Turn *your collar* down. *It's turned up on one side.*

let down (S)

1. to disappoint someone; to fail to fulfill a promise or obligation ♦ *The grant committee* let *her* down *when it failed to send the money it had promised.* ♦ *He didn't want to* let *his parents* down, *so he studied hard at the university.* ♦ *If you need help, I won't* let *you* down.

2. to allow to hang long, as with hair, or to lengthen, as with clothing ♦ *She took the clip out of her hair and* let *it* down. ♦ *Now that you've grown, we need to* let *your pant legs* down.

put down (S)

1. to belittle, insult, or say unkind things about someone or something ♦ *It's wrong to* put *someone* down *because of his beliefs.* ♦ *My friends and I sometimes* put *each other* down *playfully.*

2. to record or write information or supply specific information on a form ♦ *I* put down *the date and time of the class in my calendar.* ♦ *The questionnaire asked for my hobbies, so I* put down *tennis and reading.*

3. to put something or someone back on the ground or floor; to stop or to command that someone stop holding something and replace it to its original position ♦ Put *me* down! *I can walk just fine.* ♦ Put *that* down *before you break it!*

[See also *run down* later in this section.]

bring down (S)

1. to cause to fall; to be destroyed or killed ♦ *Superior strategies helped them* bring down *their attackers.* ♦ *The force of the earthquake* brought down *some old brick buildings.*

2. to cause someone to feel depressed ♦ *This movie is depressing. It will* bring *you* down. ♦ *I don't want to* bring *people* down *by talking about my problems.*

Keeping It Under Control

The following phrasal verbs have a general meaning: to control, restrain, or maintain. The first definition and example under each idiom show that meaning.

hold down (S)

1. to bring under control or restrain ♦ *Please* hold down *your noise.* ♦ *My son* held *the dog* down *while I gave it a bath.*

2. to have and keep a job; usually not separated ♦ *She* held down *three jobs while raising her children.* ♦ *He couldn't* hold down *a job because of his drug problem.*

ask out (S)

> to invite someone to go on a date; often put *to ask* someone *out* ♦ *Today, girls often* ask *boys* out. ♦ *I finally* asked *Joyce* out, *and she said yes!* **Note:** This idiom is used for romantic or potentially romantic dating situations. It's less often used to refer to getting together with friends or family.

go out

> to go on a date or another event ♦ *Let's all* go out *to a movie tonight.* ♦ *Would you like to* go out *with me?* **Note:** This idiom is often used for romantic or potentially romantic situations, but it's also used between friends and family. It's often put *to ask someone to go out.*

take out (S)

> **1.** to take someone on a date ♦ *Dad* took *everyone* out *to dinner.* ♦ *Lately I've been* taking out *this great girl.* **Note:** This idiom can be used in either romantic situations or between friends and family.
> **2.** to put or take something outside ♦ *Don't forget to* take out *the trash for pick-up on Monday.* ♦ *He* took *his dog* out *for a walk.*
> **3.** to remove, extract, or bring out from inside something; often put as *take something out of* ♦ *He* took *his hands* out *of his pockets.* ♦ *They had to* take out *the engine to repair it.*
> **4.** to get a license, permit, loan, or other item by applying; not generally used for a driver's license ♦ *You have to* take out *a permit to sell goods on the street.* ♦ *He* took out *a loan to build his house.*
> **5.** to subscribe to a magazine or newspaper ♦ *She* took out *a subscription to* National Geographic *magazine.*

eat (*or* dine) out

> to eat in a restaurant; often put as *eat* breakfast *out* and so on ♦ *We usually* eat *lunch* out *during the week.* ♦ *They often* dined out *at the most exclusive restaurants.* **Note:** *Eat out* can be used for any meal, while *dine out* is generally used for a more expensive dinner.

[See *eat out, dine out,* and other idioms related to restaurant dining in Chapter 3.]

Figure Out and *Find Out*

These idioms have a general meaning of to discover or learn as a result of investigation, inquiry, or experience. **Note:** *Figure out* and *find out* are often interchangeable,

keep down (S)

1. to keep under control or restrain, generally when talking about noise, dust, or other annoyances or hazards ♦ *I try to* keep down *the dust in the house by vacuuming often.* ♦ *Efforts to* keep *the mosquito population* down *help to reduce malaria.*

2. to not vomit or be sick to one's stomach ♦ *He was so sick he couldn't* keep *anything* down. ♦ *She had trouble* keeping *food* down *during the first months of pregnancy.*

quiet down (S)

1. to become quieter or calmer, to reduce noise or control one's voice; to encourage or cause someone or something to be quieter. This idiom is separable when it uses a direct object. ♦ *Okay, everyone,* quiet down. *It's time for class.* ♦ *The baby was crying, but the soft music helped to* quiet *him* down. ♦ *Giving your car a tune-up should help* quiet *your engine* down.

2. to lessen or reduce pain; generally inflammation or infection ♦ *This lotion will help* quiet down *your sunburn.* ♦ *The infection in that tooth has* quieted down *but it may come back again.*

Wear and Tear

The following phrasal verbs have a general meaning: to diminish or use up something (power, material, or energy) or to reduce the thickness of.

run down (S)

1. to stop operating or running, as a mechanical or battery-powered device because of a lack of power ♦ *Turn off the flashlight so you don't* run down *the battery.* ♦ *He left his car light on and* ran down *the battery.*

Closing Down or Just Closing?

Is the store closed or has it *closed down?* Look in the window and you'll find out. If you see merchandise inside and a sign in the window giving you the store hours, it's probably just closed (for the day) and will reopen tomorrow. But if it looks empty or deserted inside, probably the business has *closed down* (stopped operating permanently). You might see a sign in the window saying "Closing Sale" or "Going Out of Business" (an expression that means quitting business or planning to stop operating). *Shut down* can also mean to close permanently and usually refers to a factory or assembly-line process. For example, "The canneries *shut down* long ago when the fish disappeared from the bay."

2. to lessen the amount of material, usually on the sole or heel of a shoe, due to use and wear ◆ *If you* run down *your heels, a shoe-repair shop can replace them.*
3. to speak badly of someone ◆ *He's always* running *his coworkers* down.
4. to knock over (and possibly injure or kill) by driving, running, or crashing into someone or something ◆ *Those kids nearly* ran *me* down *with their bicycles!*

[See *run down* in Chapter 4.]

wear down (S)

1. to make or become worn, to lessen the thickness or height by use or friction, to diminish ◆ *The old stone steps were* worn down *from hundreds of years of use.* ◆ *The tread on his car tires was badly* worn down.
2. to weaken or lessen the resistance, to tire or get tired by stress or pressure ◆ *He argued and persisted until he finally* wore *his parents* down *and they let him get a car.* ◆ *The stress and lack of sleep while studying for exams can really* wear *you* down.

Some Positive *Downs*

A few phrasal verbs with the preposition *down* have a positive or even uplifting meaning.

calm down (S)

to become calmer or to encourage someone to become calmer, less upset, angry, or intense ◆ Calm down, *and we'll talk about the problem logically.* ◆ *Her horse was very frightened by the storm, but she was able to* calm *him* down. ◆ *This medication should help* calm down *your cough.*

hand down (S)

to pass something, usually of sentimental value or a tradition, from one generation to the next ◆ *Grandmother's wedding ring will be* handed down *to the eldest daughter in each generation.* ◆ *Customs, traditions, and beliefs were* handed down *through the generations for thousands of years.*

get down

to relax and participate in social activity, particularly dancing or music; slang ◆ *I like to* get down *with my friends on the weekend.* ◆ *The concert was great. Everyone was* getting down!

Common Phrasal Verbs Using *With*

The phrasal verbs in this section are listed in alphabetical order:

bear with (NS)

> to be patient and understanding of someone, to put up with, to endure someone or something; often used as a polite request for patience ♦ *The professor said, "Please* bear with *me while I find my notes." ♦ The sign in the lobby read, "Thank you for* bearing with *us during our remodeling."*

come with (NS)

> to be or have something added or included as an extra feature or benefit; to be or have something packaged with something else ♦ *This vacuum cleaner* comes with *a three-year guarantee. ♦ Most quality men's suits* come with *two pairs of trousers.* **Grammar Note:** *Come with* is generally put in the simple present or past tense. Don't put this idiom in a continuous tense (verb + *-ing*).

deal with (NS)

> **1.** to handle a situation or person; to try to solve a problem ♦ *Jane, would you* deal with *this customer's complaint? ♦ She has to* deal with *her problems eventually.*
> **2.** to have to tolerate or endure someone or something ♦ *I can't* deal with *him anymore; he's too difficult. ♦ Please smoke outside. We don't want to* deal with *cigarette smoke.*
> **3.** to interact with and have experience with people, things, or situations ♦ *A teacher* deals with *children all day in the classroom. ♦ I've* dealt with *this kind of research many times in my career, so it's not difficult for me.*
> **4.** (slang) to learn to accept something that seems unacceptable; to stop complaining and accept something; to take responsibility for consequences; usually said as an unsympathetic imperative, *Deal with it! ♦ You can complain about paying taxes, but in the end you have to* deal with *it. ♦ She told her younger sister, "No, you can't borrow my clothes.* Deal with *it!"*

dispense with (NS)

> to get rid of or eliminate something; to manage without something or with less, to forgo something ♦ *Let's* dispense with *the chatting and start the meeting. ♦ To save money on our vacation, we* dispensed with *our plans to rent a car and took the bus instead.*

do with (NS)

1. to manage, to do okay with less than normal or less than what's desired; sometimes phrased *can do with* or *manage to do with* ♦ *As a student, I often* did with *very little sleep.* ♦ *Camels are well designed for the desert; they can* do with *very little water.*

2. to need or want something, to be in need of something; often said as a request for help. In this context, the idiom is usually phrased *could do with*, and occasionally *can do with.* ♦ *This car* could do with *a paint job.* ♦ *We* could do with *some help moving these boxes.*

go with (NS)

1. to regularly date one person, to go out together; often phrased *going out with* or *going together*. Occasionally put as *going steady with.* ♦ *Forrest has been* going with *Paula for two years.* ♦ *She* went with *him during high school.*

2. to choose something, to make a decision in favor of something ♦ *Let's* go with *the blue paint instead of the green in the bathroom.* ♦ *I have to decide which auto insurance company to* go with.

3. to match, to be complementary, to look good or taste good together; often phrased to *go well with* ♦ *I'd like to find a red sweater to* go with *these pants.* ♦ *Some wine experts say that red wine doesn't* go well *with fish.*

level with (NS)

to be honest and truthful with someone; to speak openly and frankly with someone ♦ *I finally asked him to* level with *me; I'm tired of his lies.* ♦ *The doctor said, "I'll* level with *you. The surgery you need is risky."*

[See also *level with someone* and *on the level* in Chapter 11.]

part with (NS)

to let go of or relinquish something ♦ *The little boy won't* part with *his teddy bear.* ♦ *She didn't want to* part with *her car, but she was becoming too old to drive.*

run with (NS)

to adopt, usually an idea, as one's own; to act on something with enthusiasm ♦ *The company* ran with *his ideas for marketing the product.* ♦ *Once he decided to go into acting, he* ran with *it.*

side with (NS)

to agree with, support, or favor one person or perspective (one *side*) in a disagreement or dispute ♦ *My mother always* sided with *my sister when we had an argument.* ♦ *After hearing the arguments, I'm* siding with *the labor union in the dispute.*

Common Phrasal Verbs Using *Without*

There are just a few phrasal verbs that use *without.* They are *be without, go without,* and *do without.* These three phrasal verbs are transitive, but in some cases they are said without a direct object, because the direct object is understood. For example, in the sentence "Many poor people in the world *go without,*" the understood or implied meaning is "go without basic necessities."

Be without, go without, and *do without* cannot be separated by their direct object, but an adverb can be placed directly after the verb, as in "I never want to *go* **long** *without* seeing you." [See Chapter 18 for information on transitive and non-separable phrasal verbs.]

WHEN *WITHOUT* IMPLIES TO LACK

The three idioms using *without* generally mean lacking something, not having something essential or something that's perceived as important.

be without (NS)

> to lack or not have something that's perceived as important ♦ *One should never* be without *some form of I.D.* ♦ *I wonder how long I'll* be without *my car since it is in the repair shop.* **Grammar Note:** The idiom *be without* is sometimes used without a direct object, as in the following context where the implied meaning is to be without something that you need: "Here's some money for your first month at college. We don't want you to *be without.*"

go without (NS)

> to neglect, forgo, or sacrifice something that's perceived as a basic necessity or important ♦ *People say you shouldn't* go without *breakfast — the most important meal of the day.* ♦ *The survivors* went without *food or water for many days.* **Grammar Note:** The idiom *go without* is sometimes used without a direct object, as in the following context where the implied meaning is to manage without this item: "Please, take my coat. I'm warm enough to *go without.*"

do without (NS)

to manage or do okay although one doesn't have something perceived as important or essential ♦ *We did fine without a car when we lived in the city.*

♦ *I can't do without my cell phone when I'm on a business trip.*

WHEN *WITHOUT* HAS A POSITIVE IMPLICATION

In some contexts *without* can have a positive implication. People are happy to *be without, do without,* or *go without* some undesirable things such as pain, fear, bad habits, extra work, and so on. For example *being without* is a good thing in the sentence "I've *been without* back pain since I started doing yoga." Sometimes, being able to *do* or *go without* something can be an advantage, as expressed in this sentence, "These drought-resistant plants can *go without* water all summer."

When *Going Without* Is an Advantage

The idiom *go without* is often used to discuss the advantage of things that can operate or function well without using up a lot of resources or power. *Grammar Note: Do without* may occasionally be seen in this context in specific, limited situations. The following are some typical examples of this usage of *go without:*

♦ *A camel can* go without *water for a long time in the desert.*
♦ *With my new hybrid car, I can* go without *buying gas for weeks.*
♦ *Some divers train themselves to* go without *air for many minutes.*

When *Doing Without* Would Be Good

In the following example, *I could do without* means "I wish I could avoid or be rid of this inconvenience."

♦ *I could* do without *this extra work right now; I'm already so busy.*

The expressions *could do without* and *can do without* convey that one would be happy not to have an unpleasant, annoying, or inconvenient situation. Sometimes the situation already exists, like the extra work in the example above. In this case, the expression *could do without* implies that the situation must be endured, although it is not wanted. The following are more examples:

♦ *She's a very good friend, but I could* do without *her smoking.*
♦ *Boy! We* could have done without *that extra research paper during final exam week.*

Sometimes, *could* or *can do without* is said as an indirect request that something unpleasant be stopped, as in the following example: "'I *can do without* your bad attitude,' she told her teenage daughter."

The expression *can do without* is also used to convey that one hopes to avoid a future unpleasant situation, as in the following example: "I avoid sweet and sugary food. I *can do without* expensive dental bills!"

When *Doing* and *Going Without* Is Okay

Sometimes *doing without* and *going without* is not a problem. The expressions *can* (or *could*) *do without* and *can* (or *could*) *go without* are often used to imply that one is okay or can manage well without something. ***Grammar Note:*** In this context an adverb such as *fine, well*, or *okay* is often placed after the verb.

Here are some examples:

♦ *I* can do *fine* without *a new coat this winter; my old one still looks good.*
♦ *To save money we* could go without *buying expensive coffee drinks every day.*

Common Phrasal Verbs with *For*

Many phrasal verbs using the preposition *for* have multiple meanings and uses. Phrasal verbs with *for* are always transitive and usually non-separable. However, some of them can be separated by an indirect object, prepositional phrase, or adverb, as in this example: "He *cared* **lovingly** *for* his elderly parents." The preposition *for* serves as a transition between the verb and direct object, and helps give special meaning to the idiom.

THE IDIOMS *COME FOR* AND *GO FOR*

The idioms *come for* and *go for* have a number of meanings, and all are very common. In the first examples that follow, the idiom is expressed as either *come for* or *go for* depending on the location of the speaker or the person or thing being spoken about at the time of speaking. The next section, "Using *Come For* and *Go For* Correctly," explains when to use the verb *come* and when to use the verb *go* for these idioms.

come for (*or* go for) (NS)

1. to pick up someone, to retrieve, or to go and get something and possibly bring it back to one's starting point ♦ *What time will you* come for *me this evening?* ♦ *The landlord has* come for *the rent; we must pay him now.*

2. to attack someone or something, to run or rush toward someone or to grab at someone in a threatening manner as if to attack; also phrased *come at* someone ♦ *The boxing champion said to his opponent, "Come for me. I'm ready!"* ♦ *A mugger* went for *the lady's purse, but she kicked him and ran away.*

Using *Come For* and *Go For* Correctly

When the meaning is to retrieve, pick up, or go to get something, use *come for* to refer to the place where you or someone you're talking to is located, or will be located, at the time of speaking. Use *go for* to refer to a place where you or someone you're talking to is not located. Here are some examples:

♦ *When your plane arrives, we'll* come for *you at the airport. (The person the speaker is talking to will be at the airport.)*
♦ *It's three o'clock. Time to* go for *my friend at the airport. (Neither the speaker nor the person the speaker is talking to are at the airport at the time of speaking.)*
♦ *I'm* going for *the mail. I'll be right back. (Neither the speaker nor the person the speaker is talking to are at the mailbox at the time of speaking.)*

When the meaning is to attack, or to run or rush at someone as if to attack use *come for* when the action is directed toward or near the speaker (or someone being quoted as a speaker). Use *go for* when the action is directed somewhere away from the speaker. Here are some examples:

♦ *The dog* came for *us, but we chased it away. (The action was directed at the speakers.)*
♦ *The dog* went for *our cat, but it ran up a tree. (The action was directed at the cat and away from the speakers.)*
♦ *He told the police, "The mugger* came for *me with a knife." (The action was directed at the person being quoted as a speaker.)*

Other Uses of *Go For*

Go for has a number of other meanings and uses. The following are some of the most common:

go for (NS)

1. to choose or decide on something; to accept something for its merit or other qualities ♦ *After looking at a number of cars, we finally* went for *the Honda.* ♦ *I think they're going to* go for *my proposal.*
2. to pursue a goal or try to achieve something, to act on or pursue something enthusiastically, to encourage someone to do something; often said (slang) *Go for it!* ♦ *I'm planning to* go for *my master's degree next year.* ♦ *You finally have the chance to travel. So, I say* go for *it!*

3. to cost a specific amount, or to sell something for a specific amount ♦ *Their house* went for *$500,000.* ♦ *These shoes* go for *$20 on sale.*

4. to like or to be attracted to something or someone; often put as *really go for* or *sure go for* ♦ *I think he really* goes for *her.* ♦ *I never* went for *the grunge style.*

Grammar Note: When the helping verb *could* is used with *go for,* the meaning is *I want* or *I would like to have* something, as in this example: "I *could* really *go for* some ice cream right now."

MORE PHRASAL VERBS WITH *FOR*

The following phrasal verbs, listed in alphabetical order, are some of the most common that use the preposition *for:*

allow for (NS)

1. to leave room for, to permit or make possible ♦ *The boys' new shoes* allow for *some growth.* ♦ *Our wedding budget* allows for *only 100 guests.*

2. to consider as an influencing factor and act accordingly ♦ *We will need to* allow *an extra hour* for *traffic.* ♦ *They hadn't* allowed *time* for *possible delays when they planned their connecting flight.*

ask for (NS)

1. to request ♦ *They* asked for *a quiet table at the back of the restaurant.* ♦ *The police* asked for *everyone's cooperation with the manhunt.*

2. to invite problems or punishment by persisting in an action that may cause trouble; often phrased *to ask for it* ♦ *He really* asked for *it when he drove his mom's car without a driver's license.* ♦ *The girl told her teacher, "Yes, I did hit him, but he* asked for *it!"*

call for (NS)

1. to come to get or retrieve someone or something ♦ *I'll* call for *you around two o'clock.* ♦ *Someone from the thrift shop is here to* call for *the old furniture we're donating.*

2. to be the reason for or to deserve a special response or action; often phrased *calls for a celebration, calls for a drink,* or *calls for action* ♦ *The news of your promotion* calls for *a celebration.* ♦ *The extent and seriousness of this winter's flu epidemic* calls for *new research on immunization.*

3. (in the negative) to be unjustified; to not deserve a certain, usually harsh response or action; generally phrased *not called for* or *uncalled for* ♦ *His angry letter wasn't* called for. ♦ *It was an accident, so I think the boy's punishment was* uncalled for.

4. to require or be a necessary component of something ♦ *This recipe* calls for *five eggs.* ♦ *The zookeeper's job* calls for *someone skilled in animal behavior.*

Polite Offer and Refusal

"Would you care for..." is a common way to make a polite offer, as in "Would you *care for* something to drink?" The answer can be "Yes, I would." But don't use the idiom "care for" in the answer, because in an affirmative statement *care for* generally means to love someone or to provide care. It sounds very funny to say "Yes, I *care for* a drink."

The negative, *do not care for,* is often used as a polite refusal. For example, if offered an extra serving of food that you wish to refuse, you can say, "Thank you, but I *don't care for* any more."

The negative form is also a common and polite way to suggest dislike. For example, "I really *don't care for* that hairstyle" or "She *didn't care for* his rude comment."

Grammar Note: To avoid confusion, people generally don't say "didn't care for" when talking about providing care for someone. Saying, "I didn't care for her" sounds like "I didn't like her." Instead, use the idiom *take care of,* as in "I didn't *take care of* my mother when she was sick; my sister did." Or, another option is "I *wasn't caring for* my mother; my sister was."

5. to demand or request that certain action be taken ♦ *The workers' strike* called for *better working conditions and overtime pay.* ♦ *The Women's League for Peace and Freedom* called for *all people to get out and vote.*

care for (NS)

1. to provide care for someone, to take care of someone's needs ♦ *She* cared for *her sick mother for many months.* ♦ *When I'm at work, my aunt* cares for *my two children.*
2. to like or love someone. In this context an adverb is often placed directly after the verb. ♦ *He* cares *deeply* for *her.* ♦ *You always want to protect the people who you* care for.

head for (NS)

to go in the direction of something; for example, a location, an outcome, or the future. An adverb or prepositional phrase is often placed directly after the verb.
♦ *After school, the kids* headed *straight* for *the beach.* ♦ *If he keeps drinking, he's* headed for *big trouble.*

live for (NS)

1. to devote oneself totally to something or someone; to define one's purpose by something or someone ♦ *He* lives for *golf.* ♦ *She* lived for *her children, who where everything to her.*

2. to hope and wait in anticipation; typically phrased *live for the day* ♦ *Dan said, "I* live for the day *I can retire." ♦ We all* live for the day *someone finds a cure for cancer.*

look for (NS)

to search for or to try to find someone or something ♦ *Where have you been? We* looked for *you everywhere. ♦ I'm* looking for *some shoes to match this outfit.*

make for (NS)

to go in the direction of something with determination or possibly with haste; sometimes phrased *make for the door,* meaning to leave permanently, as with a job or a relationship, or to leave for the purpose of getting out or away from a place ♦ *When school is over, the kids grab their books and* make for *home and their video games. ♦ I* made for *the beach as soon as my plane arrived in Hawaii.*

run for (NS)

to campaign as a candidate for public office or other position ♦ *When he* ran for *president he was only 35 years old. ♦ She* ran for *governor, and won.*

speak for (NS)

1. to represent or voice another person's opinions, thoughts, or needs ♦ *He* spoke for *all of us when he said "Corporate crime must be stopped." ♦ Don't* speak for *me. I have my own opinions.*
2. to be claimed as belonging to someone; to be unavailable for dating because one is married or involved in an romantic relationship ♦ *There's only one piece of cake left, and I've already* spoken for *it. ♦ If we have to share a dorm room, I'm* speaking for *the desk by the window.* **Grammar Note:** Almost put in the passive form, as in "This seat is already *spoken for."* When this idiom means that someone is unavailable for dating, it is also always in the passive form.

stand for (NS)

1. to represent or symbolize something ♦ *In a Web address, www* stands for *World Wide Web. ♦ The stars on the U.S. flag* stand for *the 50 states.*
2. to believe in or hold as a principle; to support or uphold ♦ *Dr. Martin Luther King, Jr.* stood for *equality and justice. ♦ It's important to know what you* stand for.
3. to tolerate, allow, put up with; usually used in the negative context, phrased *do not, will not,* or *would not stand for* ♦ *We won't* stand for *any violence in our schools. ♦ My father wouldn't* stand for *any disrespectful behavior.*

Speak For Yourself!

Speak for yourself (meaning "that's your opinion, not mine") is an often-used response when someone makes a general statement or voices a general opinion that doesn't represent the feelings of everyone present. The topic can be serious or light. *Speak for yourself* is often said jokingly but can be serious also. The following are some examples:

♦ *Carm: I don't care what movie we rent, but let's not get a Western. Nobody likes Westerns. Steve: Hey,* speak for yourself. *I like Westerns.*

♦ *Nicole: No dessert for me. That meal was so filling. Ben:* Speak for yourself! *I'm going to have dessert.*

By contrast, the expression *speaking for myself* is often used to introduce one's own opinions or feelings:

♦ Speaking just for myself, *I'd rather go to the basketball game.*

People also say "I can only *speak for myself,"* which has the same meaning.

take for (S)

1. to make a mistake about someone's identity; to think that a person is someone else ♦ *With your new haircut and glasses, I almost* took *you* for *someone else.* ♦ *He's 60 years old? I* took *him* for *a much younger man.*
2. to assume something about a person's character ♦ *I had* taken *him* for *an honest person, but I was wrong.* ♦ *She thought I stole from the company! What kind of person does she* take *me* for?! ***Note:*** Often phrased "What do you take me for?!" in response to an insult or false accusation. ***Grammar Note:*** This idiom requires a noun or pronoun following the verb *take* except in the passive voice, as in "He was often *taken for* his younger brother."

Common Phrasal Verbs with *Away*

When *away* is joined with a verb, it often means to leave, depart, or separate from something, although it can have a number of other meanings. Most phrasal verbs with *away* are intransitive. The few that are transitive are also separable.

WHEN *AWAY* MEANS TO LEAVE

Many phrasal verbs with *away* mean *to leave,* in one sense or another. This section discusses these idioms and their various contexts.

One of the most frequently used phrasal verbs in this category is *go away*, which is an extended usage of the verb *to go*. It means not just to go, but to leave and be absent from someone or someplace. With this general meaning, *go away* can be used in a number of different contexts, as shown in the following examples:

go away

1. to go on a business trip or a vacation ♦ *She often* goes away *on a business trip.* ♦ *I would love to* go away *for a few days if I had the time.*
2. to leave or depart temporarily or permanently ♦ *The rain has finally* gone away. ♦ *I'll be glad when all the tourists have* gone away, *and our town is quiet again.*
3. to stop bothering someone; to leave someone alone ♦ Go away. *You're bothering me!* ♦ *I told my roommates to* go away *so I could study.*
4. to heal or be resolved, as an illness or problem ♦ *My skin rash finally* went away. ♦ *Your problems won't just* go away; *you have to deal with them.*

When *away* is added to the verbs *drive, fly, ride, walk,* and other verbs that show locomotion, it means to leave by that method of transportation:

drive away ♦ *She* drove away *in her new car.*
fly away ♦ *The bird* flew away *before the cat could catch it.*
ride away ♦ *After stopping to buy candy, the kids* rode away *on their bikes.*
walk away ♦ *He didn't want to argue, so he turned and* walked away.

[See *run away* in the later in this section.]

To *move away* is another form of leaving. *Move away* is an extended usage of the verb *to move,* and emphasizes not just moving or relocating, but leaving a former location. The following examples show the various contexts in which one can use the idiom *move away*:

move away

1. to leave one's residence, town, country or other place for the purpose of relocating to another ♦ *I'm sad because my best friend just* moved away. ♦ *We used to live in Nashville, but we* moved away *in 1997.*
2. to move back from something to avoid a dangerous situation; often said as a request or command. In this context *move away* is often followed by the preposition *from.* ♦ *The police ordered the protesters to* move away *from the building.* ♦ *You should* move away *from the workbench while I'm using this strong solution.*
3. to abandon or to begin to change from a past technology or way of doing something; generally used in reference to technology, products, trends, and approaches ♦ *Some fashion designers are* moving away *from the use of animal fur.* ♦ *Although the schools have* moved away *from bilingual teaching, many educators believe that it was very effective.*

Note: This idiom is often phrased *move away from home* when referring to a young person leaving home for the first time, as in "I'm planning to *move away from home* at the end of the summer."

Running Away from It All

Running away from it all is an expression that means to abandon a situation or to leave in order to avoid one's responsibilities or problems. The phrasal verb *run away* is also used in this context and a number of others, as shown in the following examples. *Note: Run away* is often followed by the preposition *from*.

run away

> **1.** to abandon something, often one's responsibilities or problems ♦ *You can't* run away *from your problems; they'll just follow you! **Note:** This idiom is also said as *walk away*.
> **2.** flee from one's home and family; often used in relation to a juvenile who has left the care of parents or guardians without their knowledge or approval; often phrased *run away from home* ♦ *When their son* ran away from home, *they called the police.* ♦ *The little girl said, "I'm mad at you, Mommy! I'm* running away!"
> **3.** to flee on foot, running ♦ *When the police arrived, most of the rioters* ran away. ♦ *We tried to catch the injured cat, but it kept* running away *from us.*

[See also *get away* later in this section.]

Leaving Secretly or Unnoticed

When *away* is joined with the verbs *sneak, steal,* and *slip,* it means to leave secretly or to depart without being noticed.

> **sneak away** ♦ *Let's* sneak away *from the party and go for a walk.*
> **steal away** ♦ *The newlyweds* stole away *from the reception to be alone.*
> **slip away** ♦ *The thief* slipped away *in the dark.*

Slip away also refers to the silent, steady passing of time:

> ♦ *The warm summer days are* slipping away.

Leaving This World

Another meaning of *slip away* is to die, often peacefully or while one is sleeping. Both *slip away* and the idiom *pass away* are considered polite, gentle ways of saying to die.

> **slip away** ♦ *Our old dog* slipped away *in his sleep.*
> **pass away** ♦ *My grandmother* passed away *last Sunday.*

Getting Away from It All

Getting away from it all is an expression that means to leave or escape one's daily routine and take a vacation. This expression has a more positive connotation than *running away from it all*, which is discussed in the preceding section. The phrasal verb *get away* is generally used to mean go somewhere or leave on vacation, but it has a number of meanings also, as shown in the following examples:

get away

1. to leave or escape from one's regular routine and go somewhere on vacation; to take a break from work ◆ *She* got away *for a few days and went camping.*
◆ *We're planning to* get away *for a couple of weeks in the summer.*
2. to avoid being captured or attacked, to escape from being restrained or held captive; often used in reference to being retained too long by a conversation or other social obligation ◆ *The thief tried to* get away, *but the police caught him.*
◆ *He caught a large bass, but the fish managed to* get away.
3. to move back from something or someone, to separate oneself from a harmful or stressful situation; often a request or a command; also phrased *stay away* or *keep away* ◆ Get away *from me with your pet snake!* ◆ *Anna,* get away *from the cliff. It's dangerous to be so close to the edge.*
4. to avoid, discontinue, or change a certain behavior or trend; also phrased *move away from* ◆ *I'm trying to* get away *from spending so much money on eating out.* ◆ *In today's world of cell phones, computers, and video games, we've* moved away *from spending quality time with our families.*

[See also *move away* earlier in this section.]

PUT AWAY AND TAKE AWAY

Put away and *take away* are sometimes confused because they seem similar in meaning, but they are not exactly the same. When you *put away* something, you place it in a specific location where it belongs, or you put it somewhere out of view. The main idea is that the item has been stored or placed somewhere. *Put away* is separable.

put away ◆ *Please* put away *your toys.* ◆ *Someone forgot to* put *the milk* away, *and now it's sour.*

When you *take away* something, you remove it from its current location or you confiscate it. The main idea is that the item is gone, removed, or missing. *Take away* is separable.

take away ◆ *When we finished our meal, the waiter promptly* took away *our empty plates.* ◆ *The company has* taken away *some of our benefits.*

Here are a few final examples that show the contrast in meaning between *put away* and *take away*:

> ♦ *His teacher said, "Tim, if you don't* put away *that game, I'll* take *it* away."
> ♦ *Lisa,* take *those scissors* away *from your little brother, and* put *them* away *in the drawer.*

Note: *Take away* is also used in mathematical problems and means to subtract, as in: "Seven *take away* three equals four." ($7 - 3 = 4$)

GIVE AWAY AND THROW AWAY

When you don't want something anymore — and you don't intend to sell it — you can either *give it away* or *throw it away*. *Give away* and *throw away* both mean to dispose of or get rid of one's things, but they are used to show different methods of disposal. If you *give away* something, you give one of your own possessions to another person free of charge. If you *throw away* something, you don't give it to someone else; you put it in the garbage. The following are some examples:

> **give away** ♦ *The radio station is* giving away *free concert tickets.* ♦ *I like to* give *my used books* away, *so someone else can read them.*
> **throw away** ♦ *Don't* throw away *those empty cans and bottles; recycle them.* ♦ *I had to* throw *the book* away *because I left it out in the rain.*

Grammar Note: *Give away* and *throw away* are separable. When you use the simple verb *to give,* you can say "I gave it **to someone,**" but with the phrasal verb *give away,* you don't add the words *to someone.*

Throwing Money Away

Who would actually throw money away or throw money in the trash? No one! But that's what people say about investing in a bad deal or paying for something that turns out to be useless or of poor quality. "It's like *throwing money away!*" they might say. Here are a few examples:

> ♦ *I bought my son some expensive new shoes, and now he won't wear them. I've just* thrown my money away!

> ♦ *I'm not going to* throw money away *on something I don't need.*

> ♦ *They* threw their money away *on a bad investment. Now they have nothing.*

The adjective *good* is sometimes added to the expression:

> ♦ *I just* threw good money away *on the sweater that shrunk in the wash.*

The following examples show additional meanings of *give away* and *throw away:*

give away

1. to reveal or tell a secret, to reveal the answer to a riddle or question ◆ *If you talk to Mary, don't* give away *anything about her surprise party.* ◆ *He* gave away *the answer before I had time to solve the riddle.*
2. for the father or male relative to walk with a bride to the altar or similar place where she will stand with the groom — literally, for the father to give the bride to the groom; now a symbolic gesture ◆ *She asked her uncle to* give *her* away *because her father was not living.* ◆ *Some women today don't like the traditional idea of being* given away.

throw away

to reject, ignore, or choose to miss an important opportunity ◆ *Maybe I'm* throwing away *a good opportunity, but I've decided not to take that job.* ◆ *He* threw away *his chance to be King of England when he married the woman he loved.* **Note:** A common phrase is *throw one's life away,* meaning to waste one's life, typically because of alcohol or drugs.

Phrasal Verbs with *Under* and *Over*

A few phrasal verbs are formed with the preposition *under,* while many phrasal verbs are formed with *over.* A verb plus *under* or *over* may or may not form an idiom, depending on the meaning and context.

PHRASAL VERBS WITH *UNDER*

There are only three commonly used phrasal verbs with the preposition *under.* They are *come under, go under,* and *fall under.* They have at least one meaning in common: to fit into or belong to a specific category or classification. Each idiom has other meanings also. Phrasal verbs with *under* are transitive and non-separable, as indicated by **(NS).** One exception is the intransitive form of *go under* when it means financial loss. [For more information on transitive and intransitive, separable and inseparable phrasal verbs, see Chapter 18.]

The following entries give more specifics on how these idioms are used:

come under

1. **(NS)** to belong to a category or classification ◆ *Reading instruction* comes under *the heading of Language Arts.* ◆ *Polio* comes under *the classification of viral diseases.*

2. (NS) to be in the jurisdiction or control of; to be supervised or protected by ♦ *Your job* comes under *my department.* ♦ *Minors* come under *the protection of the Child Protective Services Organization.*

go under

1. (NS) to be put into a category or classification ♦ *On the form, your financial information* goes under *the section Paying Your Tuition.* ♦ *Please file this material* under *the heading of advanced grammar.*
2. (NS) to be known as; to be called by a different name ♦ *To hide his identity, he often* goes under *an assumed name.* ♦ *When the movie star checks into the hotel, she* goes under *the name Mary Smith.*
3. to suffer financial loss ♦ *In the first two years of operation, many businesses* go under. ♦ *We're very lucky that we didn't* go under *during the recession.*

fall under

1. (NS) to be in or fit into a category or classification ♦ *Her favorite movies* fall under *the genre of film noir.*
2. (NS) to be in the jurisdiction or control of; to be supervised or protected ♦ *The town of Boulder Creek* falls under *the county jurisdiction.* ♦ *Hiring new employees* falls under *my responsibilities.*

PHRASAL VERBS WITH *OVER*

Over is used much more often than *under* to form phrasal verbs. Phrasal verbs with *over* may be transitive or intransitive depending on the verb or its meaning. For example, *think over* (to think carefully about) is transitive. You must think over *something.* On the other hand, *come over* (to come to someone's house for a visit) is intransitive. You can't *come over* something; you simply come over.

Transitive verbs with *over* are separable or non-separable, depending on meaning and usage, as indicated by **(S)** or **(NS)** below. For example, *think over* is separable. You can say *"think over* something" or you can say *"think* something *over."*

Come Over and Go Over

The idioms *come over* and *go over* have a number of different meanings and uses, and both idioms are very common.

In the first group that follows, the idiom uses either *come* or *go* depending on the location of the speaker, or the person being spoken about at the time of speaking.

come over *or* go over **(NS)**

1. to make a casual visit to someone's home or other location ♦ Come over *and visit any time.* ♦ *Would you like to* come over *for dinner tonight?*

Go Over Like a Lead Balloon!

Go over like a lead balloon is a colorful expression that means to fail to gain support, interest, or approval; to be dismissed or rejected as an idea or suggestion. This expression alludes to the fact that a balloon made of lead could never rise in the air; it would sit heavy and useless on the ground. *Go over like a lead balloon* is often used to refer to an idea or proposal that has been rejected or is very unpopular. Sometimes after making a suggestion that no one likes or supports, a person will say, "Well, that *went over like a lead balloon.*" Here are some other examples:

♦ *My suggestion that we all volunteer for community clean-up day* went over like a lead balloon *with our teenagers.*

♦ *The district proposal to extend the school day by one hour* went over like a lead balloon *with teachers and students alike.*

2. to span or traverse a space, particularly a body of water, from one side to another ♦ *My grandparents* came over *from Russia in 1897.* ♦ *As you* go over *the bridge, you'll see a wonderful view of the city skyline.*
3. to change loyalties, change sides or positions ♦ *We'll never convince him to* come over *to our way of thinking.* ♦ *The Republicans were shocked when one of their senators* went over *to the other side and became a Democrat.*

In the following examples, the idioms *come over* and *go over* have different meanings. The idiom uses only *come over* or only *go over;* the choice of verb is not dependent on the location of the speaker, as it is in the preceding items.

come over (NS)

to affect someone suddenly and unexpectedly in a profound way, often said of an illness; to cause someone to act in a certain way seemingly involuntarily
♦ *The illness* came over *him without warning.* ♦ *I don't know what* came over *me; I'm usually very polite.*

go over (NS)

1. to exceed an expected amount; also put as to *be over* ♦ *We try to stay within our monthly budget, but sometimes we* go over. ♦ *Everyone will get a bonus if the sales reps* go over *their projected sales quotas.* **Grammar Note:** This idiom can be separated by an adverb, as in "We've gone well over our budget."
2. to be accepted or approved of by others, as an idea, performance, or advice. Sometimes put as *to go over big* or *well.* ♦ *We presented our proposal to the board of directors, and it* went over *very well.* ♦ *The play has* gone over *big with audiences of all ages.*

[Also see *go over* in this section under "When Over Means With Careful Consideration"]

When *Over* Means Again

When *over* is joined with the verb *do,* or a few other verbs, it means again. To *do over* means to repeat, or do something again, often for the purpose of improving or correcting it, or just for practice. This idiom is separable and is usually put in the separable form. The expression *over and over* is often used to mean that the practice or action is repeated many times. Here are some examples:

♦ *This math problem isn't right. Please* do *it* over.
♦ *I can't figure out your card trick.* Do *it* over *again.*
♦ *We did the scene* over and over *until we had all the lines memorized.*

The verbs *write, say,* and *type* are frequently used with *over* when it means repetition of action, but some other verbs can also be used. For example

♦ *If you failed the test you can* take *it* over.
♦ *When I like a CD I* play *it* over and over *again until I'm tired of it.*

When *Over* Implies to Release or Relinquish

When *over* is joined with some verbs, the resulting idioms mean to release or relinquish something to someone else, to give something to someone, but not necessarily willingly. The following idioms have this general meaning, although there are slight variations between them. These phrasal verbs are separable.

hand over (S)

to relinquish control and put something in someone else's hands ♦ *Tomorrow, we'll* hand over *the deed to the house to the new owners.* ♦ *The mugger shouted,* "Hand over *your money!"*

fork over (S)

(slang) to reluctantly relinquish control, often of money; to return control of something to its rightful owner ♦ *When are you going to* fork over *the $50 you owe me?* ♦ *We had to* fork over *a huge sum to the government for property taxes this year.*

turn over (S)

to relinquish control or responsibility to someone else ♦ *My dad made me* turn over *the car keys after my accident.* ♦ *They* turned over *the job of fundraising to me.*

give over (S)

> to give something into someone else's possession, often in reference to money
> ♦ *The local citizens have already* given over *thousands of tax dollars to this project.* ♦ *They* gave over *some of their property for the new children's center.*

When *Over* Means with Careful Consideration

When joined with the verbs *look, talk, mull,* and *think, over* means with careful consideration. The following idioms all use *over* in this sense.

go over (NS)

> to review or look through carefully ♦ *After I give you back your tests, we'll* go over *them and discuss the errors.* ♦ *Would you please* go over *my manuscript and give me your feedback?*

look over (S)

> **1.** to look through something checking for accuracy or content ♦ *Mom, would you* look over *my essay and tell me if it's okay?* ♦ *I* looked *the report* over *and found a few problems.*
> **2.** to look at someone with specific interest, usually viewing him or her from head to foot. ♦ *Man, that girl is really* looking *you* over. *I think she wants to meet you.* ♦ *He's been* looking over *that car for ten minutes. He must be a serious buyer.* **Note:** This idiom may have a positive or negative implication, and can imply sexual attraction, as in the second example. An expression similar in meaning to *look over* is to *give someone the once over.*

talk over (S)

> to discuss an issue or problem in order to understand or solve it; to come to a conclusion or agreement. Also put as *talk things over.* ♦ *If something is bothering you, let's* talk *it* over. ♦ *Before accepting this job offer, I have to* talk *it* over *with my partner.*

mull over (*or* think over) (S)

> to think about something carefully, considering all of the pros, cons, or potential outcomes; to carefully consider before making a decision. *Mull over* often implies a more casual or longer period of thinking, possibly with no immediate decision required. ♦ *I'll* think over *your offer and let you know my decision in a few days.* ♦ *We're looking for one more person to join us on the European tour. Why don't you* think *it* over?

Turning It Over in One's Mind

An expression that means to *think it over* or *mull it over* is to *turn something over in one's mind*. Sometimes it's just said as *to turn the idea over*. For example you might say, "I've been *turning the idea over in my mind*, but I haven't yet come to a decision." *Turning an idea over* can imply a longer, more careful consideration than *mulling over* or *thinking over*. Here's another example: "We've *turned* the idea *over and over* and have finally decided to go ahead and do it."

When *Over* Means Across an Intervening Space

When *over* is joined with verbs of locomotion, like *climb, drive, fly, move, run,* and *walk,* it means to cross an intervening space or to go across a space to get from the starting point to the destination. Also, it often implies that one travels to the destination for a purpose. The first definition for each of the following idioms shows this usage of *over*. Other definitions are also included. **Grammar Note:** The idioms in this section are usually intransitive, having no direct object. In some contexts, when a direct object is required, the idiom is almost always separable and must be separated by its object.

climb over

> to climb or crawl, often carefully, to get from one place to a destination ♦ *The monkey* climbed over *to another branch to get the best fruit.* ♦ Climb over *to this side of the roof. I'll show you the damaged roof tiles. But be careful!*

drive over

> to drive from one place to a destination ♦ *I'll* drive over *to your house and pick you up in 20 minutes.* ♦ *He* drove *his daughter* over *to the park for her soccer group.*

fly over

> to fly from one place to a destination ♦ *While they were in Mexico, they* flew over *to Cuba to visit relatives.* ♦ *Our friend* flew *us* over *to one of the islands in his plane.* **Grammar Note:** *Fly over* is sometimes put in the passive voice as in this example: "Our supplies *were flown over* to the research site before we arrived."

move over

1. to relocate, moving from one locale to another locale ♦ *We* moved over *to the other side of town last year.* ♦ *Ben helped* move *his mother* over *to her new apartment.*

2. to move slightly to the left or right in order to make more space for someone; to change the location of items in a room or elsewhere. Sometimes said as *scoot over* or *slide over.* ♦ *Would you mind* moving over *a bit so that someone else can sit down?* ♦ *If we* move *the table* over *a little, we can fit the bookshelf next to it.*

Note: The idioms *move up* and *move back* are used to describe moving forward or backward.

run over

1. to run the distance from one location to another, usually to a destination ♦ *We* ran over *to see if we could help the woman who had fallen on the ground.* ♦ *To play this game, you* run over *to the table, pick up an egg in your spoon, and* run *back* over *here.*

2. to do an errand quickly; to make a quick trip, generally for some business or chore ♦ *She's not here right now; she just* ran over *to the post office to mail some packages.* ♦ *I'm going to* run over *to Dan's house for a minute.* **Note:** In this context, *run* is generally not literal. The errand or quick trip is usually done on foot (walking), by car, bicycle, or other mode of transportation.

The following are two other definitions of the idiom *run over,* definitions that do not use *over* to mean across an intervening space.

3. to exceed a time limit ♦ *The meeting* ran over, *as usual, and everyone was late leaving work.* ♦ *I'll signal you when you have one minute left so that your speech doesn't* run over *the time allotted.* **Grammar Note:** In this context, *run over* is non-separable when it has a direct object.

4. (S) to hit or bump into and possibly pass over the top of something ♦ *He felt terrible when someone* ran over *his dog.* ♦ *He was walking so fast he nearly* ran *right* over *an elderly lady.* **Note:** This context generally implies that one ran over something or someone with a vehicle, but you can also run over something or someone while walking or running.

walk over

to walk the distance from one location to another, usually to a destination ♦ *Let's* walk over *to the market and buy some fruit.* ♦ *Megan,* walk over *to that table and back to make sure that the shoes are comfortable before we buy them.*

All Over the Place

The expression *all over* is often put after the verb *climb, drive, fly, run, walk,* and others, to mean "here, there, and everywhere; in every part." If people say "We *walked all over,*" it implies that they walked to many different areas, sometimes with no specific goal or destination. But one can also *walk all over* in search of something. The expression *all over* is sometimes put as *all over town* or *all over the place.* Here are more examples:

♦ *We* drove all over *town looking for the address* (drove through many parts of town; spent a lot of time driving).

♦ *I* ran all over *the place doing errands today* (went to many places, typically by car; no actual running was involved).

♦ *The kids* climb all over *their grandpa when he comes to visit* (playfully climb in his lap, and maybe hang on his arms or shoulders).

Note: To *walk all over someone* means to take advantage of someone's generosity, kindness, or meekness.

[See *walk around, running around, drive around,* and so on, later in this chapter.]

When *Over* Implies to Remain Overnight

A few phrasal verbs — *sleep over, stay over, layover* and, sometimes, *hold over* — mean to stay or remain overnight or a few nights in a place other than home. For example, it's popular in the United States for girls, and often boys, to *sleep over* at a friend's house. Young kids often have *sleepovers* (overnight parties). *Stay over, layover,* and *hold over* are often used in reference to traveling. The following examples show how these idioms are used:

♦ *Mom, can I* sleep over *at Jenny's house tonight?*
♦ *We plan to* stay over *at my parents' house when we pass through Los Angeles.*
♦ *We'll* lay over *in Charleston, and then head down to Florida.*
♦ *They* held over *for a few nights in London before continuing on their trip.*

The idiom *held over* (generally used in the passive form) can also mean to keep or extend for a longer period of time, as an exhibit, a play, a movie, or other attraction. For example: "The play was so successful that it's been *held over* for another three weeks."

When *Over* Means for a Short Visit or Stay

The phrasal verbs *drop over* and *stop over* are used to refer to a short, informal visit to someone's residence. *Stop over* can also mean a short interruption in travel. Here are some examples:

- ♦ *Janie* dropped over *for a while today. It was nice to see her.*
- ♦ *I want to* drop over *at dad's house with these plants for his garden.*
- ♦ *We're going to have a little party tonight; why don't you* stop over?
- ♦ *We* stopped over *in Toronto to change planes.*

The noun form of *stop over, stopover,* is often used in air travel to mean the airport where a plane stops to drop off and pick up passengers before continuing on, or the airport at which a person switches planes. For example: "My ticket was cheap, but I had a long *stopover* in Phoenix."

When *Over* Implies to Recover or Overcome

The phrasal verb *get over* plus a direct object has become an all-purpose expression to mean to recover from something, to overcome or surmount something difficult, or to forget about or overlook something. *Get over* is always non-separable in these contexts. Here are specific examples that show how this idiom is used.

get over (NS)

1. to recover from an illness, a bad experience, or from emotional distress; often put as to *take time to get over something* ♦ *It took three weeks for me to* get over *my cold.* ♦ *They will never* get over *the loss of their child.*
2. to forget about, forgive, or overlook an insult or thoughtless act. People often use the expression *I'm over it* (short for *I've gotten over it*) to say that they have forgiven or forgotten an insult or difficult situation. ♦ *He's mad about it right now, but he'll* get over *it.* ♦ *He embarrassed her in public, and she's never gotten over it.*
3. to surmount or overcome a personal challenge or hurdle ♦ *He finally got over his shyness and became a radio announcer.* ♦ *We have to* get over *our prejudices if we want to live in a peaceful world.*
4. to continue to be surprised or delighted ♦ *I'll never* get over *how much you look like my brother.* ♦ *The party you gave me for my 80th birthday was so wonderful. I just can't* get over *it.* **Note:** In this context, *get over* is always put in the negative, as in the preceding examples.

Other Phrasal Verbs with *Over*

The following section includes phrasal verbs that use the preposition *over* to give special meaning to the verb. These idioms do not have a common general meaning as each has its own specific meaning and usage. They're listed alphabetically.

blow over

to subside, be forgotten, pass by; generally used to talk about weather, an argument, or ill feelings ♦ *This storm should* blow over *by tomorrow.* ♦ *We never stay mad at each other for long. Whatever the disagreement, it always* blows over *quickly.*

Get Over It!

Get over it! is a very common expression that's been popularized within the last decade or so. It means to accept the situation, deal with the situation, or live with the situation. It's used as tough advice for anyone unwilling to accept the reality of a situation, a rule, an outcome, or some other difficult aspect of life. When people say "Get over it!" they mean stop complaining, stop moping, stop blaming others, and accept it and go on with life. **Grammar Note:** *Get over it* is often preceded by the word *so*, meaning *therefore*. Here are some examples:

♦ *So, they didn't hire you. Get over it and look for another job.*

♦ *She doesn't want to go out with you. So, get over it.*

gloss over (S)

to try to make light of or downplay a lie, fault, or bad situation; to make obscure or less obvious in an attempt to deceive; often put as *gloss over the truth* ♦ *People typically* gloss over *their own faults.* ♦ *This report on this new drug is inadequate; it* glosses over *the negative side effects.* **Grammar Note:** Although this idiom is separable, it is often not separated.

pull over (S)

to move a vehicle off the road or to the side of the road and stop. In the passive form, *to be pulled over* means to be ordered to pull off the road and stop, typically by a police officer. ♦ *Everyone* pulled over *to let the ambulance pass.* ♦ *We can't stop here; there's no place to* pull *the car* over. **Grammar Note:** Although this phrasal verb is separable, its direct object (the car, bus, truck, and so on) is understood and is often not mentioned.

smooth over (S)

to soften, lessen, or get rid of difficulties or ill feelings between people; to make light of a fault or unpleasant situation. Often put as *smooth things over.* Also, *gloss over* can be used in this context. ♦ *We tried to* smooth *things* over *after their argument at the family dinner, but they stayed angry all evening.* ♦ *I know she's mad at me, but I'll talk to her and try to* smooth *things* over.

take over (S)

to take control of; to become responsible for; to do someone's job in his or her absence; also said as *take charge of* ♦ *She* took over *the position of night manager.* ♦ *I sold the car to him, and he* took over *the car payments.*

Turning Over a New Leaf

People who change their behavior or lifestyle for the better might be *turning over a new leaf* — making a fresh start or trying to improve and better their behavior. For example: "Well, I'm trying to *turn over a new leaf* and get some exercise every day."

turn over (S)

> **1.** to turn the down side up; to invert; also put as *flip over* ♦ Turn *the photo* over; *I wrote a description on the back.* ♦ *When the pancakes are cooked on one side,* turn *them* over.
>
> **2.** to make a certain amount of money selling merchandise or conducting business ♦ *They* turned over *a million dollars during the holiday sales.* ♦ *We can* turn over *a good profit in one day.*

Phrasal Verbs with *Around*

Phrasal verbs with the preposition *around* often mean to do something in a generalized or unstructured way with no immediate goal. Idioms like *drive around* (drive here and there), *look around* (look casually at everything), *mess around* (play casually, waste time, tinker), and *hang around* (loiter, do nothing) are a few examples. Most phrasal verbs with *around* are intransitive (they do not require a direct object), but there are some exceptions, which are marked with **(S)** for separable or **(NS)** for non-separable.

Grammar Note: When a phrasal verb with *around* is followed by another verb, that verb is put in the gerund form. Here is an example: "We *drove around* looking for a restaurant." In this example, *drove around* means to drive around somewhat aimlessly, without definite direction. *Looking* is a gerund.

WHEN *AROUND* MEANS HERE AND THERE

When *around* is joined with the verbs *walk*, *run*, *drive*, and *look*, among others, it means to go here and there — generally, all around an area — often with no specific goal or destination. The idioms in this group that are transitive may be separable or non-separable, depending on meaning. The following definitions explain the specifics about idioms in which *around* means here and there.

drive around

    1. to drive aimlessly or simply for the pleasure of driving, often with no specific destination; also put as *cruise around* ♦ *At Christmastime, we like to* drive around *the neighborhood to look at the Christmas lights and decorations.* ♦ *On Saturday night, we used to just* drive around *with our friends doing nothing.*
    2. to drive here and there looking for something specific or doing errands ♦ *I* drove around *downtown for half an hour looking for a parking space.* ♦ *We had to* drive around *awhile to find the freeway entrance.*

Grammar Note: When this idiom means to take someone else driving for pleasure or other purposes, it is separated by its direct object, as in, *"I'm always* driving *my kids* around *to soccer, dance lessons, and to visit their friends."*

look around (NS)

    1. to look in all directions, here and there, to enjoy a view; to pay attention, be aware ♦ Look around. *There are flowers blooming everywhere.* ♦ *When you* look around, *you can see a lot of people yakking on cell phones.*
    2. to investigate, often before a purchase ♦ *They* looked around *various neighborhoods in order to decide where they would like to live.* ♦ *Welcome to our shop. Please come in and* look around.

Grammar Note: With this idiom, the direct object is often not stated, but is understood.

shop around

    1. to look from shop to shop or store to store to compare prices, quality, service, and so on before buying something ♦ *I* shopped around *a lot before buying my computer.* ♦ *He* shopped around *for a winter coat until he found a good one on sale.* **Note:** *Comparison shop* means the same as *shop around,* in this context.
    2. to date various people casually looking for the right person for a long-term relationship; to choose one's romantic partner or spouse carefully ♦ *Don't jump into marriage with the first person you meet;* shop around. ♦ *She's not ready for marriage yet; she's just* shopping around.

walk around (NS)

    1. to take a walk; to walk leisurely and possibly aimlessly ♦ *Let's go* walk around *the museum and look at the new exhibits.* ♦ *We didn't buy anything today; we just* walked around.
    2. to stretch one's legs, get a little exercise after sitting or being immobile for a long time; in this context, the direct object is not stated, but understood ♦ *On a long car trip you should get out and* walk around *every few hours.* ♦ *Right after the operation, the nurses had him out of bed and* walking around.

[See also *get around* and *run around* later in this section.]

GETTING AROUND

The phrasal verb *get around* has many meanings and is used in various contexts. *Get around* is almost always non-separable. Following are examples of how to use this idiom:

1. (NS) to circumvent or bypass a hurdle or authority ♦ *She managed to* get around *taking the national exam by submitting her research and publications.* ♦ *We might be able to* get around *dad by asking mom instead.*

2. (NS) to travel from place to place; to be mobile ♦ *Nettie usually* gets around *the city by bus.* ♦ *He's learning to* get around *on crutches since he broke his leg.*

3. to be socially active; to know a lot of people; to have a network of friends ♦ *Dave can tell you who to talk to about this situation; he* gets around *and knows a lot of people.* ♦ *She certainly* gets around; *everyone seems to know her.*

4. to become known; to become public knowledge as news ♦ *The news of their engagement* got around *fast.* ♦ *Please don't tell anyone about it. I don't want it to* get around.

Getting around Town

The expression to *get around town* means more than just to travel around the city. People use this expression to cover all aspects of taking care of everyday errands, including getting to and from the places where one shops, works, banks, drops off and picks up kids, goes to doctor appointments, and so on. A person's ability to do those things might be expressed like this: "She's 84 years old, but she can still *get around town* and take care of the things she needs to do" or "It's impossible to *get around town* with all this road construction!"

Compact cars are often advertised as "good for *getting around town,*" meaning they are easy to park and economical for short trips to the store, school, and so on.

People often use *get around town* when referring to a mode of transportation. For example, "The college kids seem to *get around town* just fine on their bikes," or "Sometimes it's much easier to *get around town* on foot than by car."

RUNNING AROUND

One might *run around in circles* (accomplish little or nothing after much effort) or *run circles around* someone (greatly exceed someone in skill, knowledge, or other ability; be superior). Or one might simply *run around* — a versatile idiom with a number of meanings. *Run around* is generally intransitive (has no direct object), but there are a few exceptions. Here are the most common meanings and uses of this idiom:

1. (NS) to do errands; to go from place to place with purpose; taking care of various business needs. Often put as *run all around.* In this context the direct object is often not stated, but understood. ♦ *I've been* running around *all day. It's nice to come home and sit down.* ♦ *She had to* run around *all over the city to get the permits and other documents she needed for her new business.*

2. (NS) to run or move around erratically in an excited, anxious or angry way. Also *tear around.* ♦ *The dog* ran around *behind the fence barking at everyone who passed.* ♦ *He ran all* around *the house looking for his lost keys.*

3. (NS) to be up and moving around; to be out in public, specifically in certain clothing. This context is used when referring to being casually dressed. ♦ *We often let the toddlers* run around *naked at the beach.* ♦ *I usually* run around *in shorts and sandals all summer.*

4. (NS) to associate or spend time with; sometimes to date; said as *run around with.* In this context, the direct object is often not stated, but understood. ♦ *We were best friends growing up and we still* run around everywhere *together.* ♦ *He generally* ran around *with the other art students when he was in college.*

5. to be unfaithful sexually or romantically. Often put as *run around on someone.* In other words, to cheat on. ♦ *He broke off the relationship when he found out she'd been* running around *on him.* ♦ *He drank too much and* ran around *with women, and eventually his wife left him.*

Fooling Around and Other Forms of Monkey Business

The idioms *fool around, mess around,* and *monkey around* have a number of meanings in common. The example sentences that follow each definition show which of the three idioms is most often used in that context.

Fool around, mess around, and *monkey around* mean:

1. to tease or joke, possibly harmlessly; to play tricks on ♦ *I didn't mean to hurt your feelings; I was just* fooling around.

2. to engage in leisurely or idle activity; to spend time on hobbies or interests that are non-work related and that are typically pleasurable; to waste time (often said as *I don't have time to fool around*) ♦ *Dad enjoys* fooling around *in his workshop.* ♦ *We just* messed around *today and had a good time.*

Messing around in Someone Else's Business

Not minding one's own business is *messing around in someone else's business*. For example, if you give personal advice to someone who hasn't asked for it, you might get the response, "Why are you *messing around in my business?*" If you get involved with something foolish or harmful, someone might say, "Don't mess with that business." For example, a parent's advice about drugs, gangs, or other dangerous influences might be "Don't even think about *messing around with that business!*"

3. to experiment with forbidden objects or substances. Sometimes used in reference to experimenting or getting involved with drugs, alcohol, or other things that could cause harm. ♦ *Don't* fool around *with drugs.* ♦ *I wouldn't* mess around *with that parrot if I were you. It could crush your finger with its beak.*
4. to try to repair something or get it to operate; also sometimes said as *play around* ♦ *After the mechanic* fooled around *under the hood for a while, the car worked fine.* ♦ *I've* played around *with this remote for an hour, and it still isn't programmed right.*
5. to engage in casual sexual activity. Often said as a light or playful reference to sex. Also said as *mess around*. Sometimes referred to as *monkey business*.
♦ *They were* fooling around *in the back seat of the car.* ♦ *She caught her son and his girlfriend* fooling around *in the garage.*

JOKING, KIDDING, AND PLAYING AROUND

The phrasal verbs *joke around, kid around,* and *play around* mean to lightly tease or joke or to play a harmless trick on someone. This kind of joking can be fun and playful, or it can be annoying when the joking is inappropriate or carried on for too long. These idioms are intransitive.

joke around ♦ *My friends are always* joking around *and having fun.* ♦ *His father said, "Stop* joking around. *Your failing grades are a serious matter."*
kid around ♦ *He* kids around *a lot, but he's really a genuine guy.* ♦ *Hey, I'm just* kidding around. *Don't get mad.*
play around ♦ *He can be funny, but he never knows when to stop* playing around. ♦ *She's so serious. It's hard to* play around *with her.*

NOSING, POKING AND SNOOPING AROUND

The phrasal verbs *nose around, poke around,* and *snoop around* mean to investigate or to look for something hidden. These expressions are used to describe both serious investigation by police or other officials and casual investigation. Here are some examples of how these idioms are used:

nose around (NS) ♦ *The police* nosed around *the crime scene searching for clues.* ♦ *My kids are often* nosing around *the cupboards looking for snacks.*
poke around (NS) ♦ *Some private investigators were* poking around *the office asking questions.* ♦ *I like to* poke around *in antique shops to see what I can find.*
snoop around (NS) ♦ *"Get out!" She yelled at her sister. "I don't want you* snooping around *my room!"* ♦ *He came home and found a man* snooping around *his backyard.*

HANGING AROUND, STAYING AROUND, AND STICKING AROUND

The phrasal verbs *hang around, stay around,* and *stick around* mean to stay for a while, to stay or remain in a certain area or vicinity, or to linger or postpone leaving. People often say one of these idioms when they don't want someone to leave, or as an invitation to stay. *Hang around* is also used in slang meaning to loiter with friends, doing nothing.

Hang around, stay around, and *stick around* all mean more or less the same thing: to remain in the same place. With these idioms, the direct object is often not stated, but is understood. Here they are in context:

hang around (NS) ♦ *I'm going to* hang around *after class and talk with the professor.* ♦ *I wonder how long these rain clouds are going to* hang around.
stay around (NS) ♦ *The family of blue jays* stayed around *my yard all summer.* ♦ *How long are you planning to* stay around *this area?*
stick around (NS) ♦ *Don't go out. I want you to* stick around *and help clean the house.* ♦ *Can you* stick around *a little longer and join us for dinner?*

COME AROUND AND BRING AROUND

The phrasal verbs *come around* and *bring around* have a number of common meanings, but are used slightly differently, as discussed in the following note.

Grammar Note: *Come around* is intransitive and refers to one's own actions (you come around), while *bring around* is transitive, and refers to influencing the actions of someone else (you bring *someone* around). *Bring around* is almost always separated by its direct object, as in "Please *bring* your friends *around* to meet me."

Following are the various meanings and contexts in which *come around* and *bring around* are used:

1. to persuade, convert, or change someone's mind or thinking ♦ *Dad said "No" to our plan, but if we wait he might* come around. ♦ *People have* come around *to the reality that natural resources are not limitless.*

2. to stop for a casual visit or to come uninvited ♦ Come around *to the shop sometime, and I'll show you our new products.* ♦ *The raccoons* come around *every night and drink water from our little pond.*

3. to restore consciousness. Also put as to *come to* or to *bring* someone *to*. ♦ *After four months in a coma, she suddenly* came around. ♦ *When he* came around *after the operation, his family was waiting at his bedside.*

KICKING, TOSSING, AND THROWING AROUND

Kick around, toss around, and *throw around* all mean to casually discuss an idea. Here they are in context:

kick around (S) ♦ *The guys sat at the bar and* kicked around *some ideas for making money. Later they made a fortune selling Pet Rocks.*
toss around (S) ♦ *The Global Fund for Women began with two friends* tossing around *ideas for helping women in the world.*
throw around (S) ♦ *We haven't decided where to take our vacation, but we've been* throwing *some ideas* around.

Kick around, toss around, and *throw around* can also mean to be handled roughly, abusively, or carelessly, often with disrespect or disregard. *Kicked around* also means to be taken advantage of. In this context, these idioms are often used in the passive form. Here are some examples showing both active and passive forms:

kick around (S) ♦ *The boss seemed to need someone to* kick around, *and that was me.* ♦ *We were* kicked around *from one supervisor to the next. It was crazy.*
toss around (S) ♦ *Maybe he can afford to* toss *his money* around *on useless things, but I cannot.* ♦ *The little sailboat was* tossed around *in the wind.*
throw around (S) ♦ *Your clothes are* thrown around *all over the room. Pick them up.* ♦ *Everything in the house got* thrown around *during the earthquake.*

OTHER PHRASAL VERBS WITH AROUND

Here are three more common phrasal verbs with *around*:

pal around

to get together; to do things together as friends ♦ *Every Tuesday afternoon mom* pals around *with her retired lady friends.* ♦ *He* pals around *with a group of kids that his parents don't approve of.*

[See *run around* earlier in this section.]

rally around (NS)

to come together; to support a cause or a person in need. With this idiom, the direct object is often not stated, but understood. ♦ *When her partner died, all her friends and family* rallied around *to help her.* ♦ *Many people are now* rallying around *the efforts to promote the use of solar energy.*

turn around

1. to go or look in the opposite direction ♦ *I think we're going the wrong way. Let's* turn around. ♦ Turn around *and look at the beautiful view behind you.*
2. (S) to reverse the direction of one's life for the better; to stop self-destructive behavior and improve; to reverse a negative situation. Often said as to *turn* one's life *around* or to *turn* things *around.* ♦ *Getting married helped him* turn *his life* around. ♦ *There used to be a lot of anger and bad feelings at work, but the new manager has helped to* turn *things* around.

Phrasal Verbs with *Through*

When the preposition *through* is joined with certain verbs, it often gives the meaning of doing something until it is completed or resolved or until an obstacle is overcome. Some phrasal verbs with *through* are intransitive, while others are transitive and are marked with **(S)** for separable and **(NS)** for non-separable.

WHEN *THROUGH* MEANS TO SURVIVE, ENDURE, OR OVERCOME

The phrasal verbs *come through, get through, go through, live through,* and *pull through* all can be used to mean survive, endure, or overcome a difficult situation. They can refer to physical, emotional, or financial difficulties. The examples that follow describe and show the slight differences in how these idioms are used. *Come through* refers to having experienced or survived a difficult or risky time, while *get through* and *go through* stress the effort or struggle required.

come through (NS) ♦ *He* came through *the operation very well.* ♦ *It's a mystery how she* came through *that accident without a scratch.*
get through (NS) ♦ *She's having a difficult time right now, but she'll* get through *it.* ♦ *You won't believe what I had to* go through *to get these concert tickets.*
go through (NS) ♦ *They* went through *terrible hardships during the war.*
♦ *What she* went through *to get that visa! It was a nightmare!*

[See other uses of *come through* and *get through* later in this section.]

live through (NS)

1. generally used to talk about surviving or experiencing a life-threatening situation or event ♦ *He was very lucky to have* lived through *the accident.* ♦ *I've* lived through *plenty of hurricanes, so they don't frighten me.*
2. to be alive or to experience a specific historical era ♦ *Many people who* lived through *the '60s are still social activists today.* ♦ *We're* living through *an era of globalization.*

pull through (NS)

Pull through is used to talk about managing to survive a life-threatening illness or injury or a financial hardship ♦ *Grandpa had a serious heart attack, but somehow he* pulled through. ♦ *When times were especially hard, she always said: "Don't worry. We'll* pull through *this as we always do."*

FOLLOWING THROUGH WITH THINGS

The phrasal verbs *come through, follow through,* and *see* something *through* all mean to fulfill a promise; to do or to complete what one says one will do, or what others are expecting. These idioms often imply that one is reliable, dependable, and diligent.

In the following examples, the first definition for each idiom shows this meaning.

come through

1. to do what other people expect or hope, sometimes under difficult circumstances ♦ *Even though he has been sick lately, I knew that he would* come through *and finish the report.* ♦ *I didn't think that my boss would give me a raise, but she* came through *for me.*
2. to wear through, appear, or reveal itself ♦ *Oh no! My pen leaked, and the ink has* come through *onto my shirt.* ♦ *He tried to be polite, but his true feelings* came through.
3. become visible or audible ♦ *My radio picked up a station in Korea, but the sound didn't* come through *very well.* ♦ *Can you send me that fax again? It didn't* come through.
4. to materialize or be approved; often used to talk about a loan ♦ *When my student loan* comes through *I can buy my books.* ♦ *I'm waiting for a check to arrive, but it hasn't* come through *yet.*

follow through

1. to do what is necessary to complete a project or process; to complete something that other people expected or hoped for; often said as *follow through with* ♦ *Jason applied to the university, but he never* followed through *with sending his transcripts.* ♦ *She told me that she would call me about the job, but she never* followed through. ♦ *He said, "If you want people's trust, you have to* follow through *with things."*

2. to fully complete a golf stroke, tennis swing, or other similar maneuver ♦ *Her golf instructor is showing her how to* follow through *on her strokes.* ♦ *In tennis, you need to* follow through *when you swing.*

see through

1. (S) to stay with a project until it's completed ♦ *Thank you for* seeing *the project* through. ♦ *His dad said, "Don't quit now. You're almost finished.* See *it* through."

2. (S) to support, sustain, or provide for someone until the end of a specific time period ♦ *Thanks for the loan. It will* see *me* through *until payday.* ♦ *This old coat will have to* see *me* through *the winter; I don't want to buy a new one this year.*

3. (NS) to see or understand the true character or nature of something that is disguised ♦ *It was easy to* see through *his charms. Everyone knows he's dishonest.* ♦ *She pretended to be afraid, but we could* see through *that.*

GETTING THROUGH AND WORKING THROUGH

The phrasal verbs *get through* and *work through* have a general meaning of to work diligently and steadily at something until it's completed, or to work to resolve something like anger or pain.

get through

1. (NS) to manage to complete something; to finish ♦ *It took me six months to* get through *that book.* ♦ *Well, we've already* gotten *half way* through *the school year.*

2. to reach someone by telephone; to make a phone connection ♦ *You'll never* get through. *His line is always busy!* ♦ *It took awhile, but I finally* got through *to her in Rwanda.*

3. (S) to make clear or understandable; to have one's reasoning understood. Using this idiom implies that the listener has trouble understanding because of language differences, lack of intelligence or knowledge, or resistance to certain ideas. The idiom can be considered impolite or insulting depending upon the context. ♦ *The language barrier in my workplace sometimes makes it hard to* get *my ideas* through *to people.* ♦ *I've talked to my kids many times about the dangers of drugs; I hope I'm* getting through.

work through (S)

1. to work on something or exert effort until a task is complete; to solve a mathematical problem ♦ *I have a big pile of mail to* work through. ♦ *She* works through *the crossword puzzle every afternoon.*

2. to resolve problems and personal issues by working on them, by making a concentrated effort ♦ *The counselor helped her* work through *her anger.* ♦ *We've had some relationship problems, but we'll* work through *them.*

Grammar Note: Although this idiom is separable, it is generally not separated.

WHEN *THROUGH* MEANS TO EXAMINE, PAGE BY PAGE

The phrasal verbs *go through, look through, read through,* and *thumb through* mean to check or look at each page or item, either carefully or leisurely. *Check through* and *flip through* can also be used with this general meaning. The following examples show how to use these idioms and give more precise definitions:

go through (NS)

to check, look at, or read thoroughly; to review or examine; to sort ♦ *Going* through *the files, she found an old document.* ♦ *Let's* go through *your homework and check for errors.*

look through (S)

to casually look at something for pleasure, like a magazine, or to review something, like a report or essay, for information or errors. Although this idiom is separable, it is generally only separated by a pronoun. ♦ *She* looked through *my research paper and said it was very good.* ♦ *We* looked through *the color samples to choose a color for our living room.*

read through (S)

to read thoroughly and completely to check for information or mistakes. Although this idiom is separable, it is generally only separated by a pronoun. ♦ *I need to* read through *the article again to fully understand it.* ♦ *We* read through *the contract and signed it.*

thumb through (NS)

to look at or review casually while turning each page, as with a magazine, or noting each item, as with cards or photos ♦ *At the doctor's office, she nervously* thumbed through *a magazine.* ♦ Thumb through *these photos and tell me which ones you like.* **Note:** This idiom alludes to using one's thumb to turn pages or flip through a stack of papers one by one.

OTHER PHRASAL VERBS WITH *THROUGH*

Here are a few other common phrasal verbs with the preposition *through.*

break through (NS)

to penetrate or appear from behind a barrier or closure (either physical or emotional) ♦ *After five days of rain, the sun finally* broke through. ♦ *He is a very closed and private person; no one can* break through *his tough exterior.*

fall through

to fail to happen as expected; to not work out as planned ♦ *She was disappointed when her travel plans* fell through. ♦ *The deal* fell though *at the last minute.*

put through (S)

1. to successfully carry out or bring to completion; often used to talk about laws, agreements, deals, contracts, and other legally binding items ♦ *Since the bicycle helmet law was* put through, *children are suffering fewer head injuries in bike accidents.* ♦ *We were able to* put *the initiative* through *in time for voters to vote on it.*

2. to connect two or more parties by phone; often done by a receptionist or a telephone company employee ♦ *Hello. Could you* put *me* through *to the director, please?* ♦ *I'll* put *you* through *to an international operator who will complete your call.*

3. (S) to force someone to endure or experience a hardship, a struggle, a personal or physical test, or some other unpleasant situation; sometimes said lightly, as in the third example that follows ♦ *They* put *us* through *four hours of testing before we could register for our classes.* ♦ *He* put *her* through *many years of misery before she finally divorced him.* ♦ *We promise, we won't* put *you* through *all of our vacation slides. Just a few.*

run through (NS)

to rehearse a speech, song, musical or dance number, play, or other performance; to review a schedule, plan, rules, or procedures ♦ *Let's* run through *the number a few more times.* ♦ *Do you want to* run through *your speech? I can be your audience.*

sit through (NS)

to sit patiently during something; to endure a long or boring event or an unpleasant experience. In this context, one can *sit through* something without actually being seated. ♦ *It's a long movie to* sit through, *but it holds your attention.* ♦ *If I get home too late, I'll have to* sit through *one of mom's lectures.*

Putting Someone through the Wringer

There are a number of colorful expressions that people use to describe being forced to endure struggle, hardship, or challenge. Here is a list of some of the most common expressions:

put through the wringer ♦ *My dad will* put me through the wringer *when he finds out that I failed three classes.*

put through hell ♦ *The chemotherapy treatments really* put me through hell.

When people are forced to pass a challenge or test or to work or practice hard to prove themselves, they may say one of the following expressions:

put through the test ♦ *His boss really* put *him* through the test *before promoting him to manager.*

put through one's paces ♦ *We* put *the new people* through their paces, *and they did very well.*

sleep through (NS)

to continue to sleep while something loud, disruptive, interesting is happening ♦ *I can't believe that you* slept through *the earthquake!* ♦ *She wanted to watch the game on TV, but she* slept *right* through *it on the couch.*

think through (NS)

to think about or analyze until one reaches a conclusion or resolution; to analyze a problem step by step ♦ *Before making a big decision, take time to* think *it* through. ♦ *After* thinking *it* through, *he decided not to change his academic major.*

CHAPTER 20

THREE-WORD PHRASAL VERBS

Three-word phrasal verbs consist of three parts that work together as a unit, for example *get rid of* (to discard or throw away), *look forward to* (to anticipate with excitement), and *come down with* (to become sick with an illness). A typical three word–verb pattern is `verb + preposition + preposition`. The three-word verbs above show this pattern.

Another pattern for three-word verbs is `verb + verb + preposition`, such as *make do with* (to manage with limited resources). All three words of a three-word verb are necessary to create the special meaning of the idiom.

Three-word verbs are idiomatic because together the three words have a special meaning that is different from the literal meaning of the individual words. Like two-word phrasal verbs, three-word verbs cannot be translated literally. For example the phrasal verb *look forward to* doesn't mean to look or to move in a forward direction; *come down with* doesn't refer to coming or moving in a downward direction.

To summarize, three-word verbs have the following characteristics:

- The three words act as a unit to form the verb.
- The meaning of the three words together is idiomatic, not literal.
- All three parts of the verb are necessary to create the meaning.

All three-word verbs are followed by one of these structures:

- **A gerund:** For example, "We really *look forward to* **taking** a vacation."
- **A pronoun:** For example, "We really *look forward to* **it.**"
- **A noun or noun phrase:** For example, "She *came down with* **the flu**" or "He should *face up to* **what he did.**"

What Is a Three-Word Phrasal Verb and What Isn't?

Three-word verbs may be tricky to recognize because sometimes they look just like a simple verb followed by two prepositions. You can see the difference in the following examples. Compare the idiomatic meaning of the three-word verb to the literal meaning of the simple verb plus two prepositions:

Three-word verb: He *fell in with* some bad people (began associating with).
Verb + prepositions: When he was fishing at the lake he *fell in with* his fishing pole (fell into the lake, along with his fishing pole).

Other three-word verbs that end with the preposition *to* might look like a simple verb and preposition followed by an infinitive. But with three-word verbs, the preposition *to* is followed by a noun or pronoun, not by a verb. Notice the difference in structure and meaning in the following examples:

Three-word verb: He *looks up to* his father (admires and respects).
Verb + preposition + infinitive: He *looks up to see* the moon (looks in an upward direction because he wants to see something).

PLACEMENT OF THE OBJECTS

All three-word verbs are transitive, meaning they require a direct object, and are inseparable, meaning they cannot be separated by their direct object. However, some three-word verbs also require an indirect object, which generally comes between the verb and first preposition. In the following expression, the indirect object is shown in bold:

talk (someone) **out of** (something): to convince someone not to do something
For example: "We *talked* **him** *out of* buying an expensive car."

In this chapter, three-word verbs that require an indirect object are presented like the preceding example, **talk** (someone) **out of** (something), and the placement of the indirect object is shown in parentheses between the verb and first preposition. The direct object is also shown in parentheses at the end so that you can clearly see that the idiom requires two objects. Three-word verbs that require only one object (a direct object) are shown in the standard way without parentheses, for example: **get rid of.**

In some cases the three-word verb requires another type of object or qualifier such as an adjective or adverb after the verb, as shown in bold in this example: "He got **a lot** out of the workshop" (receive a benefit or advantage from something). These types of three-word verbs are also shown like the example in the preceding paragraph.

The following sections show many examples of three-word verbs categorized by their ending preposition.

Three-Word Verb "Cousins"

Some three-word verbs are a kind of extension (or relative) of a two-word verb. For example: *sit up with* (to stay awake, often during the night, with a sick or troubled person), has a very similar or related meaning to its two-word "cousin" *sit up* (to stay awake late or all night). The added preposition, "with," gives more specific meaning to the original two-word verb.

Other two- and three-word verbs are more "distant cousins," having dissimilar meanings like: *get around to* (to find time to do) and *get around* (to be widely traveled, known, or experienced). These two look very similar, but their meanings are unrelated. The addition of the preposition "to" creates a completely different idiom.

Still other three-word verbs, such as *get wind of* (to hear about something, by chance) have no two-word-verb "cousins." There is no such idiom as "get wind," which is a meaningless phrase by itself. The preposition "of" is absolutely necessary to create a meaningful expression.

Three-Word Verbs Ending with *Of*

Many three-word verbs ending with *of* follow the pattern of verb + *out of,* for example: *get out of, grow out of, talk* (someone) *out of.*

The four phrasal verbs that follow require two objects:

cheat (someone) **out of** (something)

> **1.** to cause someone to give up or to lose something by tricking or cheating
> ♦ *They trusted their employer, but he* cheated *them* out of *their retirement funds.*
> **2.** to deny oneself or someone else opportunities ♦ *If you quit school, you'll* cheat *yourself* out of *a future.* ♦ *She was* cheated out of *a normal life by the long-term effects of the accident.*

get (something) **out of** (something)

> to receive a benefit or pleasure from something ♦ *I got a lot* out of *the conference.* ♦ *He's not getting much* out of *the class. It's too easy for him.* **Grammar Note:** In this idiom, the verb *get* is generally followed by a noun or adjective such as *nothing, a lot, something, anything,* and so on.

get (something) **out of** (someone)

> to force, convince, or inspire someone to reveal a secret or to talk or give information ♦ *We finally* got *the truth* out of *him about what happened.* ♦ *The police questioned the suspect, but they couldn't* get *anything* out of *him.*

talk (someone) **out of** (something)

> to convince someone to do, or not do something; also to convince someone to give up or relinquish something, as shown in the third example that follows ♦ *He wanted to quit school, but his parents* talked *him* out of *it.* ♦ *I've made up my mind, so don't try to* talk *me* out of *it.* ♦ *I wasn't able to* talk *my dad* out of *the car keys.*

The following three-word verbs using *of* require only a direct object:

get out of

> to avoid or escape from having to do something, usually work or a commitment ♦ *I've already made a commitment; it's too late to* get out of *it.* ♦ *In my house, no one could ever* get out of *doing their chores.*

get rid of

> **1.** to eliminate, throw something away ♦ *It's difficult to* get rid of *termites. They always come back again.* ♦ *I'm going to* get rid of *these old magazines.*
> **2.** to heal an illness or pain ♦ *She finally* got rid of *her cold.* ♦ *This ointment will help you* get rid of *that rash.* ♦ *I still have a headache; I can't* get rid of *it.*
> **3.** to fire someone ♦ *When profits went down, they* got rid of *200 employees.* ♦ *I* got rid of *my incompetent accountant and found a better one.*

get wind of

> to hear some news, by chance or from an outside source ♦ *He* got wind of *the surprise party being planned for his birthday.* ♦ *When they* got wind of *the plans to divert the river, they formed a protest.*

grow out of

> **1.** to grow too tall or big to wear one's clothes ♦ *Children* grow out of *their clothes very quickly.* ♦ *I often wore the clothes that my sister had* grown out of.
> **2.** to become too mature for a childish or inappropriate behavior; used to describe a person or a pet ♦ *He used to suck his thumb, but he eventually* grew out of *it.* ♦ *Our new puppy chews everything. We hope she* grows out of *that soon.*

Three-Word Verbs in Context

The following short paragraph incorporates some of the three-word verbs in this section:

When her parents *got wind of* Leslie's decision to drop out of college, they tried to *talk* her *out of* it. "Don't *cheat* yourself *out of* a future," they said. They explained that she'd *get* a lot *out of* an education and be able to *take care of* herself as an adult.

make fun of

> to tease, mock laughingly, or ridicule ♦ *The other kids* made fun of *his interest in birds.* ♦ *Don't* make fun of *me! I'm doing the best I can.*

take care of

> **1.** to baby-sit or care for someone's needs ♦ *He* took care of *his younger brothers and sisters while his parents worked.* ♦ *She took very good* care of *him when he was sick.*
> **2.** to maintain something in good condition; to treat or be careful with a physical problem ♦ *He didn't* take *good* care of *his health, and now he has problems.* ♦ *We hired someone to help* take care of *the house.*
> **3.** to meet one's financial responsibilities; to eliminate debt ♦ *I usually* take care of *all my bills on the first day of the month.* ♦ *You need to* take care of *your overdrawn bank account.*
> **4.** to do or handle in general, such as work, logistics, or problems ♦ *I'll* take care of *all the arrangements for Chuck's retirement party.* ♦ *They asked the manager to* take care of *the problem.*

Three-Word Verbs Ending with *On*

Three-word verbs ending with *on* include these combinations following the verb: *back on, down on, in on,* and *out on.*

The three phrasal verbs that follow require two objects:

let (someone) **in on** (something)

> to allow someone to be included in a secret, plan, or endeavor ♦ *I'll* let *you* in on *a secret.* ♦ *Let* me in on *any plans for a surprise party for Ann.*

[See *get in on* (to be included) later in this section.]

422 / Phrasal Verbs

take (something) **out on** (someone)

> to make another suffer for one's own anger, frustration, bad mood, and so on
> ♦ *Hey, I know you're upset, but don't take it out on me. It's not my fault.* ♦ *He*
> took *his frustration* out on *everyone by refusing to cooperate.*

try (something) **out on** (someone)

> to test something or experiment using others ♦ *I'll try this recipe out on my*
> *family before I serve it to my guests.* ♦ *You can* try *the speech* out on *your col-*
> *leagues before presenting it to the committee.*

The following three-word verbs using *on* require only a direct object. However, some
of them, like *get in on,* may use an optional adverb or adjective between the prepositions, for example, "I want to *get in* **early** *on* the sale before the best items are sold."

come down on

> to reprimand, punish, or be angry at someone for something ♦ *The school*
> *really* came down on *them for cheating.* ♦ *His parents* came down *hard* on *him*
> *when he took the car without permission.* **Note:** This expression often includes
> *hard* or *easy* between the two prepositions.

get down on

> to criticize or reprimand someone in hopes of changing his or her behavior; often
> used as to *get down on oneself* ♦ *I sometimes* get down on *myself for not getting*
> *enough exercise.* ♦ *His teammates really* got down on *him for missing practice.*

Come Down On versus *Get Down On*

Both *come down on* and *get down on* can mean to reprimand or criticize, but here are
some subtle differences:

- *Come down on* tends to be stronger than *get down on.*

- *Come down on* implies possible punishment, legal action, or restrictions,
  whereas *get down on* implies light to serious criticism, but not punishment.

- Generally, a person of authority or one who can restrict someone else's actions
  can *come down on* someone, whereas anyone can *get down on* someone else.

Here are some examples:

- ♦ *The EPA* came down on *companies that were still polluting.*

- ♦ *He* got down on *his parents for not recycling.*

get in on

> to be included in a plan or endeavor; to take advantage of a special offer ♦ *I hope to* get in on *the meeting.* ♦ *If you buy a ticket now, you can* get in *early* on *our special fall rates.* **Grammar Note:** This idiom often has an adjective, such as *early, late, first,* and so on, between the two prepositions.

[See *let* (someone) *in on* (something) earlier in this section.]

go back on

> to take back or break a promise or agreement; to renege on. Often put as *go back on one's word.* ♦ *He* went back on *his promise to help us.* ♦ *My father never* went back on *his word.*

go in on

> to share (often equally) an expense or financial responsibility; to pool or join resources to purchase something together ♦ *If we all* go in on *a gift, we can get something much nicer.* ♦ *They* went in *equally* on *the business venture.* **Note:** This idiom sometimes has an adverb or adjective, such as *equally, halves, together,* and so on, between the two prepositions.

go out on

> to date someone while in a relationship with someone else ♦ *She* went out on *him, so he stopped seeing her.* ♦ *He* went out on *her when she was away visiting her parents.*

[See *cheat on* and other related idioms in Chapter 8.]

look back on

> to review or reassess; to remember the past, possibly with nostalgia or regret ♦ *Looking back on the decision, I think we made a mistake.* ♦ *He* looked back on *his college days as a time of freedom.*

look down on

> to regard something as inferior and oneself as superior; to consider something with contempt ♦ *They* looked down on *us because we were poor.* ♦ *He tends to* look down on *anyone who doesn't share his beliefs.*

[See *look down one's nose* in Chapter 13.]

look in on

> to check the status, safety, or progress of someone by looking at or visiting them ♦ *Before they go to bed, they* look in on *their sleeping children.* ♦ *I'll* look in on *you later to see how your sewing project is going.*

walk in on

> to enter and accidentally interrupt someone involved in a private or secretive activity, anything from a robbery to a person using the bathroom or toilet to a private argument ♦ *They* walked in on *the thieves as they were robbing the house.* ♦ *Lock the bathroom door so no one* walks in on *you.*

walk out on

> to abandon or unexpectedly leave someone to whom you have responsibility, such as a spouse or romantic partner, business partner, or one's children ♦ *He simply* walked out on *his wife and three children.* ♦ *When the business began to fail, his partner just* walked out on *him.*

Three-Word Verbs Ending with *To*

Most three-word verbs ending in *to* include the follow pattern: verb + *up to*. All of the following three-word verbs with *to* require only a direct object.

add up to

> to signify, imply, mean, or result in ♦ *It all* adds up to *one thing: We have to spend less money.* ♦ *Her hard work* added up to *a huge success.* **Note:** A common expression that is often used to summarize a point or show a result is "It all *adds up to* one thing. . . ."

come up to *or* **go up to**

> **1.** to approach someone ♦ *He* came up to *me and shook my hand.* ♦ *He told his children "Never* go up to *an unfamiliar dog; it might bite."*
> **2.** to reach or extend in height, amount, or sequence ♦ *My son now* comes up to *my shoulders.* ♦ *This alphabetical list only* goes up to *the letter L.*

[See *come up, come down* and *go up, go down* Chapter 19. For more information on correct use of the verbs *come* and *go* see Chapter 20, *Phrasal Verb Grammar,* "Coming and Going."]

come down to

1. to ultimately depend on; generally used to explain what is required for something to happen, or why something isn't possible. Often said as "It *comes down to*" followed by the ultimate factor (time, money, hard work, and so on).
♦ *We want to take a vacation, but it* comes down to *time.* ♦ *If it* comes down to *money, I'll help you out.*
2. in fact or in truth. Often put as *"When it* comes *(right)* down to *it . . ."*
♦ *When it* comes *right* down to *it, he doesn't really want to work in his father's business.*

feel up to

to feel capable physically and mentally to do something; most often used in the negative ♦ *My cold is almost gone, but I don't* feel up to *going out.* ♦ *Since she lost her husband, she hasn't* felt up to *socializing much.* **Grammar Note:** *Feel up to is generally followed by a gerund, but it can be followed by a noun when the verb in the gerund form is understood, such as "Do you* feel up to *(going to) a movie?"*

Feel Up To and *Feel Like*

Feel up to is often used in the negative when one is tired, sick, or depressed. For example: "I have a cold, so I don't *feel up to* doing anything today." When *feel up to* is used in the positive, it generally implies that one is now in a better condition, in better health, feels more rested or stronger. "Today I *feel up to* going for a walk" implies that yesterday I didn't feel well enough to go for a walk.

However, sometimes *feel up to* is used to mean that one is in the mood to do something or is interested in doing something. It might be used in a question such as: "Hey, do you *feel up to* taking a hike?"

The expression *feel like* is used to express a preference or liking. When you want to relax or you feel lazy, you might say "I don't *feel like* doing anything." *Feel like* suggests a general mood or choice, for example, "Today, I just *feel like* singing."

Compare the two expressions in the following examples:

♦ *I don't* feel up to *shopping today; I'm still a little sick.*

♦ *I don't* feel like *shopping today. It's so nice outside, let's take a hike.*

Occasionally, people do use the expression *feel like* when they're sick or tired. Their tone of voice or explanation will generally tell you if it's physical or simply a preference.

face up to

to accept something that is difficult to accept. This expression is often put as *face up to the fact.* ♦ *He had to* face up to *the fact that his grades weren't good enough for the university he wanted to go to.* ♦ *They didn't want to* face up to *their mistakes, but they had to.*

get around to

to find or make time to do something, often something that has been put off or avoided ♦ *I finally* got around to *answering my mail.* ♦ *There's no hurry. Just do it whenever you* get around to *it.* **Note:** This idiom is often said as *get around to doing something,* as in "I haven't painted the house yet, but I'll *get around to doing it.*"

hold on to

to keep, save, not spend or lose; to keep faith in something ♦ *She* held on to *her money and eventually bought a house.* ♦ Hold on to *your receipt in case you want to exchange the item.*

live up to

to act according to beliefs, expectations, or standards set by (generally) someone else ♦ *She tried to* live up to *her parents' expectations.* ♦ *He certainly* lived up to *the nickname Funny Guy.*

look forward to

to anticipate something with enthusiasm or be excited about a future event. When *look forward to* is used in the negative, the meaning is often stronger than simply meaning unenthusiastic; it means to dread or feel uncomfortable about an inevitable future event. ♦ *The kids always* look forward to *summer vacation.* ♦ *I'm not* looking forward to *having the surgery, but it's necessary.*

look up to

to respect and admire someone, to look to them as a role model; sometimes put in the passive voice, as in the second example that follows ♦ *She* looked up to *her older sister.* ♦ *Professional athletes are often* looked up to, *although many aren't good role models.*

stand up to

to be assertive or strong, often against a stronger opposition or force ♦ *The workers* stood up to *the company by going on strike, and they eventually got a better contract.* ♦ *Sometimes the only way to stop a bully is to* stand up to *him.*

Three-Word Verbs in Context

The following short paragraph incorporates some of the three-word verbs in this section:

The students quickly *warmed up to* their new teacher, because she didn't *talk down to* them, but treated them like young adults. They were comfortable *coming up to* her for help or advice. She was a strong role model, so they *looked up to* her, and they tried to *live up to* her expectations. When it *came* right *down to* it, they *looked forward to* coming to class.

talk down to

to talk in a childish, condescending or disrespectful way to someone, often as an insult or a show of disregard, but occasionally done unintentionally ♦ *Some people think it's necessary to* talk down to *children.* ♦ *I don't like how the boss* talks down to *everyone.*

warm up to

to become more comfortable with or more fond of an idea or a person, usually after being hesitant ♦ *She's beginning to* warm up to *the idea.* ♦ *They never* warmed up to *the new teacher, who was too strict.*

work up to

to gradually be able to do something after some effort, progress, or hesitation ♦ *She gradually* worked up to *running three miles a day.* ♦ *You can eventually* work up to *assistant manager after a year or two with the company.*

Three-Word Verbs Ending with *With*

Almost all three-word verbs that end with the preposition *with* require only a direct object. The first idiom that follows is one exception, requiring two objects.

take (something) up with (someone)

to discuss or address an important or difficult issue with someone; to bring a complaint to someone, often a person of authority. This idiom can also be said as *take up* (something) *with* (someone). ♦ *Let's* take *this discussion* up with *our coworkers and get their opinion.* ♦ *They* took *the matter* up with *the director.*

come down with

to become sick with a specific illness or health condition ♦ *He* came down with *malaria while he was in the tropics.* ♦ *I think I'm* coming down with *a cold.* **Note:** *Come down with* is generally used to refer to colds, flu, pneumonia, malaria and some other viral conditions, but it's not generally used to talk about more serious conditions such as AIDS, cancer, heart disease, Alzheimer's, and the like.

come up with

1. to find information after a search ♦ *I checked the Internet and* came up with *some good sources.* ♦ *Did you* come up with *anything after looking at the report?* **2.** to invent or create by thinking or teamwork; to fabricate or create and present something new ♦ *The committee* came up with *some ideas to cut overhead costs.* ♦ *After years of research, they finally* came up with *a biodegradable plastic.*

come out with

to present a new product to the public ♦ *Some auto companies are* coming out with *cars that have computer screens.* ♦ *When they* came out with *Cabbage Patch Dolls, every child wanted one.*

do away with

to eliminate or get rid of something; to fire, dismiss, or kill someone ♦ *Many banks have* done away with *their clocks, so patrons can't see how long they wait.* ♦ *They're planning to* do away with *the treasurer position.*

fall in with

to begin associating with, often by accident or misjudgment ♦ *He* fell in with *a street gang when he was just 14 years old.* ♦ *In Europe we* fell in with *some other travelers and spent time traveling together.* **Note:** *Fall in with* is often used to imply an unfortunate or bad association, but it can mean a beneficial or good association too.

Three-Word Verbs in Context

The following short paragraph incorporates some of the three-word verbs in this section:

In the past many people *came down with* hepatitis from unclean food and water. In an effort to *do away with* this disease, medical science has *come up with* a vaccine that prevents hepatitis. Since drug companies have *come out with* this vaccine, there are fewer cases of hepatitis, but it will be impossible to *do away with* this disease completely until someone *comes up with* a cure.

Three-Word Verbs in Context

The following short paragraph incorporates some of the three-word verbs in this section:

A number of local businesses have been robbed recently, the thieves *making off with* thousands of dollars in merchandise. The business community is *fed up with* this situation, saying, "We won't *put up with* this violation of our community." They've *taken* the matter *up with* state officials who, along with local police, promise that the criminals will not *get away with* these crimes.

get away with

to escape from punishment or blame for a crime or wrongdoing; to be undiscovered as one who played a trick ♦ *They let their children* get away with *too much; they're very relaxed about discipline.* ♦ *The high school seniors didn't* get away with *their prank of putting detergent in the swimming pool.*

make off with

to leave or escape, taking something that belongs to someone else, usually intentionally ♦ *The thieves* made off with *all of their money and jewelry.* ♦ *Hey, who* made off with *my stapler?*

run off with

1. to leave a marriage or romantic relationship to be with someone else, often moving to another location ♦ *He* ran off with *his wife's best friend!* ♦ *She* ran off with *her boyfriend, when her parents disapproved of him.*
2. to leave, taking something that belongs to someone else, usually accidentally ♦ *Sorry, I accidentally* ran off with *your notebook.* ♦ *Wait. Don't* run off with *my pen.*

put up with

to tolerate or endure something ♦ *She finally divorced him after* putting up with *his drinking problem for years.* ♦ *Their teacher won't* put up with *any teasing in the classroom.*

take up with

to associate or be involved with, romantically, socially, or in business ♦ *She* took up with *an artist and eventually married him.* ♦ *I wish he would* take up with *a more serious-minded crowd.*

EXPRESSIONS WITH *DO, FIX, HAVE, MAKE,* AND *TAKE*

Some of the most frequently used expressions in American English are formed with the following verbs:

do
fix
have
make
take

These simple verbs, combined with nouns, create expressions that people use to talk about everyday life, routine activities, and common personal interaction. Phrases such as *do laundry, fix dinner, have a cold, make a mistake,* and *take a bath* are examples of this category of idiomatic language. Though these expressions may seem commonplace or simple, they can be difficult for non-native speakers because of:

- **The non-literal use of the verb.** For example, the verb *fix* means repair, but *fix dinner* doesn't mean to repair it!
- **The seemingly arbitrary choice of verbs.** For example, why is it correct to say *make* a mistake, and not *do* a mistake?
- **The use of a different verb than is common in other languages to express the same idea.** For example, American English uses *have* in "Let's have our coffee," but a number of other languages use the equivalent of the verb *take* to express this idea.

Some of the expressions found here may not be considered true idioms, but are idiomatic or unconventional in some way that makes them confusing or difficult to learn and to use correctly.

This appendix is designed to help you sort out when to use *do* or *make, have* or *take,* and so on. The first (and main) section of this appendix is organized by topic. The final section is organized by verb and includes additional idioms that don't fall into one of the topic categories.

Housework Idioms with *Do* and *Make*

Most idioms related to work in and around the house use the verbs *make* and *do*. For example, the idioms *do housework* and *do chores* mean to clean and tidy about the house. Here they are in context:

> ♦ *I usually* do the housework *on Saturday morning.*
> ♦ *Come on kids, you have to* do your chores.

Grammar Note: The same idea can be expressed as *have housework to do* or *have chores to do:*

> ♦ *You boys* have chores to do *before you go out to play.*

In the following idioms, *do* means to clean or wash:

> **do the laundry** (wash clothes) ♦ *I did five loads of* laundry *this morning.*
> **do the dishes** (wash dishes) ♦ *Please* do *your own* dishes. *Don't leave them for me to do.*
> **do the floors** (mop floors) ♦ *I just* did the floors, *so don't walk on them till they're dry.*

In the following idioms, *do* means to complete or take responsibility for doing a task:

> **do the vacuuming** (vacuum the carpets and floors) ♦ *Your job is to* do the vacuuming.
> **do the dusting** (dust) ♦ *As soon as I* do the dusting, *the house gets dusty again!*
> **do the cleaning up** (clean up the house) ♦ *We* did *some* cleaning up *before our guest arrived.*
> **do the lawn** (mow the lawn) ♦ *Jared, go help your dad* do the lawn.

Grammar Note: In all of the above expressions that use the verb *do*, an adjective (such as *some*, *a little*) or a possessive adjective (such as *my, our*) can be placed between the verb and its object (the cleaning word). Such adjectives would replace the word *the*.

The following cleaning-related idioms use the verb *make*:

> **make the beds** (neatly arrange the sheets and covers on a bed) ♦ *Penny, go* make *your* bed.
> **make things neat (*or* tidy)** (clean up and tidy a little) ♦ *Let's* make things neat *before Aunt Lucy gets here.*
> **make a mess** (create a messy or disorganized state) ♦ *I always* make a *huge* mess *in the kitchen when I cook, but I clean it up.*

make work for someone (cause someone to do extra work) ♦ *Her three little children* make *a lot of* work for her.

Money Idioms with *Have* and *Make*

Most idioms related to money use the verb *make* and a few use the verb *have*. First you must *make money* (earn money), then if you've earned a lot of money, you might *have money* (be rich). The expression to *make one's money* can mean either to earn money or to become rich, depending on the context. Here are some examples of these idioms:

- ♦ *I don't* make much money *at this job, but I like the work.*
- ♦ *His family* has money, *so they bought him an expensive, nice car!*
- ♦ *She* made her money *in the computer component industry.*

Note: To *have* money also means to possess money ("I *have* some money in my pocket"), but this is the literal meaning, not the idiomatic meaning of to be rich.

The idiom *to make it rich* means to become rich (legally or illegally) through a business endeavor. For example

- ♦ *She has* made it rich *as a fashion designer.*
- ♦ *He* made it rich *selling on the black market.*

The following idioms also mean to earn a lot of money and become rich:

make a mint
make a fortune
make big bucks

For example:

- ♦ *I* made a mint *when I sold my company!*

By contrast, the following idioms mean to earn very little money at a low-paying job:

make peanuts
make next to nothing

For example:

- ♦ *I* make peanuts *working with kids, but I love the job.*

To *make a living* basically means to earn money on which to live, to earn living expenses. People sometimes say "I *make a living,*" meaning "I earn enough money to pay my bills and live moderately comfortably, but I'm not rich."

Make a living is also used to ask or talk about one's occupation or type of work. In this context, one can say either *a living* or *my living, your living,* and so on.

- ♦ *How do you* make a living?
- ♦ *I* make my living *as a photographer.*

To *make payments* means to pay one's bills and pay on one's debts:

- ♦ *Please* make your payment *on the first of the month.*
- ♦ *You'll* make payments *on that school loan for a long time.*

[See *make ends meet, make a fast buck* in Chapter 6. Also see *make bank, make big bucks, make money hand over fist* in Chapter 5.]

Appointment Idioms with *Have* and *Make*

Idioms with *have* and *make* can be used in reference to setting up a plan or scheduling an appointment, meeting, or date. Use *make* to talk about the actual arranging of the time and place, as in "I need to *make* an appointment." Then use *have* to talk about something that is already arranged, as in "I *have* a doctor's appointment for next Tuesday."

Here are some arrangements with which you can use *have* or *make:*

an appointment ♦ *I'd like to* make an appointment *with Dr. Logan.*
an agreement ♦ *My housemate and I* have an agreement *to take turns doing the dishes.*
a date (a scheduled plan to do something, or a romantic date) ♦ *We* made a date *to meet for lunch Monday.*
a plan (a scheme to accomplish or solve something) ♦ *We* have a plan, *but we don't know if it will work.*
plans (an agreement to do something at a certain time) ♦ *I'm not free on Saturday; I already* have plans.

Conversation Idioms with *Have* and *Make*

If you *make conversation,* you talk casually, usually about unimportant things. *Making conversation* is also called *making small talk.* If you *have a conversation,* you talk more seriously or for a longer period of time, possibly about an important topic. Here are some examples:

- *A reception is a good place to meet people and* make conversation.
- *Americans often* make small talk with strangers *while waiting in line.*
- *We need to* have a conversation *about your future school plans.*

When you *have a discussion* you talk seriously about something important. *Having a discussion* is a lot like *having a conversation,* and the two terms are often interchangeable, but a discussion implies a more formal situation. For example

- *We* had *an interesting* discussion *on genetic engineering in class today.*

Have is also used in the following ways to mean present or offer an idea:

have an opinion ♦ *I* have opinions, *but I can't express them well in English.*
have a (good) point ♦ *You* have a very good point, *Sue.*
have advice ♦ *Do you* have *any* advice *on how I should handle the problem?*
have something to say ♦ *I* have something to say *about this issue.*

In reference to communication problems, *have* means to engage in or experience, as in the following examples:

have an argument ♦ *We* had a big argument *about who should take out the garbage.*
have a disagreement ♦ *When employees* have a disagreement *they come and talk to me.*
have a misunderstanding ♦ *I think we've* had a misunderstanding. *Let's talk and straighten it out.*

[See also *take advice* later in this chapter.]

You can also *make a point* (state an idea well). If it's a good point it will *make sense* (be logical, rational, practical). Here are some examples of these two idioms:

- *He* made *some* good points *about the benefits of using wind power.*
- *You've* made *your* point. *Now let someone else speak.*
- *I like your suggestion. It* makes *a lot of* sense.
- *What are you talking about? You're not* making sense.

Food Idioms with *Fix,* *Make,* and *Take*

Fix and *make* can be used interchangeably to mean *prepare food to eat.* Here are some examples:

♦ *If you're going to* fix *yourself a cup of coffee, would you* make *one for me too?*

♦ *I'm going to* make *a sandwich for lunch.*

Fix and *make* can be used whether the meal is elaborate, like a Thanksgiving dinner, or less complex, like breakfast. These verbs tend to be used when the food requires very little preparation, such as instant coffee, a microwaveable meal, or a frozen dinner.

When It's Okay to *Take* a Meal

People say *take lunch* or *take dinner* in the workplace. *Take lunch* or *take dinner* is really another way of saying *take a lunch break* or *dinner break* (the verb "take" is used with the word "break"). Here are some examples showing how to use *take:*

♦ *After the meeting, everyone should* take lunch.

♦ *You can* take your dinner *after Kelly* takes hers.

Here are some other uses of *take* at work:

♦ take a coffee break

♦ take a cigarette break

[See *take a break* and related idioms later in this chapter.]

Another context in which people say *take* is when ordering in a restaurant. The server *takes the order,* and the restaurant patron *takes something from the menu.* The patron can also *have* something from the menu. Here are some examples:

Server:

♦ *May I* take *your order?*

♦ *I can* take *your drink order, now.*

Patron:

♦ *I'll* take *the roasted chicken and a salad.*

♦ *We'll* take *one child's spaghetti entrée and two adult entrées.*

Generally, *fix* and *make* aren't used when there's no preparation at all, for example when food is eaten raw or eaten right out of the package. For example, you don't say "*make* an apple" or "*fix* chips."

When referring to food that's prepared for others, here are two possible sentence structures:

- ◆ *Mom made a birthday cake* for me.
- ◆ *Mom made* me *a birthday cake.*

In American English, the verb *have* (not take) is often substituted for *eat* or *drink,* as in these examples:

- ◆ *We usually* have *dinner at 6:00 p.m.*
- ◆ *What did you* have *for lunch?*
- ◆ *I'm not hungry. I* had *a snack a while ago.*
- ◆ *Do you want to* have *some coffee?*

Time Off Idioms with *Have* and *Take*

Some idioms with *have* and *take* mean to stop working or doing other activities. They can mean to take a short break or to rest for a longer period of time.

Note: In most cases you can use *have* or *take,* but native speakers generally use *have* when talking about a standard vacation from work that others also have. For example

- ◆ *We* have *two weeks off for the holidays.*

People use *take* when talking about a break from work that one chooses or has gotten special permission to take.

- ◆ *I'm going to* take *some time off next week so that I can visit my parents.*

In the following idioms, *take* is used more often than *have,* but *have* is frequently used for the past tense, as in, "I've already *had* my break."

break (a short stop from work) ◆ *What time should I* take *my break?*
time off (days or more away from work) ◆ *I'll* take *some time off when my wife has the baby.*
day off *or* **a week off** ◆ *We only* have *one day off after New Year's.*
vacation ◆ *Cindy: Do you have much vacation time this year? Joan: I* have *two week's vacation, but I'm taking three.*

Take is used in the following idioms, all of which mean a short rest or break. Occasionally, people use the verb *have* with these expressions, as in "I had a long nap today" or "I need to have a breather" but *have* cannot be used with the idioms *take five* or, in this context, with *take a few minutes*.

take a nap ♦ *If I take a 20-minute nap, I'll feel refreshed.*
take a breather (a short break from hard or strenuous work) ♦ *Let's* take a breather. *We've been working hard all morning.*
take five (short for "five-minute break") ♦ *Okay everyone.* Take five. *We'll start again at 11.*
take a few minutes ♦ *Don't feel rushed.* Take a few minutes *to decide which service plan you want.*

A related idiom, *take it easy,* can mean to relax or stop work for awhile. The following examples show this idiom in context:

♦ *I like to* take it easy *on the weekend.*
♦ *You guys have been working hard all morning. You can* take it easy *for a while and have a cup of coffee.*

The expression *take a time out* has a number of meanings, all of which refer to taking a break in order to think or calm down.

take a time out

1. take a break from a difficult situation to think or calm oneself ♦ *You two have been arguing all morning.* Take a time out *and get away from each other for awhile. You might see things more clearly after that.*
2. a short official stop during a game for the team to discuss strategy ♦ *That team has already* taken *three* time outs.
3. a form of punishment that requires a child to sit alone, isolated from others for a period of time ♦ *If you don't stop that, you'll be* taking a time out. ♦ *When I was a kid I often had to* take a time out *on the back porch, but I usually snuck away to play.*

[See also *take time* later in this chapter.]

Illness Idioms with *Have* and *Take*

Idioms that refer to feeling sick, having a disease, and receiving treatment often use *have* and *take*.

HAVING HEALTH PROBLEMS

The verb *have* means "to be experiencing" when referring to certain pains such as a headache, a toothache, a backache, or sore throat. Here are a few examples:

- ♦ *I've* had a headache *all day.*
- ♦ *I didn't go to work today because I* have a sore throat.

Have is also used in referring to common ailments and some serious health problems, such as a cold, the flu, a heart attack, cancer, AIDS, and others. Here are some examples:

- ♦ *I always just stay in bed when I* have the flu.
- ♦ *My uncle* had a heart attack, *but he survived.*

TAKING SOMEONE'S VITAL SIGNS

In the following idioms, *take* means to check, monitor, and record:

take one's vital signs: check one's pulse, heart rate and so on
take one's pulse: check one's pulse
take a deep breath: breathe deeply
take one's temperature: check one's body temperature

Here are some examples of these idioms:

- ♦ *The nurse will* take your vital signs *before you see the doctor.*
- ♦ Take a deep breath. *I want to listen to your lungs.*
- ♦ *You feel very hot! Let me* take your temperature.

Take can also mean to swallow or ingest medicine, as in these examples:

- ♦ *I hate* taking medicine, *so I try to stay well.*
- ♦ Take two of these pills *four times a day.*

One more health-related expression using the verb *take* is the following:

take to one's bed (to be so sick that one must go to bed) ♦ *The old man* took to his bed *and never got up again.*

[See other health-related idioms in Chapter 4.]

Hair Idioms with *Do* and *Fix*

Do and *fix* can refer to styling or arranging one's hair using spray, gel, or other hair products. These idioms generally are used to describe what women do, but they can also apply to men who spend a lot of time styling their hair. Here are some examples:

♦ *I'll be ready as soon as I* do my hair.
♦ *My friends sat and* did my hair *into 100 little braids.*
♦ *It takes him 10 minutes to* fix his spiked hair *in the morning.*

Do can also mean to dye or color one's hair. Here are some examples:

♦ *She* did her hair *in a dark burgundy color.*
♦ *What color are you going to* do your hair *this time?*

The idiom to *do up* one's hair means to arrange one's hair on top of one's head or up off one's neck. Here are a few examples:

♦ *Let's* do your hair up *for the party.*
♦ *She usually* did her hair up *in a bun.*

Talking about Time

Do, *have*, *make*, and *take* are used in idioms that refer to time. You can *have time* (have enough time to do something), and *make time* (create or find the time in your schedule), but you never want to *do time* (go to prison)!

Here or some examples of each of these idioms:

have time ♦ *Dave: Do you* have time *to help me with this project? Tina: Not today. But I'll* have *some* time *tomorrow.*
make time ♦ *If I don't* make time *in my schedule to go to the gym, I never go.*
♦ *I'm really busy right now, but I'll try to* make time *next week to see you.*
do time ♦ *He* did time *for robbery.* ♦ *If you're arrested again, you'll* do time!

Another, more complicated, time idiom follows:

take time

1. stop one's routine to do something else ♦ *Take time to talk to your teenagers. It's important.* ♦ *I need to answer some letters, but I just haven't* taken the time.
2. require a lot of time to complete or accomplish something ♦ *It takes time to build a good relationship.* ♦ *Recovering from surgery takes time. You can't rush it.* ♦ *Make-up takes too much time to put on. So, I never wear it.*

Using the Phone

Have, make and *take* are used with the noun *call* in the following idioms:

have a call

> receive a call from someone ♦ *Ms. Allen, you* have a call *on line three.* ♦ *Hey Don, you* have a call. *Pick up the phone.*

make a call

> call someone on the phone ♦ *Excuse me for a minute. I have to* make a call. ♦ *I've* made three calls *to that company, but they haven't called me back!*

take a call

> to accept a call, to answer the phone in the workplace ♦ *Please ask them to hold; I'll* take the call *in my office.* ♦ *John, there's a call for you. Do you want to* take it *or call them back?*

[See *make the call* (make the decision) later in this chapter.]

Performing

Idioms with *make, do,* and *take* are commonly used to talk about performance and entertainment. The following idioms can use *make* or *do:*

> **make (*or* do) a presentation** ♦ *The fire chief* made a presentation *at school on fire safety.* ♦ *Your assignment is* to do a short presentation *on your hobby.*
> **make (*or* do) a speech** ♦ *Do you feel nervous about* making a speech *in front of so many people?* ♦ *I* did my speech *on the pros and cons of school uniforms.*

The following idioms use *do:*

> **do a performance** ♦ *We're* doing *eight* performances *of the play this week.*
> **do a number** (perform a dance, singing, or musical number) ♦ *I'll* do one solo dance number *during the show.* ♦ *At the end of the concert, she came back on stage and* did *four more* numbers!

Here are performance-related idioms with *take:*

> **take the stage** (go onto the stage) ♦ *When Nelson Mandela* took the stage *the crowd cheered and applauded wildly.*
> **take a bow** (bow to the audience) ♦ *Performers, come out and* take a bow.

[See more performance related idioms in Chapter 7.]

More Idioms with *Do*

Following are some additional idioms with the verb *do:*

do a good deed

do something nice for someone; do something charitable ◆ *My mother tried to do a good deed every day by visiting sick neighbors and helping friends.* ◆ *Thank you for returning my lost wallet. You've* done a good deed. ***Note:*** The traditional belief is that one should do a good deed every day. So, sometimes people ask, "Have you done your *good deed* for the day?"

do one's best

make one's best effort; make a serious effort ◆ *His parents said, "Just* do your very best *in everything, and you'll succeed in life."* ◆ *I* did my best *to convince her not to buy that old car, but she didn't listen.*

do well

to be adequately successful, financially and in other areas of life ◆ *They both have good-paying jobs, so they're* doing well. ◆ *Thank you for asking about my grandfather. He's* doing well *after his recent illness.*

do poorly

to be unsuccessful or to fail in something, usually school ◆ *You* did *very* poorly *on this test, Roger. What happened?* ◆ *He* did poorly *in high school, but later he excelled in college.*

do exercise

to exercise. *Do* is used with most forms of martial arts, and with exercises that are done individually in a gym, for example: sit ups, push ups, yoga, gymnastics, and so on. ◆ *I try to* do s*ome kind of* exercise *every day.* ◆ *Some older people stay strong by* doing yoga or tai chi. ◆ *He's been* doing gymnastics *since high school.*

[See *do without* in Chapter 19; see *do it* in Chapter 8.]

More Idioms with *Have*

Here are some additional idioms with the verb *have*. **Note:** The first three idioms in this group are said frequently instead of, or in addition to, *goodbye*.

have fun

> to enjoy oneself ♦ *We* had fun *playing at the beach.* ♦ *Goodbye kids. Be careful and* have fun.

have a good (*or* great) time

> to enjoy oneself ♦ *I really like him. We always* have a good time *together.* ♦ *We had a fantastic time on our vacation.*

have a good day

> to enjoy a pleasant day, good weather; a successful day financially ♦ *Bye honey, I hope you* have a good day. ♦ *Sales clerks often say,* "Have a good day!" *when you leave the store.* ♦ *The store* had a good day. *We made a nice profit.*

have a bad day

> to experience a day when nothing goes right, a hard day ♦ *You look tired. Did you* have a bad day? ♦ *When I* have a bad day, *I call a friend and talk. Then I feel better.*

More Idioms with *Make*

Here are some additional idioms with *make:*

make a decision

> to decide, usually on something important, but not always; *make a good or bad decision* means to decide wisely or unwisely ♦ *We have to* make a decision *about which health care plan we want.* ♦ *You* made a good decision *to continue your education now rather than later.*

[See also *make the call* in this section]

make a mistake

> have an error or misjudge something ♦ *I* made a few mistakes *on the test, but I got most of the answers right.* ♦ *Everyone* makes mistakes *in life. Nobody is perfect.* **Note:** Do not say "make a test." In American English, say "take a test."

make the call

> be the person responsible for deciding, choosing. Also *make a good/bad call,* meaning choose wisely or unwisely. ♦ *You* made a good call *on this restaurant. It's great!* ♦ *Both applicants are perfect for this job. I'll let you* make the call *on who to hire.*

[See also *make a decision* in this section.]

make tracks

> move, leave, or run away quickly; be in a hurry ♦ *We'd better* make tracks *if we want to catch that flight.* ♦ *The store manager caught the shoplifters as they were* making tracks *for the exit.*

make trouble

> cause problems ♦ *There are always a few kids who* make trouble *for the teacher.* ♦ *Don't listen to him. He's just trying to* make trouble *by criticizing your friend.*

make one's day

> to do something that makes someone very happy, that turns an ordinary day into a fantastic day; also sometimes *make one's week* ♦ *Your phone call has* made my day. *It's wonderful to hear your voice.* ♦ *Getting that award at school really* made her day. *It* made *her whole* week!

[See *make it, make out, make up,* and *make whoopee* in Chapter 8.]

More Idioms with *Take*

The following are some additional idioms with *take.*

TAKING A BATH

In American English people generally use the verb *take* (not *have*) when talking about bathing. They say *take a bath* or *take a shower.* Sometimes people add *my* or *your* in front of *bath* or *shower.* Here are a few examples:

> ♦ *Jenny, it's time for you to* take your bath.
> ♦ *I usually* take a shower *in the evening when I get home from work.*
> ♦ *Go ahead and* take your shower *first. I'll take mine when you're done.*

The expression *to have a bath* is most commonly used when talking about bathing someone other than oneself, such as an infant, a child, or a pet. Here are some examples:

♦ *Did the baby* have her bath *yet?*
♦ *Jason: Dad, when was the last time the dog* had a bath? *Dad: I'm not sure. But he needs to* have another one.

TAKING ADVICE

The following idioms with *take* are used to give advice or encouragement. In these idioms, *take* means to heed or follow the advice, suggestion, or warning.

take advice

listen and follow someone's advice ♦ Take my advice. *If you work hard, you'll succeed.*

take care

be careful ♦ Take care *with that fragile antique.* ♦ Take care *crossing that busy street.*

take courage *or* **take heart**

be hopeful, confident, brave ♦ *We can* take courage *that the economy will improve.* ♦ Take heart, *you'll find a job if you keep looking.*

take heed

means "listen to this warning" ♦ *Take heed* and stay away from drugs.

Here are a few more idioms with take:

take effect

begin to have an effect or influence, to begin being enforced as a law or rule ♦ *I hope that pain reliever* takes effect *soon. This headache is killing me!* ♦ *The new dress code* takes effect *immediately. No more wearing sandals or loose jewelry in the food service area.*

take note

notice something of interest, pay attention, listen to an interesting fact ♦ Take note, there *are no young people represented on this advisory board. We need to appoint some.* ♦ *Everyone* take note, *the tour leaves an hour earlier than the time listed on the tour schedule.*

take part

participate in, be part of; also *take part in* ♦ *We're going to put on a fund raising event. Do you want to* take part? ♦ *In the 1960s, thousands of people* took part in *the civil rights demonstrations.*

take place

to happen, occur ♦ *When and where will the event* take place? ♦ *The accident* took place *at the corner of Eighth Street and Market Road.*

take turns

alternate in doing something ♦ *In our house, we* take turns *doing the dishes.* ♦ *Kids, don't fight over that toy.* Take turns *playing with it.*

DIFFERENCES BETWEEN AMERICAN IDIOMS AND BRITISH IDIOMS

American English and British English are, of course, similar in many respects, but they also have many differences. There are some differences in spelling, pronunciation, accent pattern, wording, and usage. Idioms and slang develop and change in a social context, so they are often very different in American English and British English.

This appendix presents some of the more common and problematic idioms, expressions, and terms that British English speakers encounter in American English.

Idioms with Different Prepositions

The American and British idioms in this section share a common meaning but use a different preposition with the verb or adjective to form the idiom. For example, the American idiom *fall down,* as in "The boy fell down and cut his knee," is said as *fall over* in British English. This is a small but important difference because in American English *fall over* is generally only used in reference to inanimate objects such as a vase or lamp, not in reference to people. Most of the following idioms are phrasal verbs (two-word verbs that include a verb and a preposition), and some are adjectives.

American Idiom and Example	American and British Common Meaning	British Idiom
come over ♦ *Come over* anytime. You're always welcome.	to visit someone's house	**come round**
different from ♦ This food is really *different from* the food we eat in my country.	not the same as, distinguished from	**different to**

continued

American Idiom and Example	American and British Common Meaning	British Idiom
fall down ♦ The little girl *fell down* and scraped her knee.	to fall on the ground or floor *Note:* In American English *fall over* is generally used for an inanimate object, such as a vase or lamp.	**fall over**
in school ♦ I'm not working because I'm still *in school.*	to be a student, attending school, usually college or university	**at university**
knock something out ♦ We *knocked out* the project in one week.	to make or create hurriedly *Note:* In American English the expression *to knock someone up* means to impregnate someone.	**knock something up**
move around *or* **get around** ♦ My father was in the military, so we *moved around* a lot.	to relocate often, be mobile; have a wide network of friends or acquaintances	**move about** *or* **get about**
it's up to someone ♦ She asked my advice, but *it's* really *up to her* how she invests her money.	means "it's your decision, responsibility, choice." *Note:* In American English *down to you* means you are the last one, the only one left, as in "Everyone else has gone home, so now it's just *down to you* and me."	**it's down to someone**
wait on tables ♦ When I was a student, I *waited on tables* to earn money.	to be a waiter or waitress; also, to *wait tables*	**wait at tables**

Idioms with Different Verbs

The American idioms and British idioms in this section share a common meaning and some common words, but they use different verbs to form the idiom. This can be a very important difference for example, the British idiom *take a decision* makes no sense in American English. If you said or wrote *take a decision,* it would be considered an error. Most of the following expressions are phrasal verbs (two-word verbs that include a verb and a preposition).

American Idiom and Example	American and British Common Meaning	British Idiom
call someone up ♦ I'll *call you up* tonight. What's your phone number?	to telephone someone *Note:* In American English to *ring someone up* means to total someone's purchases at a cash register.	**ring someone up**
check something off (a list) ♦ He *checked off* his grocery list as he chose the items.	to mark an item on a list as done, completed *Note:* The American English idiom *tick someone off* means to annoy someone or make someone mad, as in "His comments at the meeting really *ticked me off*."	**tick something off**
line up ♦ The kids *lined up* on stage to receive their awards.	to form a line, get in a line	**queue up**
make a decision ♦ I finally *made a decision* about my career plans.	to decide	**take a decision**
nab ♦ The police *nabbed* the suspect as he was leaving the store.	to catch or arrest a criminal	**nick**
run a red light ♦ Did you see that car?! It just *ran a red light!*	to fail to stop for a red light, to go through a red light	**jump a red light**
set the table ♦ She *set the table* with her best china for the party.	to put dishes and silverware on the table	**lay the table**
take a bath *or* **shower** ♦ After working in the garden, she likes to *take a* hot *bath*.	to wash oneself in the bath or shower *Note:* In American English people occasionally say *have a bath* or *shower*, but generally this is used when pets or children are bathed by someone, as in "The dog had a bath today."	**have a bath** *or* **shower**

Idioms with Different Nouns

The following abbreviations, slang expressions, and informal terms are quite different in American English and British English. The difference can be very important; for example, the British English slang term for friend, *mate*, means romantic partner or spouse in American English. All of the idioms in this section are nouns or adjective and noun combinations.

American Idiom and Example	American and British Common Meaning	British Idiom
ATM ♦ I need to go to the *ATM* and get some money.	automated teller machine, money machine	**cash dispenser** *or* **cash point**
backup lights ♦ One of his *backup lights* isn't working.	red lights on the back of the car that glow when going in reverse	**reversing lights**
bathroom, restroom ♦ Excuse me, where is the *restroom* located?	room that contains the toilet ***Note:*** American English speakers sometimes consider it a bit crude to refer directly to the toilet in this context.	**loo, toilet, lavatory,** *or* **W.C.**
bill ♦ I don't have any change in my pocket, just *bills*.	dollar bill, paper money ***Note:*** In American English a *bank note* refers to a specific type of promissory note issued by the bank.	**bank note**
buddy, pal ♦ He usually goes out with his *buddies* on Saturday night.	friend ***Note:*** In American English *mate* refers to one's spouse or romantic partner. It implies a sexual relationship and, often, life partner, as in "He wants to settle down and find a mate."	**mate**
a busy signal ♦ Maybe he's on the phone or his computer because I'm getting *a busy signal*.	repeating tone indicating the phone that one called is in use	**the line's engaged**
dishwashing detergent ♦ You'll find the *dishwashing detergent* on aisle 7 next to the soap.	liquid detergent for washing dishes	**washing-up liquid**

American Idiom and Example	American and British Common Meaning	British Idiom
grammar school	school for children aged 6 to 11 or 12 years old *Note:* In the United States, the *primary grades* are grades 1 through 3, for children who are approximately 6 to 8 years old.	**primary school**
half bath ♦ We've just redecorated the *half bath* for our guests.	room with toilet and sink but no bath *Note:* In American English a *cloak room* is a closet or small room where one hangs coats, umbrellas and so on.	**cloakroom**
high school	academic school for students who are approximately 13 to 18 years old *Note:* In the United States, *grammar school* is for children who are approximately 6 to 11 years old	**grammar school**
merry-go-round ♦ Children love to ride the horses on the *merry-go-round*.	carousel	**roundabout**
nail polish ♦ Her daughter has 20 different shades of *nail polish*.	paint for finger- and toenails	**nail varnish**
newsstand ♦ I'm going to the *newsstand* to pick up a paper.	small stand or stall where one buys newspapers	**newsagent** *or* **bookstall**
private school	a school that charges tuition and is not funded by the government *Note:* In the United States, a *public school* does not charge tuition and is funded by the state government.	**public school**
rest stop *or* **rest area** ♦ After driving 400 miles, they stopped for a break at a *rest stop*.	place along the highway to stop, use the bathroom, rest	**lay by**
(shopping) cart ♦ My *cart* was full of items for our holiday meal.	metal cart for holding grocery items one wants to buy	**shopping trolley**

continued

American Idiom and Example	American and British Common Meaning	British Idiom
soft drink ♦ They bought some *soft drinks* to take to the beach.	soda, carbonated drink	**fizzy drink**
take out ♦ When we're too tired to cook, we order *take out.*	food ordered, often by phone, from a restaurant and taken home to eat	**take away**
waste (paper) basket ♦ We can toss all these old files in the *waste basket.*	small container for throwing away paper	**dustbin**
zits ♦ He tried different medications to get rid of his *zits.*	acne, pimples	**spots**

Idioms with Very Different Wording

These expressions are worded very differently in American English and British English, but they have the same meaning. Some of them are verb phrases, some are adverbs, and others are expletives.

American Idiom and Example	American and British Common Meaning	British Idiom
catch red-handed ♦ They *caught* the shoplifter *red-handed* as she put merchandise in her purse.	to catch or discover people while they are committing a crime	**bang to rights**
cut in line ♦ Hey! No *cutting in line!* Go to the end of the line and wait your turn.	to get ahead of other people already waiting in a line	**jump the queue**
do the dishes ♦ My son's job is to do *the dishes* after dinner.	to wash the dishes ***Note:*** In American English to *wash up* means to wash one's face and hands or to clean oneself up, usually before a meal or after working or playing outside. For example, "She helped her little sister *wash up* before lunch."	**wash up**

American Idiom and Example	American and British Common Meaning	British Idiom
fill in the blanks ♦ In part two of the test, *fill in the blanks* with the correct word.	to complete a form; to complete test questions	**fill in the gaps**
get going ♦ Our trip was delayed, but we finally *got going* around noon.	to hurry, leave, go	**move off**
give something up ♦ I quit smoking. It was time to *give it up.*	to quit, stop doing something	**give something a miss**
go bad ♦ Ugh! This milk *has gone bad!*	to spoil, rot, turn sour **Note:** In American English to *go off* means to ring, as an alarm, or to explode, like fireworks, a gun, or a bomb. For example, "My alarm *goes off* every morning at 6:30 a.m." and "The gun *went off* accidentally."	**go off**
go belly up ♦ During the recession a lot of businesses *went belly up.*	for a business to fail, go bankrupt	**go all up**
go on *or* **go ahead** ♦ Okay, kids. *Go on.* There's the school bus.	encouragement to proceed; leave, go	**off you go**
hang up ♦ Susan, *hang up* the phone now and come eat dinner.	to end a phone conversation	**ring off**
all at once ♦ The raft tipped, and everyone fell out *all at once.*	all happening at the same time	**all in one go**
happen only once ♦ In our lifetime, seeing this comet will *happen only once.*	to happen just one time, no more	**be a one-off event**
look sharp ♦ He always *looks sharp,* no matter what he wears.	to be well dressed, fashionable **Note:** In American English to *look smart* means to look or appear intelligent, as in "He thought that his glasses made him *look* very *smart,* like a scholar."	**look smart**

continued

American Idiom and Example	American and British Common Meaning	British Idiom
miss one's turn ♦ He *missed his turn* at bat when he went to the food stand to get a soda.	to miss one's chance to do or try something in a succession of turns with others	**miss one's go**
next to last ♦ You're scheduled to speak *next to last,* so you can relax for a while.	the one before the last, second to last	**last but one**
Period! ♦ No! Your father and I won't allow you to buy a motorcycle. *Period!*	that's final; that's the end	**Full stop!**
right away ♦ I'll put that report on your desk *right away.*	immediately, without delay	**straight away**
a run ♦ Oh no! I have *a run* in my stocking.	a line of unraveled weave in nylons, pantyhose	**a ladder**
sleep in ♦ I can't wait for Saturday when I can *sleep in.*	to sleep later than usual, deliberately	**have a lie-in**
be stuffed ♦ Everyone *was* completely *stuffed* after the Thanksgiving meal.	full of food, satisfied	**be full up**
take a turn ♦ Everyone *took a turn* at flying the kite.	to have a chance to do or try something in succession with others	**have a go**
wash up or **get washed up** ♦ While we were camping, we *washed up* in a small basin.	to wash, generally one's hands and face	**have a wash**

Caution! Differences to Watch Out For

Heads up! Attention! Here are some idioms that could cause embarrassment or at least confusion and odd looks if you aren't aware of the differences in meaning. In some cases, the British expression is considered vulgar or impolite in American English. In other cases, a crude or impolite British expression may have a perfectly acceptable and common usage in American English. In some cases, the same words have opposite meanings, like the word *bomb*, or they may have slightly different usage, like the word *fetch*.

SAME MEANING, DIFFERENT WORDS

American Idiom and Example	American and British Common Meaning	British Idiom
do it ♦ The threat of AIDS has made people more cautious about *doing it* casually.	to have sex *Note:* In American English *on the job* is only used to mean while at work or working diligently.	**on the job**
give someone a call ♦ I'll *give you a call* tonight.	to telephone *Note:* In American English *tinkle* is a child's word for urinate, as in "Mommy, I have to *tinkle*."	**give someone a tinkle**
get it on ♦ Movies show everything today, even people *getting it on*.	to have sex *Note:* In American English *have it off* means to have a day off from work, as in "Monday is a holiday; we have it off."	**have it off**
horny ♦ It's one of those movies about a bunch of *horny* college guys at a party.	to be sexually excited or easily aroused *Note:* In American English *Randy* is only used as a man's name.	**randy**
keep your chin up ♦ Don't get discouraged about it. *Keep your chin up.*	don't get discouraged; keep hopeful *Note:* In American English *pecker* is slang for penis.	**keep your pecker up**
pouring down rain ♦ It's been *pouring down rain* all day.	raining very hard *Note:* In American English *pissing* is crude slang for urinating.	**pissing down with rain**
a screw up ♦ Because of a *screw up*, the project went badly.	a mix-up, a big mistake *Note:* In American English *cock* is slang for penis.	**a cock up**
a smoke ♦ Hey, can you give me *a smoke?*	slang for cigarette *Note:* In American English *fag* is a derogatory slang for homosexual. [See *fag* in the next section.]	**a fag**
tired out *or* **tuckered out** ♦ The kids were really *tuckered out* after Little League practice.	exhausted, very tired	**fagged out**

SAME IDIOM, DIFFERENT MEANING

American English Meaning	Idiom	British English Meaning
a failure, as a movie, a play or a plan ♦ The play was *a bomb* and got very poor reviews. *Note:* A modern slang expression in American English, "You're the bomb," means "You're the best!"	**a bomb**	a success
derogatory slang for a gay man, homosexual ♦ Many gay men have been harassed and called *fag.*	**fag**	cigarette
a command, usually to a dog, to go get something ♦ I've trained the dog to *fetch* the newspaper for me.	**fetch**	a request to a person to go get something
an attractive and sexy man or woman ♦ I met a great guy last week. He's smart, interesting . . . and a *hottie!*	**hottie**	a hot water bottle
crude slang meaning to get someone pregnant unintentionally or carelessly ♦ He married his high-school girlfriend at 17 because he *knocked her up.*	**knock someone up**	come to get or pick up someone
a condom ♦ Using *rubbers* has helped decrease the incidence of AIDS.	**rubber**	an eraser
crude but often acceptable slang for angry, annoyed. Often said as *pissed off.* ♦ I was really *pissed* when I saw the mess those kids made in the house.	**pissed**	drunk

INDEX